A HISTORY OF
THE LAND LAW

A HISTORY OF
THE LAND LAW

A. W. B. SIMPSON

SECOND EDITION

CLARENDON PRESS · OXFORD

1986

Oxford University Press, Walton Street, Oxford OX2 6DP
London New York Toronto
Delhi Bombay Calcutta Madras Karachi
Kuala Lumpur Singapore Hong Kong Tokyo
Nairobi Dar es Salaam Cape Town
Melbourne Auckland
and associated companies in
Beirut Berlin Ibadan Nicosia

Oxford is a trade mark of Oxford University Press

Published in the United States
by Oxford University Press, New York

© A. W. B. Simpson 1961, 1986

First published 1961 under the title
An Introduction to the History of the Land Law
Second Edition 1986

British Library Cataloguing in Publication Data
Simpson, A. W. B. (Alfred William Brian)
A history of the land law.—2nd ed.
1. Real property—Great Britain—History
I. Title II. Simpson, A.W.B.
344.1064'3'09 KD829
ISBN 0-19-825537-3
ISBN 0-19-825536-5 Pbk

Library of Congress Cataloging in Publication Data
A history of the land law.
Rev. ed. of: An introduction to the history of the
land law. 1961.
Bibliography: p.
Includes index.
1. Land tenure—Law and legislation—Great Britain.
2. Real property—Great Britain. I. Simpson, A. W. B.
(Alfred William Brian). An introduction to the history
of the land law. II. Title.
KD833.S56 1986 346.4204'3 85-28510
ISBN 0-19-825537-3 344.20643
ISBN 0-19-825536-5 (pbk.)

Set by Downdell Ltd., Oxford
Printed in Great Britain
at the University Printing House, Oxford
by David Stanford
Printer to the University

Preface

In this revised edition of a book first published back in
1961 I have attempted to pursue the same modest aim: to
write a short simple book which will introduce its readers
to the history of a very complicated subject, and provide
guidance to the literature. The revisions take account of
more recent scholarly work, and the notes provide a select
list of further reading. The emphasis is upon the legal
doctrines and institutions, and I hope this will prove
useful not simply to those, if any there be, whose interests
are so confined, but also to readers whose interests lie in
wider questions of social or economic explanation. I have
tried to resist the temptation to inflate the size of the text,
and, though the chapter on nineteenth-century law has
been enlarged, I have not duplicated accounts to be found
in standard current legal texts.

A.W.B.S.

Contents

Contents

I

Tenure

EVEN today the two most striking doctrines of the land law, at least on first acquaintance, are the doctrines of tenure and of estates. Modern writers are at pains to warn the student of the comparative unimportance of tenure in the modern law, and point to a series of statutes which have eliminated from our law almost all the direct effects of the tenurial relationship of lord and tenant, and reduced the types of tenures which can still exist. Indeed, so unimportant have tenures become that nobody certainly knows what sorts of tenure can still exist, and in practice this matters not at all.[1] But although the importance of tenures is now minimal, the basic doctrine of tenure is still with us; all land whatsoever is held, mediately or immediately, that is directly or indirectly, of the Crown.[2] Intimately connected with this axiom, *nulle terre sans seigneur*, is the doctrine of estates, whose development, in part at least, was forced upon the common lawyers by the theoretical difficulties raised by the doctrine of tenure. The doctrine of estates too is still with us, though in a guise which would hardly be intelligible to a medieval lawyer. But although the fundamental nature of these two doctrines is avowed in the leading modern textbook on real property,[3] estates no longer have the fascination that once they had, and tenure is little discussed. The emphasis of the modern law passes both doctrines by, and rightly so. If we go back into the history of the land law the emphasis changes. In the eighteenth and early nineteenth centuries the ablest property lawyers are concerned to work out the subtleties of the rules governing the limitation of estates, particularly in connection with the elaborate family settlements of the time;[4] when we reach the fifteenth

---

[1] Megarry and Wade, *Real Property*, p. 33, note 84 and pp. 36–7.

[2] The doctrine that all land is *owned* by the Crown is a modern one; it is quite misleading. See below p. 47.   [3] Megarry and Wade, *Real Property*, p. 14.

[4] Thus the two great books of the period are Fearne's *Essay on the Learning of Contingent Remainders and Executory Devises* (1772) and Preston's *An Elementary Treatise on Estates* (1791).

century Littleton's treatise on the law of real property is traditionally called *Tenures*,[5] and though he deals at length with the doctrine of estates it is the tenurial quality of the law which bulks largest in his analysis. Indeed the farther back we travel in time the more important does tenure become.

Feudalism and the Conquest

The doctrine of tenure has its origin in the state of social organization known as 'feudalism'. 'Feudalism' is undoubtedly a vague and imprecise term, with a number of connotations. For our immediate purpose it is sufficient to note that the feudal structure of society, which was firmly established in England after the Norman Conquest, involved dependent land holding —the holding of land in return for the rendering of services, typically military service. What was involved was both a personal relationship between superior and inferior, lord and vassal, marked by reciprocal duties of protection and service, and the granting of a benefice, that is, a parcel of landed estate to be enjoyed upon favourable terms, so long as the service due was faithfully performed. In cases where the tenant failed to observe the customary feudal obligations involved in his tenure he could be disciplined, even to the extent of losing his status as tenant and thus his land, and the feudal or seignorial court of his lord, whose function it was to see that custom was observed, resembled a modern military tribunal in that it was concerned as much with discipline as with justice. Even before the Conquest land tenure of a sort was known; the *loan* of land[6] created a relationship between lender and holder which closely resembles the feudal relationship between lord and tenant of post-Conquest times, and the relationship between the Saxon lord and the village community where he held sway could be described in tenurial terms. How widespread tenure was in Anglo-Saxon

[5] Sir Thomas Littleton (*c.* 1415–81) wrote his book, so it is said, for the instruction of his second son Richard; father and son were of the Inner Temple. The date of compilation is unknown; it was certainly finished by 1480, when a manuscript copy was sold for the considerable price of 10*s.* 6*d.* The first printed edition appeared in about 1481; there have been many editions since, for the *Tenures* rapidly became the standard elementary introduction to the law of property. Coke's *Commentary on Littleton* appeared in 1628. The best edition of Littleton is by E. Wambaugh (1903), and this includes a life. The text presents a number of difficulties, and it seems likely that the book is unfinished. See generally Holdsworth, II, pp. 571 *et seq.*

[6] For an illustration see Digby, *Real Property*, p. 57.

England is a moot point, and a somewhat artificial one; until there was a theory of tenure the question can hardly be asked.[7] What is clear is that the Norman administrators did have a theory of tenure, and applied it universally; all land whatsoever was held of some lord, and ultimately of the Crown. This is fully recognized in Domesday Book (1086) and certainly no such rigid doctrine could possibly have existed before 1066; indeed, in England alone was feudalism so universalized.[8] On the Continent feudal land-holding did not engulf all land; some tracts of land—called allodial lands—escaped the net. In Domesday Book the compilers sometimes seem puzzled by a landholder who seems to have no lord, but such puzzlement is assumed to arise rather from ignorance of the facts than from any exception to the universal application of the concept of tenure. The consequence of this was that feudal law did not simply become the law of the knightly, aristocratic class, nor the law of some parts of the country alone; it became the common law of England.

This triumph of order was made possible by the Conquest, and by the high degree of administrative efficiency attained by King William's staff. The invasion of England by a band of military adventurers made it necessary to quarter this military aristocracy on the conquered land; William had to reward his followers and preserve his military strength for the future. He was able to achieve both these ends by parcelling up the land of the country amongst his followers, who became his tenants for their land, holding by his grant.[9] In return he bargained for services; and most of his tenants were bound to serve in the royal army and bring with them a specified number of knights. The tenure thus created was knight-service, the typical feudal

[7] For accounts of pre-Conquest land laws see Plucknett, *Concise History*, pp. 516–20, 'Bookland and Folkland', 6 *Econ. Hist. R.* 64; Jolliffe, 'English Book-Right', 50 *E.H.R.* 1; Maitland, *Domesday Book and Beyond*, pp. 220 *et seq.*; John, *Land Tenure in Early England*; J. O. Prestwich, 'Anglo-Norman Feudalism and the Problem of Continuity', *Past and Present*, Vol. 26, p. 9. For illustrative material see Robertson *Anglo-Saxon Charters*. For a study of social conditions after the Conquest, and an account of the tenurial system in practice see Lennard, *Rural England*. For a general account of feudalism see Ganshof, *Feudalism*. See also S. D. White, 'English Feudalism and its Origins', 19 *Am. J.L.H.* 138.

[8] Scotland came very close to England, but some allodial land survives; see C. D'O. Farran, *The Principles of Scots and English Land Law*, pp. 19 *et seq.*

[9] A few Saxon lords were permitted to retain something of their former position; they too became tenants and vassals of the King, but the lords of post-Conquest England were predominantly Norman.

tenure, and it was wholly Norman.[10] The tenant who owed the service of ten knights was said to hold ten *knight's fees*,[11] and so on; there is some evidence to show that the quota of knights due was fixed in multiples of five or ten knights.[12] The immediate tenants of the Crown were called his tenants in chief, and there were probably about fifteen hundred of these tenants by 1086.

Now when it is said that the country was granted out by the King to his tenants in chief it must not be imagined that any process of wholesale eviction took place; a system of parasitism was involved, and parasites cannot survive the destruction of their hosts. At the bottom of the social scale were those humble peasants who actually wrested the agricultural wealth of the country from the soil; it was their labour which made the whole paraphernalia of knights and castles possible. At the time of the Conquest many were slaves, the property of some Saxon lord; some were free men who had a lord, but who did not hold their lands of their lord, for their personal relationship of dependence was unconnected with their enjoyment of land. Others perhaps could be regarded as tenants, who held of their lords. The greater part of these peasants would be bound by custom to perform various duties of a public nature, such as to repair bridges, and also other duties which were of personal benefit to the Saxon lord of the village community in which they lived—for example they might be bound to provide him with a food rent, or to labour on the land of their lord. The tendency before the Conquest had been for the peasants of a village community to become increasingly dependent upon the local lord, and it has been suggested that it may have often happened that the peasants surrendered their lands into the local lord's hands and received them back again in return for an obligation to labour on their lord's land; in return for a greater degree of subservience the peasants received the protection of a powerful man. In general

[10] For a different view see John, *Land Tenure in Early England*, Chs. V–VIII.

[11] Later the word *fee* connotes heritability, as in *fee simple*. This was not always so; the fee (fief, *feudum, feodum*) of early times is simply a *holding*, perhaps being limited in normal usage to the holding of a tenant of some importance.

[12] For the early history of knight-service see Stenton, *First Century of English Feudalism, passim*, Sanders, *Feudal Military Service in England, passim*. For examples of early grants of land see *English Historical Documents* II, pp. 896–7, 916–36, and cf. the passage from Glanvill at p. 937.

the effect of the Norman Conquest was only to substitute a new, alien, lord for his Saxon predecessor; a new system of parasitism was substituted for the old. What a tenant in chief acquired by the King's grant was not the enjoyment of land so much as the enjoyment of rights over land and services due from peasants who cultivated that land; to the peasant it may not have seemed that anything very momentous had occurred. But we know very little of the immediate effect of the Conquest on the Saxon peasantry.[13]

The King's immediate grantee—the tenant in chief *ut de corona*[14]—could retain his land and provide knights by paying for them, and keeping them in his household, but more frequently he provided his quota by subinfeudation. This took the form of a grant by the tenant in chief of one parcel of land to some lesser man, X, the land to be held of the grantor in return for the service of one or more knights in the royal army. The grantee, X, in his turn could again subinfeudate to another, Y, a part or the whole of his parcel of land, and in this way any number of rungs in the ladder could be created. Upon such a subinfeudation the grantor and grantee could reach any bargain they wished as to the services, but this in no way concerned the lord of whom the grantor held, for the service due to him remained burdened on the land, unaffected by subinfeudation. The terms '*forinsec*' and '*intrinsec*' were devised to describe the contrast. Thus in our example the service due to the Crown was, as between X and Y, *forinsec*; it was outside the scope of their bargain and unaffected by it, whereas the service they agreed was *intrinsec*—within the scope of their negotiations. Into whosoever's hands the land came the Crown could distrain upon it for the *forinsec* service. Normally the grantor would undertake to indemnify the grantee against the *forinsec* service, and the writ of mesne[15] was devised to give effect to this arrangement; thereby the occupant of the land sued his immediate lord so as

---

[13] For an account of conditions in England on the eve of the Conquest see Stenton, *Anglo-Saxon England*, esp. pp. 463 *et seq.*, and for the effects of the Conquest, pp. 614 *et seq.* See too Douglas, 'The Norman Conquest and English Feudalism', 9 *Econ. Hist. R.* 128.

[14] The term is used in contradistinction to a tenant in chief *ut de honore*, who became the King's tenant in chief through the operation of the doctrine of escheat, which is explained later.

[15] The writ is first found in the early thirteenth century.

to secure an indemnity against the *forinsec* service. The need for the writ of mesne was aggravated by the rule that the *forinsec* service was charged upon each and every part of the land, so that a sub-tenant, in theory at least, might find his one acre distrained upon for services reserved on a grant of five hundred; by the use of the writ a cumbersome justice could be done.

The Diversity of Tenures

The provision of an army was but one of the requirements of medieval society. By the creation of tenures involving other forms of service the land, which was the major source of wealth, could be made to yield to lords whatever goods or labour they required. It is important to realize that no fixed rules governed the type or nature of the services which could be stipulated for upon a grant of land. The result was the creation of tenures which range from the ludicrous to the obscene and from the onerous to the nominal. A few examples will illustrate this diversity.[16] In the reign of John we find that William, Earl Warren, granted lands in Stamford to be held for the service of finding annually a mad bull to divert his lordship, whilst there are several grants of land for the service of holding the seasick King's head on his trips across the channel. Straw for the royal privy had to be found by one unfortunate landholder, and the tenant of lands in Suffolk, one Rolland, was obliged upon Christmas Day to make a leap, a whistle and a fart *coram domino rege*, a service subsequently commuted for a less embarrassing money payment. At the other end of the scale come really heavy burdens—tenants in chief who owe the service of forty or more knights, those who hold at substantial rents in kind, and those who hold in return for onerous services, such as the duty of caring for falcons and hounds.

Upon this diversity of social relationships the medieval lawyers imposed a deceptively simple classification of tenures. The basis for this classification—which was only achieved by degrees—was the nature of the service due. The need for classi-

---

[16] Comical tenures are to be found collected in Blount, *Ancient Tenures*, from which the examples are taken. Coke (Co. Litt. 86a.) observes, 'Nay, the worst tenure I read of this kind, is to hold lands to be *ultor sceleratorum condemnatorum, ut alios suspendio, alios membrorum detruncatione, vel aliis modis iuxta quantitatem perpetrati sceleris puniat*, that is to be a hangman or executioner. It seemeth in ancient times such officers were not voluntaries, nor for lucre to be hired, unless they were bound thereto by tenure.'

fication arose largely because the customary *incidents*, or spasmodic liabilities, attached to the various tenures differed. These incidents of tenure, which will be discussed more fully later, took a variety of forms—for example *relief*, a money payment, was due when tenants who held by certain types of tenure inherited from their ancestors. Since the incidents due depended upon the nature of the tenure, some for example being appropriate to military tenures only, it became necessary to devise a classification based upon the nature of the services due, which alone distinguished tenures into identifiable types. In the course of the Middle Ages the economic importance of the services gradually declined—largely because they were fixed burdens which a lord could not vary unilaterally when a change in money values or social needs made them outdated. The incidents, as we shall see, tended to maintain their value and keep pace with inflation, and so the classification of the various types of tenure became very important financially. The type of tenure had other incidental legal effects—for example upon the power of alienation. Finally the distinction between *free* and *unfree* tenure had the immense importance of determining whether or not the tenant could sue in the royal courts for the protection of his interest in the land, for until the end of the fifteenth century the royal judges did not trouble themselves with the misfortunes of tenants who held by unfree tenure.

Littleton's Classification of Tenures

Littleton adopted a scheme[17] which has substantially been accepted ever since. The classifications to be found in modern textbooks are mere simplifications of his treatment. He divides tenures in the following way:

Knight-service. In the fifteenth century the distinguishing feature of this tenure was the obligation to pay scutage, a form of direct tax, by then never in practice exacted. The obligation to pay scutages, if and when levied, was therefore purely notional. This may seem a far cry from the obligation to fight as a knight in the royal army, but since the Conquest a great deal had happened to knight-service. The system of depending upon personal attendance by tenants for the provision of an army broke

[17] Littleton, secs. 95–171.

down quite soon, for reasons which belong more to military than to legal history.[18] In place of personal service the Crown came to accept money payments instead, and these were called scutages, or shield money; they were levied from time to time in proportion to the number of knights due from the tenant in chief, who in his turn would exact scutage from his sub-tenants, and so on down the ladder. In some cases quite humble persons would pay the scutage appropriate to a fraction of a knight's fee, persons whose social status made them impossible candidates for actual knighthood.[19] Persons holding land charged with the service of a fraction of a knight (e.g. half a knight's fee) must always have had their service expressed in money or goods. We first meet with examples of scutage being accepted in the early twelfth century, and the practice soon became common. At times the great tenants in chief might also have to pay a fine as well as scutage—probably this represented a recognition that in accepting scutage in lieu of personal service the Crown was granting a favour, for which the tenant might reasonably have to pay extra. From the middle of the thirteenth century onwards the payment of scutage became the normal practice, and the Crown ceased to rely upon tenure by knight-service to provide an army directly. Scutage came to be regarded as a form of direct taxation, and in the fourteenth century it fell under the control of Parliament. The last scutage was levied in Edward III's reign, and indeed only some forty scutages are known to have been levied in the whole history of the institution.

Escuage, or Scutage, and Castle-gard. Littleton, through his somewhat disorderly treatment of the matter, might give the impression that tenure by escuage (i.e. by scutage) was regarded as being separate from tenure by knight-service, and some controversy has arisen as to whether or not a separate tenure by escuage was recognized.[20] The key to the confusion in Littleton seems to be this: Littleton sometimes uses the term knight-service to describe tenures where there was an obligation to pay

[18] Poole, *Domesday Book to Magna Carta*, pp. 10–27; Powicke, *The Thirteenth Century*, pp. 540 *et seq.*, *Mediaeval England*, ed. Poole, Vol. I, p. 128.

[19] Note also that no particular size of holding was appropriate for a knight's fee.

[20] Littleton, secs. 95, 99, 103, 111, 153, 158. See also Pollock and Maitland, I, p. 274, note 1.

scutage, and sometimes to describe tenures of a military nature generally (called tenures in chivalry). Used in the first sense, tenure by knight-service and tenure by escuage are synonymous terms; used in the latter sense, tenure by knight-service includes forms of tenure (notably grand serjeantry and castle-gard) which were military but did not involve the obligation to pay scutage. It is when he is using the term knight-service thus widely that he contrasts knight-service (meaning military tenure generally) with escuage (meaning that particular form of military tenure in which the tenant was bound to pay scutage).

A tenant who held by castle-gard[21] was obliged to serve in the defence of castles; by the end of the thirteenth century such service was almost always commuted for a money payment, but such payments were not scutages. Some such payments lingered on in the form of a sort of rent, called ward money, centuries after the castle in question had crumbled into dust, and where the service had been thus commuted the tenure was treated as socage. With the decline in the military importance of castles, castle-gard too ceased to have much importance.

Grand Serjeanty. This was the tenure by which lands were held in return for some service of a personal nature, which was to be performed for the lord of whom the lands were held. In the early Middle Ages the grant of a parcel of land was a common method of ensuring that useful services were performed,[22] but in the course of time it became more usual to pay wages for service instead; here as elsewhere contractual arrangements came to perform functions which had in earlier times been tenurial. Thus serjeanty soon fell into decline, and the services originally reserved ceased to be exacted at all, or were commuted for a money rent. By the close of the fifteenth century the only ser-jeanties which actually survived were those where the service was of some honourable kind—carrying the King's sword at his coronation, or being his Marshal or Constable. Some of these honourable services lingered until recent times. At the coronation of George VI in 1937 the Lord of the Manor of

---

[21] For an account of castle-gard see Stenton, *The First Century of English Feudalism*, pp. 190–215.

[22] See Poole, *Obligations of Society*, pp. 57–76, for an entertaining account of the medieval serjeants.

Worksop performed his service of presenting an embroidered glove for the sovereign's right hand. At the coronation of Elizabeth II the Lord of the Manor was out of the country, and was unable to perform the service in his proper person; as a substitute the Royal College of Needlework presented the glove, but it was embroidered with the arms of Worksop. Grand serjeanty was subject to a number of peculiarities. In the thirteenth century it was established that serjeanties were inalienable and impartible, and at some time in the fourteenth that they could only exist as tenure in chief of the King. The restriction of this tenure to tenure in chief was really a move in favour of free alienation, for it meant that all other serjeanties became assimilated, in all but name, to socage, and socage lands could be freely alienated. An essential characteristic of grand serjeanty was that the tenant must be obliged to serve in his own person—an obligation to provide some object, such as a spear, created socage tenure and not serjeanty. So long as this requirement was satisfied the nature of the services mattered little, and although most were military in character this was not of necessity the case; the honourable characteristic was satisfied by the fact that the service was due only to the King, and the most menial services to royalty, then as now, were regarded as conferring honour.

These tenures were predominantly military. The next two tenures are curious in that they exemplify the uniform application of the doctrine of tenure, for in reality neither involve the rendering of any tangible services at all.

Frankalmoin. This tenure was created when lands were granted in return for an obligation to perform spiritual services on behalf of the grantor, and it came to be essential that no secular services be reserved in the grant. But this simple principle was not clearly settled until the fifteenth century, and at an earlier period secular services were in fact not infrequently reserved in grants which were accepted as being grants in frankalmoin.[23] Furthermore it came to be the rule that the only possible grantees were religious persons or institutions. Two types of frankalmoin were distinguishable. A gift *in free, pure, and perpetual alms* gave rise to an obligation on the part of the grantee

---

[23] See Poole, *Obligations of Society*, pp. 6 and 57–8.

to pray for the souls of the grantor and his ancestors, and if the tenant defaulted the only remedy was for the lord to complain to the ordinary, for the royal courts would not interfere. If, however, specific services were reserved—for example ten masses a year—the tenure was called tenure by divine service, and the lord could enforce the obligation in the royal courts. The effect of the statute of *Quia Emptores* in 1290 was to make tenure in frankalmoin rare, for the tenure could not subsequently be created anew, and although it has never been abolished, few examples can exist today.[24]

Frankmarriage. Littleton does not clearly treat this as being a separate form of tenure, but he implies that it was in one passage.[25] A gift in frankmarriage created a peculiar sort of estate, which will be discussed in connection with the entail, but such a grant also had tenurial peculiarities, in that no services were due to the grantor for three generations, except fealty (normally regarded as an incident rather than a service).[26] Nevertheless such a grant created a tenure, though it was tenure in which no service might be due for nearly a century.

Socage Tenure and its Variants. Finally we come to the group of tenures of which the leading example is socage, the only tenure of any importance met with in modern land law. Socage was the great residual category of tenure, and its characteristics can only be defined negatively. By the time of Littleton a miscellaneous collection of tenures, some of which had originally been regarded as quite distinct, and had represented quite diverse economic and social relationships, had been bundled together under a single classification, and described in this rather unilluminating way: 'Tenure in Socage is, where the tenant holdeth of his lord the tenancie by certeine [i.e. definite]

---

[24] On frankalmoin see Maitland, 'Frankalmoin in the Twelfth and Thirteenth Centuries', 7 *L.Q.R.* 354, Kimball, 'Tenure in Frankalmoin and Secular Services', 43 *E.H.R.* 341; Douglas, 'Tenure in Elemosina: its Origins and Establishment in Twelfth-century England', 24 *Am. J. L. H.* 95.

[25] Littleton, sec. 138.

[26] But see Littleton, secs. 138-9. In reading Littleton note the absence of any clear-cut distinction between services and incidents; thus both homage and fealty are treated as services. See secs. 85, 138, 139 and Co. Litt. 83a.

service for all manner of service, so that the service be not knights service.' Later Littleton adds, '. . . for every tenure which is not tenure in chivalrie is a tenure in socage.'[27] This mode of definition is not very complete, for it hardly serves to distinguish frankalmoin, which to Littleton was certainly not to be included in the bundle, from socage; here again all that can be said is that so long as the services are not spiritual then the tenure will be socage. A socage tenant, therefore, might hold at a rent which was nominal or substantial, and the rent might be payable either in kind, or money, or labour. He could even be liable to pay a form of scutage, so long as his liability was to pay a fixed and invariable sum, so that the amount he had to pay was not dependent upon the sum assessed as scutage for each knight's fee. Similarly a tenant who had compounded with his lord to pay a fixed rent in lieu of rendering personal service in the form of castle-gard was treated as a tenant in socage. Although infinite variety was possible, by the middle of the fifteenth century the socage tenant usually owed a money rent, such rents being known as 'quit rents', for by paying the rent the tenant was quit of other service.[28] In attempting to give the derivation of the word 'socage' Littleton writes:

In ancient time, before the limitation of time of memory, a great part of the tenants, which held of their lords by socage, ought to come with their ploughs, every of the saide tenants for certain daies in the year to plough and sow the demesnes of the lord. . . . And because that such services were done with their ploughs, this tenure was called tenure in socage. And afterwards these services were changed into money, by the consent of the tenants and by the desire of the lords, viz. into an annual rent. But the name of socage remaineth, and in diverse places the tenants yet doe such services with their ploughs to their lords. . . .[29]

[27] Littleton, secs. 117–18.

[28] In the earlier Middle Ages one who took land in return for an agreed money rent was called a *firmarius* or *farmer*, the rent payable being the *firma*, and the transaction was described by saying that the lands were *ad firmam*. The arrangement made might differ—the farm might be for years or for life or for a number of lives, or the tenant might hold heritably. In the latter case he was said to hold in fee farm. The position of a *farmer* was at first treated as *sui generis*; the *firmarius* was not a socage tenant, and the lawyers think of fee farm, for example, as a special kind of tenure. Farmers who held in fee or for life came to be protected in their landholding like feudal military tenants, and their tenure came to be treated as a form of socage, but farmers for years were never really fitted into the feudal structure of things, as we shall see; they were only beginning to be thought of as feudal tenants in Littleton's time. Much interesting material on *firmarii* is discussed in Lennard, *Rural England*, Chs. V, VI, and VII.

[29] Littleton, sec. 119.

The connection between the word 'socage' and the old French word 'soc', meaning a plough, seems to originate in Bracton, and although it is now thought to be erroneous, yet the underlying idea which prompts this theory is sound, for socage tenure is essentially agricultural and non-military; it is the tenure of the sokemen, the free peasants. The sokemen form a recognized class in Domesday Book; literally they are 'men who are under a Lord's jurisdiction' or 'men who owe suit of court'[30]. Those forms of socage where the only duty on the tenant's part was to do fealty, or to pay annually a nominal rent, such as a rose, are symptomatic of the unreality produced by the universal application of the doctrine of tenure; for example a son whose father gives him entailed lands to assist him in founding a family may be made to hold of his father in socage at a nominal rent, but nobody would expect the relationship between them to be that of lord and vassal. Into the spacious category of socage were placed those tenures which were tenures in name only, and with the disappearance of the realities of feudal tenure from society it was natural that socage should in the end become the sole surviving tenure of any importance; today it is still the law that all land is 'held', and since it must be held by some tenure we say it is held in free and common socage. This is only another way of saying that it is just held, for socage which is free (of services) and common (in the sense of immune from special customary incidents) has no positive characteristics. The requirement that the service must be certain distinguished the free tenure of socage from the unfree tenure of villeinage, which later came to be known as copyhold tenure. This test of certainty was adopted in Littleton's day after some earlier vacillation. From an early period the landholding of those who held in villeinage was not protected in the royal courts, so that the law governing the villein tenant was not common law; in so far as the villein tenant was protected at all he was protected in the court of his lord. In the fifteenth century the traditional attitude to the villein tenant began to change, and by the end of the sixteenth century he was as well protected as the freeholder.[31]

---

[30] See Stenton, *Anglo-Saxon England*, pp. 507 *et seq.*, Maitland, *Domesday Book and Beyond*, pp. 66 *et seq.*

[31] See below, p. 155 *et seq.*

Littleton mentions two other tenures which by his time (as he indeed admits) are better classified as forms of socage rather than as separate tenures. These forms of socage were:

Petit Serjeanty. When it became settled in the fourteenth century that the peculiar incidents of serjeanty only applied to tenure in chief, all mesne[32] serjeanties became assimilated to socage. There remained a number of tenants who held in chief of the Crown in return for services which took the form of providing the King with some small article pertaining to war—a lance for example or a pair of gloves. The connection with warfare and knightly accomplishment involved in such service made the lawyers hesitate from calling such tenures socage, for socage was predominantly an agricultural tenure, appropriate to peasants. Thus the special class of petit serjeanty was devised, and distinguished from grand serjeanty because the latter involved personal service by the tenant, whereas the former involved merely the supply of some warlike article. In its consequences, however, petit serjeanty did not differ from socage.

Burgage. This arose when free tenants in ancient boroughs held their lands either from the King directly or from some other lord in return for some certain rent. Such tenure, as Littleton admits, amounts to no more than a form of socage. Many boroughs had their own special customs[33]—for example the custom of borough english whereby the youngest son instead of the eldest inherited, and the customary power of devise attached to lands in a number of boroughs.[34] Such peculiar customs were not confined, however, to lands held in burgage, as we shall see, and in Littleton's time there seems to have been no purpose in retaining the separate classification of burgage tenure for purely legal purposes.[35]

[32] A mesne tenure is any tenure which is not in chief; similarly any lord but the King is a mesne lord.

[33] For borough customs see *Selden Society*, Vols. 18 and 19. For the history of burgage see Hemmeon, 'Burgage Tenure in England', 26 *L.Q.R.* 215, 331, 27 *L.Q.R.* 43.

[34] The effect of some of these borough customs, especially the customary power of devise, was that borough lands were subject to a more intense ownership than was land generally; not only were tenants exempt from the burdensome incidents of military tenure, but they had powers in relation to their land which were greater than those allowed at common law.

[35] For other tenures see Littleton, sec. 156 (cornage) and note Pollock and Maitland,

Fee farm—this is discussed in note 28 above and later in Chapter III.

The Incidents of Tenure

The main purpose of classifying tenures is the help it affords in determining the incidents which the tenant must pay. They were as follows:

Homage and Fealty. Homage was the ceremony by which the tenant became the lord's man, and in the early days of the common law, when this relationship was the basis of social organization, it had extremely important consequences in the field of public and criminal law. Thus a breach of the duty of faithful service which was created by homage was the early felony. Later the relationship of lord and man ceased to correspond to the facts of social life, and the consequences of homage lay more in the field of private law, the most important being the duty of the lord who had received homage to warrant (i.e. guarantee) the title of the tenant. Warranty is discussed more fully later in this book, but briefly a person who had warranted another's title was bound to provide compensation if the title proved defective in litigation, and was himself barred from asserting any claim to the land. In Littleton's time this obligation to warrant gave rise to a peculiar relationship known as homage ancestrel, which arose when a tenant and his ancestors had held land from the same lord and his ancestors time out of memory; if this was the case an obligation to warrant arose by implication of law. At an earlier time, however, the imposition of an obligation to warrant title was not peculiar to tenure by homage ancestral, but arose whenever homage was accepted. At a time before the statute of *Quia Emptores* in 1290 when most alienation took place by subinfeudation (so that the grantor and lord was the same person), the doctrine of warranty greatly assisted the free alienation of land, for the grantor having warranted his tenant's title, his heir could hardly be allowed to dispute it. Express covenants of warranty replaced warranties arising by implication through homage in the course of the

I, p. 279 (Thegnage, Drengage, and tenure by barony), and Chew, *Ecclesiastical Tenants in Chief*, Ch. V (tenure by barony). The position of tenants in ancient demesne is discussed later.

fifteenth and sixteenth century, and the ceremony became obsolete.

Fealty was the oath of faithful service taken by the tenant in favour of his lord; it had no importance in private law. Fealty was incidental to all the free tenures, but homage was in origin confined to tenure by knight-service, where it was appropriate as between the leader of a military force and his men. It later spread into the other free tenures, almost certainly because of the desire of tenants to secure the advantages of having done homage. Thus even a woman could perform the ceremony, Littleton noting, somewhat primly, that she did not say that she became the lord's woman, since this would be inconvenient. Only tenants for an estate of inheritance, that is an estate like a fee simple which descends to the tenant's heir, could enforce their right to do homage.

Aids. Aids were sums payable to lords at irregular intervals to help the lord out of some financial emergency, and in origin symbolize the 'stand or fall together' relationship of lord and man. Early they became a mere exaction, and tenants secured a limitation upon the emergencies which justified an aid; they were confined to the ransoming of the lord from his captors, the knighting of his eldest son, and the marrying of his eldest daughter. These occasions were defined in 1215 by *Magna Carta*, and in 1275 the appropriate sum in the last two cases was fixed by statute;[36] at first the fixing of these sums did not, however, bind the Crown. Aids could be freely given by tenants in other circumstances, or ordered by the Common Council of the Realm. As late as Elizabeth I's reign impoverished aristocrats occasionally kept the wolf from the door by levying an aid, much to the irritation of their tenants. Aids were not peculiar to tenure by knight-service only; socage tenants also were liable for *aide pur faire fitz chevalier* and *aide pur file marier*, but tenants in grand serjeanty were not.[37]

Relief and Primer Seisin. Relief was the sum paid to the lord by a tenant who inherited his holding from an ancestor. In the

---

[36] 3 Edw. I, st. 1, c. 36, 25 Edw. III, st. 5, c. 11.

[37] Aids are not mentioned by Littleton, no doubt because he thought them obsolete; Henry VII revived them, levying an aid for the knighting of his son. See Co. Litt. 76a, 106a.

period immediately following the Conquest the principle of heritability, especially in the case of land held by military tenure, was not established. To allow an heir to inherit military lands irrespective of his ability as a knight was open to obvious objection, so we find that the military tenant is originally thought of as having something in the nature of a life interest only, his heir having, at best, a strong claim to succeed him. This claim, if it was recognized, could be exercised only if he were willing to buy back the land from the lord for a large payment. But Henry I in his Coronation Charter (1100) enunciated the rule that the heir need not buy back the land, but take it up on payment of a just and lawful relief, and this amounts to a recognition of the right of the heir to inherit, or perhaps to be regranted the lands. Much difficulty was experienced in fixing an appropriate sum. In Glanvill's time the relief on a knight's fee was fixed at 100*s*., and that of a socage tenant at a year's rent. Holders of baronies[38] by Edward I's time owed a hundred marks. Tenants in grand serjeanty were long left to make their own bargain—as personal servants the heritability of their holding was not so firmly established. In a case in 1410[39] we learn that they too must pay one year's value of the land.

The King, as often was the case in medieval law, had an additional right against his tenants in chief, for he was entitled to the first seisin (primer seisin) of his tenant's lands before the heir entered. In the case of tenure in chief *ut de honore*, the King, if the heir was of full age, was entitled to the mesne profits of the land until the relief was tendered. If the tenure in chief was a tenure *ut de corona* then the King was entitled to a year's seisin of the lands, or a payment in lieu. Furthermore, if the tenant had been in ward to the King, then, if he held *ut de corona*, he must sue for the delivery (livery) of the land to himself upon attaining his majority, and this cost half a year's profit of the lands, and if he held *ut de honore* he must sue the lands out of the King's hands (*ouster-le-main*) and again pay half a year's profits. These royal rights applied to all lands held in chief except in one case: where a socage tenant was under age at the time of his ancestor's death, a relief alone was payable. Liveries and

---

[38] On the term 'barony' see Chew, *Ecclesiastical Tenants in Chief*, Ch. V. In later law thirteen and a third knight's fees was said to consitute a barony; see Co. Litt. 69b.
[39] Y.B. 11 Hen. IV Trin. pl. 9, f. 72.

ouster-le-mains both attracted fees, and, with primer seisins, formed valuable perquisites of the Crown;[40] their evasion occasioned much ingenuity.

Wardship and Marriage. Wardship was the lord's right to have the custody of the lands or person of an heir who inherited before attaining his majority. In the case of a tenant in knight-service or grand serjeanty the lord had the custody of the lands until the heir became twenty-one (if the heir was male) or fourteen (if a female and married) or sixteen (if female and unmarried). The lord was not accountable for the profits of the land, but could treat the wardship as an assignable right; in fact, wardships were bought and sold as investments and were the most lucrative of all the incidents of tenure.[41] The lord also had the wardship of the body of the heir, whom he was obliged to maintain and educate, and with his wardship of the body went the right to sell the marriage of the ward. This right was subject to some degree of regulation; the lord could not tender a marriage to a person of lower rank, nor was the ward compelled to accept the marriage. But refusal was a serious matter, for the heir might then have to forfeit the value of the marriage to his lord. The process by which military wardship became so debased is an interesting story which cannot be told here, but it can be seen how the lord's rights had some rational basis at a time when the identity, character, and education of his tenants mattered to him, and when an inheritance was safer in the hands of the lord than in the hands of an infant;[42] only by degrees does wardship become degenerate but not wholly commercialized.[43]

Wardship of socage lands and tenants stood upon an entirely different footing. The guardianship fell upon the nearest relative, who was made liable to render an account of his ward-

[40] See the tables in Appendix II to Bell, *The Court of Wards and Liveries.*

[41] For a rosy account of the merits of education by the lord of the fee see Fortescue, *De Laudibus*, p. 107 and for the system in action see Hurstfield, *The Queen's Wards.*

[42] Yet curiously enough the lord's right to wardship is first generally recognized in 1176 by the Assize of Northampton, c. 4; earlier the wardship of military lands passed to the widow or kin of the deceased tenant, as is laid down in the Coronation Charter of Henry I (1100); see *English Historical Documents*, II, p. 400.

[43] But for some redeeming features see Bell, *The Court of Wards and Liveries*, Ch. VI; Hurstfield, *The Queen's Wards.*

ship; indeed, as Littleton realizes, the guardian's position was closely analogous to that of a trustee. The law safeguarded the heir by the provision that a person upon whom the lands might descend could not be guardian, and the Statute of Marlborough in 1267 gave the action of account against a guardian when the heir reached the age of fourteen.[44] Coke treats the guardian in some respects as a sort of bailee of the profits of the land, and indeed a guardian in socage, a life tenant, a trustee, and a bailee of goods have many points of resemblance in the common law.[45]

The Crown also has a peculiar right of prerogative wardship, which resolved in its favour the difficulties which arose when a tenant under age held lands of various lords, one of whom was the King. Here the King had the wardship of the body and of all the lands; if the King was not one of the lords, then the lord from whom the tenant held by the oldest feoffment (i.e. grant) triumphed. This doctrine, as might be expected, applied only in the case of military tenures.

Escheat and Forfeiture. Escheat is of two kinds. If a tenant dies without heirs, then the land comes back to the lord from whom it is held, and this is escheat *propter defectum sanguinis*. Some difficulty is met within distinguishing between an escheat of this kind and a reversion, and this difficulty troubled the lawyers of the thirteenth century just as it troubles modern students.[46] The simple rule is that escheat depends upon tenure and tenure alone, and so occurs only where a tenant in fee simple dies without heirs general. If, say, a life tenant dies, the land comes back to his lord, but this is not the result of the tenure but because the residue of the fee simple remains in the lord in his capacity of grantor, not in his capacity as lord. Escheat *propter delictum tenentis* occurred when the tenant committed felony, and when felony involved a breach of the tenant's obligation to serve his lord faithfully it was reasonable that the land should be forfeit to the lord. By the time we reach the end of the twelfth century the term felony had come to embrace a wide range of

---

[44] For the action of account see Fifoot, *History and Sources of the Common Law*, pp. 268–88.

[45] Co. Litt. 89a; for the analogy with a trustee see Littleton sec. 123.

[46] See P. Bordwell, 'Estates in Land', 18 *Iowa L.R.* 425.

crimes unconnected with the feudal bond between lord and man, so that the chance of a fortuitous gain by the lord was profitably increased, and the rational basis of the rule was lost. Later, lawyers attributed the escheat in cases of felony to the curious and biologically absurd notion that the felon's blood was 'corrupted', whatever that may mean, so that inheritance was impossible through him.

The lands of a traitor were forfeited to the Crown, as were his goods, so that, unlike escheat, forfeiture could not be of benefit to a mesne lord (i.e. a lord, other than the King, from whom the lands were held). Even in cases of escheat for felony the Crown acquired the right to waste the land of the felon for a year and a day—a partial recognition of the notion that felony involved a crime against the state. Forfeiture was limited to cases of high treason, which is peculiarly an offence against the King personally, and the famous Statute of Treasons in 1352 represents an attempt to delimit the ambit of treason so that dispute as to the respective scope of the lord's right to escheat and the King's right to forfeiture should cease. Earlier attempts by the Crown to extend forfeiture to felony, either by an open extension of doctrine or by a deliberate extension of the scope of treason, failed through baronial opposition.[47] Escheat and forfeiture were incidental to all the free tenures.

Tenure and Local Custom

The growth of centralized royal jurisdiction at the expense of the baronial courts created the uniform land law which Littleton analysed; the tendency during the two centuries before his time had been for local custom to be swallowed by the common law —the common custom of the whole realm.[48] Some local custom did, however, survive to affect the landholding of free tenants, and its continued existence posed a considerable problem of analysis. Littleton treated the land law of his time under two basic rubrics—tenures and estates. Tenures he subdivided into a small number of wide categories which were capable (without great difficulty) of containing most forms of tenure which existed;

---

[47] The medley of offences known as petit treasons led to escheat and not to forfeiture.
[48] For the attitude of the common law to custom see Plucknett, *Concise History*, pp. 307–14; see also N. Neilson, 'Custom and the Common Law in Kent', 38 *H.L.R.* 482.

upon estates he imposed a similarly simple classification. But local and particular customs were difficult to fit into an analysis based upon a clear distinction between the doctrine of tenures and the doctrine of estates. Thus in some boroughs there was a custom called borough english, whereby the youngest son and not the oldest inherited lands subject to the custom. Littleton, thinking of this and of other borough customs, vacillates between saying that borough lands are held by a special tenure, tenure in burgage, and saying that lands subject to borough customs are held by socage tenure subject to special customs.[49] Yet since the custom of borough english affects the heritability of lands subject to it, one would expect Littleton to treat the custom as affecting the nature of the estate of the tenant of the lands. The theoretical difficulties which faced Littleton in this connection were a persistent source of uncertainty of classification until modern times.[50]

Besides the custom of borough english, that of gavelkind was sufficiently widespread to be of considerable importance.[51] The custom applied, prima facie, to all lands in Kent, but would be recognized as applying to lands elsewhere if specially proved. The chief peculiarity of gavelkind lands was that they were partible—that is to say the lands would descend to all male heirs of a tenant in equal degree so that they shared the land, rather than descending upon the eldest male to the exclusion of the others, but there were other special rules affecting alienability, escheat, dower, and curtesy. The survival of this anomalous system of landholding in Kent has never been satisfactorily explained, but it is usually attributed to the strategic and economic importance of the county, which lent its inhabitants strength to resist the imposition of common-law uniformity.

Stages in the History of Tenure

The history of tenure passes through a number of stages. In the early formative period before and after the Conquest the relationship of lord and man forms the basis of the social organization of the country, and the tenures created form the

---

[49] Littleton, secs. 162, 165.
[50] Cf. Williams, *Real Property*, pp. 43, 60, and Challis, *Real Property*, p. 14.
[51] For an account of gavelkind see Holdsworth, III, pp. 259 *et seq.*

bond of economic, military, and spiritual co-operation between high and low. With the decline in the value of the fixed services and the rise of an economy based upon contract and the payment of wages, the feudal structure tends to become an archaism. The incidents of tenure, viewed essentially as a form of taxation, assume an increasing importance; in the field of private law a ceaseless battle is waged between those who seek to evade them, and those who seek to profit from them. This battle over what has been appropriately called 'fiscal feudalism' becomes more and more a conflict between the Crown on the one hand and the landowners on the other, and the reason for this is the statute of *Quia Emptores* (1290), which forbade the creation of new tenures upon the grant of a fee simple.[52] Before the statute let us suppose a situation in which A holds of B, and B holds of the Crown. If A wishes to sell his land to Z he will almost certainly do so by *subinfeudating*; that is to say he will make Z his tenant, and the length of the ladder will be increased by another rung. The other possible method is substitution—a grant so designed that Z steps into A's shoes and becomes B's tenant. The statute laid down that in future when a fee simple was granted the grant should always take effect by way of substitution. The reasons for this provision we shall explain later; at present it is important to note that in the course of time the result will be that nearly all tenures will come to be tenures in chief, for the consequence of the doctrine of escheat will be for rungs to be knocked out of the ladder, and the statute of *Quia Emptores* forbids their replacement. The profits of feudalism became to an increasing degree Crown profits, and on the death of a landholder a special inquiry, the inquisition *post mortem*, could take place in which a special official, the escheator, sought to discover what was due to the Crown. By the time we reach the Tudor period[53] mesne lordships had become uncom-

---

[52] For the text see Digby, *Real Property*, p. 236.

[53] For an account of fiscal feudalism see Bean, *The Decline of English Feudalism 1215–1540*, Bell, *The Court of Wards and Liveries*, *passim*; J. Hurstfield, 'The Profits of Fiscal Feudalism', 1541-1602, 8 *Econ. Hist., R. 2nd Ser.* 53, 'The Revival of Feudalism in Early Tudor England', 37 *History* (N.S.) (1952), 131.

For the social effects of this revival see R. H. Tawney, 'The Rise of the Gentry', 11 *Econ. Hist. R.* 1, 7 *Econ. Hist. R., 2nd Ser.* 91. H. Trevor Roper, 'The Gentry', 1540-1640, *Econ. Hist. R. Supplement* No. 1, 3 *Econ. Hist. R., 2nd Ser.* 279, L. Stone, 'The Anatomy of the Elizabeth Aristocracy', 18 *Econ. Hist. R.* 1 and 4 *Econ. Hist. R., 2nd Ser.* 302.

mon, whilst at the same time the technique of evading incidents had reached a perfection which a modern income tax practitioner might well envy. The effect and purpose of the Statute of Uses (1536) was largely to prevent this evasion, and in the late sixteenth and early seventeenth centuries the collection of the feudal revenues of the Crown was brought to heights of efficiency never before attained. A special institution, the Court of Wards and Liveries, was established in 1540 to administer the system; the 'liveries' were the deliveries of lands held in wardship to the heir when he attained his majority. These burdensome feudal dues had become entirely anachronistic, and with other expedients, helped the Crown in its attempt to dispense with the need to rely upon Parliament for revenue. The unpopularity of feudal exactions was probably greatest with the smaller landowners, and they were abolished under the Commonwealth.[54] At the Restoration there was some danger that they too would be restored, but in 1660 the Statute of Tenures[55] finally abolished them. This ill-drafted and obscure Act[56] seems to have been intended to convert all tenures by knight-service, serjeanty, and frankalmoin into free and common socage—that is to say socage which was subject to no services and which was free from customary peculiarities. The poor draftsmanship led, perhaps, to the preservation of frankalmoin. At the same time the honourable services of grand serjeanty were retained, though the tenure itself was no longer allowed to exist. Tenure by socage in chief, which had some peculiar features, was also converted into free and common socage, but whether other tenures in socage were affected is obscure, and in practice unimportant. The better opinion is that they were not touched.

The only important residuary effects of free tenure left after the Act came into force (it was retrospective to 1645) were escheat, forfeiture, and those few incidents and services connected with socage: customary variants of socage such as gavelkind, ancient demesne, and borough english. Forfeiture was abolished in 1870, as was escheat *propter delictum tenentis*,[57]

---

[54] A resolution of the Long Parliament in 1645 was confirmed by an Act in 1656.
[55] 12 Car. II, c. 24.
[56] For the text see Digby, *Real Property*, p. 396.
[57] 33 and 34 Vict., c. 23, The Forfeiture Act.

escheat *propter defectum sanguinis* went in 1925.[58] Other forms of escheat may have survived the 1925 reforming legislation, but these forms are of modern invention and are hardly justifiable upon historical grounds.[59] In 1967 there was a proposal to repeal the Statute of *Quia Emptores*, but this failed. Had this not been so, there would have arisen the strange possibility of the creation of a new tenurial system, for subinfeudation upon a freehold grant would have become possible again.

[58] 15 Geo. V., c. 23, ss. 45, 46, The Administration of Estates Act.

[59] See Megarry and Wade, *Real Property*, p. 34, notes 93–8. Escheat on the dissolution of a chartered corporation, which last took place in the case of Hertford College Oxford, may be historically justifiable. See Challis, pp. 65, 66, 226, 467, *Re Wells* [1933] Ch. 29.

II

The Real Actions

THE common law of land grew up around the forms of action[1] which brought litigation concerning land before the royal justices, and thus enabled them to begin to impose a uniform system of rules of landholding upon the whole realm; eventually in this century the legislature has completed the task, and local customary departures from the common law have been all but totally extinguished. In the period immediately following the Conquest the scope of royal jurisdiction, and therefore of the common law, was probably extremely narrow. Amongst the duties of the feudal lord was the duty to hold a court for his tenants, in which their disputes could be determined. What was a duty was also conceived to be a right; the administration of justice was a profitable business, and to deprive a lord of his court was to usurp a property right which he would not wish to lose. Primarily, then, it was the duty of the King to hold a court for his tenants, the tenants in chief, and not to usurp their functions by meddling with the disputes of lesser tenants.

Had this theory (if one can call it such) been maintained there could have been no common law as we know it. The earliest inroad into it is first stated by Glanvill.[2] He states that according to the custom of the realm, no man need answer in any court for his freehold land unless commanded to do so by the King's writ.[3] This rule was probably based upon two vague

---

[1] For an elementary but now somewhat superseded account see Maitland, *Forms of Action*. The early history of the writ system has been greatly illuminated by R. C. Van Caenegem's *Royal Writs in England from the Conquest to Glanvill*, Selden Society, Vol. 77, which has supplanted much earlier work on the subject. Baker, *An Introduction to English Legal History*. Ch. 4 and Milsom, *Historical Foundations of the Common Law*, I, Ch. 2, give general accounts.

[2] Glanvill's *Tractatus de Legibus et Consuetudinibus Regni Angliae* was written c. 1187–1189. There is a modern edition with translation by G. D. G. Hall, who discusses the authorship and nature of this book in his introduction.

[3] For the scope and history of this rule see Glanvill, XII, 2, 25; Selden Society, Vol. 77, pp. 212–31. The rule was enacted in the Provisions of Westminster (1259), c. 18, and again in the Statute of Marlborough (1267), c. 22.

but important conceptions. The first is the idea that in some sense all free tenants were the King's tenants. This idea had found expression in William I's reign in the famous Sarum oath of 1086, when 'all the land-owning men of any account that there were all over England, whose soever men they were' swore fealty to William, and became his men, accepting a duty to serve him faithfully, even against their own lords.[4] The second is the idea that the King is the fount of all justice, exemplified in the undertaking of William I to maintain the law of King Edward.[5] Now once a royal writ becomes necessary to initiate certain litigation, it is easy to see that the King will be in a position to claim an interest in seeing that the litigation is properly conducted. We can see the recognition of this notion in the form of the writ of right (called the *Breve de Recto*), which is the oldest form of writ which initiates litigation in the court of a mesne lord.[6] It runs:

The King to Lord X, greetings! We order you that without delay you do full right to D concerning one messuage with its appurtenances in the Manor of Dale which he claims to hold of you by the free service of a rose at midsummer for all service, of which T deforces him. And unless you do so, the Sheriff of . . . will do so, lest we hear further complaint on the matter for want of right.

The King has clearly taken freeholders under his wing, and if their lords will not do them justice the case will be moved into a court where a royal officer will ensure that right is done. In the developed system a writ of tolt will move the case from the seignorial Court Baron into the County Court, and if there is a defect of justice there the writ of pone will transfer the action into the Common Pleas.[7] A somewhat different hypothetical explanation for the principle has been put forward by S. F. C. Milsom.[8] He has argued that it merely expresses the essential

[4] For the Sarum oath see *English Historical Documents*, II, pp. 161–2; the story comes from the Anglo-Saxon Chronicle. Cf. Stenton, *The First Century of English Feudalism*, p. 111.

[5] See *English Historical Documents*, II, pp. 399–400.

[6] For detailed discussion see Selden Society, Vol. 77, pp. 195–223; for illustrative material see pp. 413–24.

[7] For the use of pone and tolt see Selden Society, Vol. 66 (*Brevia Placitata*), Introduction *passim*; strictly, tolt is a procedure, not a writ.

[8] Milsom, *The Legal Framework of English Feudalism*, pp. 57–9 and *passim*; *Historical Foundations of the Common Law*, pp. 133–4.

logic of the feudal relationship, in which a lord owed a duty of protection to his tenants. Hence a feudal lord could not, on his own authority, permit that the rights of one of his own tenants be questioned in his own court. Thus if Hugo's court is Robert's seignorial court, this must be because Robert is Hugo's tenant; it would be logically absurd for Robert's status as tenant to be questioned before his own lord's court. If this view is correct the function of the royal writ was presumably to license, on the authority of the monarch himself, an assumption of jurisdiction by a feudal lord which would otherwise amount to a disreputable breach of a lord's obligation to his tenant.

At first the King limited himself in general to indirect protection of freeholders. In the case of his own tenants in chief, direct protection was extended in the royal court. To bring litigation by the tenant in chief into the royal court the appropriate writ was the *praecipe in capite* (sometimes confusingly called a writ of right), which took this form:

The King to the Sheriff of X, Greetings! Order T that justly and without delay he render to D one messuage etc. which he claims to be his right and inheritance held of us in chief, and whereof he complains that the aforesaid T unjustly deforces him, as he says. And unless he does so, and so long as D gives you security to prosecute his claim, then summon the aforesaid T by good summoners to be before our justices at Westminster on such and such a day to show why he has not done so. And have there the summoners and this writ.

Both in seignorial courts and in the King's court trial after the Conquest would normally be by battle, the parties fighting either in person or by champion; the appeal to force was ultimately an appeal to God, who would ensure that right prevailed; formally the theory of battle was that it tested the validity of a witness's oath.[9] In practice the threat of battle may often have led to a compromise. Perhaps in 1179 Henry II took the bold step of introducing generally a form of jury trial, known as trial

---

[9] For an account of trial by battle see *Lowe* v. *Paramour* (1571), Dyer, p. 301, and see Thayer, *A Preliminary Treatise on Evidence*, p. 39, Selden Society, Vol. 62, 113–22, V. H. Galbraith, 'The Death of a Champion, 1287', *Studies in Mediaeval History presented to F. M. Powicke*, p. 283. Battle was abolished in 1819; it was obsolete by the fifteenth century. It was last offered in land litigation in *Claxton* v. *Lilburn* (1638) Cro. Car. 522.

by the grand assize; the tenant who was impleaded in a writ of right or *praecipe in capite* could choose to have the issue tried by a jury composed of twelve or sixteen knights of the neighbourhood. This new procedure had to be supervised by royal officers, and so in any case in which the tenant put himself upon the grand assize the lord's court was bypassed. We do not certainly known the date of this innovation, if innovation it was; the procedure seems well developed by the time Glanvill was written (that is between 1187 and 1189 or thereabouts). It seems quite possible that Henry II merely allowed generally a method of trial previously used in litigation involving tenants in chief in somewhat exceptional circumstances.[10] Naturally enough this reform of procedure was attractive to those who were impleaded by writ of right, and led to an extension of royal justice at the expense of seignorial justice.

The Petty or Possessory Assizes

More important still were the petty or possessory assizes. The earliest of these[11] is the assize of novel disseisin, and its origin remains uncertain and controversial. One view attributes the procedure to a legislative act, perhaps in 1166. Another sees the regular procedure emerging out of intermittent investigations of disseisins, these being originally more like criminal than civil proceedings. The writ, which invariably initiated litigation in the royal courts, took this form:

The King to the Sheriff, Greetings! D has complained to us that T has disseised him of his free tenement in the Manor of Dale unjustly and without a judgment since . . .[12] And so we order you that, so long as D shall give you security for prosecuting his claim you should cause that tenement to be reseised with the chattels which were taken in it (i.e. that the chattels should be restored), and the same tenement with the chattels to be in peace until the first assize when our justices shall come into those parts. And meanwhile you should cause twelve free and lawful men of that neighbourhood to view that tenement, and cause their names to be put into the writ. And summon them by good

[10] See Selden Society, Vol. 77, pp. 82 *et seq.*

[11] The writ became a writ of course in 1179. See Selden Society, Vol. 77, pp. 261–365; Sutherland, *The Assize of Novel Disseisin*, Ch. I; Milsom, *Historical Foundations of the Common Law*, pp. 137–43.

[12] A short limitation period was written into the writ; thus the disseisin had to be *novel*, i.e. recent.

summoners that they be before the justices aforesaid at the assize aforesaid ready to make recognition [*recognitio*] thereupon. And put by gages and safe pledges the aforesaid T, or if he shall not be found, his bailiff, that he be there to hear that recognition. And have there the names of the summoners, the pledges, and this writ.

Now a comparison between this writ and the writs *de recto* and *praecipe* reveals a number of important differences. The new form of procedure has some obvious advantages. If the tenant resists the claim, then the assize jury will be summoned at once; there is no option of trial by battle, and no delay in calling the jury together. Similarly the view of the land is ordered at once, and no separate writ has to issue to secure the view. The tenant cannot just disappear for if he cannot be found his bailiff will be attached instead. In short, the new form of action is designed to be expeditious. Furthermore, novel disseisin only lies in the royal courts; there is no form of writ corresponding to the *breve de recto*. If we go beyond the form of the writ and compare the substantive law which grew up around it, then the differences are more striking still. In the writs of right the demandant[13] claims the land as his right and inheritance (*ius et hereditatem*); in the developed law this always involved a claim to a heritable interest.[14] Furthermore it became the rule that to make good such a claim the demandant must base his claim upon the seisin of some ancestor of his, from whom he must trace a title by hereditary right. The writs of right were appropriate for the assertion of the demandant's best possible title, for the demandant was allowed (within very generous limits) to delve as deeply as he cared into ancient history in setting up his title, and so he could claim that an eviction or other loss of possession happened many years ago, perhaps in his great-grandfather's time. The old lawyers had a striking way of expressing this; they said that the writs of right went highest in the right. The same generous limits in resisting the claim applied to the tenant. After judgment in so solemn an action the parties and their heirs were not allowed another chance to put their titles in issue; the losing party and his heirs would be barred for ever. This drastic result was not

---

13 In real actions the plaintiff is called the demandant and the defendant the tenant.

14 For discussions of the nature of the claim see Selden Society, Vol. 77, pp. 306–13, Vol. 66, lxix *et seqs.*

to be brought about lightly, and the courts took extreme care to prevent anybody being taken by surprise. The tenant was given endless time to appear, and a large body of law grew up around the various essoins, or excuses for failure to appear, which the tenant could plead.[15] He could for instance, retire to bed ill, and stay there for a year and a day, whilst the action hung fire. The writ of novel disseisin, however, initiated litigation of a much less ponderous and drastic sort. The demandant alleges a recent, novel, dispossession, a disseisin, by the person who is now seised of the land in dispute. The jury is summoned to answer a simple question of fact—did the tenant disseise the demandant within the short period of limitation in force?[16] If the answer is that he did, then the *status quo ante* will be restored. That is all. There is little apparent scope for the development of a great deal of law connected with the writ, but the disseisin must be unjust, and the land must not have been adjudged to the tenant (*iniuste et sine judicio*)—and these words in the writ obviously envisage the possibility of some defences to the action in point of law, as opposed to a mere denial of the fact of disseisin. In the course of time the inevitable happened, and legalistic elaboration of this form of action pursued its stultifying course, so that a mass of complex law grew up around the writ. But in its origin and for many years after-wards, novel disseisin afforded a speedy and efficient remedy.

Bracton tells us that sleepless nights were spent in devising the writ; others have been devoted to a search for the source of the new procedure which remains, as we have seen, controversial. Controversy also exists as to the primary original function of the assize: early actions were not infrequently taken against the claimant's own lord or his steward, and this suggests that it was primarily designed to protect tenants from their lords rather than from third parties. A feudal lord could in some circumstances disseise his own tenant for breach of his feudal obligations, but, as the words of the writ indicate, not 'unjustly or without a judge-ment'—of the seignorial court. Like many other new forms of action, the procedure, or something like it, was available in

---

[15] For essoins see Selden Society, Vol. 62, pp. 378–94.

[16] The medieval technique of limitation seems odd to us; an ultimate date was fixed from time to time, and the modern technique of fixing a period of limitation which runs from the time at which the cause of action accrued was not employed at all.

extraordinary cases before the writ became a writ of course. It soon came to be used against mere strangers who ejected land holders, even if this was not its original function. At a time when there were men who were little more than professional disseisors, it is not surprising to find a strong King prepared to take vigorous steps to check this pernicious form of conduct, which is almost wholly unknown to modern society. The disseisor who lost the action was treated as a criminal and imprisoned, and quite soon we find the demandant recovering damages as well as his land.[17] It is perhaps mistaken to conceive of Henry II's policy as a policy of protecting seisin as an abstract state of affairs. He seems rather to be concerned to prevent disseisins. Inevitably, however, the new writ conferred upon seisin a new importance. In the early years the writ could protect *any* seisin, even if it was purely vicious; a disseisin by a person who has right on his side is still a threat to public order, and as such cannot be tolerated in an ordered society. But self-help was not wholly forbidden. Once ejected, so Bracton tells us, a person had four days to re-enter, if he could, upon the land. After that he lost his right of entry,[18] and must bring novel disseisin (or a writ of right), for if he forced his way back on to the land he himself would be liable to have novel disseisin brought against him, and he would lose such an action, for his opponent did not have to show that he had any right to the land. Ultimately there could be no unfairness in this, for a judgment in novel disseisin did not bar the unsuccessful party from later bringing a writ of right, which would put the question of title in issue generally. In the majority of cases there would, in practice, be no need for such double litigation; as a rule disseisors would have no real claim to the land and knew it. Such disseisors would not be likely to waste their time by claiming the land by writ of right, and the judgment in novel disseisin would thus settle the dispute permanently. The new writ soon became very popular, and the need to bring a writ of right, either in a royal or seignorial court, did not frequently arise. Landholders could no longer be put to proof of their title by any rogue who cared to throw them out of possession.

17 The earliest case is in 1198, but before this the successful demandant obtained an order that he be reseised of his chattels and the fruits of the land.

18 See Bracton f. 163, and Maitland, 1 *Coll. Pap.*, pp. 415 *et seq.* A right to enter land must be kept quite distinct from a right to land; a person has a right of entry when his entry is lawful, being in law neither a disseisin or some other wrong.

The principle underlying novel disseisin was applied to other spheres. In the assize utrum[19] a jury was summoned to decide whether land was held by lay or spiritual tenure—a preliminary question to any litigation about it, for the Church claimed jurisdiction over spiritual land. Later the Church was to lose this jurisdiction, and the assize utrum became the parson's substitute for the writ of right. This curious development was brought about in this way. A parson could not use the writs of right, for, like a life tenant, he could not trace his title back to the seisin of an ancestor. The assize utrum could be made to serve the parson, however, for the question asked in the writ was whether certain land in a parish was 'the free alms of the Church of X'. If the answer was 'yes', then it followed that it was the parson of the parish's land.[20] The assize of darrein presentment[21] was also connected with matters ecclesiastical. If a dispute arose as to who had the right to present a clerk to a cure of souls, the writ lay to decide who of the contestants presented last, and adjudged to that person the right to present again; the title of the advowson (which is what this right is called) could be tried later by writ of right, but in the meantime the parishioners would not lack a parson to perform the rites of the Church. Both these two writs decide issues of a preliminary sort in a cheap and expeditious way by submitting to a local jury a closely circumscribed question of fact, unlike the older writs of right which do not circumscribe the issue to be determined at all. Like novel disseisin they do not supersede the writ of right by attempting to do its job in a better way; rather they perform a function for which the older writ was ill-adapted.

Finally Henry II introduced the assize of mort d'ancestor.[22] Novel disseisin only lay between disseisor and disseisee. If a

[19] For detailed discussion see Selden Society, Vol. 77, pp. 325 *et seq.* It was in existence in 1164, being mentioned in the Constitutions of Clarendon, c. 9. For the text see *English Historical Documents*, II, p. 721. In later terminology it is frequently called the *Iuris Utrum*.

[20] Thus Fitzherbert (*Natura Brevium* 49R) says it is 'a writ of the highest nature that a parson can have'. The form of the writ was suitably modified, but even in its final form the original function of the writ is visible.

[21] For detailed discussion see Selden Society Vol. 77, pp. 330 *et seq.* The action probably dates from 1179.

[22] Introduced in 1176 by the Assize of Northampton, c. 4; for the text see *English Historical Documents*, II, p. 412. For detailed discussion see Selden Society, Vol. 77, pp. 316 *et seq.*

tenant of land died and a stranger entered the vacant tenement before the heir was able to do so, the stranger was not a disseisor, for he had disseised nobody. He was called an abator and in the law as it developed the new writ lay at the suit of an heir against such a person; in origin, however, this was not the primary function. The assize of Northampton only talks of an action by an heir against his lord. The aim is to regulate matters when a tenant dies and his lord adopts a difficult attitude to his heir.[23] The writ ran as follows:

The King to the Sheriff of X, Greetings! If D shall give you security etc. then summon by good summoners twelve free and lawful men from the venue of X . . . prepared to recognize upon oath if A, (the father, or mother, brother, sister, uncle or aunt) of the aforesaid D was seised in demesne as of fee of one messuage with its appurtenances in X on the day upon which he died, and if he died since the last passage of the King into Normandy, and whether the aforesaid D is his next heir. And in the meantime let them view the aforesaid messuage.

It must be noted that the writ only lay within narrow limits, for the heir must be within the specified degree of relationship,[24] and his ancestor must have died seised. But if it was available, it enabled the heir to recover the land without having recourse to a writ of right. The new form of action was clearly trespassing into the domain of the writs of right, for the demandant was claiming the land by setting up a title to a heritable interest which was derived from the seisin of an ancestor, for he claimed as heir to an ascendant of his. Yet unlike the wide generality of the claim advanced by the older writ, the newer form of action only permitted the claimant to set up a circumscribed title; he might be able to show that the land had been in the family for generations, but he was not allowed to do so if he chose to litigate by the assize; this was the price he had to pay for the more modern procedure.

[23] For a discussion see Thorne, 'English Feudalism and Estates in Land', [1959] *Camb. L. J.*, 193. In Glanvill (*c.* 1187) the action lies against any abator except a kinsman of the demandant.

[24] This was not apparently originally the case, but the rule is established by Bracton's time. In the early thirteenth century writs of *aiel* (grandfather), *besaiel* (great-grandfather) and *cosinage* were invented to supplement the assize.

The Writs of Entry

This device of inventing newer writs appropriate for a narrowly defined category of claim was enormously elaborated in the real actions known as the writs of entry. Like the petty assizes these writs bypassed the seignorial courts, and their common feature lies in the fact that the demandant alleges a specific flaw in the tenant's title to the land. He asserts that the tenant has no entry upon Blackacre except through a specified person, and then goes on to assert a particular flaw in that person's title. Thus one form (called *'Entry sur disseisin in the per'*) contains an allegation that the tenant has no entry on Blackacre except through (*per*) Z who demised the land to him, and then alleges that Z disseised (*sur disseisin*) the demandant's father, whose heir the demandant is. The possible flaws in titles to land were very numerous, and we can only give examples of the writs of entry designed to cover them. A large number of writs alleged a disseisin as a flaw, but there were others too. Thus the allegation might be that the tenant's title came to him from an intruder (one who entered wrongfully on land after the death of a life tenant), or from an alienation by a lunatic (called *'Dum non Compos Mentis'*), or from an alienation by a husband of his wife's lands during marriage (called *'Cui in Vita'*). We first meet with writs of entry in the late twelfth century; the earliest example seems to be a writ of gage.[25] In this writ it was alleged that the demandant had conveyed his lands to the tenant as security for a debt, and that since he was now ready to pay the debt the tenant ought not to continue to hold the land; the writ therefore specified how it was that the tenant had entered the lands, and gave a specific reason why he should not remain there. The petty assizes, and particularly mort d'ancestor, may have helped to suggest the idea of confining the issue to some single flaw in the tenant's title. At first the scope of the writs of entry was closely confined; the land must not have passed from hand to hand too many times since the defective title arose. Thus the demandant might either sue 'in the *per*', where he alleged an entry *through* X, who had a defective title, of 'in the *per* and *cui*', where he alleged an entry *through* X, *to whom* Z,

---

[25] This is given in Glanvill, X, 9, and has behind it a history of spasmodic royal intervention; see Selden Society, Vol. 77, p. 260.

whose title was bad, granted (or whatever it was) the lands. The Statute of Marlborough (1267) removed this limitation by allowing the writs to be framed 'in the *post*'; this allowed the demandant to refrain from specifying how many changes of hand had occurred *after* the defect arose. Once this is permitted it is obvious that writs of entry may be made to serve much the same purposes as the writs of right, and the tendency to use them in preference to the older writs was encouraged by the better procedure employed in them. Indeed, in Richard II's time it was even thought worthwhile to invent a writ of entry to do the job of novel disseisin, called a writ of entry 'in the nature of an assize' or '*in le quibus*'.

The invention of these new writs contributed much to the extension of royal justice at the expense of the seignorial courts, but this usurpation did not pass without some opposition. The thirty-fourth chapter of *Magna Carta* (1215) laid down that in future the writ called *praecipe* should not issue so as to deprive a free man of his court.[26] This clause was perhaps intended to apply to both the writs of right and the writs of entry, which were both in the *praecipe* form. A mystifying feature of this provision, which was maintained in later issues of the Great Charter though limited to the writ *praecipe in capite*, is its apparent ineffectiveness. It has usually been thought to have been included in the Charter at the instance of the barons for purely selfish motives, to protect their valuable rights of jurisdiction from encroachment; it is at least possible that the intention was to protect tenants, as well as lords, or even instead of lords, from the inconveniences of centralized justice. In the thirteenth century it came to be settled that the clause was to be construed so as to give a lord a right to intervene to preserve his right to a court, but the tenant appears to have been unable to object if he was sued by a *praecipe* writ when he did not hold in chief of the Crown; a lord who wished to object must sue out a special writ to establish his claim, called the writ *De Non Intromittendo*. The practice also grew up of issuing *praecipe* writs which included a clause saying that the lord, in whose court the

---

[26] For a discussion see Selden Society, Vol. 77, pp. 248–51, and N. D. Hurnard, 'Magna Carta cl. 34', *Studies in Mediaeval History presented to F. M. Powicke,* p. 157; Milsom, *The Legal Framework of English Feudalism,* pp. 69–71; Clanchy, 'Magna Carta, Clause Thirty-Four', 79 *E. H. R.* 542.

action should normally have been tried, had waived his court (*'quia dominus remisit curiam'*), even if in fact he had done so. The royal power to control defects of justice in seignorial courts was also abused; instead of waiting to see if the lord was prepared to do right to his tenants, writs of tolt and pone were issued at once, and the writ *praecipe* might not even be issued at all. By the time we reach the fourteenth century the triumph of the royal courts is all but complete, and in its triumph the barons appear to have generally acquiesced.

The Origin of Proprietary Rights

The rise of the royal common law of land, expressed through the medium of the real actions commenced by royal writ issued out of the Chancery, undoubtedly involved a major transfer of jurisdiction over land disputes; so far as free tenure was concerned, the seignorial courts lost out to the centralized royal system of justice, which came to be centred in the Court of Common Pleas at Westminster. It has been convincingly argued by S. F. C. Milsom in *The Legal Framework of English Feudalism* that the eclipse of the seignorial courts, and with it the destruction of the mechanism whereby the personal link between lord and free tenant was overseen and made vital, was not an intended consequence of the evolution of the writs of right, of novel disseisin, and of mort d'ancestor. The reciprocal feudal relationship, with obligations defined by custom and justiciable in the seignorial court, was open to abuse, and the original function of these royal procedures was to provide a sanction against such abuse by lords who failed to observe feudal custom. What had started as a mere system of royal judicial review by degrees became a take-over. Freehold tenurial disputes came to be settled exclusively in the royal courts. Milsom's thesis goes further, however, in arguing that this transfer of jurisdiction did not simply mean that old feudal customary law came to be administered, quite unchanged, in the royal courts, just as it had been in the seignorial courts. The transfer of jurisdiction brought in its train a radical transformation in ideas; customary feudal law was supplanted by a new body of legal ideas of a different character. Most fundamentally, what was involved was a movement from a world in which the central concept was one of reciprocal *obligations*, to one in which lord and tenant were conceived of as independently holding *property rights*, good against the world. Milsom argues that in the world of feudal custom, the notion of property rights (rights as it is said *in rem*) had no place; seignorial courts dealt in terms of the personal relationship of tenure between lord and man, and no more. So it was that the invention of the common law of land held by freeholders, operating through the real actions, produced, as an incidental consequence, the invention of proprietary rights in land as well as the destruction of the underpinnings of the feudal bond. This thesis is not easily, or, indeed, perhaps appropriately, distinguishable from another, which is that the rise of the common law, operating through the early real actions, brought about a transfer of entitlements from lords to tenants. What was once the lord's fief therefore became in reality the tenants' land, over which the lord retained residual, and increasingly archaic, rights. Milsom's thesis is more complex than this short summary can reflect, and any attempt to understand the significance of the rise of the early common law is inevitably hampered by the fact that the early seignorial courts left no records; what went on in them must therefore be largely a matter for intelligent speculation. But that is a problem which Milsom has of course recognized. His interpretation of the evidence is very persuasive, and needs to be studied in the original.[26a]

Title and the Real Actions

The medieval scheme of real actions, as developed in the thirteenth and fourteenth centuries, poses some difficult problems of classification. The title protected by novel disseisin we should be tempted to describe as a possessory title, and that protected by the writs of right as proprietary. In some ways this distinction is apt, but in others it is misleading. Clearly it leaves us in hopeless quandary over the writs of entry and the writs of mort d'ancestor, aiel, besaiel, and cosinage, for how are we to classify these actions? In order to avoid conundra of this sort it is necessary to abandon the simple dichotomy of 'proprietary' and 'possessory', which is the source of all our difficulty, and talk of English Law in English terms. Now the first point which must be grasped is this—in a real action what is recovered is

[26a] See now R. C. Palmer, 'The Origins of Property in England', 3 Law and History Review, 1-50.

not the ownership of land, nor the possession of land, but the seisin of land. Whatever the real action, the end product is the same. For many purposes seisin and possession need not be distinguished, but it is as well to use the correct term, since this will repel the temptation to think in terms of a Romanistic contrast with *dominium*. In the writ of right it is not *ownership* of land, but *seisin* of land, which is sought, and the same is true of novel disseisin at the other end of the scheme of writs. Furthermore, in all the real actions the claimant must establish some reason why he is entitled to seisin; he must show that he has a title. The common law came to recognize a variety of ways in which a person could show title, but all these ways had one feature in common. All involve an assertion, expressly or by implication, of an earlier seisin, either the seisin of the claimant himself (as in novel disseisin) or the seisin of some other person, from whom the title is derived (as in the writs of right). Thus it is said that seisin was the only root of title recognized by the common law, just as today it is probably correct (statute apart) to say that possession is the only root of title recognized. The curiosity of novel disseisin lies in the fact that it allows a claimant to rely on his own seisin as a title, and the introduction of the action gives rise to the doctrine that any person who acquires seisin acquires thereby a title, though a poor title; it matters nothing by what roguery he acquires seisin. If he conveys the land the transferee will be able to use the rogue's earlier seisin as a good root of title; if he dies seised, his son may bring mort d'ancestor against an abator, or even, if he cares, a writ of right.

Once the law has accepted the doctrine that any seisin counts as a good root of title, it must clearly devise some guiding principle which enables one to say how conflicting claims to seisin are to be resolved. The simple rule is that the oldest title is the best, or, to put it another way, the person who can base his title upon the earliest seisin is best entitled to recover seisin. Hence, an investigation into the strength of a title is a historical undertaking. A great body of law grows up as to how titles can be derived; thus to derive a title by inheritance, the claimant must show that he is the heir at law under the complicated rules which govern the descent of lands, and so forth. In the writs of right the naked question, which of the parties to the action has the better title, is finally decided. Since the demandant will recover by showing a better title than the tenant, it will not always be necessary for him to show as good a title as he might be able to do, but the awful finality of the writ of right will be a strong encouragement for him to do the best he can. The evolution of the petty assizes introduces a new idea. Why should the disastrous consequences of losing a writ of right terrify demandants into having to establish their best title when in many cases much less would suffice? A seisin of three months' duration confers a better title than that of a stranger who entered the land two months ago. The action is of limited scope, and it proves to be very successful; in the course of time a large number of these limited actions are invented. In using them to recover seisin the demandant limits himself to a precise reason why he should recover the seisin, and the tenant is similarly limited to a denial of the force of this reason, either in point of fact or law. The demandant's case will rest upon an allegation of a title derived from a seisin earlier in time than a specific flaw in the tenant's title. If we are attempting to classify these actions it would be misleading to say that in some the demandant asserts a possessory title and in others a proprietary title, as if the law recognized different qualities of title or different types of title divisible into two kinds. Consider the situation if Jones, whose land has descended to him peaceably since his great-great-grandfather's time, is disseised by Smith. Whether be brings a writ of right or novel disseisin he asserts the selfsame title; all that he does if he chooses the petty assize is that he spares himself the trouble of tracing it as far back as he might; he does not go so 'high in the right'.[27]

If we try to draw a division between possessory actions and proprietary actions, we end up by drawing a line between actions where the demandant bases his title on his own seisin, and actions where he bases it upon somebody else's. In the first group comes action like novel disseisin and some of the writs of entry, and in the latter the majority of the writs of entry, mort d'ancestor, and the writs of right. Our line drawing will have obscured the real point, which is that the hierarchy of real actions does not naturally fall into two basic categories, any

[27] R. C. Palmer, *The Whilton Dispute 1264–1380*, gives a fascinating account of the use of the various forms of action in a prolonged property dispute.

more than titles do. Titles are better or worse as they are more ancient or more recent, and the gradation is a gentle one. It is not possible to divide titles into two groups without the risk of falsification, so we can hardly attempt to do the same to the actions in which titles are used to justify a claim to seisin.

The Concept of Seisin

The conception of seisin must bulk large in any account of the real actions—the seisin which is the root of titles, and the seisin which is claimed by showing title.[28] The transitive verb 'to seise' appears originally to have been used to characterize the action of a feudal lord in establishing his vassal on land as tenant. But the noun, as Milsom has put it, denotes 'a condition rather than an event, a relationship between person and land'. So far we have not suggested that there is any great difference between this conception of seisin and the conception of actual (or *de facto*) possession, and in the twelfth century there was not; the person seised of land was simply the person in obvious occupation, the person 'sitting' on the land. At one time the curious position of the tenant for years was thought to raise a difficulty. Undoubtedly in the twelfth century he could not use the assize of novel disseisin, whilst the tenant for life could, and this rule was never relaxed. Clearly both are equally in *de facto* possession, and the explanation at one time given for the rule was that the tenant for years, though possessed, was not seised. If this explanation had been correct, then clearly there was some mysterious distinction drawn between seisin and possession as early as Glanvill's time. As we shall see later this is not the correct explanation; the tenant for years was seised but not *'seised of a free tenement'*, and thus he did not fall within the terms of the writ. Broadly speaking therefore, seisin and possession were identical conceptions, and it was quite unobjectionable to talk of persons being seised of chattels. Since the conception was a simple, descriptive one, seisin and disseisin were appro-

---

[28] The classic studies of seisin are those of Maitland—'The Seisin of Chattels', 1 *L.Q.R.* 324, *Coll. Pap.* I. 329, 'The Mystery of Seisin', 2 *L.Q.R.* 481, *Coll. Pap.* I. 358, 'The Beatitude of Seisin', 4 *L.Q.R.* 24, 286, *Coll. Pap.* I. 407, and Ames, 'The Disseisin of Chattels', *Lectures in Legal History*, Lect. XVI. See also N. D. Hurnard, 'Did Edward I reverse Henry II's Policy upon Seisin?', 69 *E.H.R.* 529, P. Bordwell, 'Seisin and Disseisin', 34 *H.L.R.* 592, 717, Milsom, *The Legal Framework of English Feudalism*, esp. pp. 39–41; Sutherland, *The Assize of Novel Disseisin*, esp. pp. 40–2.

priate matters to be understood by laymen, who could well say whether Jones was seised of Blackacre on the day when he died, and whether Smith had been disseised by John Doe. By the end of the Middle Ages all this is changed. The lawyers have refined, modified, and elaborated the concept, so that an immense body of law has grown up on seisin. To speak of the seisin of chattels has become a solecism; seisin has become a term appropriate only to those forms of property recoverable in the real actions—Real Property—and to speak of a lessee's seisin became a gross error; again, on any manor a large part of the land is clearly occupied by unfree tenants, but it is not they who are seised but their lord. Seisin has become a great mystery, and to know who is seised you must know the law. It is easy to see how this came about. The conception of seisin lay at the root of the real actions and at the root of the conception of title. As the law on these subjects is elaborated to serve the needs of policy and justice, the conception of seisin suffers elaboration and loses its primitive simplicity. It becomes a matter on which there is an expert opinion, and the legal concept becomes distinct from the lay concept from which it developed.

In Bracton's time[29] it was said that it took four days for a disseisor to become seised *vis-à-vis* the person he had ejected; the disseisee had a right to enter the land during this time, whilst the situation remained fluid, and if he did so the disseisor could not bring the assize against him. In the course of time the duration of this right of entry was extended. The motive behind this was clear enough—it was to prevent the use of the assize to protect the vicious seisin of the disseisor against the person he had ejected, who would normally be 'the true owner' (to use a dangerous phrase!) By Littleton's time the right of entry of the disseisee endured until it was 'tolled', or determined. This would happen if the disseisor died and his

[29] Bracton, f. 163. There were longer periods available to those who were away from the land at the time of the disseisin. Henry of Bratton or Bracton's supposed book, *De Legibus et Consuetudinibus Angliae*, was written in the thirteenth century; Bracton died in 1268. Many manuscripts of the book survive, and there is much doubt amongst scholars as to the precise date and manner of compilation. The only modern edition (untranslated) of the text is by Woodbine; a reprint of this with a translation and elaborate notes and commentary has been published under the editorship of S. E. Thorne, and amounts to a new edition. It is now thought that Bracton took only a small part in the story. See Baker's entry in Simpson, *A Biographical Dictionary of the Common Law*, pp. 69–71.

heir succeeded him (called a 'descent cast'), but even here the disseisee could preserve his right to enter by making continual claim to the lands, a procedure quaintly described by Littleton, '. . . if he dare approach the land, then he ought to go to the land, or to parcell of it, and make his claime; and if he dare not approach the land for doubt or feere of beating, or maiming, or death, then ought he to go and approach as neere as he dare toward the land, or parcell of it, to make his claime'.[30] Another way in which a right of entry could be destroyed was by certain forms of alienation, and these were called 'discontinuances'.[31] All this made for a complicated body of law. Disseisin ceased to mean simply ejection from land, for the entry on to land of a person who had a right to enter was not a disseisin. 'And note,' says Littleton, 'that disseisin is properly, where a man entreth into any lands or tenements where his entry is not congeable, and ousteth him that hath the freehold.[32] To expound when an entry was 'congeable'[33] would take a book. Indeed, so common was it for persons to have rights of entry, and to be disposed to take steps to exercise them, that forcible entry on land became a social problem which the assize no longer served to prevent, and statutes of Forcible Entry had to be passed to make it a criminal offence to enter on land violently even if the entrant had a right of entry, and to serve the same function of discouraging self-help which novel disseisin had originally served.[34]

But this was by no means the only complication. From the beginning, seisin was a relative conception. The disseisor became seised *vis-à-vis* the disseisee after the fifth day; *vis-à-vis* rest of the world he was probably seised at once. The abator and the intruder did not become seised *vis-à-vis* the heir or reversioner for a year and a day, but once again they probably became seised *vis-à-vis* others at once; nobody else had a right to enter upon them. This relativism was accentuated as the dura-

[30] Littleton, sec. 419. See also secs. 385 and 414.

[31] A discontinuance turned a right of entry into a right of action. See Littleton, sec. 592, and Co. Litt. 325a. The typical illustration is a feoffment in fee simple by a tenant in tail; this makes it necessary for the heir in tail to bring an action to recover the land, for he cannot enter upon the feoffee.

[32] Littleton, sec. 279.

[33] i.e. lawful.

[34] Statutes of Forcible Entry date from the reign of Richard II. The statutes are 5 Ric. II, c. 7, 15 Ric. II, c. 2. 4 Hen. IV, c. 8, 8 Hen. VI, c. 9.

tion of rights of entry became extended. Further complexity was introduced when a distinction between seisin in deed and seisin in law grew up. Seisin in law was attributed to those who had an immediate right to enter upon land, but had not yet exercised it; an example would be an heir who had not entered after the death of his father, the land remaining vacant. The purpose of this doctrine was simply to enable some of the advantages of seisin to be conferred upon such a person without minimizing the importance of seisin; the lawyers took the time-honoured step of inventing a 'constructive' seisin. Another interesting application of this concept is to be found in Coke on Littleton. The Statute of Uses had purported to transfer seisin from one person to another by legislative power. Clearly the impertinence of Parliament in meddling with the common law had to be kept in some bounds, and so Coke only says that the seisin 'in law' has been transferred.[35] Parliament cannot turn a man into a woman, but it can *deem* that a man be a woman, or turn men into 'women in law'.[36]

Finally there are those who are clearly in *de facto* possession, but not seised. Originally the tenant for years was denied novel disseisin because he had no free tenement. If the tenant could not bring the assize, for this technical reason, then common sense led to the conclusion that the lessor should, for otherwise the existence of a lease would greatly favour disseisors. To give the lessor the action it was necessary to attribute seisin of the freehold to him, rather than to the tenant, and so in time the force of the argument that both landlord and tenant could hardly be seised at the same time gave rise to the doctrine that the lessee was not seised, though he was 'possessed'. The denial of seisin to the lessee was never taken quite to its logical conclusion, and the eventual situation was that he was seised for some purposes and not for others; Littleton was not so far wrong when he says in one passage that the lessee is seised, and in another that he is not.[37] Rather similar problems arose over the unfree tenants. The royal courts were not prepared to protect

---

[35] Co. Litt. 266b, and on seisin in law see Littleton, sec. 448. On the doctrine of disseisin at election, where a person who was not disseised in fact could choose to be treated as if he was disseised, see the note by Butler, Note 1 to Co. Litt. 300b.

[36] See Simpson, 'The Analysis of Legal Concepts', 80 *L.Q.R.* 535.

[37] See below, Ch. III.

landholding by unfree tenure until the late fifteenth century brought a change of mind; thus villein tenants could not bring the real actions. Since it was sensible to allow somebody to bring these actions for manorial land the lord was allowed to do so, and to square this with legal theory the seisin was said to be in the lord, and not in the tenant. It will be recalled that the assize of novel disseisin speaks only of a *'liberum tenementum'* and it may well be that the deliberate exclusion by Henry II of the *'villanum tenementum'* from protection had a great deal to do with the later attitude of the courts to the unfree tenants.

The Decline of the Real Actions

As the law grew more complicated the old real actions became less and less satisfactory; particularly striking is the decay of novel disseisin though, as its historian D. W. Sutherland has pointed out, it enjoyed an active life of something near three hundred years, and did not become wholly obsolete until about 1650[38]. The other actions suffered too. The supreme example of dilatory procedure is to be found in the process known as 'fourching in essoins'. If two joint tenants were sued, say by writ of right, each could tender excuses (*essoins*) for non-appearance. They could both be ill in bed for a year and a day, but after that they must appear to answer the action. The ingenious idea occurred to somebody of contriving that each be ill alternately, and the courts accepted this practice. In one case the two tenants keep at it for eight years, and we never find out if they ever stopped until the death of one caused the writ to abate, and the demandant had to begin all over again. The alternating excuse was suggestive of the two prongs of a fork; hence the name. But in spite of grave procedural defects of this sort, which were from time to time remedied by statute, the old real actions had to be made to work after a fashion when no alternative to them existed, and dilatory litigation has been accepted as an inevitable incident of life until comparatively recent times. Those who are amused by the case in Dyer *'Que depend thirty ans sans discussion'*[39] would do well to reflect on conditions in our own time,[40]

---

[38] *The Assize of Novel Disseisin*, 1–2. In Ch. 5 he discusses the reasons for the decline in the use of the action.

[39] *Coningesby* v. *Throckmorton*, Dyer 174b.

[40] Cf. Megarry, *Miscellany at Law*, pp. 244–6.

particularly in the courts of the U.S.A., where litigation flourishes and can be prolonged more or less indefinitely, or at least until the money runs out.

None the less the real actions did become grossly unsatisfactory. In the fifteenth century considerable use was made of trespass and other personal actions to try title to land. Before the action of ejectment was devised in the sixteenth century trespass *quare clausum fregit*, for example, could be employed; by appropriate pleading, in which the alleged trespasser justified his entry, a question of title would arise, and the court would have to settle it. Specific recovery of the land could not be ordered, but a judicial decision as to title would often in practice settle a dispute. The action of detinue of charters was also used; the principle of law was that the title-deeds of land belonged to the person who had the best title to the land, and so in an action to recover such deeds the title of the parties to the dispute came in issue. Very frequently actions were brought on the statutes of Forcible Entry. These statutes had made forcible entry a criminal offence; the courts allowed a civil action to lie upon them, and these actions performed in the fifteenth century much the same function as the assize of novel disseisin had performed at an earlier period. The popularity of these actions is an indication of the state of decay to which novel disseisin had come. Yet for all their archaic procedure and complexity the old real actions were still in quite frequent use until late in the sixteenth century.

To a very considerable degree the rules and concepts of English property law have been permanently influenced by the procedural forms of the old real actions—thus the very distinction between the real and personal property[41] in one sense originates in the distinction between real and personal actions. The entail of the common law can be viewed as a conception developed to explain doctrinally the situation produced by the real actions of formedon, which we shall discuss later in this book.[42] The peculiar position of the copyholder right up to his century stems from the fact that the twelfth-century villein could not use the real actions; so too does the position of the

---

[41] For a discussion see T. C. Williams, 'The Terms Real and Personal in English Law', 4 *L.Q.R.* 394.
[42] See below, Ch. IV.

lessee for years, whose interest is the bizarre 'chattel real'.[43] The student of property law will constantly come across other examples. Yet there is a danger in attributing too much importance to the influence of procedural technicalities over the substantive law. It would not be obviously true to say that real property became heritable simply because the heir acquired appropriate real actions, for in this context, as in others, it is never quite clear whether the rules of law, themselves based upon what was felt to be right, were sanctioned by an appropriate procedure, or whether the rules were developed to explain the existing procedure. The truth no doubt in many cases was that law and procedure grew together, reflecting what society regarded as important entitlements. Sometimes, indeed, one cannot help wondering whether the popular antithesis between substantive law and mere procedure is a very helpful guide to the understanding of legal development. And furthermore, many rules which have a procedural expression really go deeper—chattels and land are treated differently by the law because movables and immovables *are* different from each other; the forms of action only give this difference legal expression.

[43] See below, p. 247 *et seq.*

III

The Tenant's Interest in the Land

AN obvious consequence of the tenurial system is that a number of persons have interests of some sort in the same parcel of land. Confining our attention for the time being simply to free-holders, at the bottom of the feudal ladder there will be a tenant who has seisin of the land and is called the tenant in demesne, and at the top there is the King. In between there may be a string of mesne lords, who are lords and tenants at the same time. This all posed something of a problem in analysis to the early lawyers, and it might have been solved in a variety of ways. One solution would have been to conceive of the tenant in demesne as the 'owner' of the land, and to treat the interest of the lords in the land as *iura in re aliena*. But this was not the way in which the position was looked at, and perhaps the expla-nation lies in the materialism which is a striking feature of medieval legal thought in England. As A. D. Hargreaves put it: 'This materialism is a phenomenon which pervades the whole of the mediaeval land law. Whenever it meets with a conception which we should now regard as a right, it tends to transform it into an almost concrete *thing*.'[1] This attitude of mind also encouraged the rejection of any theory which would say that the lord 'owned' the land, and that the rights of tenants in the land were *iura in re aliena*. Such a theory would have led inevitably to saying that the King, who was ultimately lord of all land, was the 'owner' of all land.

The lawyers never adopted the premise that the King owned all the land; such a dogma is of very modern appearance. It was sufficient for them to note that the King was lord, ultimately, of all the tenants in the realm, and that as lord he had many rights common to other lords (e.g. rights to escheats) and some peculiar to his position as supreme lord (e.g. rights to forfeit-ures). Naturally they catalogued these special rights, but they

---

[1] Hargreaves, *Introduction to the Principles of Land Law*, p. 48.

did not so differ in kind as to make it necessary to put the King in an entirely separate category; he was supreme lord, and that was enough. They treated the bundle of rights vested in mesne lords as if they were material things, and called them *seignories* or manors, and to these 'things' they applied the notion of seisin just as they applied it to land itself; thus they spoke of a lord who held a seignory in Blackacre as being seised *in service* of Blackacre, and of the tenant in occupation of Blackacre as being seised *in demesne* of Blackacre. For the protection of the various rights which formed the substance of a seignory real actions lay, and like the real actions which protect the tenant in demesne, these too involved the adjudication upon conflicting titles based upon seisin. The lord could sue his tenant for the services by the writ *de consuetudinibus et servitiis*, and claim on the seisin of his ancestor; seisin here will mean *de facto* receipt of the services due. As against the world at large the lord could bring a writ of right for a seignory against one who had wrongfully obtained seisin of the services, or bring novel disseisin if the wrongful acquisition was of recent date. This materialistic approach to the description of the tenurial hierarchy of land-ownership is to be found in Bracton. It makes it possible for the lawyers to say that the tenant in demesne of Blackacre and the lord of whom the tenant holds the land are both 'owners' or, better, 'tenants' of Blackacre and are both entitled to seisin. The subject-matter of their 'ownership' differs, however, for the lord owns the seignory and the tenant the land itself, so that their claims to seisin need not conflict. There is a passage in Bracton which clearly illustrates this point. The discussion centres upon the question whether the lord suffers an injury if his tenant in demesne makes a gift of the land he holds.

If he says that an unlawful entry [i.e. by the donee] has been made into his fee this is not so, for it is not his fee in demesne but the fee of his tenant, and the lord has nothing in the fee except the service. Thus it will be the fee of the tenant in demesne and the fee of the lord in service. . . . And so it is that one who enters upon the homage and service does the lord an injury, and not one who enters upon the tenement. . . .[2]

2 Bracton, f. 46. See also Digby, *Real Property*, pp. 158 *et seq.*

The Heritability of the Fee

Now the doctrine of tenure is based upon the notion of a vassal holding land in return for homage and service, and the holding of the tenant is called his fee or fief (*feodum*). Once homage is taken, the lord is bound to respect the tenant's rights for his lifetime; this obligation, so far as the lord is concerned, is certainly lifelong. But beyond that, the position was originally less clear. Let us forget for a while the complexities of the feudal structure, and concentrate upon the relationship between the man on the land, who we will call the tenant, and his immediate lord, and examine this relationship. Immediately after the Conquest it seems that the tenant's fee was not regarded as heritable of right,[3] though as a matter of fact the fee would often pass down from father to son, subject to the payment of a relief as the price of the succession and regrant.[4] The tenure between lord and man was very much a personal affair, which came to an end when the tenant or the lord died. To what extent lords had a really free choice in selecting a new tenant, and to what extent they were constrained by customary entitlements, must remain obscure, but a tenure could only be created by actual acceptance of homage. In 1100 the Coronation Charter of Henry I introduced a new element of stability by providing that the heirs of a tenant in chief need no longer buy back their lands, but could in future 'take them up' upon the payment of a just and lawful relief, and the same principle was applied to other tenants.[5] This amounts to a recognition that such fees were heritable, but when a tenant died some traces of the older system survived; the lord had certain rights in the land until the heir was ascertained and the tenure reestablished by the payment of a relief and the performance of homage by the heir. To secure his rights the lord might seize

---

[3] The whole question of the heritability of the tenant's interest is examined by S. E. Thorne in his article 'English Feudalism and Estates in Land', [1959] *Camb. L. J.* 193. The conclusions which he reaches differ from those expressed in the text; in particular, Professor Thorne reaches the conclusion that the heritability of the tenant's interest was not established until after Glanvill's time. The matter is discussed by Milsom, *The Legal Framework of English Feudalism*, Ch. 5.

[4] See Thorne, *op. cit.*, pp. 195–6, Pollock and Maitland, I. p. 314.

[5] See Plucknett, *Concise History*, pp. 523–4; for the text see Stubbs, *Select Charters*, p. 118.

the land into his own hands until the formalities were observed, and naturally there was a degree of conflict between heirs who claimed to succeed as of right and lords who were anxious to protect their own interests against the demands of heirs. In this conflict the rights of the heir were strengthened as time passed.[6] Thus when the heir was a minor the lord was entitled to hold the lands in wardship, but by Glanvill's time his right is qualified; he is only entitled to do so if he had received the heir's homage, and has thereby recognized his right to have the lands. In Glanvill we find that the heir's right to succeed is firmly established, so long as he tenders the relief and does homage, and he can indeed compel the lord to accept the relief and homage by writ.[7] But the seisin does not pass automatically from the deceased tenant to his heir, and upon the death of the tenant there may ensue something in the nature of an interregnum; the heir may not be on the scene, or there may be dispute as to who is the heir. In situations of this sort the lord may well seize the lands himself.[8] But after 1176 the true heir is *entitled*, he can demand the seisin from his lord by mort d'ancestor, and he can do so even if he has not yet paid his relief, for the lord has lost his right to retain the lands as a security for the relief. If the heir happens to have acquired the seisin he is entitled to resist the lord if the lord attempts to take it from him.[9] But as the lord is the person who should look after the orderly succession to fees he still retains some rather vague rights in the land, and he is said to be entitled to a 'formal' seisin, the relic of the time when the tenure came to an end on death. It is not surprising to find that the King as lord retains

---

[6] The problem raised by Thorne is really one of definition—'how scanty have the lord's rights over the land to become before one can say that the tenant's heir *inherits?*' Milsom's discussion (*op. cit.*, p. 180) raises another similar problem, for he treats customs about inheritance as defining whom the lord in his court should choose as heir, but as not conferring rights. I find this contrast difficult to understand.

[7] Glanvill, IX, 5; see *English Historical Documents*, II, pp. 937 and 941.

[8] Lords continued to do this, even when they ought not to have done so, long after Glanvill's time; see the Petition of the Barons (1258), c.1 (Stubbs, *Select Charters*, 373). In 1267 the heir was given a remedy in damages against a lord who entered the inheritance and wasted it by the Statute of Marlborough, c. 16. See Pollock and Maitland, II, pp. 310-11.

[9] See Selden Society, Vol. 77, pp. 316 *et seq.*; Glanvill, IX, 6, and read the passage in *English Historical Documents*, II, pp. 937-43, and in Digby, *Real Property*, pp. 77, 79, 80, 83.

from an earlier period rather more than other lords; he has the right to a real first seisin (primer seisin) of the lands upon the death of one of his tenants in chief.

At what point in time we say that the heritability of the fee is established is rather an analytical than a purely historical question, but in Glanvill's time it seems to have been quite settled that to hold in fee was to hold heritably.[10] At the same time the rule of primogeniture was established clearly enough in the case of the military tenures,[11] though it had a harder struggle where the land was held in socage. Glanvill is a little unclear on the subject, but seems to treat the descent of the entire holding to one son, either the oldest or the youngest, as the general customary rule, whilst admitting that socage lands anciently subject to a custom of equal division amongst sons should descend according to the custom. But by Edward I's time primogeniture had become the common law of all tenures, and exceptions to the rule were treated as anomalous customs in opposition to common right.

The Right to Alienate

The alienability of the fee took longer to establish. When it becomes accepted that the fee is heritable it is clear that an alienation by the tenant deprives the heir of his hopes; indeed, the heritable quality of the fee makes it tempting to say that even before the death of the tenant his heir has some sort of interest in the land. Glanvill is quite clear that there are some limitations upon the power of tenants to disinherit their heirs, but he does not commit himself very specifically as to what precisely they are, or indeed as to what an heir can do if they are infringed.[12] He grasps hold of a very intelligible idea when he says that the power of alienation is wider over acquired lands than it is over inherited lands; one must not take advantage of the right of inheritance and then deprive one's heir of the same advantage. By Bracton's time, however, these family restrictions upon alienation have wholly disappeared, and Bracton does not even mention them. The protection of the

[10] For other discussions of the subject see Pollock and Maitland, I, p. 314, and Plucknett, *Concise History*, pp. 523–4.

[11] Glanvill, VII, 3.

[12] Glanvill, VII, 1; the passage is discussed by Plucknett, *Concise History*, p. 526.

family is limited to the widow's right to dower and the widower's right to curtesy, which entitle them to life holdings of a part or all of the deceased spouse's land as against the heir or lord. Incidentally, however, the tenant's freedom of alienation has an effect in mitigating the harshness of primogeniture. Thus in Glanvill it is recognized that a tenant can grant away some of his land with his daughter as a marriage portion. But the tenant who wishes to grant lands to his younger sons and thus modify the results of the adoption of primogeniture is in a difficult position; he cannot give them any of his inherited lands without his heir's consent. When the heir's consent ceases to be necessary the tenant is able to provide for all his children; the heir is only entitled to what is left when his father dies. This position is reached in the thirteenth century, and legal theory has to accommodate itself to the position. Thus arises the dogma that when land is granted 'to A and his heirs'—the normal way of granting a fee—the words 'and his heirs' are words of *limitation* and not of *purchase*; they mark out or delimit what is given to A, but confer no interest by way of grant upon the heir. The heir takes land by *descent* from his ancestor, and not by way of grant or purchase from the grantor. Thus Bracton says: 'the heir acquires nothing from the gift made to his ancestor because he was not enfeoffed with the donee'.[13] Later this doctrine is reinforced by the acceptance in the early fourteenth century of the rule that a living person can have no heir, for until his death his heir cannot be certainly ascertained. The heir cannot take an interest because he is not identifiable, and a grant with no identifiable grantee is something which the lawyers could not swallow.

The disappearance of the family restraints upon free alienation was closely connected with the doctrine of warranty.[14] The receipt of homage gave rise to an obligation by the lord to warrant or guarantee the tenant's holding, and as an incidental effect the lord was barred from claiming the land from the tenant in litigation. By Glanvill's time this bar had come to be extended to the lord's heir. Thus if Robert had alienated some of his land, his heir was barred from claiming it back so long

[13] Bracton, f. 17; extracts from a long discussion are given in Digby, *Real Property*, pp. 164, 170.

[14] On this complex subject see a series of articles by S. J. Bailey in 8 *Camb. L. J.*, 274 and 9 *Camb. L. J.* 82 and 192.

only as Robert had alienated by subinfeudation and accepted the homage of the alienee. Glanvill does add a proviso—the gift must have been a reasonable one—but this qualification seems to have disappeared rapidly.[15] The duty of the lord to look after his tenant and protect him thus assists the growth of a power of free alienation.

The existence of tenure gives rise to specifically feudal objections to free alienation by the tenant. If the tenant alienates by way of substitution, the lord may be saddled with a bad tenant who is unfit to perform the service due; he might even find that the alienee is a personal enemy. If the tenant is allowed to subinfeudate, the lord can hardly complain upon personal grounds, for he retains the same tenant, but he may be seriously harmed financially in relation to the incidents of tenure. Suppose, for example that Osbert, who holds of Robert, wishes to alienate his holding to Richard, and does so by subinfeudating. If the alienation takes place on account of a sale, then Osbert will receive the purchase price and grant the lands to Richard to hold of him at a nominal service of, say, a red rose at midsummer. Osbert will be left seised of a seignory, worth one rose annually, and it is on the value of the seignory that the amount due in incidents to Robert, his lord, will be calculated. Thus if Osbert dies and his heir, a minor, succeeds him, Robert will be entitled to the wardship over a seignory of trivial value; if Osbert commits felony, the seignory, and not the land, will come to Robert by escheat. In theory at least the services due to Robert will not be affected, for he can distrain on the land if they are not performed, and no bargain between Osbert and Richard can deprive Robert of them; in practice the remedy of distress might not be so effective, for the tenants of the land might be poor men, unable to perform the service, and distraint to compel them to do so would be a waste of effort. But as time goes on the incidents of tenure become financially increasingly important, and lords become increasingly reluctant to be deprived of them.

Particularly grave disadvantages ensued when a tenant alienated to a religious corporation; such a body never died, never committed felony, and never left an infant heir, so that

---

[15] Glanvill, VII, 2.

the lord was permanently deprived of the most valuable incidents of tenure even if the alienation was by substitution. If it was by subinfeudation the tenant's heir was just as hardly hit, for he too was deprived of the chance of a windfall such as an escheat, and he might find himself the tenant of so depleted a holding that he could not discharge the services due to his lord. Objections to grants 'in mortmain'—to a dead hand—are thus based upon a desire to protect both feudal lords and the family.

Quia Emptores

In Glanvill's time it is doubtful whether a tenant was entitled to alienate his holding without the consent of his lord; to be on the safe side it was wise to secure the lord's consent to a gift, but it was not perhaps essential if the gift was a reasonable one which did not seriously affect the lord's interests.[16] In the Great Charter of 1217 an attempt was made to define the lord's rights, and it is laid down that, 'No free man shall henceforth give or sell so much of his land that the residue shall be insufficient to support the service due in respect of the fee.' This is the first specific statement on the subject, but it probably was only intended to state what the barons thought was the existing rule. In Bracton's time it appears that in practice a lord could not do anything about an alienation which displeased him,[17] and thus from the mid-thirteenth century onwards the fee has become an alienable fee; this situation was finally recognized by the statute of *Quia Emptores* in 1290,[18] which lays down that, '. . . from henceforth it shall be lawful for every freeman to sell at his own pleasure his lands and tenements, or part of them'. But the statute was devised so that lords should in future suffer no loss by alienation, for it provides that in all unconditional grants of a fee (later this means grants in fee simple) the grantee shall, by operation of law, take by substitution, and hold of the grantor's lord, and not of the grantor. This solution to the problem is a striking illustration of the lack of importance which by this time

16 See Pollock and Maitland, I, pp. 329-49, for a general discussion of the subject.

17 The passage quoted above from Bracton, f. 46, amounts to a recognition that this is so.

18 For the text see Digby, *Real Property*, p. 236; for comment Plucknett, *Legislation of Edward I*, p. 102.

was attached to the personal relationship of lord and tenant; lords were more interested in protecting their incidents than in selecting their tenants.

The recognition of the freedom of the tenant in fee simple (as we would call him) to alienate freely led to the abandonment of grants in which the grantor expressly by the form of the gift conferred on the grantee a power of free alienation, by making the gift not simply 'to A and his heirs' but 'to A, his heirs and assigns'. Before *Quia Emptores* there seems to have been some doubt as to whether or not the land ought to come back to the grantor when the heirs of the original grantee died out, whether he had alienated or not; Bracton seems to vacillate on the question.[19] If the courts in the fourteenth century had decided that it should then the doctrine of estates would have been very different, but by 1306 the other view was quite settled, as this dialogue shows:[20]

Bereford C. J. See that there is no deceit in your pleadings: for from what you have said we understand that the tenements were given to William and Agnes and to the heirs and assigns of Agnes, and there is no force in that word 'assigns' but simply in those words 'heirs of Agnes'.

Herle. That say we: and in a fine no one puts the word 'assigns'; and yet an assign can vouch him [i.e. the grantor] or the heirs of him that granted by fine. . . .

This had probably been the accepted law for some time, and it illustrates the important fact that it is not only in the case of a pre-*De Donis* conditional gift that a grantor can be deprived of his having the lands back by the alienation of the tenant.[21]

Grants in mortmain, however, were excepted from the tenant in fee's power of free alienation. The development of a legislative policy can be traced back to the Great Charter of 1217. The provision which has been quoted was probably directed particularly against such grants, and Chapter 43 strikes at collusive arrangements with religious houses designed to evade feudal incidents, but does not specifically restrict straightforward

---

[19] See Bracton, f. 17b, 23b, 48b, discussed in Holdsworth, III, p. 106 and Pollock and Maitland, II, p. 14.

[20] Y. B. 33–5. Edw. I (R.S.), at p. 362.

[21] See below, p. 65.

grants in mortmain.[22] In 1258 the barons at Oxford protested that men of religion were entering their fees without their consent, and a year later the Provisions of Westminster required a licence from the immediate lord for a gift to a religious house.[23] Finally the law was settled by the statute *De Viris Religiosis* (1279),[24] which made lands granted to religious bodies liable to forfeiture and allowed the immediate lord of the land which had been alienated in mortmain to enter into it and hold it himself, and if he failed to do so the next lord was allowed to enter, and so on up the chain of lords. The statute did not, however, prevent alienations in mortmain, for the Crown adopted the practice of granting licences in mortmain which removed the risk of forfeiture, and these licences were freely granted. What in effect checked excesses of piety in the medieval period was the inability to devise land.

The Concept of the Fee Simple

By the end of the thirteenth century, therefore, the normal fee, which had been granted to a man and his heirs with no special provisions in the grant, had become an alienable and heritable interest. In a year book of 1294 the reporter notes: 'A fee pure is when anyone has a frank tenement which he can give, sell, alienate or assign, and which will descend to his heirs.'[25] To distinguish such a fee from other fees the expression fee *simple* comes to be used. At first what is indicated by the term *simple* is that the *grant* is unconditional, but soon the idea is that the *interest granted* is a simple fee. Such a fee, besides being alienable, will descend upon both the lineal and collateral heirs of the tenant. The rules of inheritance are complex, but in their developed form they can be summed up in the following propositions,[26] which we can appropriately discuss now at the expense of a strictly chronological arrangement.

---

[22] It deals with grants to religious houses where the grantor has arranged to receive the lands back again by regrant and so become the tenant of the house; some religious bodies were specially exempt from liability for temporal service, and the effect of such an arrangement was to reduce the resources of the fief permanently. For the text see Digby, *Real Property*, p. 133.

[23] For texts see Stubbs, *Select Charters*, pp. 375, 393.

[24] For the text see Digby, *Real Property*, p. 219.

[25] Y.B. 21-2 Edw. I (R.S.), p. 364. The expression 'pure fee' is more commonly used at first than the expression 'fee simple'.

[26] Based upon Blackstone, Bk. II, Ch. 14.

(*a*) Inheritances lineally descended to the issue of the person who last died seised, but never lineally ascended.

The person who died seised is called the stock of descent, and the rule is expressed in the maxim *seisina facit stipitem*. The tracing of descent from the person last seised is very ancient, and almost certainly first arose because of the form of claim sanctioned in the assize of mort d'ancestor, in which, it will be remembered, the demandant must show that he is the heir of the person who died seised of the lands in issue.· The rule lasted until 1833, when it was altered by the Inheritance Act, which altered the stock to the last purchaser—that is the last person to come to the land otherwise than by descent. This was always the rule at common law for tracing the descent of an estate tail; the heir in tail had to make himself heir to the original donee in tail, not to the last tenant. The old rule still applies, of course, to the descent of title to the throne.

The denial of the right of lineal ascendants is a curiosity which has provoked some speculation. In the simplest case it means that if John buys some land and dies childless leaving a father Hugo alive, Hugo cannot under any circumstances inherit the land; it will sooner escheat to the lord than go to him. This rule was not settled until the very end of the thirteenth century; Britton[27] indeed denies it. The simplest explanation of the rule is purely doctrinal; inheritances descend, they go down, not up. This indeed may well be the root of the matter, the early lawyers accepting what seemed to them to be the *natural* rule. Maitland,[28] in an ingenious and conjectural mood, devised another explanation. In Glanvill and subsequent writers there is a rule that a man cannot be both lord and heir, at least if he has taken homage.[29] The receipt of homage, which imposes on the lord the duty to warrant the tenant's title, debars him from claiming the land back as heir; he may only retrieve the land by escheat, when all other possible heirs fail. Maitland points out that in the twelfth century, in practice,

---

[27] Britton, II, pp. 319, 325.

[28] Pollock and Maitland, II, pp. 286 *et seq.*

[29] Glanvill, VII, 1; Bracton, f. 65b; Britton (II, pp. 33-4) advises lords to be careful not to take homage if they have a chance of claiming as heir. Glanvill's statement of the rule is extremely difficult to follow; Hall, in his edition (pp. 72-3, notes), attempts to make sense of the text.

sons who acquired land would normally do so from their fathers by subinfeudation; in our example Hugo would be John's lord in most cases, and thus be unable to claim as heir. If he took at all he must take by escheat, when all other possible heirs have failed. The common case gave rise to a general rule that fathers cannot inherit from sons and, wider still, that lineal ascendants cannot inherit. After *Quia Emptores* (1290) stopped subinfeudation the newer generalized rule lived on, divorced from its earlier basis in the older rule that a man cannot be both lord and heir.

There are difficulties in Maitland's view,[30] and he never claimed more than plausibility for it. We can note that neither the writ of right (where a claim must be based on an *ancestor's* seisin) nor mort d'ancestor (where the same is true) afforded a procedure in which an ancestor could claim from a descendant, but whether procedure moulded the law, or the law moulded procedure, is anybody's guess.

The rule forbidding lineal ancestors to inherit was abolished by the Inheritance Act of 1833.

(*b*) Male issue were admitted before female, and where there were two or more males in equal degree the eldest only inherited, but the females inherited together as co-parceners.

We need an example. Hugo dies seised, leaving an elder daughter Matilda, then Mary, then a son John. John is the heir. If John had died before his father, Matilda and Mary take jointly as co-parceners.

The preference of males to females hardly needs explanation; obviously the rule is natural where land is held by knight-service, but it is older than Norman feudalism. Of primogeniture we have already said something; the equal treatment of heiresses, who together constitute one heir, is not at all easy to explain, for the rule applied even when the land was held in knight-service and the military arguments for keeping the fief together would have seemed likely to produce primogeniture amongst daughters. In Glanvill's time the practice was for the eldest daughter to do homage for the lands, whilst the younger daughters held of their elder sister. A royal writ of 1236 had the

---

[30] Plucknett, *Concise History*, p. 716, note 3, where it is pointed out that Maitland's explanation is hard to square with Britton.

effect of altering this practice, and thereafter all the daughters did homage directly to the lord; probably the practice changed because it was more profitable to the lord to have all the daughters directly under his wing, for it made it easier for him to sell their marriages and enjoy his wardship over their lands.[31]

(*c*) The lineal descendants *in infinitum* of any person deceased represented (i.e. stood in the shoes of) their ancestor.

Suppose John dies seised, leaving a grandson Peter (whose father, Hugo, was John's eldest son, but is now dead) and a second son Richard. Peter will be the heir, and not Richard, for Peter stands in the shoes of his father.

This rule was settled late, in Edward I's time, though earlier legal opinion had inclined towards it. The delay in accepting the rule was the result of the precedent set by the accession of King John in 1199. On Richard I's death the claimants to the throne were Arthur and John. Arthur was the grandson of Henry II by his third son Geoffrey, who was dead, and John was Henry's fourth son. Under the rule of representation Arthur had the best claim, but John in fact obtained the Crown. The lawyers could hardly do anything but follow this royal precedent whilst it would have been near treason to depart from it.[32]

(*d*) On failure of lineal descendants of the person last seised the inheritance descended to his collateral relatives (subject to rules (*b*) and (*c*), being of the blood of the first purchaser.

Suppose this to be the family tree, deceased persons being indicated by the names in brackets.

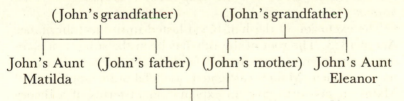

Now suppose that John's mother was the first purchaser—perhaps she bought the land. John died seised; Aunt Eleanor

[31] See generally Pollock and Maitland, II, pp. 274-6.
[32] See Pollock and Maitland, II, pp. 284-6, or Plucknett, *Consise History*, 716-18, for a fuller account; the point was entangled in high policy until 1241.

will be the heir, for she alone is related by blood to John's mother, whereas Matilda is not. Even if Matilda was changed in our example to Uncle Hugo, the same bar would exist to his inheriting. The result of the rule is that land which has come down on one side of the family will go back to that side, and this is thought to be its *ratio*; the principle was established, apparently, in the thirteenth century.

(*e*) The collateral heir of the person last seised must have been his collateral kinsman of the whole blood.

The exclusion of the half-blood of course only applies to collaterals. The standard example of the rule is this: Hugo marries Eleanor, and has a son John, and a daughter Matilda. He marries again, this time Elizabeth, and has a son Peter. Hugo is seised of Blackacre and dies seised, and John, his eldest son, inherits. John enters and dies seised. We have to discover *his* heir; it will be Matilda, for she is of the whole blood, and not Peter, who is of the half-blood. Not only is Matilda preferred, but Peter cannot under any circumstances inherit.

Suppose the story was different, and that when Hugo dies John is abroad on a crusade, and that John dies before he can get home and acquire seisin of Blackacre. Now we have to find not John's heir (for he did not die seised) but his father Hugo's heir. Hugo has a lineal descendant Peter and a lineal descendant Matilda; the half-blood rule is quite irrelevant, and boys are preferred to girls. Peter is the heir. The difference between this and the first example is summed up in a tag—in the first case *possessio fratris* (i.e. John's seisin) *de feodo simplici facit sororem esse heredem.*

The exclusion of the half-blood lasted until the Inheritance Act of 1833. The root of the rule has been the subject of elaborate controversy. Blackstone defended it,[33] and gave an explanation which Maine castigated as 'elaborate sophistry',[34] Maine in his turn gave an explanation in terms of a theory of an agnatic scheme of relationship which was dismissed by Maitland,[35] Maitland rejected all rationalizations—there had

---

[33] Blackstone, Bk. II, pp. 228 *et seq.*

[34] Maine, *Ancient Law*, 10th ed. (by Pollock), p. 165. Maine thought that the original exclusion was only of uterine half-brothers (i.e. those with the same mother, but different fathers); these were not related at all under an agnatic scheme. The judges became confused, and in time excluded all the half-blood.

[35] Pollock and Maitland, II, pp. 302 *et seq.*

to be a rule one way or the other, and the fourteenth-century lawyers just happened to adopt this rule. Plucknett in his turn rejected Maitland's account,[36] the rule is as old as primogeniture, and the acceptance of primogeniture and the acceptance of the principle *seisina facit stipitem* (descent is traced from the person last seised) necessarily led to the exclusion of the half-blood. Holdsworth[37] also portrayed their exclusion as a deduction from two principles. Like Plucknett, he thought that the rule *seisina facit stipitem* was one, but in place of primogeniture he adopts the rule that the heir must be of the blood of the first purchaser as the other, an idea which comes from Blackstone. The reader must go to these writers and make up his own mind.

(*f*) In collateral inheritance the male stocks were preferred to the female, unless the lands in fact descended from the female.

This is an extension of the preference of males; if, for example, Hugo dies seised and leaves no issue, his heir must be sought amongst the collaterals. In the search you 'hunt back'[38] in the male line—the father, the father's father, and so on, only having recourse to the female line if the male fails to produce an heir. This hunt for collaterals under the English scheme of inheritance was carried out (subject to rules (*b*), (*c*), (*d*), and (*e*)) according to what is called the parentelic scheme. This is best illustrated by an example. Suppose the following family tree, in which John has just died seised, and the living members of the family are indicated by the absence of a bracket.

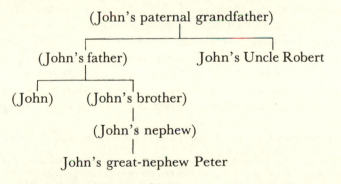

(John's paternal grandfather)

(John's father)   John's Uncle Robert

(John)   (John's brother)

(John's nephew)

John's great-nephew Peter

---

[36] Plucknett, *Concise History*, pp. 719–22.
[37] Holdsworth, III, pp. 183–5.   [38] The expression is Blackstone's.

If you count the steps from John to his Uncle Robert there are three, from John to Peter there are four. It would appear that Robert is the nearest collateral relative, but at common law he is not the heir. Instead, the rule is that you exhaust all the descendants of John's father, however remote, before you look at the descendants of his grandfather at all; thus Peter is the heir. The name 'parentelic' arises because a person's issue constitute his *parentela*. John has no *parentela*, his father and grandfather have. Under the parentelic scheme you take each *parentela* one by one and do not examine a more remote *parentela* until you have disposed of the less remote. In our example there is no need to go to the grandfather's *parentela*, for the father's contains a living person, Peter, and he is the heir.[39]

The descent of heritable interests in land to the heir marked off real property from personal property,[40] around which there grew up a wholly different body of law which determined what was to be done on death. The descent to the heir could not be interfered with by will. Local custom apart, wills of land were rejected utterly by the common law, whereas it was sinful not to execute a will of personal property; the rule that land was not devisable was settled in Glanvill's time. Death-bed gifts were also excluded. To the rule that real property could not be devised was added the rule of primogeniture, which spread outwards from the military tenures until it governed land held by any tenure, except only where local custom, as in Kent, resisted the imposition of uniformity. The power of a landholder to interfere with descent was at first very limited; devices such as adoption were not recognized, for 'God alone can make an heir'.[41] Alienation *inter vivos*, a poor substitute for a will, was the safest technique available. In the course of time better methods were evolved. The creation of an entail in effect modifies the course of an inheritance, though only in a restrictive way. In the later Middle Ages, as we shall see, the *use* of lands was popular in that in effect it gave a power of devise,

[39] For the contrast between the parentelic scheme and the gradual scheme see Pollock and Maitland, II, pp. 295 *et seq*.

[40] Chattels real, such as leaseholds, followed the rules for personal property. For the history of succession to personalty see Plucknett, *Concise History*, pp. 725–46.

[41] Glanvill, VII, 1. Note that the descent of an entail could not be affected by will until 1926.

and in the end devisability was conferred on landowners by statute.[42] Yet the old rules continued to apply in cases of intestacy, subject to some modification, until 1926, though they were almost always superseded by will.[43]

Modifications of the Fee in the Age of Bracton

So far we have dealt only with what we would call the fee simple, where the grantor of the estate makes a gift to 'A and his heirs' *simpliciter*. The law of the thirteenth century displays a generous freedom in its attitude to variant forms of gifts, for there were then no very precise rules as to the possible forms of gifts of lands. Bracton's approach to the vagaries of donors[44] is to enunciate the principle that by granting lands in other ways—say 'to A and the heirs of his body'—the donor was able to establish a sort of private law which would govern the descent of the lands, just as today the parties to a contract are sometimes thought of as making their own private law to govern their business dealings. Such a special provision will have the effect of enlarging or restricting the class of heirs capable of inheriting the land. Let us confine our attention to gifts restricting the class of heirs, gifts where the heirs are restricted to descendants of the grantee by a particular wife and the like. The origin of such peculiar gifts is to be found in the institution of the *maritagium*.

Though in one sense a Norman institution, the *maritagium*, or marriage portion, is a feature of most societies. The foundation of a new family must be assisted by some initial endowment of property, and in a society where land is the chief source of wealth we may expect to find gifts of land being made on account of marriage.[45] In particular, younger sons, who would not inherit under primogeniture, needed provision when they married. In

---

[42] See below, pp. 191–199.

[43] The Land Transfer Act of 1897 modified the law by providing that upon the death of a tenant (of a heritable interest) intestate the real estate should devolve upon and vest in the personal representatives, to be held on trust for the heir, whose interest thus became equitable only. See this explained, Williams, *Real Property*, pp. 218–21.

[44] For texts see Digby, *Real Property*, pp. 163 *et seq.*, 101 et seq. See also Plucknett, *Consise History*, p. 516.

[45] See Glanvill, VII, 18. For an Anglo-Saxon marriage agreement which seems to anticipate some features of the Norman *maritagium* see Robertson, *Anglo-Saxon Charters*, p. 148. See also *English Historical Documents*, II, pp. 921–2, 929, for examples of early marriage settlements.

the thirteenth century any such gift counted as a *maritagium* so long as the connection with an existing or contemplated marriage was specified at the time of the grant, and so long as the gift did not consist in a grant of dower by the husband to the wife; essentially the *maritagium* came from somebody other than the parties to the marriage. Since the purpose of such a gift was to found a family, it is natural that donors wished to ensure that the land should stay in the new family. Hence the normal form of such a gift would include a limitation restricting the class of heirs who could inherit the land to the issue of the original donees, corresponding to the heirs capable of inheriting under the entail (in its various forms) of later law. A very usual form would be a gift by the bride's father to the bridegroom and the heirs of his body begotten on the wife-to-be. But many variants are found; the parties to the marriage might be given the land jointly or the heirs might be limited to the issue of the husband by any marriage. Any variation which might occur to the donor was acceptable. Such gifts might also have tenurial peculiarities, for the donor might undertake to acquit the donee of liability for feudal services (that is, for the forinsec service), and this could be effected by expressing the gift to be in frank or free marriage, instead of in marriage only.

The results in law of gifts in marriage were established by custom in the course on the twelfth and thirteenth century. Until the third heir entered, the donees were not liable to do homage. This meant that the donor did not have to warrant their title, and removed the risk that the donor would be unable to get the land back if the new family died out. It also would probably have the effect of making the land difficult to alienate, and it has been suggested, on no very good authority, that in Glanvill's time *maritagia* were in fact inalienable.[46] That this was the intention of the donor can hardly be doubted. But it seems very dubious whether there was anything that could be done about it if the donee did alienate to a person who would take the risk; indeed, the rules which Bracton states on the subject, which have caused much discussion, probably represent an attempt to explain theoretically what for better or worse existed in practice—the donee's power to disinherit his children,

---

[46] Plucknett, *Concise History*, p. 546.

which so obviously frustrated the donor's intention. If the gift was in free marriage the feudal services revived when the third heir entered, and homage was then due.

The limitation of the possibility of descent to the issue of the donee gave rise to a right in the donor, who would also be the lord, to have the land back if issue capable of inheriting failed at any time. Since reversions and escheats are hardly distinguished before *Quia Emptores* it is a nice, and perhaps artificial point what the donor's right should be called.

Bracton on Conditional Gifts

The recognition of *maritagia* probably had some influence upon the growth of the practice of making grants which cut down the class of heir when no marriage occasioned the gift, and such gifts too would have the effect of giving the donor the right to have the land back if issue of the prescribed class failed. Bracton subjects all gifts of *maritagia* and all analogous gifts to a lengthy analysis, which can easily be misunderstood. In the first place he lays down that only the class of her specified in the gift can inherit, and that if the heirs at any time fail, then the land will revert (or escheat) to the donor. He then has to explain the absence of any remedy to prevent the donee defeating the reversion by alienation, a gap in the law which must have struck contemporaries as curious, and he has also to explain the right to disinherit the issue which the power of alienation obviously involves. The power of disinherison he explains here in the same way as in the case of the fee simple; the heirs take nothing by the gift, for the word 'heirs' is a word of *limitation* and not of *purchase*, as we would say. The destruction of the reversion to the donor he explains by having recourse to Roman learning on conditional gifts, though it seems now to be admitted that he was not the first to do so. If there is a gift to A and the heirs of his body by a particular wife (which might or might not be a *maritagium*) this gives A a freehold (what we to-day would call a 'life estate') until the birth of issue, which will swell into a fee (not a fee *simple*, since only the heirs stated can inherit) if issue are born alive, and shrink into a life estate if issue predecease the donee A. In effect this means that A may alienate and destroy the reversion only whilst issue are alive, and this rule will apply to any issue of A who succeed to the land; if A alienates when no child is alive and dies childless, then the donor can recover the land from an alienee. This appears to have been the law of the time, and Bracton's analysis fits it. If a grant was made to A and his heirs if he have heirs of his body, then the gift is expressly a gift of a fee conditional upon the birth of issue to the donee; thus the donee obtains a life interest at once, and he will obtain the fee once issue is born, and which will never shrink again into a life estate. In such a case the heirs general will succeed, precisely in accordance with the terms of the gift. In contemporary terms the donee obtained the freehold, the *liberum tenementum*, at once, but only obtained the fee, the heritable interest, if the condition was realized. This again fits what we know of the contemporary law. The writ which protected the reversioner was called formedon in the reverter, and it appears to have been available in just those circumstances in which Bracton's analysis indicates that it ought to lie.[47]

Conditional Fees

Later lawyers were to argue that before the statute *De Donis* in 1285 the common law knew only one sort of fee, the fee simple, though such a fee simple might be granted conditionally, and thus be properly called a conditional fee, or, more confusingly, a conditional fee simple. There is a degree of unreality in such a dogma, for before the statute the modern analysis into the doctrine of estates had not been attempted, and although we can perfectly well *impose* this analysis upon the law of Bracton's time (indeed, every reference to an estate in his book so far is an example of such imposition) yet we must not forget that in doing so we are being unhistorical. The developed doctrine of estates involves a 'fragmentation' of ownership, and in Bracton's time the implications of fragmentation had hardly been realized. Bracton works with two conceptions—the fee and the freehold. The fee, the heritable interest, might be temporarily separated from the freehold, as occurred when there was a grant for life, which had the effect of putting the freehold in the life tenant and leaving the fee in the grantor. Usually they were united, as when a tenant in fee held in demesne. The old

---

[47] S. F. C. Milsom, 'Formedon before De Donis', 72 *L.Q.R.* 391.

real actions were adapted to these two conceptions; thus if one who held for life was impleaded in a real action there was a procedure which enabled him to call upon 'him in whom fee and right reside' to assist him. But there was no procedure which envisaged the possibility that two people might simultaneously hold fees in the same land, nor that there could be different types of fee. Bracton only thinks in terms of *different ways of granting a fee*—conditionally or unconditionally—and he has not reached the point of saying that different types of grant create different types of fee, the fee tail and the fee simple.

Even if we do employ the modern terminology it is quite wrong to speak of one type of fee alone in Bracton's time, and call it the fee *simple*. If we compare the later entailed estate with the fee simple[48] we may note three distinctions of basic importance. One is the fact that the entail is inalienable. Now in Bracton's time if there was a grant to A and the heirs of his body begotten, and the condition was satisfied by the birth of issue, the donee could alienate, and it is this alienability which led later lawyers to say that the donee's estate was in effect a fee simple subject to condition precedent, for alienability was characteristic of the fee simple. In doing so they forget that the two other characteristics which later distinguished between the entail and the fee simple affected the donee's estate in Bracton's time too, even after the condition was realized. These are the limitations upon the class of heir capable of inheriting, and the reversion to the donor upon failure of that class of heir. Now the doctrine of estates is a way of classifying interests in land according to the possible theoretical time on the land—a fee simple is capable of lasting longer than an entail or a life estate. Just before the statute *De Donis* we find the germs of this notion affecting the terminology used to describe the interest of one who has received a grant to himself and the heirs of his body, instead of a grant to himself and his heirs simpliciter. The heritable interest of the donee—his fee—is said to be a *feodum talliatum*, a cut-down fee in contradistinction to a *pure* fee; it is

---

[48] In the pre-1926 law a fee was designated *simple* because of its capacity of descending to the heirs general. Nobody has really faced up to the effects of the 1925 legislation upon the old doctrine and terminology of estates, which is today inappropriate as a tool for a presentation of the English law of property. If one retains the old concepts in all strictness the fee simple has been abolished. New wine manages somehow or other in old bottles.

less in quantum than other fees, and this is because the class of possible heirs is smaller. From this it is a small step to saying that the interest of one whose fee is *talliatum* is less because it is inherently shorter in possible duration.

Dower and Curtesy

In the early common law there were two forms of life interest which arose through operation of law.

A wife's right to enjoyment life of her husband's lands after his death was called 'dower'. In origin the right arose only if the husband voluntarily endowed his wife at the solemnization of the marriage at the church door,[49] and the right was limited, whatever the actual endowment, to a third of the lands of which the husband was then seised.[50] The limitation to a third is intelligible enough, for dower operates to the harm of both heirs and lords, whose wardship will be reduced by the widow's rights. The law, however, grew more favourable to widows, and in the absence of an express endowment the wife came to be *entitled* to a third.[51] In the late thirteenth century the precise form of the rule changes, and the wife becomes entitled to a third of the lands of which her husband was solely and separately seised at any time during his life,[52] though if her husband wished to do so he could endow her of a lesser share at the church door. Soon afterwards the rule changed again[53] and the wife became entitled to at least a third of the lands of which her husband was solely seised during the marriage which children

---

[49] On the early history of dower see Plucknett, *Concise History*, p. 566. See also the *Coronation Charter of Henry I* (1100), c. 4, printed in Stubbs, *Select Charters*, p. 118, and *English Historical Documents*, II, p. 401. The marriage portion which the wife brings into the marriage and the dower which she is given by her husband are frequently called by the same title, *dos*, in the earliest documents: see Co. Litt. 31a and Glanvill, VII, 1. In both instances the wife is intended to have a life interest, the land being heritable through the husband.

[50] Glanvill, VI, 1.

[51] The growth of the rule is obscure. Glanvill (VI, 1) recognizes the wife's entitlement, and there is a writ of dower *unde nihil habet* (VI, 15) by which a widow may claim a reasonable dower, but the writ presupposes a gift by the husband; perhaps there was a fiction, and the gift was presumed. Britton (II, p. 236) assumes this, and says that 'a wife is sufficiently endowed if the husband say nothing'.

[52] Magna Carta (ed. 1217), c. viii, 'and for her dower shall be assigned unto her the third part of all the lands of her husband which were his during his life, unless she has been endowed of less at the Church door'.

[53] For the developed law see Littleton, secs. 36, 37, 40, 41.

of the marriage might inherit, and the husband could not reduce her rights by an express endowment of a lesser share. The rule which gave the widow a third probably originated in the military tenures, but spread into socage tenure, where the wife was indeed at one time generally entitled to a half or more.[54] A variety of methods of barring the wife's right to dower were developed; the most usual was a conveyance by fine to which the wife consented in court, and the employment of joint tenancies, out of which no dower arose because the husband lacked the sole and separate seisin which alone gave his widow her estate.

Tenancy by the curtesy of England arose where a husband survived his wife. He was then entitled to a life estate in a half of her lands. Unlike dower this is not mentioned by Glanvill except in connection with a wife's marriage portion (*maritagium*),[55] but in Bracton's time it extended to any lands of which the wife had a heritable interest. The husband acquired the right if issue was born alive—if a cry was heard within four walls, as the old writers quaintly put it. It mattered nothing that issue did not survive. Curtesy was regarded as a peculiarly liberal and specifically English right,[56] and there is some evidence that it originated in a royal concession granted by Henry I. The husband is in early times said to be entitled by the law (*per legem*) of England, which may suggest a legislative origin. If this is so, then curtesy must be earlier than Glanvill, and Maitland suggested that this can be inferred from Glanvill's treatment of the subject.[57]

[54] See Pollock and Maitland, II, p. 421; for the later rule see Littleton, sec. 37, where the possibility of customary variations is noted.

[55] Glanvill (VII, 18) makes the point that the husband is entitled to curtesy of the wife's *maritagium*; he says nothing of the wife's inherited land. For a possible explanation of this see Pollock and Maitland, II, p. 420, note 1. The right is said to extend to inherited land in Bracton, f. 438, and in Y.B. (R.S.) 20, 21 Edw. I 39.

[56] The expression curtesy is found in the early year books; before this the husband is said to be entitled 'by the law of England', *per legem Angliae*. For this curious title see Pollock and Maitland, II, p. 414. For Bracton's account see Digby, *Real Property*, p. 175.

[57] See *The Mirror of Justices*, Selden Society, Vol. 7, p. 14, and cf. Pollock and Maitland, II, p. 415. The peculiarity of the husband's right to curtesy was that it defeated even the lord's right to wardship. The husband is entitled to do homage for his wife's land, and once homage is received the lord cannot take the lands into his own hands. For an explanation of the origin of curtesy in a form of guardianship see Pollock and Maitland, II, p. 419, Plucknett, *Concise History*, p. 571, esp. note 5.

Dower and curtesy both mitigate the effects of feudalism and primogeniture upon the family, and particularly in the case of dower, a long struggle was waged between those who wished to protect the widow and those who wished to deprive her of her rights.

Life Tenancies

Life tenancies which arose through express grant have a rather obscure early history, which is bound up with the whole question of the development of the fee from something like a life interest into a heritable interest. In early feudalism all feudal holdings, all fiefs, were probably for the lives of lord and vassal and no more. In the twelfth century it is clear that express grants of a life interest were made,[58] but Glanvill hardly mentions the effect of such grants, and it seems that he would have regarded a life tenant as a commodatary, who held the land of another as a temporary arrangement; the land was not the tenant's land, for the situation created was analogous to that which arose when land was pledged or hired or held in ward, which Glanvill regards as examples of *iura in re aliena*.[59] Those who did not hold in fee (meaning heritably) did not own.

But by Bracton's time the position of one who had been granted lands for life was fairly well settled. Like the tenant in fee the life tenant had seisin. He achieved a position which holders for a term of years or in wardship did not achieve, through obtaining a right to bring novel disseisin; this was denied to the termor and the lord who held in ward. Technically this was because the life tenant had a free tenement, and thus came within the very words of the writ. In consequence a life tenancy, being specifically recoverable by a real action, did not become a chattel interest, but came to be regarded as an estate in land, and although Bracton does not talk of estates the substance of this development has been reached by his time.

[58] See for example *Curia Regis Rolls*, I, p. 430, where the existence of a life tenancy defeats mort d'ancestor (a case of 1201), also Madox, *Formulare Anglicanum*, No. CX-CV (*c.* 1175).

[59] This view is controversial; it is based on the interpretation of Glanvill, III, 1, XIII, 11 (where it seems that Glanvill is discussing the existence of a life-tenancy as an exception to mort d'ancestor), and I, 4 (where a fee and a free tenement are contrasted).

The estate *pur autre vie* is also discussed by Bracton; it is the greatest interest a life tenant can lawfully confer upon an alienee. In Bracton's view such a tenant did not acquire a freehold,[60] for the duration of his interest was not measurable by reference to his life. Involved in the conception of a freehold is the idea that a freeholder must be entitled for his own lifetime at the least. Bracton's view did not prevail in the fourteenth century, and the tenancy *pur autre vie* came to rank as a freehold estate. This produced complications, for what was to happen if the tenant died before the estate determined? A freehold estate could not be left by will, and the grantor could hardly retake what he had given away. The tenant's heirs could not take the land, for the estate was not heritable. The solution adopted was to let the land go to the first occupant, called the general occupant, or to the tenant's heir as special occupant if the estate had been granted to A and his heirs during the life of B.

The Term of Years

The term of years has a strange history. The termor, farmer, or lessee for years, as we would call him, never seems to have been allowed to use the assize of novel disseisin. When the decision to deny him the assize was taken we have no record; it is usually assumed that this was the rule from the very beginning. The tenant for life, on the contrary, seems always to have been able to use the assize, and this differentiation between the two forms of tenancy is one of the great mysteries of the early common law. Maitland thought that the explanation for the termor's lack of remedy lay in 'a youthful flirtation with romanism'.[61] Looking into the Roman texts for some guidance as to the position of the termor, the early lawyers, he thought, found an analogy in the position of the *conductor* or the *usufructuarius*; neither had possession, and from this it was deduced that the termor did not have possession, or, what came to the same thing, seisin, so that it was impossible for him to complain of disseisin. Maitland's theory has been denied by more modern writers, notably by Joüon des Longrais, who has shown that the assize was denied to the termor not because he lacked

---

60 Bracton, f. 13, reproduced in Digby, *Real Property*, p. 164.
61 Pollock and Maitland, II, p. 114.

seisin, but because he could not bring himself within the terms of the writ which required seisin *of a free tenement*.[62] This explanation, of course, raises a mysterious question—what was the implication of the expression 'free tenement'? Des Longrais thought that there was a distinctive conception of a free tenement as being the property which supported a family for at least as long as the lifetime of one person. He argued that early leases did not fall within this conception, for they were normally created to serve as investments, and were designed to evade the ecclesiastical prohibition of usury. In contemporary literature the termor is treated as a thoroughly undesirable person. In such a climate of opinion it was natural, he thinks, that the assizes should not be made available to termors, and the inclusion in the writ of the words 'free tenement' ensured that the new remedy should avail only to protect family property.

That it was the lack of a free tenement, a *liberum tenementum*, and not the lack of seisin which militated against the termor can hardly now be doubted, and an economic explanation of the termor's position does certainly bring out a striking analogy between his position and that of a holder of a wardship, who was also denied the assize. Wardships and leaseholds were both held as investments, and both were treated in the same way by the law; neither fell within the conception of a free tenement.[63]

But it is still odd that a life tenancy was regarded as a free tenement, and was protected by the assize of novel disseisin. Des Longrais devised his suggested conception of a free tenement to fit the fact that the life tenancy was included in it, and it is difficult to extract Des Longrais's elaborate conception of a free tenement from the simple expression *liberum tenementum*, which on the face of it says nothing at all about family holdings. Although an economic explanation helps to explain why the term of years was treated as it was, such an explanation does not obviously explain why the term for life was treated differently. Both forms of term were frequently employed in the

---

[62] Joüon des Longrais, *La Conception Anglaise de la Saisine*, and see Plucknett, *Concise History*, p. 571, and a review in 40 *Harv. L.R.* 921.

[63] Cf. the position of the pledge creditor or gagee of land as stated in Glanvill; though he is seised he still cannot use novel disseisin, even if the debtor ejects him; he has no free tenement.

thirteenth century to create leases at economic rents in favour of farmers, and the lease for life was not obviously a 'family' interest[64] furthermore, the long lease for years might well endure beyond the tenant's life, and provide the economic basis for a family, and both Bracton and Britton are struck by the anomalous treatment of the long term, and are at pains to point out that even a long term is still not a freehold.[65] Now when the assize of novel disseisin was originally limited to protect those who were seised of *a free tenement* the limitation, on the face of it, was a tenurial one, and was designed to exclude those who held by unfree tenure—the villein tenants—and those who did not have a *tenement* at all. If this is so, then the termor for years was excluded from the protection of the assize because of some tenurial ground. It is suggested that the original reason for the unfortunate lot of the termor for years was simply this, that a lease for years was not conceived of as creating a tenurial relationship between lessor and lessee at all; thus the lessee, so far from having a *free* tenement, did not have a tenement at all. In a transaction whereby an individual hired land in order to exploit it economically, no feudal relationship of subservience and protection, sealed by homage, was included: the social significance of the transaction was quite different. The life tenancy on the other hand had once been the normal military tenancy, and the life tenant who in the twelfth century secured the use of novel disseisin owed his favoured position to a memory of a time when all the military fiefs had been little more than life tenancies, heritable of grace only. The same reasoning would explain the treatment of the holder in wardship and the pledge creditor, or gagee. The *tenementum* of the lord who holds in wardship is the seignory. Again the Glanvillian gagee does not become the tenant of the gagor; the relationship between them is not a feudal relationship.[66]

---

[64] 'Farmers' could also hold in fee at a rent; their interest was called a fee farm; thus terms of years, for life, and holdings in fee were made to serve the same economic purpose; see further p. 77 below.

[65] See the passage from Bracton reproduced in Digby, *Real Property*, p. 163.

[66] Another explanation has been presented by W. M. McGovern, 'The Historical Conception of a Lease for Years' 23 *Univ. of Cal. Los Angeles L.R.* 501; the original point was to prevent a situation in which both landlord and tenant could sue the ejector.

In Littleton's time it was said, though with some doubt, that the tenant for years was a feudal tenant;[67] the proof of this lay in his obligation to swear fealty to his lord. In the twelfth and thirteenth centuries it is not at all clear that it would have been thought appropriate for such a lessee to swear an oath of faithful service to his lord; the idea of a person becoming a vassal for a term of years hardly fitted into the feudal structure of things. The lessee never did become liable to perform homage, and this is a fact hard to reconcile with the view that he was a tenant. For if a tenure was created between lessor and lessee, that tenure could be classified only as a tenure in socage, and by Bracton's time socage tenants had begun to do homage to their lords, and in the end this became the normal rule. But the tenant for years never did homage, nor indeed is he ever spoken of as a socage tenant.[68] The idea that the termor had a *tenementum* is indeed an afterthought of the common law, whose implications were never really worked out with any consistency.[69] If in the twelfth century he had been thought of as a feudal tenant he would surely have been said to hold a free tenement, for the tenure by which he held could only have been free socage. But instead the lease was thought by Glanvill to create a purely contractual relationship, and not a tenurial one.

The Protection of the Termor

The lack of the assize put the termor in a weak position, and this could hardly be tolerated as the growth of the husbandry lease and the growing tolerance towards capital investment conferred respectability upon the termor. About the close of the twelfth century the introduction of the writ of covenant gave the termor a remedy against his lessor in which the land itself could be recovered. Conceptually this treated his rights as contractual, though the contract was as we would say specifically enforceable. In about 1230 a new writ of *quare ejecit infra terminum* gave him a remedy against any ejector claiming title through a

---

[67] See Littleton, sec. 132, and the illuminating note of Challis, 'Leaseholds: Are they Tenements?' 6 *L.Q.R.* 69, reprinted as Appendix I to Challis, *Real Property*.

[68] Though Littleton's hesitant view that he should perform fealty comes at the end of the section on socage tenure.

[69] Thus the normal definition of a tenement is 'that which can be entailed under De Donis'; in the sixteenth century it was settled that leaseholds could not be entailed.

sale by the lessor.[70] Soon after this a form of trespass or tort action called *eiectione firmae* was developed, and this action could be brought for damages against any wrongful ejector. It left the termor fairly well protected, though he could not recover the land itself in such an action, which, like all actions of trespass, lay for damages only. In the course of the fifteenth century, as we shall see, the law was changed by the courts, and by the end of the century specific recovery of the land came to be allowed in *eiectione firmae* just as it was allowed in *quare ejecit*. So it was that by the close of the Middle Ages the leaseholder came to have a fully protected interest in the land leased to him.[71]

The classification of this interest provoked not a little difficulty. In the early fourteenth century the lessee's interest was sharply distinguished from a real property interest in that the lessee could not use the real actions, and lawyers began to call it a chattel interest.[72] The lessee was at this time protected against the lessor by the writ of covenant,[73] and for a time this action could lead to the award of specific recovery.[74] This might have confused analysis still further, but the courts gave up the practice of making such awards, so that the violation of the lessee's interest protected by covenant was a mere contractual wrong, sounding in damages only. It was only in *quare ejecit* that the lessee could obtain specific recovery; even this was doubted in the fourteenth century. The termor's interest was therefore closely analogous to a man's interest in a chattel which would primarily be protected by detinue, in which action the defendant could always pay damages rather than deliver the chattel back again. As a chattel

---

[70] The writ was said to have been invented by William Raleigh, Bracton's master. Bracton (f. 220) thinks that it will lie against any ejector, but its scope was limited by later lawyers. Britton (I, p. 417), writing about 1290, denies the termor any remedy at all except against one claiming title through the lessor. On the relationship between *quare ejecit* and *eiectio firmae* see Milsom, 'Trespass from Henry III to Edward III', I, 74 *L.Q.R.* 195 at pp. 198–201.

[71] The protection of the termor was also advanced by the statute of Gloucester (1278), c. 11, which allowed the termor to intervene in collusive litigation by real action when it was designed to oust him from his term. The statute only applied where there was a written lease, and the collusive action was lost by default. The defects in the statute were not remedied until 1530 (21 Hen. VIII, c. 15). For an example of the use of a common recovery to oust a lessee, employing a technique very similar to the common recovery used to bar entails, see Y.B. 7 Hen. VII, Pasch. pl. 2, f. 10.

[72] Y.B. 33–5 Edw. I, (R.S.), p. 165.

[73] On which see Simpson, *History of Contract*, pp. 9–52.

[74] Fitzherbert, *Natura Brevium*, 145 I.

interest it was therefore classified, and like other chattels it could be bequeathed.[75] Nevertheless, lawyers could not get away from the fact that the lessee's interest was an interest in land; he was seised, and at least in Littleton's view there was thought to be a tenure between landlord and tenant, so that the lessee owed fealty to his lord but never homage. The eventual solution was to call his interest a 'chattel real', so recognizing the fact that it partook both of the nature of real property and of chattels. Such recognition was more or less forced upon the law when the 'real' character of the interest was forced into prominence in 1499 with the decision that the term was specifically recoverable against the whole world.[76] It was left to the sixteenth-century lawyers to put the final touches on this hybrid creature of the law.

Legal theory had to accommodate itself to the different treatment of the termor for years and the life tenancy, and as it came to be thought that the termor held the land from the lessor and was a tenant of sorts the distinction had to be sought in the definition of a free tenement or freehold. Bracton's suggested definition is a heroic attempt to fit the various contrasts which were suggested by the expression:

 . . . a free tenement is a tenement which a person holds to himself and his heirs in fee and in inheritance, or in fee only to himself and his heirs. Likewise a tenement held as a free tenement, as for life only, or in the same way for an indeterminate time without any certain predetermined time. . . . But a tenement cannot be called free which he possesses for a certain number of years . . . although for a term of a hundred years, which exceeds the life of a man. Likewise a tenement cannot be called free which he holds at the will of lords, precariously. . . . Likewise a tenement is called free to distinguish it from villeinage. . . .'[77]

Both historically and analytically it would have been better had the lawyers used the term 'freehold' to differentiate holdings by free tenure from holdings by villein tenure, and had explained the treatment of the lessee for years, the guardian in chivalry, the holder at will, and the holder in gage, all of whom were denied novel disseisin, by denying to them a feudal tenurial holding involving the relationship of man and lord at all. But

[75] See Pollock and Maitland, II, p. 115.
[76] See p. 93 below.
[77] Bracton, f. 207. See the passage in Digby, *Real Property*, pp. 138, 141.

this was not the way in which the theory of the law did develop, and so the term freehold was forced to accommodate an assortment of connotations. It could be used to differentiate free and unfree tenure, but it came more and more to be used to differentiate interests in land (soon to be called estates) which were of uncertain duration from those interests to which a fixed term had been limited.

Fee Farm

There was another form of landholding at a rent known to early English law, and it has an odd history; the institution is known as fee farm.[78] A tenant was said to hold at fee farm when he held heritably[79] (in fee) in return for a perpetual rent due to his lord. The relationship was feudal, between lord and vassal. The rent was rent *service*, and not a rent *charge*, for it was a tenurial service due to the lord, and carried with it a right to distrain at common law, or as the old books put it, 'of common right'. A rent charge due to someone other than the tenant's lord did not carry with it the right of distraint unless this was expressly provided for when the charge was imposed. Fee farm was treated by Bracton and by contemporaries[80] as a tenurial arrangement distinct from tenure in socage. Socage tenure was the tenure of the free but humble peasant, the better-class villager, whereas the *firmarius* who held in fee farm belonged to a somewhat higher rank in society; he was a man of some substance. It would be misleading, however, to suggest that the distinction is clearly understood today, and it may be that contemporary terminology itself was hardly precise.

Fee farm was killed by the statute of *Quia Emptores* (1290). The nature of the fee which the tenant had was unmodified; we would say the tenant's interest was a fee simple. After *Quia Emptores* it was no longer possible for a subject to subinfeudate for a fee simple, so that grants in fee farm, reserving rent service to the grantor as lord, could no longer be made. What had previously been a common practice passed almost wholly out of use, and previously created tenures in fee farm became treated

[78] The fullest discussion of fee farm is in Lennard, *Rural England*, especially Ch. V.
[79] Cf. Lennard, *op. cit.*, pp. 111–12, for life tenures described as fee farm in the twelfth century when the normal feudal relationship was lifelong only.
[80] E.g. see the passage in Digby, *Real Property*, p. 123 (Magna Carta, c. 37).

as a type of socage tenure.[81] In Scotland, where *Quia Emptores* did not apply, *feu-farm* has become the predominant tenure today.[82] Yet even in England the practical effects of *Quia Emptores* could be bypassed to some extent; land could be granted in fee simple but be charged with a perpetual rent-charge in favour of the grantor, and this practice has survived until modern times in the north of England.

The position of the tenant in fee farm can be contrasted with that of the tenant for years. Both hold at a rent; both are *firmarii*, but they are quite differently treated by the law. The fee farm tenant holds by a recognized tenure; he has a free tenement, fully protected by the real actions; he escapes the shabby treatment meted out to the lessee for years. Yet fee farm becomes obsolescent in 1290, and only a shadow of it survives. In the end it is the term of years which carries the day. And in the course of time the relationship between the aristocratic landowners and their farm tenants came to take on at least some of the characteristics of the original feudal relationship of early Norman times, with reciprocal obligations which were none the less real though not necessarily enforceable at law. Thus the nineteenth-century farmer could rely upon customary entertainment at the tenants' dinner, and other good things might come his way so long as he voted correctly in elections, attended funerals, and discharged a variety of deferential duties. Modern feudalism, built up around the lease for years, is not wholly gone today. But it is in the main a social and political institution, not one legally sanctioned.[83]

Future Interests

We have already noted that if one who has a fee dies without heirs of any sort then the land will come back to his lord, and that since his lord and his donor (or their heir) will be usually the same person, there is some confusion of terminology over this right to have the land back; sometimes it is called an escheat and sometimes a reversion.[84] Similarly the land will

[81] See Littleton, secs. 117, 215, 216; also Co. Litt. 143b, and note 5 by Butler.

[82] See C. D.'O. Farran, *The Principles of Scots and English Land Law*, pp. 53–6, 80–2.

[83] See generally F. M. L. Thompson, *English Landed Society in the Nineteenth Century*, and for the previous century, G. E. Mingay, *English Landed Society in the Eighteenth Century*.

[84] See Milsom, 'Formedon before De Donis', 72 *L.Q.R.* 391.

come back when the holder of a *maritagium* dies without heirs capable of inheriting under the terms of the gift, and again it is not settled in Bracton's time which term is appropriate here. In the case of the death of a life tenant, too, the land will come back, and in these cases there is no need for the donor to expressly lay down that the land is to revert.[85] After the statute of *Quia Emptores* (1290) the distinction between reversions and escheats rapidly becomes clear, for the result of that statute is that donees of fees 'simple' will hold not of their donor but of the donor's lord; lord and donor will always be different people, for all such grants are substitutionary.[86] Thus if the land is to come back upon failure of heirs general it will be to the lord that it comes, and it becomes obvious that escheat depends upon tenure and upon tenure alone; the term 'escheat' is reserved to describe what happens when a tenant in fee simple dies without heirs. The term 'revert' is used to describe the coming back of the land to the donor; this will happen when a life tenant dies or a tenant in tail (after *De Donis*) dies without heirs in tail.

Just as the word 'revert' is used to describe the coming back of land, so the word 'remain' is used to express the fact of land staying away from the grantor; it remains to some other person. Thus besides its modern use one can talk of land remaining to the heir of a tenant in fee simple. The limitation of remainders in the modern sense is quite common in the century before *De Donis*. But the validity in law of such limitations long remained controversial amongst historians. Maitland found many examples of the limitation of remainders after conditional fees, and argued that such limitations would not have occurred if the law had not recognized their validity. Challis, who treated the pre-*De Donis* conditional fee as a conditional fee simple, regarded such limitations as absurdities, since, according to the developed doctrine of estates, no remainder can be limited after the grant of any type of fee simple; once a man has given away the fee simple there is nothing else left for him to alienate, for the fee simple

---

[85] When a gift analogous to a *maritagium* is made, the reversion must be expressly saved according to the law of the fourteenth century; see Y.B. 30-1 Edw. I (R.S.), pp. 250, 384.

[86] Generally see P. Bordwell, 'The Common Law Scheme of Estates', 18 *Iowa L.R.* 425 and 33 *Iowa L.R.* 449.

represents the maximum quantum of interest possible. That Challis's view represents the mature law cannot be doubted, but the time under discussion did not know the mature doctrine of estates, and the argument is misplaced.[87] In more recent times Humphreys claimed to have discovered a writ of formedon in the remainder dating from just before *De Donis*, but his identification was open to considerable doubt.[88] In 1975 P. Brand published a plea roll entry dating from 1279 which is certainly evidence of the existence by that date of formedon in descender, but it still remains open to doubt whether the writ was regularly available by that date. His article shows too the earlier abuse of formedon in reverter and descender to supply the lack of a more appropriate remedy.[89]

[87] The controversy can be followed in the following writings: Maitland, 'Remainders after Conditional Fees', 6 *L.Q.R.* 22, *Coll. Pap.* II, 174, Challis, *Real property,* Appendix II, Pollock and Maitland, II, p. 23.

[88] W. H. Humphreys, 'Formedon in Remainder at Common Law', VII *Camb. L.J.* 238. Humphreys' conclusion has been doubted by Professor Bailey in VIII *Camb. L.J.* at p. 275, note 9. He suggests that the writ is perhaps designed for the survivor of one of two joint tenants in tail, and further than even if it is formedon in remainder it may not have been a writ *de cursu.* But see Milsom's comment in 72 *L.Q.R.* at pp. 391-2.

[89] 'Formedon in the Remainder before "*De Donis*"', 10 *Irish Jurist* 318.

IV

The Statute De Donis *and the Invention of the Doctrine of Estates*

THE title of this chapter indicates that the statute *De Donis* had a great deal to do with the formation of the characteristic doctrine of the land law and this is indeed so. But an account of the narrower effect of the statute must precede any discussion of its wider implications. We have seen how *maritagia* and other forms of conditional fee could be alienated once the condition was satisfied, and how this right of alienation clearly defeated the intention of donors of such gifts. This state of the law provoked strong protest in 1258, in the Petition of the Barons.[1] The precise form of the barons' complaint is interesting. They say that when land is given to a husband and wife jointly in marriage, with a limitation to their issue, wives who survive their husbands alienate the land during their widowhood and destroy the reversion, and that no writ exists to enable the grantor to recover the land from the alienee. Furthermore, such alienations take place although issue has failed. It is clearly the alienability of *maritagia* which is the cause of complaint, and the statute *De Donis Conditionalibus* in 1285[2] is directed solely at the prevention of alienation by holders of conditional fees, though it is not confined to the particular case which the barons mention. The preamble instances three cases:

A gift to a man and woman jointly and to the heirs of their bodies begotten.

A gift 'in frank marriage', which expression by then has come to be interpreted as implying a similar limitation to the heirs of the body of the donees.

A gift to one and the heirs of his body.

---

[1] For the text see Stubbs, *Select Charters*, p. 377, and Plucknett, *Concise History*, p. 551.

[2] For the text see Digby, *Real Property*, pp. 226, 229.

It states that in all three cases a reversion to the donor or his heir exists, whether expressed (as in the first and last cases) or implied (as in the second case), and goes on to say that it is obviously wrong that once issue has been born the donee can alienate, and thus disinherit the heir and destroy the reversion. The statute then lays down the general principle that in future the will of the donor, as expressed in the *forma doni*, is to prevail. To protect the reversioner the writ of formedon in reverter already exists,[3] but the implication is that in future this is to lie against an alienee of the donee, a substantial change in the law. To the issue the statute gives what it calls a new remedy, the writ of formedon in descender, which will enable the issue to recover the land if it has been alienated. In fact, a writ of formedon in descender did exist before *De Donis*,[4] but its function was limited, and it did not restrain alienation. It existed to cope with a different problem. If a tenant of a conditional fee died seised, but his heir was unable to enter on the land because an abator had got on to it first, the remedy we might expect him to use would be mort d'ancestor. But only the heir general could bring mort d'ancestor, and sometimes the heir entitled to a conditional fee would not be the same person as the heir general.[5] To meet this rare situation formedon in descender was devised, so that the special heir under the form of the gift could claim. Before *De Donis*, however, this writ did not lie against an alienee; the previous tenant must have died seised. So the legislation radically altered the function of the action. The statute says nothing whatever about remainders or the writ of formedon in remainder which, as we have seen, existed before *De Donis* but may not have been available of course.

The Interpretation of De Donis

So far the statute is quite clear, but unfortunately it suffered from bad draftsmanship, and the word 'issue' is used in such

[3] For this writ before 1285 see Milsom, 'Formedon before De Donis', 72 *L.Q.R.* 391.

[4] For this writ before 1285 see Milsom, *op. cit.;* also Y.B. 6 Edw. II, Selden Society, Vol. 34, p. 44, Y.B. 5 Edw. II, Selden Society, Vol. 31, p. 177, Vol. 33, p. 225.

[5] For example, suppose land is granted to H and W and the heirs of their bodies begotten, and they have issue S; H has been previously married and has a son Y by his earlier marriage. Y is heir general to H, but S is heir in tail.

a way as to make it possible to argue that only issue in the first generation is intended, and not issue *ad infinitum*. If this was the intention then only the first donee was restrained from alienation, but a general survey of the statute makes it probable that this was a mistake on the part of Chief Justice Hengham, to whom the draftsmanship is attributed.[6] For a long time, however, there was doubt as to the interpretation of *De Donis* on this point,[7] and the process by which the entail of limitless duration was built up is one of the curiosities of the land law.[8] In 1311 Bereford C.J. and his colleagues were faced with the difficulty, and Herle argued that the statute only forbade the first donee from alienating; formedon in descender, he said, was a purely statutory remedy and was only given to the heir of the first generation—thus subsequent heirs must rely on mort d'ancestor or nothing. Herle's argument was designed to show that subsequent heirs could not sue unless their ancestor had died seised, and thus could not prevent alienation. Bereford C.J. would have none of this. He denies, correctly, that formedon in descender originated in *De Donis*, and says that mort d'ancestor is never an appropriate remedy for an heir in tail, citing a case to prove this. Herle tries to distinguish the case cited upon the ground that it concerns a gift 'in frank marriage', but Bereford C.J. replies that the law is the same in cases concerning gifts 'in frank marriage' as in cases expressly limiting an entail; in both the intention is that the inalienability is to endure for three generations, and it was only by error that the statute failed to say so.[9] The implications behind this enigmatic discussion seem to be as follows. It is already accepted that a gift of land 'in frank marriage' is inalienable for three generations—that is to say, as long as it retains its peculiar tenurial quality. This result is attributed to the fact that the heir to lands so given must use formedon in descender, and not

---

[6] The late G. D. G. Hall suggested to me that this attribution is dubious; when Hengham C.J. said that he and his fellow justices had made the statute he was only referring to one chapter of the statute, and this was not *De Donis*. See Y.B. 33 and 35 Edw. I (R.S.) 78.

[7] See Sayles, Selden Society, Vol. 58, p. xxxv, and p. cxx.

[8] See Plucknett, *Statutes and their Interpretation*, pp. 51-2, *Concise History*, pp. 552-4, *Legislation of Edward I*, pp. 132-5, Updegraff, 'The Interpretation of "Issue" in De Donis', 39 *Harv. L. R.* 200.

[9] Y.B. 5 Edw. II, Selden Society, Vol. 31, p. 177, Vol. 33, p. 226.

mort d'ancestor, a rule of common law origin.[10] The statute *De Donis* makes formedon in descender available against alienees, and so any heir who can bring formedon in descender may, as a result, recover land which his ancestor has alienated. This ingenious reasoning is carried farther in a case in 1344.[11] There the theory is advanced that the entail only lasts until the first heir enters, and Stonore J. accepts this. The majority view is, however, that the entail will retain its peculiar characteristic of descending to a limited class of heirs indefinitely; this implies that the heirs *ad infinitum* must use formedon in descender, which lies against alienees, and not mort d'ancestor, and in consequence that the inalienability will last for ever. In 1346 the indefinite continuance of the entail seems to be accepted,[12] and in 1410[13] it is held that this indefinitely prolonged prohibition of alienation and capacity of descending to a limited class of heirs applies to a gift 'in frank marriage' which has lasted longer than three generations. This in effect means that a grant 'in frank marriage' confers an entail[14] upon the grantee with tenurial peculiarities which absolve the donee from services for three generations, and since by the fifteenth century the services are no longer very important the practice of making gifts in this form dies out.

Apart from a solitary entry on the plea rolls in 1279[15] it is not until about 1291–2, that we first meet in Britton with a mention of formedon in remainder,[16] and the writ is referred to in a year book case in 1305.[17] As early as 1310 we meet the beginnings of a dispute which has lasted ever since when Toudeby argues, as

[10] Cf. Y.B. 6 Edw. II, Selden Society, Vol. 34, p. 44, where Bereford C.H. says that Hengham C.J. took the view that the heir in tail cannot ever bring mort d'ancestor, and Inge J. holds that before the statute the correct writ was formedon in descender.

[11] Y.B. 18 and 19 Edw. III (R.S.) 194; cf. Y.B. 4 Edw. III Trin., pl. 4, f. 29.

[12] Y.B. 20 Edw. III (R.S.) ii, p. 202.

[13] Y.B. 12 Hen. IV Mich., pl. 15, f. 9.

[14] But a curious form of entail, created without words of limitation. For a short account see the Reading of Robert Constable in 1489, Selden Society, Vol. 71, pp. 174–6. It was not possible for a remainder in fee simple to subsist after a gift 'in frank marriage', for this would have destroyed the tenure between grantor and grantee, and the tenurial relationship was essential.

[15] See above, p. 80.

[16] Britton III, Ch. XIII, p. 120, who speaks of the right 'descending' to a remainderman if tenant in tail dies without issue living, and notes that the remainderman must use formedon.

[17] Y.B. 30 Edw. I (R.S.), p. 180, 33–5 Edw. I (R.S.), pp. 20, 130, 157.

Maitland was to argue some four centuries later, that the writ existed at common law before the statute.[18] In the early fourteenth century it was used to protect remainders limited after a life estate, as well as remainders after a fee tail.

The Measurement of Interests by Time

Now it is at the close of the thirteenth century that we first meet indications of the organization and professionalization of the common law, just at the same time as the series of law reports known as the year books begin to give us some insight into the processes of legal reasoning in the courts, through which the technical doctrines of the law became established. As soon as the year books start we find lawyers using the word 'estate' to describe the quantum of interest which a tenant has in his land. The word is connected with the latin *status*; it is used of the *legal position* of the tenant, and from this usage slides imperceptibly into the modern technical meaning, which is not very different.[19] In Bracton's time the basic distinction had been drawn between the fee—the heritable interest—and the freehold less than the fee, which was typically the interest of the life tenant. Just before *De Donis* the use of the expression 'fee tail'[20] indicates a consciousness that there might be different sorts of fee, and the statute of *Quia Emptores*, by forbidding subinfeudation only in the case of lands held *in feodo simpliciter*, marked off the fee which had been granted unconditionally, the fee 'simple'[21] from fees which were not 'simple'. Lawyers began to see that a simple or unconditional grant of a fee created a different sort of fee from a conditional grant. The courts could perhaps instead have held that only one sort of heritable interest was known to the law—the fee—but recognized that grants of this interest could be conditional or absolute. Alternatively they could recognize, as they did in the end, that there were two sorts of fee—the fee tail and the fee simple.

---

[18] Y.B. 3 and 4 Edw. II, Selden Society, Vol. 22, p. 41, Selden Society, Vol. 22, p. 280. See also Selden Society, Vol. 69 (*Casus Placitorum*), p. lxxxviii/37, where formedon in remainder is mentioned in a student's notebook, probably before *De Donis*.

[19] For early examples see Y.B. 20 and 21 Edw. 1 (R.S.), pp. 12, 34, 38, 50.

[20] It occurs in c. 4 of the statute; cf. Maitland's example from a De Banco Roll of Mich. 11–12 Edw. I, '*Emma non habuit . . . nisi feodum talliatum secundum formam donationis praedictae*'.

[21] In Bracton's time more often the expression *pure fee* is used.

This recognition was not immediate, nor was it inevitable. For the statute *De Donis* dealt on the surface only with the right of alienation, and it would have been possible to have treated the interests governed by the statute as being no more than fees, granted conditionally, of a temporarily inalienable kind. Alternatively the courts could have held that the statute only forbade alienation (for more than his life) by the first donee and said that the effect of the statute was to give the donee a freehold (we would say 'life estate') and his heir a fee, a suggestion made by Serjeant Toudeby in court.[22] But once it was settled that the inalienability is to endure for longer than the lifetime of the donee, first for three generations, and then for ever, such theories as these become difficult to work; the second theory would need modification so as to make every tenant a life tenant only, for as each heir entered the fee would shift to *his* heir, and so on.[23] Such explanations were abandoned in the course of the fourteenth century, and in their place attention was concentrated upon the other characteristic of the interest protected by the statute (as interpreted), which was, not that the interest could only be alienated for the tenant's life, but rather the fact that the interest descended on a limited class of heirs *ad infinitum*. Its heritable quality was different from that of a normal fee; it was indeed a different sort of fee, a fee tail and not a fee simple. This notion itself involves a recognition that it is a fee which has been cut down, and which is lesser in *quantum* than a fee simple, and so the lawyers are led to measure fees *by their possible duration in time,* for the wider the class of heir who can inherit the less is the chance that the fee will ever end. And the classic statement of the nature of an estate, which is found in *Walsingham's Case* (1573), is that 'An estate in the land is a time in the land, or land for a time.'[24]

Now this alone is not the whole basis of the doctrine of estates. For that doctrine further involves a recognition not simply that

[22] See the valuable discussion in Plucknett, *Concise History*, pp. 554–7. As late as 1490 the notion that a tenant in tail has a fee simple subject only to a restriction upon alienation is advanced by counsel; see Y.B. 5 Hen. VII. Hil., f. 14, pl. 5. The theory is ridiculed by the court. Cf. Y.B. 12 Edw. IV Pasch., f. 2, pl. 7.

[23] But Serjeant Toudeby never went this far; his theory was produced to explain the results of *De Donis* on the supposition that only the first donee was restrained from alienating.

[24] 2 Plowden 547 at 555.

STATUTE *DE DONIS* AND DOCTRINE OF ESTATES 87

the sum of possible interest—the fee simple—may be cut up into slices like a cake and distributed amongst a number of people, but that all of them will obtain present existing interests in the land, though their right to actual enjoyment, to seisin in demesne, may be postponed. The slice of cake may be shrink wrapped, not to be actually eaten yet. In Bracton's time it was recognized, as we have seen, that land might be granted in such a way that it would revert to the donor, as where a life estate was granted, and that it might also be made to remain away from the grantor. But here the notion is rather of a cake being passed about than of one being sliced up. The change in thought occurs when lawyers start to talk of *reversions* and *remainders*, rather than of *persons to whom the land may revert* or *remain*, for this terminology involves a recognition that reversions and remainders are *existing interests* rather than rights to obtain an interest. The new approach seems to be the direct result of the introduction of the new actions of formedon in remainder and formedon in reverter in the late thirteenth century, and the clarification of the distinction between reversions and escheats after *Quia Emptores* in 1290. Since reversioners and remainder-men have real actions to protect their interest, they must have an interest to protect. This feeling was so strong that it very nearly led lawyers to say that since the issue in tail had a real action, formedon in descender, they too must have an estate. Since all these interests related to the same piece of land, it was natural to regard them as parts of the sum total of possible interests in that land, and the greatest possible interest known was the fee simple; their co-existence was only explicable by the fact that some estates gave a present right to seisin and others a future right to seisin, and by the notion that the greatest possible interest, the fee simple, had been cut up and parcelled out.[25]

[25] For Holdsworth's view see Holdsworth, II, pp. 350, 352. See also P. Bordwell, 'The Common Law Scheme of Estates and the English Justinian', 33 *Iowa L.R.* 449, and cf. 18 *Iowa L.R.* 425, A. D. Hargreaves, 'Shelley's Ghost', 54 *L.Q.R.* 73. The old procedure in the real actions catered happily only for the distinction between the fee and the freehold severed from the fee (e.g. a life estate), and in the fourteenth century there was great difficulty when litigation arose on settlements which gave fees to two or more people—for example a gift to A for life, remainder to B in tail, remainder to C in fee simple. The problem was this: did B or C have the fee? The procedures of the real actions hardly catered for the obvious answer that *both* had fees, for they had become fixed before the idea that this was possible had occurred to anyone. Note too that it was

Seisin and the Doctrine of Estates

Seisin is the conception which connects the person who has an estate with the land itself. We have seen that the real actions produce the English conception of title. Titles are better or worse according to the age of the seisin upon which they are based, and even a very recent (and perhaps transparently wrongful) seisin is to some extent protected. Thus any person who is seised of land has a protected interest in that land, good against all but those who have a title based on an older seisin. From this it is deduced that one who is seised must have an estate, and unless he claims through some gift which cuts down his estate then it will be a fee simple. Conversely, anybody who has an estate granted to him (or to an ancestor from whom he claims) has a right to seisin, either now or in the future. This right to seisin may be enforceable through entry (as for example when A, who is seised of Blackacre, is disseised by B who is still alive and seised) or by action (for example if A was tenant in tail of Blackacre and alienated to B, and now A's heir after A's death is claiming the seisin from B), and there is much subtle learning upon the distinction. Broadly speaking, the law favoured holders of estates who were prompt in claiming seisin; their right began as a right of entry and in time would become a mere right of action, and eventually be destroyed entirely by the rules as to limitation of actions; similarly the position of the person seised improved as time went on, since the same process obviously worked to the advantage of the sitting tenant.[26]

We must note one final point: the medieval lawyers never spoke of a person *owning* an estate in lands. It is reasonable enough for moderns to speak of owning land, but to introduce the notion of owning estates simply complicates an already complex terminology in a pointless way. Freeholders are all tenants, so they *hold* the Manor of Dale (or whatever the property is called). Their interests are measured by time; they hold the manor *for* an estate in fee tail, or *for* life, or whatever, either *in possession*, or *in remainder*, or *in reversion*. Nothing further need be

a long time before it was settled that a remainderman (who of course had never had seisin) could alienate see Y.B. 21 and 22 Edw. I (R.S.), p. 184, and cf. Plucknett, *Concise History*, p. 556.

[26] See Maitland, 'The Mystery of Seisin', *Coll. Pap.* I, at p. 362.

said about anybody owning anything for the legal position to have been fully stated.

Heritable Estates: the Fee Simple

By the second half of the fifteenth century, when Littleton wrote his *Tenures*, the common law estates had on the whole assumed the form which they were to retain until the 1925 legislation. With the fee simple Littleton began his work, writing, 'Tenant in fee simple is he that hath lands or tenements to hold to him and his heirs for ever', and he adds, 'And note, that a man cannot have a more large or greater estate of inheritance than fee simple'.[27] From this follows a basic rule: once a fee simple is granted no further limitation of an estate is possible, for the grantor has alienated his whole interest, which is eternity. For the purpose of this rule even a determinable fee simple (e.g. a gift to A and his heirs, lords of the Manor of Dale) is assimilated to a fee simple absolute, and the grantor of such an estate is left with no existing interest, but with a 'possibility of reverter' only. In theory a fee simple can (and, indeed, theoretically must) last for ever; under the rules of inheritance there is no limit to the remoteness of relationship through which an heir can establish his claim. So long as he is prepared to claim through Adam there must be an heir. In practice technicalities concerned with the writ of right prevented any claim being made through a person seised outside the period of limitation of that action,[28] and this, coupled with the obvious difficulties of proof, established reasonable limits to the remoteness of relationship which would found a claim; were this not the case escheat for failure of heirs would never have occurred.

Apart from its duration the fee simple is notable for its alienability. In the thirteenth century the grantor of a fee simple might impose restrictions upon the grantee's power to alienate, and there was no clear law upon the validity of such restraints. In the fourteenth century it was settled, in accordance with the policy underlying *Quia Emptores*, that a general restraint upon alienation of a fee simple was bad.[29] This marks off the fee

---

[27] Littleton, sec. 1, sec. 11.

[28] Until 1237 the period went back to 1135, between 1237 and 1275 it went back to 1154; in 1275 it was fixed as 1189.

[29] 33 *Liber Assisarum*, pl. 11.

simple from the fee tail as strikingly as does the different extent of the heritability of the two estates. Partial restraints upon alienation were, however, permissible, and still are.

Entailed Interests

The statute *De Donis* mentions only three sorts of entailed limitation, but the courts allowed other types; later lawyers attributed this to 'the equity of the statute', a conception which legitimized the extension of a statute by analogy beyond the scope of its actual text. These are divisible into tail male (where only the male heirs can inherit), tail female (female heirs only) and tail general (male and female heirs), and any of these forms could be made special by limiting the issue to the issue by a particular wife or husband. Not all these permutations are actually met in practice. As we have seen, these various types of entail were potentially of perpetual duration, and they possessed another curious characteristic, that of being protected against attachment for debts incurred by the tenant in tail. Indeed so far as powers of management and the rest of the world were concerned, the tenant in tail was treated as a mere life tenant, so that he could not, for example, grant leases binding for longer than his own life. Nor was his misconduct allowed to damage his descendants—entailed property was not forfeitable for treason beyond the lifetime of the traitor. In a sense entailed lands were treated as family property, not the property of any individual, but the theory of the law did not explicitly recognize the family as an entity capable of owning. So an underlying conception of family ownership had to be expressed in terms of individuals holding estates in land. In one form or other entails developed all over Europe, permitting landowners to arrange for the transmission of their property in a unit. As Brissaud puts it in relation to France: 'They made the patrimony inheritable, indivisible, inalienable and incapable of being distrained upon . . . they only gave the head of the family a limited right of ownership.'[30]

---

[30] Brissaud, *History of French Private Law*. See also Simpson, 'Entails and Perpetuities', 24 *Juridical Review* (N.S.) 1, for a comparison with Scots law. On the medieval law an invaluable source is Constable's *Reading* (1489) on the statute *De Donis*; it is printed with a translation by S. E. Thorne in Selden Society, Vol. 71, at p. 171.

By the middle of the fifteenth century a variety of methods had been found which enabled entails to be barred;[31] that is to say, which enabled the tenant in tail to alienate in such a way as to prevent his issue, or remaindermen, or reversioners, or all of them, from claiming the land back from the alienee when their interests accrued in possession. Looking at the matter from the point of view of the forms of action these devices barred the right to bring formedon in descender, remainder or reverter. They will be described more fully in the chapter on conveyancing, but here we must consider their effect upon the doctrine of estates. If the issue and both remaindermen and reversioners were all barred it is quite easy to see that the alienee obtains a fee simple; there is nobody left to later cut short his interest. If only the issue is barred, then a theoretical problem arises. The alienee will be safe until the issue of the alienor who were capable of inheriting under the entail die out. If that should ever happen the remainderman or reversioner will become entitled in possession, and be able to recover the land back from the alienee, who thus obtains an odd sort of interest which is like a fee simple except in this one particular. Not until the middle of the sixteenth century is the first (and only) definition of this curious interest attempted in court by the learned Edmund Plowden, who calls it a base fee.[32] By Coke's time it was settled that base fees could arise by operation of law, but could not be expressly granted. Thus if land was granted to A and his heirs for so long as B has heirs of his body, A obtains a determinable fee and the grantor is left with a possibility of reverter. The grantor cannot limit remainders after the gift to A, nor does he retain a reversion. A does not obtain a base fee, for it is a defining characteristic of a base fee that there should be remainders or reversions or both expectant upon it. Base fees could also arise in ways unconnected with the alienation of estates tail.

[31] Constable points out that in strictness alienation is not forbidden—'alienation is not prohibited but suffered, and the heir given a remedy for it'. An alienation by a tenant in tail which put the heir to his action is called a *discontinuance*; it discontinues the heir's title, by destroying his right to enter the land and converting it into a right of action.

[32] *Walsingham's Case* Plowden 547 at 557, and see Challis, *Real Property*, p. 325. Coke (Co. Litt. 18a) calls a base fee a fee simple determinable.

The Life Estate and the Estate pur autre vie

Since a life tenant held only for the term of his life he could not rightfully alienate for any longer period; a rightful alienation created an estate for the alienor's life—the estate *pur autre vie*. This rule produced a difficulty, already mentioned: what was to happen if the alienor lived longer than the tenant *pur autre vie*? This problem was solved by the rule that the first occupant could have the land for the rest of the life of the alienor: 'He that shall first hap it, shall enjoy out the term'. In later law this result could be avoided if the grantor at the outset granted the estate *pur autre vie* 'to A and his heirs'; this gave A's heir a right to the land not as an heir taking by descent but as *special occupant*. The complicated law of occupancy was largely worked out after Littleton's time, and indeed Coke himself hardly mentions the doctrine.[33] General occupancy was virtually abolished by the statute of Frauds (1677);[34] special occupancy lasted up to the 1925 reforms.

The Term of Years

We left the termor in an unsteady position, denied novel disseisin, and reduced to using *quare ejecit* against ejectors claiming title through the lessor, covenant against the lessor himself, and bringing trespass for damages only against any stranger who turned him out or interfered with his possession. This position could hardly be regarded as satisfactory, especially as the husbandry lease became more and more common as the old manorial economy broke up. In the fifteenth century a very important step forward was taken when the lessee was allowed to recover the land itself from any ejector in the peculiar form of trespass called *eiectio firmae*, which had been developed originally to give the lessee merely a remedy in damages. In 1455 Serjeant Choke, later a judge, had suggested that this was possible, and this view was accepted by Serjeant Fairfax in 1468. Brian, who

---

[33] See Littleton, sec. 739, and Co. Litt. 41b. The earliest reference to general occupancy seems to be in 1449 (Statham, *Abridgement*, Reconusannz, pl. 1); cf. Y.B. 38 Hen. VI Pasch, f. 27, pl. 9. The custom of appointing a special occupant is earlier; see Y.B. 17, 18 Edw. III (R.S.) 76. It has been stated incorrectly that special occupancy was unknown to Littleton, but see the passage cited.

[34] 29 Charles II, c. 3.

became Chief Justice of the Common Pleas in 1471, agreed.[35] In 1499 there was a decision to this effect in the Common Pleas upheld on a writ of error in the King's Bench, and a decision of the Common Pleas in 1525-6;[36] thereafter specific recovery was never called in question. We do not know the reasoning which lay behind this development, but we may hazard a guess. About this time it became accepted (wrongly) that *quare ejecit* had developed out of *eiectio firmae* under the *Consimili Casu* provisions of the statute of Westminster, and after some doubt it was settled by the fifteenth century that in *quare ejecit*[37] the term itself was recoverable. It was probably argued that since the term was recoverable in *quare ejecit*, a *fortiori* it must be recoverable in the action out of which *quare ejecit* developed.

However the change was justified, it was to have the most important effects upon the land law. *Eiectio firmae* was a form of trespass, the simplest and most satisfactory action in the Register of Writs. Soon freeholders came to compare their misfortune in having to use the older real actions, if they wanted specific recovery, with the happy position of the termor. In the course of the next two centuries a series of fictions enabled them to use the termor's remedy, which came to be called the action of ejectment. 'And so, by a curious twist of history, the freeholder was glad in the end to avail himself of remedies originally designed for the protection of the humble termor.'[38]

Tenants at Will and at Sufferance

The doctrine of estates ran into difficulties over a variety of persons who were undoubtedly in occupation of land, and who could not be called trespassers or disseisors, since their entry was lawful, who yet did not have any interest of a nature which the courts were prepared to protect fully. We have already

[35] See Y.B. 33 Hen. VI Mich., f. 42, pl. 19, 7 Edw. IV Pasch., pl. 16, f. 5. Hussey J. agreed in 21 Edw. IV Mich., pl. 2, f. 10.

[36] The decisions are noted in Fitzherbert, *Natura Brevium*, 220 H. See J. H. Baker, Selden Society, Vol. 94, pp. 180-3 for detailed discussion. Plucknett, *Concise History*, p. 373, note 5, refers to a case in 1389 when the term was recovered, but this cannot have settled the matter. No doubt Brian, as Chief Justice, was largely responsible for the first decision. Cf. Kiralfy, *Source Book*, pp. 110 *et seq.* (On p. 113, line 15, read *Eiectione vi et armis* for *quare ejecit*.)

[37] Y.B. 33 Hen. VI Mich., pl. 19, f. 42. See generally Milsom in 74 *L.Q.R.* at pp. 198 *et seq.*

[38] Plucknett, *Concise History*, p. 574.

mentioned the villein tenant, whom the royal courts would not protect with the real actions; another example is the *cestui que use*[39] who is in possession, and who was also denied protection at common law by real action. In the case of the villein tenant the freehold was said to be in the lord; in the case of the *cestui que use* the freehold would be in the tenant of the legal estate out of which the use arose—the feoffee to uses or trustee as we would call him to-day—and the courts refused to protect the occupant of the land against the lord or feoffee. Thus he was said to be a tenant at the will of him who had the freehold. Tenants at will are discussed by Littleton[40] in terms which make it clear that he saw some analogy between their position and that of a tenant for years, and it is easy to see why. Like termors they lacked the freehold, and had therefore no power to use the real actions, yet like termors they had possession, if not seisin, and so could bring actions against third parties based upon possession, notably the action of trespass. But the position was not quite the same, for a tenant for years was protected against his lessor, for he was entitled for a fixed term, whereas a tenant at will was not. Tenancies at will could arise in other ways, whenever a person was let into possession of land without being granted any sure or certain estate known to the law.[41]

A tenancy at sufferance arises when a person obtains possession of land through the acquiescence of the freeholder but without his consent, in such a way that his entry does not amount to a trespass—for example a tenant for years who holds over after a term has expired. The distinction between a tenant at sufferance and a tenant at will is not mentioned by Littleton.[42] The major point of practical difference, as was later recognized, arose in connection with what were called emblements. A tenant at will who had sown crops was allowed to re-enter to reap them, the profits of what had been sown, even after his tenancy was determined. A tenant at sufferance was not so favoured,

---

[39] Roughly a beneficiary under a trust; see Ch. VIII below.

[40] See Littleton, secs. 68, 71.

[41] For example Littleton, sec. 70. Tenants at will were not liable for permissive waste, but if they committed voluntary waste they could be treated as trespassers and sued for damages; this was justified by the fiction that the tenancy determined automatically at the moment when the tenant misbehaved himself. See Co. Litt. 57a.

[42] See Co. Litt. 57b.

for he was a wrongdoer of a sort, although he was neither a disseisor nor a trespasser.

Contingent Remainders

By Littleton's time the distinction between remainders and reversions could be stated in its modern form.[43] But the courts had not yet made up their minds about contingent remainders. A variety of reasons complicated the issue here. Firstly when a contingent remainder is granted there is a grantor, but no grantee. Thus suppose a grant to 'A for life, remainder in fee simple to the first son of B to attain 21' and suppose that no son of B has attained the age of 21 at the time of the grant. The grantor has alienated the whole fee simple, but to whom? It might be said that this does not much matter, but there are tenurial difficulties—who now holds the fee simple of the grantor's lord? And who is the lord of the life tenant? It should be the remainderman in fee simple, but there is for the time being at least no remainderman in fee simple. These theoretical difficulties are neatly summed up by Thirning C.J. and Hill J. in the remark, 'Terre hors de ma person ne puit my passer *in nubibus*'.[44] So for reasons of this sort we may well agree with Paston J. who in 1430 expressed the opinion that contingent remainders could not be justified by reason.[45] There were also possible objections on grounds of policy. Once it is recognized that a living person can have no heir,[46] only an heir *apparent* or *presumptive*, it follows that any limitation to the heir of a living person is contingent. Consider a gift to A, with a remainder to his heir in fee simple. The remainder is contingent, but this is not the only possible objection to such a limitation. If it is valid, then the heir looks as though he is going to take the fee simple not by descent from his father but by force of the grant—by purchase—and if he does not take by descent his lord will not

---

[43] The classic definitions are Coke's, however; see Co. Litt. 49a (remainder) and 22b (reversion).

[44] Y.B. 11 Hen. IV Trin., pl. 14, f. 74.

[45] Y.B. 9 Hen. VI Trin., pl. 19, f. 23.

[46] The dogma is obviously connected with the rule that the word 'heir' is always a word of limitation and not of purchase; thus in a gift 'to A and his heirs' one cannot tell who is the heir until A dies, so the word 'heirs' cannot designate a grantee. The rule *nullus est heres viventis* is settled in the early fourteenth century; see for example Y.B. 32 Edw. I (R.S.) 236.

be able to claim a relief. This is simply a tax-dodging trick, and early contingent remainders were often tainted by connection with evasion of this kind. One can well see that the courts were predisposed to treat them with caution, and the learned Littleton regarded them as always invalid,[47] though Littleton's view was hardly law in his own day, and did not prevail after his time.

Origins of the Rule in Shelley's Case

Now the only sort of contingent remainder met in practice in medieval settlements took the form of a limitation to the heirs of a living person, and with this alone the courts concerned themselves. Such a remainder was contingent because a living person could have no heir; thus the remainderman was not identified until after the death of his ancestor. In the course of the fourteenth century the courts, after some early vacillation,[48] built up a fairly clear body of doctrine on such remainders, and this doctrine was based upon a simple classification of such remainders into two types. The first type arose if the living person whose heir was to take the remainder *was himself granted some estate.* Here the limitation was allowed to take effect, but a curious construction was put upon such limitations, which substantially meant that although the limitation *prima facie* created a contingent remainder, yet, as construed by the courts, the creation of a contingent remainder was avoided. This is the embryonic 'rule in *Shelley's Case*', one of the deepest mysteries of the common law. The celebrated rule takes its name from a case decided in 1579,[49] but the doctrine it embodies was fairly well settled by the middle of the fourteenth century. We can distinguish the settlements falling under the rule into three types.

(*a*) Those involving a limitation 'to A for life, with remainder to his right heirs' (i.e. in fee simple) or 'to A for life, with remainder to his heir and the heirs of his body' (i.e. in tail).

---

[47] This is clear from Littleton, sec. 721.

[48] There is a long discussion in *Saltmarsh* v. *Redeness* (1317) Selden Society, Vol. 54, p. 35, Vol. 61, p. 12.

[49] 1 Rep. 88b. The case does not concern an ordinary gift 'to A and his heirs' and the rule named after the case is not concerned with such a gift; it is not correct to say that the rule in *Shelley's Case* applies to such a gift, having the effect that A takes the fee simple. Nevertheless there is a close doctrinal connection between the rule in *Shelley's Case* and the effect of the limitation 'to A and his heirs'.

Such forms of limitation were rare in practice, and probably arose through unskilful conveyancing; they were treated as mistakes by the courts and benevolently construed as if they read respectively 'to A and his heirs' and 'to A and the heirs of his body'.[50] Thus A took the fee simple, or the fee tail, himself. There is nothing surprising about such a construction, which does no more than recognize the practical result of what the settlor has done. Even if you construe such a limitation at its face value, and *call* A a life tenant, A will not *in practice* be in the position of a life tenant. Thus if he commits waste nobody can complain or do anything about it, for until he dies he has no heir who can complain, and then it will be too late. Again, in the case of a gift to A for life, remainder to his heirs, if A alienates in fee simple his heir will be unable to get the land back, for he will be bound by his ancestor's warranty. The courts thus recognized the realities of the matter in construing such gifts as they did, and the construction they adopted had other advantages. It avoids saying that such grants create a contingent remainder in favour of the heir, which would have involved invalidity, and it therefore avoids all the doctrinal difficulties which contingent remainders involved—a grant with no grantee, land in which nobody had a fee, an heir whose ancestor had been seised claiming as a purchaser and not as an heir,[51] and so on. Further it prevented a very obvious device for evading feudal dues, for only a person who came to land by descent would be in ward to the lord of that land, and would be liable to pay relief. There are therefore very understandable reasons for the attitude taken by the courts to such limitations.

   (*b*) Those involving a gift to A in tail with remainder to his right heirs (i.e. in fee simple). On the face of it such a gift wears a strange look, but the reason why such limitations occur is

---

[50] Y.B. 13 Edw. II 392, 33 Hen. VI Hil., pl. 16, f. 5. *Hall's Reading* (1481), Selden Society, Vol. 71, p. 149, *Constable's Reading* (1489), Selden Society, Vol. 71, p. 177. Cf. 39 Lib. Ass. 20, f. 238, where lands were limited to H and W for life, remainder to one heir of their bodies begotten, remainder to one heir of that heir, and so on. It seems that this curious limitation was construed as a gift in tail to H and W. The approach of the courts was to do their best to carry out the settlor's intention, however badly the conveyance was drawn.

[51] Particularly in the fourteenth century the courts found this a very worrying conception; the word 'heirs' was a word of limitation, and heirs should claim by descent, especially if their ancestor had been seised. For a person to claim *as heir* and yet to claim *as purchaser* seemed contrary to all principle.

plain. If A is tenant in fee simple of Blackacre and wishes to entail it, he must do so by some device which involves his granting the fee simple to a friend who at once grants it back again to him in tail; this is because of the technical rule that a tenant cannot by himself change the estate by virtue of which he is entitled to seisin. In such a case A will not, of course, wish to give the friend any interest in Blackacre—to use the hoary legal metaphor the friend is used as a 'mere conduit pipe'—but if the friend does no more than regrant the fee tail he will be left with the reversion in fee simple. To avoid this result the settlor adds the ultimate limitation to the right heirs of A. Now if the limitation is to be given a simple and obvious construction, then the most curious result will follow. A and his issue will be tenants in tail, but if A's lineal descendants ever fail, at however remote a time, then the limitation of the remainder will vest the fee simple in possession in the collateral heirs of A. The practical result of this will be that A is trying to have it both ways, for he is trying to obtain the benefit of entailing the land, which lies in the inalienable quality of entailed land, but is trying to avoid the disadvantage of an entail, which is that the entail will end when the lineal heirs fail. According to the terms of the settlement Blackacre will descend in most cases in exactly the same way as a fee simple, for when the lineal heirs fail the collateral heirs will take, and the way in which the settlement is framed amounts to nothing more than an attempt, though perhaps not a conscious attempt, to make a fee simple inalienable by A's lineal heirs.

The courts found such limitations very puzzling, and various constructions were mooted. One was that once A was dead the remainder in fee simple vested in his heir general, but his heir general would almost invariably be the same person as the heir in tail, and the prospect of a single person being tenant in fee simple and tenant in tail at the same time raised all sorts of difficulty of a theoretical kind. So in the end they held that A obtained both estates at once, and that the two estates merged, leaving him simply as tenant in fee simple.[52]

---

[52] This doctrine was in doubt in the fourteenth century; see Y.B. 24 Edw. III Mich., pl. 79, f. 70. It is clearly stated in *Hall's Reading* (1481), Selden Society, Vol. 71, at p. 149.

(c) Those involving a gift to A for life, remainder to B for life, remainder to the heirs of A.[53] Here the courts, by the time we reach the fifteenth century, were prepared to be benevolent. They let the settlement take effect as it stood, but developed an involved theory to explain why it did so. The gift was construed so as to confer both the life estate and the fee simple upon A, but the estate granted to B prevented the merger of these two estates until B died.[54] Thus if A survived B, A would hold as tenant in fee simple; if B survived A, then B would have the land for his life and A's heir would have to wait for it. It was said that so long as B was alive his vested estate had the effect of making A tenant for life in possession, and tenant in fee simple in interest only, no merger occurring. A similar doctrine applied when the gift was to A in tail, remainder to B in tail, remainder to the right heirs of A.

The Decision in Shelley's Case

All this theory was eventually summed up in the rule in *Shelley's Case* in 1579.[55] What was significant about the decision was that the context had now changed; sixteenth century law was not hostile to contingent interests. The medieval rules had been developed in a spirit of benevolence, to prevent limitations failing because of the common law's reluctance to accept contingent remainders.[56] By 1579 the courts did accept the validity

[53] Such a settlement might be employed if B was a brother for whom the settlor wished to make provision.

[54] This doctrine is to be found in the fourteenth century, though it was then hardly settled. See for example Y.B. 23 Edw. III Mich., pl. 17, f. 32, 38 Edw. III Mich., f. 26, 41 Edw. III Trin., pl. 10, f. 16, 42 Edw. III Pasch., f. 8, pl. 4. It is settled in the fifteenth; see for example II Hen. IV. Trin., f. 74, pl. 14, *Hall's Reading* at p. 149. The question arises in complicated ways; usually some procedural point is in issue.

[55] 1 Co. Rep. 88b. Coke's report of the case should be compared with the reports in Anderson 71, Moo. K. B. 136, and Dyer 373b, and it must be said that there is grave doubt as to its reliability. Of it Anderson C.J. said, 'Nota le Attorney Master Coke ad ore fait report en print de cest case ove arguments and les agreemehts del Chanceler and auters Juges, mes rien de c. fuit parle en le Court ne la monstre.' In Dyer much greater stress is laid upon a desire to carry out the settlor's intention. But for better or for worse it is Coke's polished report, as usual, which has been the root of the later law. See Megarry and Wade, *Real Property*, pp. 1161–3 for a summary of the later doctrines.

[56] The most usual explanation of the year book cases is a supposed judicial policy of preventing tax evasion or of encouraging freedom of alienation; I doubt if either played more than a trivial part, even supposing them to have existed. A connection has also been suggested with a supposed rule that an heir cannot take by purchase from his own ancestor; but no such rule ever existed in so unqualified a form. See

of contingent remainders, so that the reason for the old rules of construction had gone. Why then were these old rules given a new lease of life? Two new grounds of policy may lie behind the restatement. The first was the fact that the medieval rules had the effect of allowing free alienation. Thus in a gift to A for life, remainder to his right heirs, the medieval doctrine gave A the fee simple, so that he was free to alienate the land. By 1579 the courts had become very worried about settlements which restricted freedom of alienation, and were thus perhaps inclined to uphold the old rules. The second reason was perhaps that the rules prevented evasion of feudal incidents. In our example, under the rule, A's heir will take by descent, and have to pay a relief and (if under age) be in ward. In 1579 the Crown was very anxious to stamp out any evasion. This is conceivably why the Queen took a personal interest in the outcome of the celebrated case, though a personal connection is more likely.

Quite different considerations applied when a settlement included a limitation to the heirs of a stranger (i.e. somebody who was not himself given any estate), and the stranger was living when the conveyance took effect. In the fourteenth century such a remainder was simply void, and no benevolent construction avoided this.[57] In the fifteenth century the law relating to this second class of remainder was changed. In

Courden v. *Clerke* (1603) Hob. 29, Co. Litt. 22b. The very obvious evasive device whereby a father simply enfeoffed his eldest son (cf. the modern gift to avoid death duties) was in part checked by the Statute of Marlborough, c. 6 (1267), see Co. Litt. 88b, note 11, and cf. Y.B. 20 Edw. I (R.S.) 217 (1292)—'Note that if the father enfeoff his eldest or youngest son of his land, the lord shall not have a relief or heriot from him after the death of his father, by reason of the feoffment. And the eldest son can claim two estates.'

[57] Plucknett, *Concise History*, pp. 562-4, suggests that from 1336 contingent remainders were upheld if they vested before the precedent estate determined, but the cases do not support this, and in his discussion he does not distinguish limitations to the heirs of a stranger from limitations to the heirs of a person who is also given an estate. Thus the case cited by him in 1336 is of the latter type and needs separate consideration. The case of 1388 does discuss a limitation to the heirs of a stranger, but the validity of the limitation does not arise on the pleadings. The case in 1410 only holds that a gift to the heirs of a stranger is good if the stranger is dead *at the time of the gift*; this is treated as an odd exception to the rule that the word *heirs* should be construed as a word of limitation and not of purchase, for the stranger's heir was allowed to claim *as heir* yet by purchase and not by descent. No decision in favour of a remainder which was contingent when the gift was made is to be found before 1453. See the cases: Y.B. 10 Edw. III Mich., f. 45, pl. 8, 11 Ric. II (Ames Foundation) 283, 11 Hen. IV Trin., f. 74, pl. 14, 9 Hen. VI Trin., f. 23, pl. 19 (see Kiralfy, *Source Book*, p. 100).

1453[58] it was held according to one inadequate report of the case, that a gift to the heirs of a living stranger was good if the stranger died in the lifetime of the grantor. We might express this rule in modern terms by saying that contingent remainders must vest *in the lifetime of the settlor*[59]—a very sensible principle. Other reports[60] suggest the rule that certainly became law in Henry VII's time: that such a remainder will be good if it vests before the determination of the precedent estate.[61] Thus a gift to A for life, remainder to the right heirs of B, will confer a life estate on A and a fee simple on B's heir so long only as B dies before A; if this did not happen, then the remainder failed. Beyond this the courts were not prepared to go, and it will be seen that the recognition of such remainders avoided any possibility of there being a time when nobody was entitled to seisin of the land—to put it technically there could be no abeyance of seisin. The fact that the remainder must be preceded by an effective grant of a freehold estate (only a freehold estate—it was seisin of the freehold which was vital), and that the remainder must vest before the precedent estate determined, produced this result. With remainders which depended upon other contingencies than the death of a living person—for example a gift to A for life, remainder to B *at 21*—the medieval courts did not have to deal, and it is only in the sixteenth century that we first come across any recognition of their validity. In so far as the fifteenth-century lawyers considered grants of this sort at all they classified such limitations as raising problems concerned with estates granted on condition, and in Littleton's time it was settled law that only a grantor or his heirs could reserve a power of entry for breach of condition, and that such a power could not be reserved in favour of a stranger;[62] looked at in this way such contingent remainders were obviously void. In the sixteenth century the milestone is *Colthirst* v. *Bejustin* in 1550,[63] which recognized the validity of contingent remainders

---

[58] Statham, *Abridgement*, Done pl. 6.

[59] If a settlor can vest estates after his death by a settlement executed in his lifetime he is in effect exercising a concealed power of devise, and a common law legal estates could not be devised; the decision prevents evasion of this rule.

[60] Fitzherbert, *Feffements and Faits*, pl. 99, Brooke, *Done et Remainder*, pl. 37.

[61] See Y.B. 2 Hen. VII Hil., pl. 16, f. 13, 12 Hen. VII Trin., pl. 7, f. 27, 21 Hen. VII Hil., pl. 12, f. 11.

[62] Littleton, sec. 347, 723.   [63] Plowden 21.

whatever the contingency involved; as we shall see, however, this recognition was to be hedged about with elaborate restrictions.[64]

Finally we must note a terminological point—to say of a person that he has an estate is to describe his legal position *as tenant*. A person who had been disseised ceased to be a tenant, and so in the classical common law there could be no question of saying that a disseisee had an estate. Thus it is that estates can be divided into estates in possession, in reversion and in remainder, but there is no category into which one can fit the disseisee; he has a right to obtain seisin by entry or action and become tenant for an estate again, but in the meantime it is the disseisor who is tenant for an estate in fee simple.[65]

[64] On the subject-matter of this chapter see P. Bordwell's articles on the common-law estates in 18 *Iowa L.R.* 425, 33 *Iowa L.R.* 449, and 34 *Iowa L.R.* 401.

[65] For a general analysis of ownership in English law see A. M. Honoré, 'Ownership', *Oxford Essays in Jurisprudence*, 1st. Series (ed. Guest) Ch. V.

V

Incorporeal Things

ANALYSTS have always been unhappy about the property-lawyer's classification of hereditaments into corporeal and incorporeal; their unhappiness is quite misplaced, for the classification represents a perfectly sensible distinction, though perhaps the distinction could be better expressed, and indeed more fully elaborated. But different writers have adopted different criteria for drawing the distinction, and thus the subject is beset with difficulty.[1] The basis of the subtle analyses of later theorists is to be found in Bracton, who took the distinction between *res corporales* and *res incorporales* from Roman writers, and attempted to use it to provide a framework for describing a heterogeneous collection of rights which were recognized in contemporary law. The difficulty which confronted him may best be seen if we consider the content of some of these rights.

Rights as Things

A person might have the right to present a cleric to a vacant church—this was an advowson. A person might have a seignory as lord of land of which another man was seised in demesne, and this seignory comprised a whole bundle of rights to services, to feudal incidents, and to jurisdiction. A person might have a right to sustenance from a religious institution—this was called a corody. A person might have a right, in common with others, to pasture his beasts upon the land of another—a common of pasturage. This by no means completes the list.[2] Now contemporaries, and the lawyers who had to develop some law about these valuable rights, talked and thought of them as *things*, rather than as *rights*. No doubt they were quite conscious that

---

[1] For discussions see Challis, *Real Property*, Ch. V, and the note by Sweet at p. 52; cf. Williams, *Real Property*, pp. 30–2, Megarry and Wade, *Real Property*, pp. 813–17, Lawson and Rudden, *The Law of Property*, Ch. 2.

[2] See Pollock and Maitland, II, pp. 124–49; there is a useful list in Megarry and Wade, *Real Property*, pp. 814–17.

these were *abstract* things; we must not overemphasize their materialism, and suppose that they saw no difference between a gift of a cow and a gift of, say, a corody. The same is true to some extent today, and is reflected in common speech; we speak of giving a person a contract, or an annuity. But medieval man carried the treatment of rights as *things* to rather greater lengths. A good example is the advowson. Bracton ridicules the layman for the way in which he says in a charter that he grants a church, when he really means that he grants a right of presentation to a church, but the layman's attitude to the advowson, rather than Bracton's analysis, was what carried the day.[3] It was recognized that they were a form of property which could be transferred by grant, and of which the grantee, by enjoyment, could indicate to the world the fact of his seisin, just as the tenant of Blackacre could show his seisin to the world by visibly enjoying the fruits of his property. For interference with the seisin of an advowson the writ of darrein presentment—the counterpart of novel disseisin—was available, and it was clear enough that a presentation by a stranger was an interference with the seisin. So valuable were advowsons that they early acquired a proprietary writ in the nature of a writ of right, and thus became recoverable in action.[4] In short they were treated as pieces of property like land itself, or perhaps we should say as the subject-matter of property.

Many other such rights were treated as *things* in much the same way, and their economic importance was such that they were protected in the royal court from an early period. Thus in Glanvill we find writs to protect those who hold rents, advowsons, commons, and easements generally, and it is explained that writs of right can be varied to make them appropriate for the recovery of services.[5] In the predominantly agricultural economy of the twelfth century, land and rights connected with land were equally important and so were equally protected by

[3] Bracton, f. 53.

[4] Glanvill, II, 13, IV, 2, and see Selden Society, Vol. 77, at p. 330, and at p. 507 (No. 181). Cf. Glanvill, XII, 15, where there is a writ addressed to the Sheriff in this form: 'I command you that without delay you command R that justly and without delay he permit H to have his easements in the wood and pasture of such a vill, which he ought to have, as he says; as he ought to have them, and usually has had them, and that you permit not the aforesaid R or any other to molest or injure him.'

[5] For texts see Digby, *Real Property*, pp. 112–15, Fifoot, *History and Sources*, pp. 11–15.

real actions of one sort or another. At this time the law of contract was rudimentary, but many transactions which might
have been regarded as contractual were given legal effect by
being treated, and conceived of, as grants of property—of
course a contract can even be thought of as involving the grant
of things or 'choses' in action, though this is not the way in
which modern lawyers do think about contract. Thus today if a
farmer wishes to pasture his animals upon another man's land
he will make a contract with him; in the twelfth century such a
transaction would more probably have been effected by the
grant of a profit of pasturage.

Incorporeal Rights as Real Property

It was natural that these incorporeal rights, most of which
were closely connected with land, should be governed by the
same rules as land itself; it could hardly be otherwise. Thus
they could be granted for equivalent interests—for life or in fee
—and they could be inherited, devolving according to the rules
governing the descent of landed property. Hence the word
'hereditament' is used, to indicate this capacity of descending
to the heir. The concept of seisin was applied to them, so that a
man could complain of a disseisin of a common of pasture just
as he could complain of a disseisin of Blackacre. Glanvill clearly
sees nothing strange in this, but in Bracton's book the peculiarity is recognized, and Bracton attempted to provide his readers
with an analysis of the subject-matter of ownership which
would place the facts of contemporary law upon an intellectually
satisfactory basis. As we have seen, he drew on the Civil or
Roman Law for the basic distinction between *res corporales* and
res incorporales:

There is also another and second division of things, for some are corporeal and others incorporeal. Corporeal things are such as may be
touched, as land, ground . . . but incorporeal things are such as
rights, which cannot be seen or touched, as the right of going, or of
driving, or of leading water, and such like, which cannot be possessed,
but only quasi-possessed.[6]

Bracton is thus unhappy about the way in which the law talks
of seisin of incorporeal things; he regards it as something of a

---

[6] Bracton, f. 7; elsewhere he speaks of true possession after enjoyment.

fiction. We might like to express our feelings on the matter differently, but there is substance in Bracton's suspicion that there was an element of incongruity in assimilating corporeal and incorporeal property. Indeed the contemporary law did not succeed in effecting a complete assimilation. Thus unlike corporeal things, incorporeal things, as Britton puts it, '. . . do not admit of livery of seisin, as gross, coarse and material things do'.[7] Thus they could not be physically transferred, but had to be conveyed by deed—they lay in grant, and not in livery. In Britton's day the correct method of grant was delivery of a charter in view of the lands to which they related, which was about as near to livery of seisin as one could get. But the grantee, if he wanted to alienate, must acquire seisin by enjoying the right before he alienated, and until he did so his title was imperfect.[8]

Incorporeal Rights as Servitudes

Bracton was also not prepared to accept incorporeal things in the air, as it were; they had to be connected with a corporeal thing.[9] This requirement was satisfied fairly easily in the case of most of the rights by the existence of something in the nature of a servient tenement, as in the case of a right of way or right of pasture. In the case of an advowson the church itself is the thing to which the right attaches, though we would hardly regard the church as a servient tenement. Bracton thought of all incorporeal rights as rights in the nature of servitudes. This approach can hardly be said to have been followed in the later law with any consistency, though it is true that of the incorporeal hereditaments which the common law came to recognize in its developed form (listed by Blackstone[10] as advowsons, tithes, commons, ways, offices, dignities, franchises, corodies, annuities, and rents) all are in some respects analogous to servitudes, whilst of course most of them are servitudes.

Of the host of incorporeal things known to medieval law easements and profits are the most important left today. Both

[7] Britton, II, 8. See L. O. Pike, 'Feoffment and Livery of Incorporeal Hereditaments', 5 *L.Q.R.* 29.

[8] Britton, II, 9. But incorporeal rights appurtenant to land will pass if the land itself is conveyed by livery of seisin.

[9] Bracton, f. 53; see also Digby, *Real Property*, pp. 185, 189.

[10] Blackstone, II, 21.

Bracton[11] and Britton[12] include in the class of servitudes those natural rights of a property owner which arise through the partial acceptance in the law of the maxim *sic utere tuo ut alieno non laedas* (so use your own that you do not harm another). They do so because the application of this principle imposes a burden upon the tenant of the servient land of adjoining land-owners. Interference with such 'servitudes' was remediable from Bracton's time onwards by the assize of nuisance, a modified form of the assize of novel disseisin.[13] It is true that the distinction between such natural rights and servitudes *stricto sensu* is already appreciated—natural rights arise through operation of law, they are 'of common right', and do not depend upon express grants or prescription. But since natural rights and servitudes proper were remediable by the same action it was natural enough to put them both in a single category; and Bracton's analysis was not finally rejected until the nineteenth century.

Neither Bracton nor Britton attempted to list all the possible servitudes. Thus Britton says: 'A person may subject his tenement to a servitude in several ways, as by granting that another, who has nothing therein, shall have a right of pasturing or mowing or fishing or of driving cattle or of way or of carrying therein or by other servitudes, which may be infinite and numberless. . . .'[14] But with the exception of rights of way and rights to water, medieval law did not have much experience of easements; profits were much more common and important. Profits differ from easements in allowing the holder of the right to take away something of value—turf, wood, grass, fish—from the burdened land. A right of way, a typical easement, does not have this characteristic.

Rights of Common

The most characteristic profits were the rights of common which arose in manors and were enjoyed by freeholders.[15] The origin of these rights has been disputed. The orthodox theory of the later law is that they arose through grants by the manorial lord to his tenants, and support for this theory is to be found in

[11] See Digby, *Real Property*, pp. 187, 190.   [12] Britton, II, 23.
[13] Fifoot, *History and Sources*, Ch. 1.   [14] Britton, II, 23, 3.
[15] For texts see Digby, *Real Property*, pp. 195–210.

Bracton. It is much more probable, however, that such rights simply arose as customary rights associated with the communal system of agriculture practised in the primitive village communities. At a very early period such villages would be surrounded with tracts of waste land, not yet brought into cultivation. Of the land which was cultivated some parts would always be lying fallow, or be temporarily unused after the harvest had been gathered. On such land the villagers as a community would pasture their beasts and from it they would gather wood and turf and so forth. In the course of time, when the increase of population and reduction in the quantity of uncultivated land started to produce crowding and conflict, their rights would tend to become more clearly defined but would still be communal rights, principally over waste lands regarded as the lands of the community itself. The tenurial system converted the villagers into tenants, and the theory of the law placed the freehold of most of the lands of the manor in the lord. Some of his tenants, it is true, will be freeholders, but the majority hold unfreely in villeinage, and the pre-eminence of the lord makes it natural to treat him as the 'owner' of the waste lands. Thus a theory of individual ownership supplants earlier more egalitarian notions. The freehold tenants of the manor are able to assert their rights over the lord's lands in the royal courts, and the theory of the lawyers says that these rights originated in the grant of the lord. But the rights of the freeholders of the manor do not differ in kind from the rights of the unfree tenants, which, as the lawyers recognize, depend not upon any grant but upon the custom of the manor. It is unlikely that as a general rule the freeholders' rights had a different origin, though there is no doubt that some rights *in alieno solo* which were enjoyed by freeholders did in fact arise through actual grants, for examples of such grants are known. What is not historically correct is the legal theory which asserts that *all* arose in this way.[16]

Classification of Profits

Although the profits which formed so characteristic a part of the manorial system of agriculture were the typical profits of medieval law, it was perfectly possible for profits to arise by

[16] See Vinogradoff, *Villainage in England*, pp. 260–72.

grant or long user outside the framework of the manor, and a considerable body of law grew up around them. Bracton recognizes two types of profit—those that pertain to (or are 'appurtenant' to) a freehold tenement, and those that are not—the profit in gross. Bracton is not too happy about the profit in gross, and he does not regard it as a full-blooded property right.[17] But his successors in the law were quite prepared to accept such profits, and their view has prevailed. Bracton states a simple body of rules which govern the acquisition of profits. They arise either through express grant or reservation, *pur cause de vicinage*, or through long user. On this straightforward basis the common lawyers, in the course of time, have built up the elaborate body of law which exists today, riddled as it is with fiction and absurdity, but in the Middle Ages only the germs of the disease are apparent, and the law was on the whole lucid and rational.

Prescriptive Titles

Bracton gives an admirable definition of the user which is needed to found a prescriptive title. Profits may be acquired, '. . . by user for a long time with peaceful, continuous and uninterrupted enjoyment of the right, the lord knowing of it and neglecting to interfere; for this is regarded as equivalent to a legal transfer, provided that the enjoyment has not been by violence, or clandestinely or by request and permission . . .'[18] The long user became the common law's 'time whereof the memory of man runneth not to the contrary', and until after the time of Littleton there were lawyers who were prepared to take this phrase sensibly and literally.[19] Unhappily, the view which prevailed, and which is to be found in the early year books,[20] required user to be shown since 1189,[21] with the absurd

---

[17] See Digby, *Real Property*, p. 205.

[18] Bracton, f. 222.

[19] See Littleton, sec. 170, and for Coke's comments, Co. Litt. 113a–115b.

[20] E.g. *The King* v. *Breaux* (1313), Selden Society, Vol. 29, p. 180.

[21] In effect this means that the plaintiff will fail if the enjoyment of the right can be shown to have been impossible at some point of time after 1189; in the case of rights connected with buildings this can often be done. Coke seems to envisage disproof only by a record or by written evidence or by human memory, whereas in the modern law any form of disproof is acceptable. The acquisition of rights has thus become more difficult.

results all know. The date was selected by analogy with the period of limitation fixed in 1275 for the writ of right; until the Prescription Act (1833) the only attempt to mitigate the resulting injustices was the judicial invention of the fiction of the lost modern grant.

It is clear that in Bracton there is no theory that acquisition by prescription depends upon any fictional presumption of a lost grant; long user of itself founds a right of property. Not until the seventeenth century is the modern doctrine of a presumed grant found in the reports.[22] The earlier theory of the law was more closely analogous to the modern theory of local custom. A local and particular custom, established by long user, creates local, peculiar law, at variance with the common law; similarly prescription was thought to establish a private law, also at variance with the common law, which applied to the person who was able to prescribe for the right in question. Prescription was the equivalent of a sealed charter, which too could abrogate common law, and set up a private law; this was the way an entailed estate was created by the form of the gift, expressed in the charter. The close analogy between local custom and prescription may be most clearly seen in the rules which still govern the acquisition of common *pur cause de vicinage*. If the unfenced waste lands of two manors march together it is obviously impossible to prevent beasts straying from one manor to the other. In recognition of this a freeholder who had a right of common in one manor acquired a similar right in the adjoining manor 'because of proximity'. In order to prescribe for this right the claimant had, in effect, to show not long user by himself and his predecessors in title, but a local custom, enjoyed by all the commoners, which permitted beasts to 'intercommon', to wander from one common to another. Thus in this instance the distinction between prescription and acquisition by local and particular custom disappears. Indeed, in many cases in which a right of common is claimable by pres-

---

[22] See *Gateward's Case*, 6 Co. Rep. 59b at 60b, where it was held that 'every prescription ought to have by common intendment a lawful beginning'. Earlier cases had drawn the distinction between the personal nature of prescription and the local nature of custom; from this had come the rule that a fluctuating body of persons could not prescribe. This rule, in its turn, had fitted easily into the lost grant theory of prescription, for a fluctuating body of persons could not receive a grant. See Y.B. 15 Edw. IV Trin., pl. 7, f. 29, *Withers* v. *Isham* (1553), Dyer 71a.

cription the sort of evidence which suffices to ground a prescriptive claim would as well found a claim for the existence of a
local custom. What differs is the theory of the significance of
the evidence.

Common Appendant

One class of profit was treated anomalously; this is the class
of profits *appendant*. In the developed law of Coke's day a freehold tenant of a manor could claim common of pasture over
the manorial waste as an incident annexed by operation of law
to his tenure.[23] He did not have to go beyond proving the
tenure, which must, of course, have been created before *Quia
Emptores* (1290); it was not necessary to prescribe or show a
grant. Not until the sixteenth century is the adjective 'appendant' used technically to characterize this type of profit, but the
basis of the doctrine is to be found very much earlier. In Bracton
common of pasture is treated as the most usual and important
profit, for a manorial tenant who did not have the right would
hardly be able to farm at all. The existence of a right of common
could be shown in various ways. A claimant might rely upon a
specialty, or upon long user, which, as we have seen, was
treated as its equivalent. Alternatively he could claim the right
as an adjunct to his holding. In the latter case he was said in the
fourteenth century to claim a profit which was 'appurtenant' or
'appendant' to his freehold—the two terms are used quite
interchangeably—and the basis of such a claim was that the
claimant had a profit because he was seised of land to which the
right was annexed. The annexation could be shown in a variety
of ways, but the most usual way was for the claimant to rely
upon ancient use. Quite early—in the statute of Westminster II
(1285)[24]—we find traces of the idea that a freehold tenant of a
manor might have a right of common of pasture attached to his
freehold by law, or as contemporaries would put it, 'of common right', a phrase roughly equivalent to the modern 'by the
law of the land'. In a case in 1317[25] there is a long discussion as

---

[23] Co. Litt. 122a.

[24] 13 Edw. I, st. 1, c. 46.

[25] *Solers* v. *The Parson of Dorstone* (1317), Selden Society, Vol. 61, p. 91, and cf.
p. 65, where it seems that common *pur cause de vicinage* is 'of common right'. See also
Y.B. 27 Edw. III (R.S.) at p. 353, where (in 1343) common appendant is spoken of as
'of common right'.

to whether this is true of freehold land purchased by the acre, or only true of hidated land; it is clear that the extent of 'common right' is not very clear and, perhaps because of this uncertainty, claimants continue to show that pasture rights are annexed to their lands in particular by prescribing; the law is not yet settled that *any* freeholder of a manor can claim common of pasture. As time passes the effects of *Quia Emptores* become more obvious; the freeholders of manors are a select class who cannot be increased, for the creation of new tenures has ceased. The fifteenth-century judges came around to the view that all such freeholders have a right of common of pasture by operation of law. In 1462 Newton C.J. and the whole court enunciated the doctrine that there is no need to prescribe for common appendant, and the year book reporter makes a special note of this rule.[26] Thereafter the term 'appendant' comes to be used as a term of art to designate the right of pasturage which arises by operation of law in favour of freeholders, whilst the term 'appurtenant' is used to designate profits which are associated with a dominant tenement but which do not arise 'of common right' and so have to be claimed by prescription or grant; they are *appurtenant* in opposition to profits in gross, which do not enure to the benefit of a particular piece of land, and which are not annexed to a particular tenement.[27]

When it is settled that common *appendant* arises by operation of law in all manors it becomes necessary to fix its precise limitations. The right only attached to arable land, and was limited to 'beasts commonable'—horses and oxen, cattle and sheep—and only to those beasts which were *levant* and *couchant* on the claimant's land. The right passed automatically to any tenant of the land to which it was appendent, and would be apportioned if the land was split up. It was impossible for a tenant

---

[26] Y.B. 22 Hen. VI Mich., pl. 13, f. 9, at f. 10.

[27] Thomas Fitzwilliam's *Reading* (1465) on the Statute of Merton, c. 4, divides rights of common into common in gross and common appendant; there is no third category. Common appendant, in his view, is 'of common right', but common in gross is not. Yet he thinks it necessary to prescribe for common appendant, and by the term he only seems to mean common attached to a dominant tenement. He does not think that such attachment or annexation can be produced by an express grant: it can arise only through prescription. See Selden Society, Vol. 71, at p. 58.

to sever the right from the land, and alienate it separately, whereas this could be done in the case of common appurtenant.

Profits Appurtenant and in Gross

Into the category of profits *appurtenant* were placed all profits created by act of the parties, or claimed by prescription, which were annexed to a dominant tenement; in practice, claims based upon prescription are much the most common. The profits which fell into this class form a heterogeneous collection, some of fairly modern origin, but most of them of immemorial antiquity just like common appendant. Thus on many manors the freeholders had enjoyed a right to gather turf for just as long as they had enjoyed a right to pasture their beasts, and the two rights originate in the economic structure of the village community in the same way. For the right of pasture they need not prescribe—this is common *appendant*—but for the right of turbary they must, for it is common *appurtenant*. There is nothing particularly rational about the limitation of common appendant to common of pasture only.

The courts also accepted the validity of profits in gross, in spite of Bracton's unease about them; they were always rare and somewhat anomalous, more usually arising through the severance of a profit appurtenant from the dominant tenement than from deliberate creation. From the earliest times too it was recognized that profits could be created in severalty as well as in common; a typical early example would be a several fishery. Historically several profits are almost always the result of an actual grant, though the grant will often have been lost, so that a claimant may have to rely upon prescription; in this instance the modern doctrine that prescription gives rise to a presumption of a grant is not so much of a fiction as it is in the case of profits enjoyed in common.

Approvement

At a very early period the village community was probably surrounded with such extensive waste land that there was more than was needed for the villagers. When the communal rights of the village community gave way to the individual property rights of imposed feudalism, it was natural enough that the power of enclosing such waste land should be acquired by the manorial lord, and equally natural that the lord's right to do this should be resented by the villagers as a form of expropriation. The Statute of Merton in 1235[28] gave, or more probably confirmed, the lord's right to approve the waste lands of the manor so long as sufficient was left for the commoners. This right to approve was extended in 1285.[29] It is probable that the intention was that the lord could only approve against the type of common rights which came to be called common *appendant*, and not against common *appurtenant*. By Coke's time, however, the only restriction was in favour of common *in gross*. The right to approve only existed against the freehold tenants of the manor. As against the unfree tenants the lord's rights were limited by the custom of the manor. Thus approvement by the lord only led to a partial discharge of the waste lands of a manor from rights of common. Approvement must be distinguished from inclosure under private Acts of Parliament, which normally involved not only the waste of the manor but also the common fields, and led to a complete discharge of rights of common existing either at common law or under the manorial custom applicable to the unfree tenants.

Easements

The law of easements, though less developed, mirrored the law of profits. Thus easements could exist in gross as well as being appurtenant to land, and could be claimed by prescription as well as by express grant. There could, of course, be nothing to correspond precisely to the doctrine of common appendant, though the right to a way of necessity was thought of as arising by operation of law, 'of common right', like common *appendant*. The distinction between natural rights, local customary rights, and easements was not at all clearly formulated. This was in part the result of the fact that the assize of nuisance and the action on the case for nuisance lay equally to protect natural rights and easements, and partly because the rule that only a capable grantee can prescribe, and not a fluctuating body of local people, was not settled in medieval law[30] for it is a conse-

---

[28] For the text see Digby, *Real Property*, pp. 198, 206, and for discussion see Plucknett, *Legislation of Edward I*, pp. 83 *et seq.*

[29] Statute of Westminster II, c. 46.

[30] See *Withers* v. *Isham* (1553), Dyer 71a.

quence of the modern theory of prescription. The basis of the more modern law, largely borrowed from Roman law, was there in Bracton, but it cannot be said that much progress had been made in incorporating it into the common law. Even in Coke's time the subject of easements was only scantily explored, and is hardly mentioned in Coke's commentary on Littleton.

Incorporeal Rights and the Doctrine of Estates

It has sometimes been suggested that there is some connection between the development of a doctrine of estates in the fourteenth century and the treatment of incorporeal hereditaments by the early medieval lawyers. The argument is this. The lawyers treated land and rights connected with land in much the same way; the same actions to some extent protected both, the same rules about inheritance applied to both, the same conception of seisin was employed in both instances. The similarity in the treatment of land and rights over land made it convenient to analyse the conception of ownership in a way which would fit both. In order to produce a satisfactory analysis ownership had to be divorced from the subject-matter of ownership and conceptualized. The curious solution adopted by the common-lawyers was the doctrine of estates, which makes it possible to say that Jones owns a life estate in his land and a life estate in, say, an easement which is appurtenant to his land, and thus expressing the similarity in the legal treatment of the land and the right over land which he is entitled to enjoy. The dissimilarity is expressed by saying that his life estate in his land is a life estate in a corporeal thing, whilst his life estate in the easement is a life estate in an incorporeal thing. This analysis can be summed up by saying that in the common law of realty ownership is always ownership of an incorporeal thing—an estate—but that estates can subsist in both corporeal things, such as houses and fields, and in incorporeal things such as advowsons and profits. The argument suggests that once the law took the course of treating land and rights over land on the same footing this analysis was in some way inevitable. The plausibility of this theory is considerable, but it is by no means clear that there is any truth in it; the flaw in the reasoning lies in the suggestion that the early medieval lawyers took over the Roman conception of ownership, of *dominium*, and then took the ingenious step of saying that the Englishman *owned* an incorporeal thing called an estate. They never did; talk of ownership of estates is modern talk. Instead they speak of a tenant being seised in fee simple (or fee tail or whatever it is) of Blackacre, or of a several fishery in the Usk, and this description is entirely adequate for their purposes and does not strike them as in any way incongruous, though it includes no mention of anyone owning anything. If it had, then it would perhaps be true that a doctrine of estates which said that English ownership was always ownership of an incorporeal thing—an estate—would have been the way out of the incongruity. But there is little reason to suppose that they did find it strange to treat corporeal and incorporeal hereditaments in much the same way, and thus little reason to suppose that the doctrine of estates represents an attempt to dispose of the problem.

Covenants Affecting Land

Covenants which affect land have a close affinity with easements, and there are obvious resemblances between the law which governs them. Historically, however, the two are quite distinct. Easements from a very early period rank as a form of property, and the law which governs land itself is extended to them through the medium of the assize of nuisance, which is an extension of the assize of novel disseisin. The law of covenants affecting land is an extension of the medieval law of contract, which grew up around the action of covenant.[31] The model for this extension was the ancient law of warranty.[32] Upon a subinfeudation by feoffment (the normal mode of conveyance before *Quia Emptores* (1290)) it was normal for the feoffor to warrant the land to the feoffee, and even if he did not do so an obligation to warrant arose by implication on the receipt of homage; this is an illustration of the feudal notion that a lord has a duty to protect his tenants. The obligation to warrant, which was the consequence of the tenure created by the grant and receipt of homage, descended to the heirs of the feoffor, and the benefit passed down to the heirs of the feoffee;[33] thus it

[31] For an account of this action see Fifoot, *History and Sources*, Ch. 11, Simpson, *History of Contract*. Pf. I Ch. I.

[32] The law of warranty is discussed in Ch. VI.

[33] See S. E. Thorne, 'English Feudalism and Estates in Land', [1959] *Camb. L.J.* 193, for the effects of homage and the relationship between homage and warranty in early law.

provided an example of an obligation which passed down like real property. In the course of time the reliance upon implied warranties gave way to a reliance upon express warranties. Partially this was the result of *Quia Emptores* (1290), which limited subinfeudation to estates other than the fee simple.[34] After 1290 no tenurial relationship was created between grantor and grantee of a fee simple, to which the obligation to warrant could be automatically attached. Where a fee simple was granted by substitution, so that the grantor was not the lord of the grantee, the duty of the grantor to warrant the grantee's title only lasted for the lifetime of the grantor. Express warranties in a charter could be sued upon as covenants in the action of covenant; by being inserted in charters they automatically became promises under seal. Naturally enough they were treated as covenants annexed to the estate of the covenantee, they guaranteed the actual estate granted, and by an extension of the normal rules governing the action of covenant they could be relied upon by persons other than the original covenantee, so long as he had the estate to which the benefit of the covenant had been originally attached. The recognition of the rule that the benefit of an express warranty would run with the estate to which it was annexed for the purposes of the writ of covenant merely copied the same rule which applied for the purposes of the writ of *warrantia cartae* (the special writ for enforcing warranties), for voucher, and for rebutting a claim to the land.[35] In the fourteenth century it was settled in *Pakenham's Case* (1369) that the benefit of other sorts of covenant could be annexed to the estate of the covenantee; the covenant enforced in that case was held to bind the defendant to celebrate divine service in the chapel of the plaintiff,[36] who was a successor in title of the

[34] This was enacted, or confirmed, by the statute *De Bigamis* (1276). *Quia Emptores* in 1290 enacted that all grants of this sort should be by substitution. Where lesser estates (e.g. a life estate) were granted there could still be an obligation to warrant on tenurial grounds, for the grant would create a tenure between grantor and grantee.

[35] A warranty is thus defined by Coke: 'A warranty is a covenant real annexed to lands or tenements, whereby a man and his heirs are bound to warrant the same: and either upon voucher, or by judgment in a writ of *warrantiae cartae*, to yield other lands and tenements to the value of those that shall be evicted by a former title, or else may be used by way of rebutter.' Co. Litt. 365a. Coke carefully distinguishes a covenant annexed to land, 'which is to yield but damages' from a warranty, which is a 'covenant real', that is a covenant which can be specifically enforced. See Co. Litt. 384b.

[36] Y.B. 42 Edw. III Hil., pl. 14, f. 3.

original covenantee. Thus the power of running with the estate in land of the covenantee was extended outside the original context of warranties. This breach of the ordinary rule of privity of contract was limited to the benefit of covenants affecting land.

On the running of the burden of covenants there is little known of the medieval law, but we can perhaps guess what a medieval lawyer would have said by looking at the law of warranty. The obligation to warrant descended upon the heirs of the warrantor; it could not be annexed to land, for on an alienation the land passed to the alienee who took the benefit. By the thirteenth century it was settled that it was not possible to alter this rule about the obligation to warrant by making contrary provision in a deed.[37] Though there is an absence of authority upon whether upon a feoffment, a burden (such as a *duty* to say divine service) could be annexed to the land of the feoffee by mere covenant[38] the probability is that this could not be done, by analogy with the law of warranty.

Thus it was the rule that the benefit of a covenant could be annexed to the estate in land of the covenantee, but it is unlikely that a burden could be imposed. It must be noted that the medieval law on this point does not depend upon the existence of privity of estate (that is a tenure) between the parties to an action on the covenant, for this does not exist between grantor and grantee of an estate in fee simple. The rules which govern the landlord and tenant relationship, where in modern law there is privity, do not develop until the sixteenth century. It seems probable, however, that the benefits of covenants in a lease ran with the land at common law in the medieval period, by analogy with the decision in *Pakenham's Case*. At the same time it is not likely, though there is little authority on the matter, that covenants could in medieval law be annexed to a reversion. Certainly this was not established until after the medieval period.[39]

---

[37] Y.B. 32, 33 Edw. I (R.S.) 516.

[38] Upon a feoffment a burden could be imposed on the land in favour of the feoffor by way of reservation so long as it fell within some recognized category of property right. An example would be a rent-charge.

[39] See generally Holdsworth, III, pp. 157 *et seq.*

VI

Medieval Conveyancing

THE classical-medieval conveyance was the feoffment with
livery of seisin. Back in Anglo-Saxon times it seems that some
land[1] could be conveyed by delivery of a written instrument, a
charter, but with the Norman invasion this practice, which was
probably never quantitatively common, died out, and an actual
physical delivery of land became the normal mode of private
conveyance. Naturally one cannot hand over a tract of land in
the same way as one hands over a horse, but the law encouraged
alienors to make conveyances of land as like the delivery of a
chattel as possible. The expression 'feoffment with livery of
seisin' does not indicate any twofold ceremony; a grant of a fee
is implied by 'feoffment',[2] and livery, or delivery of seisin, is
the mode in which the grant is made. This delivery of seisin
must be an actual delivery of vacant possession and not a mere
symbolic delivery alone, and in order to make a livery of seisin
the feoffor must be seised so that he can relinquish his seisin to
the feoffee on the land itself. It is obvious that this mode of conveyance gave to dealings in land a notoriety which no symbolic
delivery or delivery of a deed could ever give.

Capacity to make a Feoffment

In order to make a feoffment the feoffor must be seised; conversely, any person who was seised could make a feoffment.
From this principle some curious results followed. If a tenant in
fee simple in possession was disseised he was quite unable to

---

[1] Called *bookland*, as opposed to *folkland*, which was held not by charter and in
accordance with a special law of the charter, but by popular custom. The institution
gave rise to the fairly common place name, Buckland. In the nature of things little is
known about folkland; indeed the word only occurs three times in surviving literature.
See Plucknett, 'Bookland and Folkland', 6 *Econ. Hist. R.* 64, *Concise History*, p. 518,
Jolliffe, 'English Book Right', 50 *E.H.R.* 1, John, *Land Tenure in Early England*, Chs. I–
III.

[2] A life estate, which in the developed law is not a 'fee', is passed by feoffment; the
term 'fee' originally did not connote heritability, and a man might hold feudally and
therefore 'in fee', for life only.

convey any interest in the land until he recovered his seisin by entry or action. The disseisor, on the other hand, was able to make a feoffment, and although his alienee was vulnerable to an action by the disseisee yet he obtained an estate which was good until it was upset by action. Again, a life tenant or anyone who was seised could make a feoffment, and in the absence of any provision to the contrary such a feoffment would pass a fee simple to the feoffee which similarly would be good until upset by the reversioner or remainderman; such a feoffment was wrongful; it was a tortious feoffment, but it was not void or invalid. The capacity to make a feoffment was a capacity to clothe with a fief, and the normal fief was heritable; the capacity to make a feoffment derived from the fact of seisin, and from nothing else. A tortious feoffment, however, had the important incidental effect of working a forfeiture; the feoffor's interest in the land was totally destroyed through his wrong. Thus if a life tenant made a tortious feoffment the reversioner (or remainderman) in whom was the next vested interest could at once take steps to recover the seisin without having to await the death of the life tenant.

Charters

The delivery of a charter or deed would normally accompany a feoffment, though no document was needed to perfect such a conveyance. Documentary evidence was obviously valuable to establish the terms of the feoffment. Such a deed would identify the land and the names of the parties to the conveyance, and then go on to state the donee's interest (using the appropriate words to convey a fee simple, life estate, or whatever it was), the lord of whom it was to be held, and the services due. The deed would then normally include an undertaking on the part of the grantor to warrant the grantee's title, and would conclude with the grantor's seal and perhaps a list of witnesses to its attachment.[3] Naturally more complicated transactions produced longer and more complicated charters of feoffment, whilst simple conveyances might not be accompanied by any charter at all, though to dispense with one was to ask for trouble

---

[3] For examples of charters of enfeoffment see *English Historical Documents*, II, pp. 916–36, esp. nos. 235 (*c.* 1066), 244 (1121), 250 (*c.* 1130), 263 (1155); see also p. 846, no. 196 (1187). And see S. E. Thorne, 'Livery of Seisin', 52 *L.Q.R.* 345.

in any litigation which might arise. The security of conveyances executed by feoffment accompanied by charter was a
continuous source of worry to landowners, for both theft of
charters and forgery of them were common. In one fifteenth-
century case we hear of charters being kept in a chest too heavy
to be brought into court, and the chest had no doubt not been
made so massive for nothing. Other expedients were tried to
increase security. One was to pay royal clerks to enrol a copy of
a charter on the close rolls where the office copies of closed up
royal communications were preserved. Such copies are safely
preserved in the public records to this day. Another was to
execute duplicate deeds on the same piece of parchment, cutting the two copies apart with a ragged cut. The word 'chiro-
graphum' might be written across the line of the tear. If forgery
was alleged, then it could soon be seen if the two documents fitted together. Such charters were called indentures from the in-
dented line of the cut, and contrasted with deeds poll, which
had a smooth or polled top edge. The best expedient of all, as
we shall see, was to employ an entirely different form of conveyance, the fine, which combined both advantages with others
peculiar to itself.

Interests which Lay in Grant

Some interests in land simply did not admit of livery of seisin
—for example incorporeal rights such as advowsons. In cases
of this sort the grantor delivered to the grantee a deed of grant,
and this operated as a conveyance. But the grantee was in some
respects in a weak position until he had actually enjoyed the
right; for example a grantee of an advowson who had never
presented was unable to use the assize of darrein presentment,
and since he could not show enjoyment in any ancestor he was
unable to bring a writ of right to recover the advowson. Thus,
although it was impossible in such cases to deliver seisin, yet
the notion of seisin, manifested by enjoyment, could well be
applied to such interests, and a title was imperfect until there
had been such enjoyment. A reversion is another example of an
interest which does not admit of livery of seisin, for the conveyance of a reversion must take place over the head of the person
who is actually seised of the land—for example a life tenant—so
that the grantor will have no seisin to deliver. So it becomes

settled that a deed must be allowed to operate to convey the land, but to perfect the conveyance the life tenant, or whoever it is who is in actual seisin, must acknowledge the new reversioner; he must attorn tenant to him. The result of all this was the growth of an important classification of interests in land into those which were susceptible of livery of seisin and those which were not—those which lie in grant and those which lie in livery,[4] the latter could be conveyed without a deed, whilst the former could not. Interests which lie in grant might be further subdivided into interests where a deed alone gave the grantee a perfect title, and those where something more, such as attornment, was needed. Interests which lie in grant are usually treated as the same interests as those called incorporeal hereditaments, but the correct classification has been the subject-matter of some arid and inconclusive dispute.[5]

Fines of Land

Early in the history of conveyancing the search for a really secure mode of conveyance led to the evolution of the fine or final concord. Such a conveyance took the form of a compromised fictitious personal action; the terms of the compromise, which are in fact the terms of the conveyance, are drawn up under the superintendence of the court and preserved in its records. The advantages of some such system are obvious, and as early as 1195 we find a regularization of the procedure adopted over these fictitious actions. The terms of the fine were in future to be drawn up in a tripartite indenture. One part each went to the parties to the action—the grantor and grantee—and the third, which was called the foot of the fine since it was cut off the foot of the skin, was preserved amongst the court records. These feet of fines, which were the ultimate protection against forgery, remain in the public records in a series from 1195 up to

---

[4] See Co. Litt. 9a, and L. O. Pike, 'Feoffment and Livery of Incorporeal Hereditaments', 5 *L.Q.R.* 29.

[5] See Challis, *Real Property*, p. 47, and Sweet's note at p. 49. Students should note the distinction between situations where livery of seisin is not necessary, and a grant by deed will suffice, because seisin has already passed out of the grantor (e.g. a grant of a reversion in fee simple expectant upon a life estate) and cases where livery in an obvious sense is inappropriate (for example where the grant is a grant of an advowson).

1833,[6] when the system, which had worked in much the same way for six hundred years, was finally abolished. It is possible that fines originated when the concurrence of a court—a lord's feudal court—was required for the validity of transactions by tenants. If so they did not originate in the context of litigation at all.

Varieties of Fine

There were a number of varieties of fine, and a great deal of complicated law about their operation.[7] Basically the procedure differed little. The action, which came to be begun by writ of covenant, or writ of *warrantia chartae*, was brought by the prospective grantee, who was called the querent, since he was doing the complaining, against the prospective grantor, called the deforciant as the individual notionally deforcing the querent of the land. After the action had been begun the parties applied for the court's permission to compromise the action, and were granted a licence to compromise. The terms of the compromise were drawn up in the final concord. Once the concord is made the names of the parties change. The grantor is now called the conusor (or cognizor) and the grantee of conusee, the whole process being described as 'levying' a fine. The main varieties of fine differ in the grounds upon which the grantor (deforciant, conusor) pretends he has had to compromise. In the fine *sur cognisance de droit come ceo que il ad de son done* the conusor admits that the lands in question belong to the conusee on the ground that he, the conusor, previously gave them to the conusee. Such a fine was said to be 'executed'; this meant that since it is admitted that the lands are already the lands of the conusee there is no need for any livery of seisin to him.[8] This was the most commonly used type of fine. A variety of this type of fine, that *sur done grant et render* would be used to create settlements in this way. Smith wants to settle Blackacre, of which he is tenant in fee simple, by making himself life tenant

---

[6] 4 and 5 Will. IV, c. 74. The feet of fines are a valuable source of local history; the parts preserved by the parties turn up often in the bindings of old books. For an example of a fine *sur cognisance de droit come ceo que il ad de son done* see Kiralfy, *Source Book*, p. 99.

[7] There is a clear account in Blackstone, II, Ch. 21.

[8] For the early history see Pollock and Maitland, II, 94-105. Blackstone, II, Appendix IV gives a specimen.

and his son remainderman in tail. He secures the co-operation of Jones, and they levy a fine, with Smith as conusor and Jones as conusee. Smith admits that the lands belong to Jones in fee simple because (so it is pretended) Smith has previously given them to Jones. Jones at once regrants the lands to Smith for life with remainder in tail to his son, remainder in fee simple to whoever Smith has designated. The whole settlement is embodied in the fine, and is secure against forgery and theft, whilst the court will not accept the fine unless the terms of the settlement are valid. Such a fine was however executory only. Executory fines differed in that the fine did not become effective until the sheriff had delivered seisin to the conusee. Another example is the fine *sur cognisance de droit tantum*, in which the conusor simply recognizes that the lands are the right of the conusee, without there being any pretence that the conusor has ever given the lands to the conusee. This type was used to pass reversionary interests. Yet another type, the fine *sur concessit*, involved a grant by way of compromise to the cognisee, without any admission of prior right.

The fine was the most secure of all medieval conveyances, and around so useful an institution for the security of men's lands there grew up an almost superstitious reverence. So long as one of the parties was seised of the lands no one could dispute the fine after a period of a year and a day from the execution of it, except those under some disability. This gave opportunities for fraudulent practice, and in 1360 it was enacted that a fine should not affect the rights of strangers to it.[9] This did much to destroy the value of conveyances by fine, and in Richard III's reign a compromise was reached.[10] So long as a fine was accompanied with proclamations it would bar strangers as well as parties and privies after a period of five years; remaindermen and reversioners were allowed a period of five years after their estates fell in to assert their rights. Henry VII re-enacted the substance of this statute.[11] Extensions of time were given to married women, prisoners, persons gone overseas, and lunatics, time running against them when their disability ended—for example when the husband died, or

---

[9] 34 Edw. III, c. 16.
[10] 1 Rich. III, c. 7.
[11] 4 Hen. VII, c. 24.

the prisoner was released. Fines were particularly valuable as a mechanism whereby a married woman could effectively alienate her lands, after examination by the court.

Collusive Recoveries

Differing from the fine, in that the collusive litigation was begun by real action and not by personal action, was the collusive or feigned *recovery*. The term 'recovery' is used to describe successful litigation by real action in which the demandant recovers the land, and collusive recoveries could be used as a form of conveyance. In the Middle Ages feigned and collusive recoveries never became an approved form of conveyance in the way fines did. They were normally tainted with fraud of one sort or another, and the efforts of the courts and the legislature[12] was directed rather to restricting such frauds than to encourageing the use of recoveries for conveyancing. A typical fraud which could be attempted would be this. Smith is a life tenant but wishes to sell the land for a fee simple to Jones. He and Jones reach agreement, and Jones brings a writ of right against him on a bogus title claiming the fee. Smith 'pleads faintly'—that is, he puts in a plausible but inadequate defence to the action—and if nothing is done about this Jones will recover the land in fee. The law, however, develops a counter to such a fraud by allowing the reversioner or remainderman who is really entitled to the fee to pray to be received to defend his title, and if he does this the fraud will be prevented. A large variety of other frauds were tried from time to time, but they were usually dealt with by the development of procedures which enabled the victims of the frauds to 'falsify'—that is, to avoid—the feigned recovery. Only in one special sphere did the courts give any encouragement to the use of false recoveries for conveyancing purposes, and this exception to the general pattern was, as we shall see, the result of very special circumstances.

---

[12] Feigned recoveries were a well-known technique of ousting lessees for years; the landlord would be impleaded by a friend who would lose the action by default, and the friend would then reconvey the land to the landlord free of the term. This abuse was checked by the statute of Gloucester (1278), but the statute only applied to recoveries by default where the lease was written, and was easily evaded. For other statutory provisions restraining fraudulent recoveries see Plucknett, *Concise History*, pp. 620–1.

Conveyancing Devices and the Entail: Warranties

As soon as it became clear that an entail would endure for as long as there were heirs of the prescribed class, conveyancers started to search for some method of breaking entails—that is to say, some method whereby a tenant in tail could alienate the entailed lands for a fee simple, or secure a power of disposal over the fee simple, which is not the same thing. He might wish to sell the land or he might simply wish to alter his own estate into a fee simple, perhaps with a view to its ultimate disposal. Or, and this perhaps was more usual, he wanted to resettle the land within his family, commonly when an alliance by marriage was under way. In either circumstance he must secure the power to alienate indefeasibly something he has not got, and if he is to do this he must find some way of barring the claims of his own issue (i.e. of depriving them of the possibility of bringing formedon in descender), those of any remaindermen, and those of the reversioner. The statute *De Donis* had foreseen the risk of such attempts and provided that a fine should be no bar to the issue in tail or to the reversioner.[13] Probably a fine would not bar the remaindermen either,[14] but the point would hardly arise, for a conveyance which only barred the remaindermen's rights would not be of much use to a tenant in tail. Tenants who wished to break entails therefore had to turn to some other device. In the fourteenth and early fifteenth centuries the best hope was to be looked for in the doctrines surrounding warranties.

On any conveyance it was normal for the alienor to warrant, or guarantee, the title of the alienee.[15] Thus if Smith, tenant in fee simple, alienated to Jones, he would warrant Jones's title. This warranty had important consequences. The benefit of it would enure to the benefit of Jones and his heirs, and the burden descend to the heirs of Smith. If Smith or an heir of his ever brought a real action against Jones or one of his heirs for the land the action would fail, for the warranty would act as a bar. This ruling obviously assisted the doctrine that a fee simple

---

[13] See the text in Digby, *Real Property*, at p. 230.

[14] Doubted in Y.B. 11 Edw. II, 18, Selden Society, Vol. 61.

[15] On the whole subject of warranties see S. J. Bailey, 'Warranties of Land in the Thirteenth Century', VIII *Camb. L. J.* 274, IX, 82, 'Warranties of Land in the Reign of Richard I', IX *Camb. L. J.* 192.

was freely alienable. Again if Jones were sued in a real action by a stranger who disputed his title, he could call upon Smith (or whoever now had the burden of the warranty) to fulfil his warranty. This was called voucher to warranty, and the result of successful voucher[16] would be that Smith had to defend the action; if he lost, then he must convey to Jones lands of equal worth to those lost to the stranger. Of course, if he won then Jones retained the lands as before.

The most obvious way to use warranties to bar entails would be for the tenant in tail to alienate in fee simple with warranty. The burden of the warranty would descend to his heir, and his heir general would almost always be the person prima facie entitled to bring formedon in descender to recover the lands from the alienee. It would seem on principle that the heir would be barred from his action by the warranty. Neither remaindermen or reversioners would be barred, of course, so that the alienee would get what later lawyers called a base fee. Whether this simple device was ever countenanced by the courts (it would have driven a coach through *De Donis*) we may doubt, but in 1306[17] a generous interpretation of the statute of Gloucester definitely settled that such a warranty was no bar. About the same time, however, a new doctrine emerges. It becomes the law that such a warranty will bar the issue in tail provided lands held in fee simple, and of equivalent value to those which were subject to the entail (and which have been alienated), descend to the heir in tail. This doctrine is hinted at as early as 1292, and soon after this becomes accepted.[18] We can only guess at the reasoning employed, but it was probably something like this. *De Donis* does not in terms have anything at all to say about warranties, but its purpose would be entirely frustrated if a simple warranty were to bar the issue in tail, so that a consideration of the underlying purpose of the statute leads to saying that such a warranty will not act as a bar. If the heir in tail is compensated for the loss of the entailed lands through the descent to him of lands of equal value, there is not

---

[16] The person vouched could question his obligation to warrant; this was 'demanding the lien' or 'counterpleading the warranty'.

[17] Y.B. 33–5 Edw. I (R.S.) 388.

[18] See Y.B. 20 Edw. I (R.S) 302, 33 Edw. I 24, 5 Edw. II, Selden Society, Vol. 63, p. 36.

the same temptation to restrict the ordinary rule that a warranty operates as a bar, for the heir in tail has been looked after well enough. The alienor has not disinherited his line. So a 'lineal warranty with assets descended' becomes a recognized bar to the issue. A warranty was said to be lineal in a person if the following conditions were satisfied:

(*a*) His claim to the lands to which the warranty related must be a claim by descent.

(*b*) His obligation to warrant must come to him from some person through whom he can trace a title by descent.

To put this another way, he who has the obligation to warrant must be able to claim the lands to which it relates as heir to the person who made the warranty.

Warranties which were not lineal in a person were collateral.[19] A simple example of a lineal warranty arises where A, tenant in tail male general of Blackacre, enfeoffs B in fee simple with warranty. He dies, and the obligation to warrant descends upon S, his eldest son, and heir general. S is also heir in tail, and his title to the lands is traceable by descent from his father, so that the warranty is lineal in him. An example of a collateral warranty is afforded by this example. D settles land in tail on his eldest son A, with remainder in tail to B his younger son. A enfeoffs X in fee simple with warranty and dies childless. The obligation to warrant descends upon B as heir general to his elder brother, but B's claim to the land is by purchase from D. The warranty is *collateral in B* to his title to the land.

The importance of the distinction between lineal and collateral warranties lies in the fact that it became settled in the fourteenth century that a collateral warranty alone would bar the claim of issue in tail, remaindermen, or reversioners to entailed land.[20] By ingenious conveyancing it was possible for tenants in tail to break the entail completely. But the use of col-

---

[19] This negative definition provides the simplest solution to the problem of differentiation. See Co. Litt. 373b, note 2 (by Butler), for a valuable discussion.

[20] See Y.B. 20 Edw. III (R.S.), Pt. II, 202, and cf. Littleton, sec. 712. An attempt was made in 1377 to abolish the bar by collateral warranty by statute, but this failed; the doctrine became all but obsolete by 4 Anne, c. 16. See Co. Litt. 373b.

lateral warranties for this purpose was so set about with complication and uncertainty that at best it provided only a dangerous
and speculative expedient, and at worst it might be entirely
impossible.

At first sight it seems difficult to see why a collateral warranty
should be allowed this force. The reason is not to be found in
any initial theoretical premise based upon the distinction between lineal and collateral warranties, but arises from the basic
common-law principle that one who is bound to warrant
another man's title to land cannot be heard to claim that land
for himself. Unless altered by statute this principle was maintained throughout the Middle Ages. *De Donis* did not expressly
abrogate the basic rule, but it was soon seen that unless *De
Donis* was to be interpreted as if it did, then it would be entirely
nugatory. In holding that the effect of *De Donis* was to reverse
the common-law rule, by making a lineal warranty no bar to
the issue in tail, the courts were giving a generously wide interpretation to that enactment, which was in accordance with its
spirit if not with its letter. Beyond this they were not prepared
to go. In the case of lineal warranty with assets descended, the
social purpose of the statute was fairly well served by allowing
the warranty to act as a bar. The issue in the first degree were
not left landless, and it was not at this time clear that the statute
intended to protect the remoter issue. Collateral warranties
were not frequently met in practice, and it does not seem to
have occurred to anyone to suggest that *De Donis* restricted
their barring effect. The bar by collateral warranty is not therefore a peculiar new doctrine evolved by the courts in the fourteenth century but a residual survival of a basic common-law
rule which escaped abrogation; the wide interpretation of the
statute *De Donis* was never carried so far.

Collusive Common Recoveries and Entails

The search for an efficient method of barring entails eventually met with success around the middle of the fifteenth century
in the use of an ingenious device known as the common
recovery, but which is better described as a *collusive* common
recovery. A *common* recovery was in technical language one in
which there was voucher to warranty, though the adjective
'common' seems to have become used to describe collusive

recoveries since they were available to all, using vouchees available to all. The collusive common recovery worked in the following way. Suppose Smith to be tenant in tail in possession of Blackacre, which he wishes to sell for a fee simple to Jones. A collusive real action is brought by Jones against Smith on a feigned title, Jones having already paid or agreed to pay Smith for the land. In this action Jones claims a fee simple in the land. Smith appears in court and vouches one Brown to warranty. Brown does not dispute his obligation to warrant Smith's title, and the action then proceeds between Jones and Brown. Instead of putting up a defence Brown asks for 'leave to imparl'—that is, he asks the court for an adjournment whilst he talks the matter over with Jones in the hope of reaching a settlement, and he and Jones leave court to have their imparlance. Brown promptly disappears. This is a contempt of court, and when Jones arrives back before the Justices and tells them that Brown has absconded, they at once give judgment in favour of Jones. The judgment is that Jones recovers the land, and that Brown is to convey to Smith lands of equal value to those recovered. Unfortunately Brown, who has been carefully selected for this reason (and paid for his trouble), has no land, so that the judgment can never the satisfied. If it ever was satisfied, then the land conveyed would be held on the same terms as that lost to Jones; it would be subject to the entail and to any interest in remainder or reversion after Smith's estate. Thus *if the judgment had been satisfied* neither the issue in tail nor the remaindermen or reversioner would suffer any loss, and although everybody knows that it never will be satisfied, the court's view is that it has done its best, and cannot be blamed if Brown is a man of straw. A blind eye is turned to the fact that the whole procedure is an obvious fraud, and neither the issue nor the remaindermen are allowed to do anything about it.

Around the common recovery hangs a great mystery. In the first place we do not really know when it was evolved, and in the second place there is no full understanding of the theoretical justification which allowed its entrance into the law. As Plucknett puts it, '. . . if the theory of the recovery is obscure, its history is even more so'.[21] We first meet a clear indication of the

[21] Plucknett, *Concise History*, p. 621. Baker in Selden Society, Vol. 94, p. 204 *et seq.* has added much information.

acceptance of the device in *Talcarn's* or *Taltarum's Case* in 1472.[22]
The facts of the case are extremely complicated, but the point
decided was that a common recovery with a single voucher—the
form of common recovery which we have described—did not
always suffice to bar the issue in tail from bringing formedon in
descender against the recoveror of the land. The recovery was
'common' only in the sense that there was voucher to warranty,[23]
not in the sense that the procedure was available to all. The case
concerned such a recovery which had been suffered in 1465, and
this was held to be ineffective. It was, however, assumed that a
common recovery with single voucher would effectively bar the
issue in an appropriate case, though what quite was an appropriate case produced some diversity of opinion. Chief Justice
Brian would only admit that such a recovery barred the issue if
the donor or his heir was vouched to warranty. Now the success
of the collusive common recovery (in its developed form) as a
method of barring entails depends upon the vouchee being not
the donor, or his heir, but some landless stranger who can never
satisfy the judgment, so that if Brian's view had prevailed we
should never have had the classical common recovery. What
Brian was prepared to allow (and it is clear that he was merely
stating the settled position in 1472) was the use of common
recoveries to bar entails when there really was going to be a
recompense of lands of equal value; such recoveries would be
used when it was wished to disentail one parcel of land and
substitute another for it with the co-operation of the original
settlor. But Choke and Littleton JJ. were prepared to go farther
than this; they seem to have taken the view that the issue would
be bound even if a person other than the donor or his heir was
vouched, so long as there had been judgment against him. Their
view came to be accepted, and it opened the way to the trick of
vouching a stranger who was a mere man of straw; indeed J. H.
Baker has shown how two individuals regularly acted as

---

[22] Y.B. 12 Edw. IV Mich, f. 14, pl. 16, f. 19, pl. 25, 13 Edw. IV Mich., f. 1, pl. 1.
The spelling *Taltarum* is traditional, and the belief in a 'correct' spelling of a fifteenth-
century name is anachronistic. The text is in Digby, *Real Property*, p. 255, and, with
pleadings in Kiralfy, *Source Book*, p. 86.

[23] Baker in Selden Society, Vol. 94, p. 204, note 6, denies that the recovery was
'common'; he there means that the vouchee was not the later professional man of
straw.

vouchees in the 1470s.[24] At first such a stranger could be bound
to warrant by getting him to execute a deed of release in favour
of the tenant in tail with warranty; the release could be a release
of wholly imaginary rights, but was none the less effective, and
gave an air of plausibility to the business.[25] By the mid-sixteenth
century even this cover was abandoned; one simply vouched the
court crier.[26] The final step was to hold that the collusive common recovery would bar not only the issue, but also the
remaindermen and the reversioner; this was finally decided in
1581 in *Capell's Case*.[27] Common recoveries thus became 'common assurances'—that is, everyday conveyances for the breaking of settlements. The evolution of the common recovery,
originally used only to resettle, into a device which could be used
to wholly alienate the family lands, remains somewhat obscure.

The Theory of Recoveries

The doctrinal theory of the common recovery too is not wholly
clear, for we lack a sufficient body of fifteenth-century authority
through which to trace the history of the matter, but the bones of
the theory are not impossible to reconstruct. Back in the early
fifteenth century attempts were made by tenants in tail to use
collusive recoveries (without voucher) to bar their issue; the
alienee brought a real action on a feigned title against the tenant,
and the tenant let judgment go by default.[28] Now *any* recovery in
a real action prima facie bound the losing party's issue, for the

[24] See Selden Society, Vol. 94, p. 205. The chronology is uncertain, but it would be
a mistake to think that the device appeared in the mid-fifteenth in its fully developed
form. Thus Littleton does not write of the entail as a barrable estate, and Constable in
his *Reading* (1489) does not envisage a general use; to him collateral warranties are the
normal mode of barring entails. See his *Reading*, Selden Society, Vol. 71, at pp. 182,
185, 190, 199, and cf. Keilwey's *Reports*, p. 123b. Again the clauses of perpetuity of the
fifteenth century are not designed to check the use of common recoveries.

[25] See the judgment of Brian C. J. in Kiralfy, *Source Book*, p. 92. Littleton and
Choke JJ. thought that a stranger could be vouched, so long as he bound himself to
warrant by deed, as happened in *Taltarum's Case*, see pp. 95, 98, 99.

[26] The common vouchee, the court crier, first appears in the printed reports *Anon*
(1538), Dyer 35a where one Webster acts in this capacity but the first monopolist was
Denis Guyer in the 1480s. See also St. Germain, *Doctor and Student* (1523) Ch. XXVI.

[27] 1 Rep. 61a.

[28] See Y.B. 7 Hen. IV Trin., f. 17, pl. 13, 3 Hen. VI Trin., f. 55, pl. 33, 7 Hen. VI
Trin., f. 38, pl. 3. See also Elphinstone, 'The Alienation of Estates Tail', 6 *L.Q.R.*
280, but note that the case he cites in 1340 (14 Edw. III R.S. 104) is an example of a
genuine common recovery, for all that the report tells us.

recoveror had, after all, won a real action, and it was thus presumed that he was better entitled to the lands than the issue of
the losing party. This general principle applied to the case of
recoveries against tenants in tail just as it applied elsewhere in
the law. In certain cases, however, persons who were prima facie
bound by recoveries could *falsify* the recovery—we would say
avoid—if the recovery was pleaded in subsequent litigation. It
was decided that recoveries by default had against tenants in tail
could be falsified by the issue in tail, so that they were not an effective device. Thus if Hugo, tenant in tail of Blackacre, was impleaded by Robert, and lost by default, his issue were none the
worse. His heir in tail could bring formedon in descender
against Robert, and when Robert pleaded that he was entitled
by the recovery, which bound Hugo's heir, the heir could reply
by falsifying the recovery on the ground that it was a recovery by
default, and he would win his action. The ground given for this
rule was that the default through which Robert recovered the
land was an act of Hugo, the tenant in tail, and by *De Donis* no
act by a tenant in tail could be allowed to prejudice his issue.[29]

This rule was neatly sidestepped in the collusive common
recovery, where the act which leads to the loss of the action is the
act, not of the tenant in tail, but of the vouchee; it is he who
defaults and departs in contempt of court, not the tenant.[30] *De
Donis* said nothing, of course, about the act of a vouchee, and it
could thus be argued that a common recovery in which the
vouchee defaulted was not open to falsification.

Yet it seems surprising that falsification was not possible on
some other ground. Why should not the issue falsify on the
ground that the tenant had vouched the wrong man—not the
donor but a stranger? This line of argument was originally easily
blocked by getting the stranger to bind himself to warrant by
deed of release with warranty, so that technically he was not the
wrong man to vouch; only when the common recovery had been
established was this precaution dropped. Again, why could the
issue not falsify on the broad general ground that the whole

[29] The words of *De Donis* replied upon appear in the preamble, which speaks of the
deed or *act* of the donee in tail.

[30] The use of a collusive *common* recovery is first met in a case in 1459, Y.B. 37 Hen.
VI, pl. 15, f. 31, but the case as reported is inconclusive, being adjourned; this is a
clear indication that the collusive common recovery was not yet established.

collusive common recovery was nothing else but an obvious fraud? It is commonly said that the real reason was the desire of the judges to permit the breaking of entails, and encourage free alienation. This all suggests a judicial enthusiasm for free trade in land which is quite anachronistic, though judges might well have favoured a policy of allowing heads of families to reorganise their land holdings as family needs changed. A technical, theoretical, justification of a refusal to allow falsification was not impossible, and a technical ground for allowing it was correspondingly difficult to discover. It was an old principle of the common law that the issue in tail could obtain redress only against acts which were detrimental to them,[31] and the collusive common recovery was cunningly moulded around this principle. The vouchee, it is true, never contested his obligation to warrant, and he always defaulted, but in theory his behaviour could even be said to benefit the issue in tail rather than harm them, for the result of it was that they could look to him for their recompense. Of course the vouchee never in practice did satisfy the judgment, and it was futile for the issue to attempt to enforce it against him. But the courts took the view that they had done their best, and treated the vouchee's failure to satisfy the judgment as irrelevant. Indeed, the fact that the vouchee is a man of straw—which seems to us the basic point about the common recovery—is never so much as mentioned in the early cases. But this need not surprise us, for the loss which is suffered when a judgment goes unsatisfied through the defendant's lack of means is not in the nature of things remediable by the courts, and it would be odd in any branch of the law to question the validity of a judgment simply upon the ground that the losing party was penniless or landless.

The introduction of the collusive common recovery is often thought of as an act of naked judicial legislation inspired by strong views of public policy; indeed, Pigott suggested that the litigation in *Taltarum's Case* was instigated by Edward IV in the hope that the destruction of the system of entails (which were

---

[31] *Octavian Lumbard's Case* (1371), Y.B. 44 Edw. III Trin., f. 21, pl. 24. Pigott thus states the gist of the case: 'tenant in tail . . . to one that had a prior right to the estate a rent-charge, in consideration of a release of his right; this being for the benefit of the issue, held he could not avoid it'. The normal rule was that only a tenant in fee simple could grant a rent-charge binding upon his heirs.

not forfeitable for treason) would restore peace and stability to the country. It is much more likely that the judges were not so much influenced by a desire to establish a free market in land, or a commitment to the landowner's freedom to alienate the family patrimony, as by the difficulty of finding any technical flaws in a very ingenious device which was principally employed to resettle family lands. Though many writers have ridiculed the common recovery, I have never yet seen one who has set out a technical argument against its efficacy which a fifteenth-century court could have accepted, though this is not to say that no such argument could have been composed by a contemporary.

Recoveries with Double Voucher

Some very elaborate law grew up around the common recovery, particularly concerning the extent of the bar created by it. In *Taltarum's Case* the common recovery with single voucher was, as we have seen, held ineffective to bar and issue in tail. The basic theory of the extent of the bar was this: only those persons who could possibly obtain a recompense from the vouchee in the form of an equivalent estate in lands provided by him were barred from claiming estates in the land recovered from the tenant suffering the recovery. Now in the recovery with single voucher, suffered by a tenant in tail who was seised, it was the tenant who vouched the man of straw, and the man of straw never of course contested his obligation to warrant the tenant's title, and the courts naturally enough assumed that his failure to contest the obligation ('demand the lien') amounted to an admission that he was bound to warrant the title by virtue of which the tenant was seised at the time of the recovery. It followed that the lands he was ordered to convey to the tenant were to be held under that particular title and no other, and only those claiming by that particular title would be barred. Sometimes the issue of the tenant might contrive to claim by a different title, and if so they would not be barred. An example of this situation could arise under the doctrine of remitter. Suppose T is tenant in tail by force of a gift from D; T tortiously (wrongfully) enfeoffs F in fee simple, and F regrants the land in tail to T with remainders over, the whole transaction being an attempt to resettle the land upon slightly different terms. Later on T runs short of money, and wishes to sell the land to P for a fee simple, and break the settlement; he suffers a common recovery with single voucher and P recovers the land. T's son S will not be barred. When T suffered the recovery he was seised by virtue of a title based upon the gift from F; he could not claim to be seised by virtue of a gift from D, for this older, better, title had been previously discontinued[32] or interrupted by his own wrongful alienation in fee simple. His son S can, however, claim by the older title—he was no party to the wrong—and he is said to be *remitted* or put back to his older and surer title. This older title has not been barred, and the common recovery has failed of its object.

To meet this difficulty the recovery with double voucher was invented.[33] In our example T would first enfeoff G; P would bring his action against G who vouched T, who vouched the man of straw. Here the tenant in tail T is not seised at the time of the recovery, and the rule restricting the scope of the bar to the title by which the tenant was seised could not apply. For some time the courts were a little puzzled as to how the scope of the bar could be determined. T, as first vouchee, had not contested his duty to warrant, so the scope of the duty was never determined, and it was difficult to see how the scope of the bar could be delineated. The rational solution would have been to say that it was uncertain what title was barred. After some doubt it was settled in the end that the bar must he held to extend to any title by which T ever had been seised, or by which any ancestor of his (whose heir he is) had ever been seised; thus in our example the son S would be barred. Even more complex devices were evolved. Common recoveries with treble vouchers were used when it was prudent to bar the issue in tail of two different people, as might happen if under a complex series of settlements it was not clear who was entitled as a tenant in tail.

Under the classical strict settlement which, as we shall see, was evolved in the seventeenth century and lasted until our

[32] The root meaning of 'discontinued' is 'interrupted'; the technical meaning of 'discontinuance' is 'an act which turns a right of entry into a right of action', here the right of S to bring formedon in descender.

[33] Brooke, *Abridgement, Taile*, 32 (1532), seems to contain the earliest reference to the use of double voucher. Until it was invented the common recovery would frequently be useless.

own time, there would normally be a life tenant, L, in seisin, and a tenant in tail, T, in remainder; here the procedure would be slightly different. Since a common recovery was a real action, and a real action had to be brought against a person who was seised of the land, it was essential for T, if he wanted to bar the entail, to secure the co-operation of L. Having done so, the life tenant would enfeoff G (often the family governess) and G became the 'tenant to the praecipe'—the person against whom P would bring the real action. G then vouched T, and T vouched the court crier. In this form the common recovery survived until it was abolished in the nineteenth century.

Clauses of Perpetuity

The results of the invention of the collusive common recovery were very considerable, for the entire nature of the entailed estate was now altered. Any tenant in tail in possession, once he became of age and could therefore litigate in the real actions, could bar his entail, and any tenant in tail out of possession could do so with the consent of whoever was seised— normally a life tenant. By the late fifteenth century, conveyancers, employed by settlors who wished to counter this development, had already attempted to devise means of restraining the alienation of entailed lands. The expedient they employed was called a clause of perpetuity, and though such clauses might vary in detail, they all relied upon the donor of the entailed estate reserving a power of re-entry, exercisable if the tenant in tail alienated. At first such clauses are usually directed against direct alienations with warranty (which relied on the collateral warranty rule) rather than against the use of the common recovery, but in Henry VIII's reign, when the use of common recoveries becomes more frequent, attempts were made to insert into conveyances clauses of perpetuity which were drafted to prevent their use. For a time the validity of these clauses was accepted by the courts, but their utility was limited by the rule, settled by Littleton's time, that only a donor or his heirs could take advantage of such a power of re-entry. Now a settlor will normally want to provide that if the eldest son, who is granted the first entail, attempts to break it, then the next son may enter, but since the next son will not be either the donor or his heir a clause of perpetuity will not be very helpful to the settlor. In the late sixteenth century, ambitious conveyancers tried to get round this disadvantage, but we must leave an account of this to a later chapter.[34]

Fines to Bar Entails

The perfection of the common recovery as a mode of barring entails led to a legislative modification of the effect of a fine. Once it was accepted that an entail could be barred, it seemed absurd to require tenants in tail to go through the rigmarole involved instead of allowing them to produce the same effects by fine. In Henry VIII's reign it was settled that a fine would bar the issue in tail. This was decided in 1527 in a case on a statute of 1490,[35] and soon after the decision was confirmed by statute, in 1536.[36] At this date the common recovery only barred the issue, for the position of remaindermen and reversioners had not yet been settled, so that the effect of both methods of barring entails seemed to be the same. When it was settled that the recovery would bar remaindermen and reversioners the sensible thing would have been to pass legislation to give a fine the same effect, but this was never done. This anomaly became important in the later law of the strict settlement.

Wills

The medieval law did not recognize the validity of a will of lands. In Anglo-Saxon times it is clear that 'bookland'—land held by written charter—could be devised, and this power of devise was the chief peculiarity of such land. After the Conquest a power of testamentary disposition of land continued to be recognized for a while in the *post obit* gift. In the twelfth century this power was discountenanced by the royal court. Glanvill seems to have in mind a death-bed gift, rather than a will in the modern sense, when he justifies the attitude of the royal court in denying validity to such gifts, which he says are made by persons *in extremis* who are not in full command of their faculties, and are therefore not truly voluntary.[37] Once it

---

[34] For the early history see Baker, Selden Society, Vol. 94, p. 206.
[35] 4 Hen. VII, c. 24, *Anon* (1527), Dyer 2b.
[36] 28 Hen. VIII, c. 36.
[37] Glanvill, VII, 1.

became clear that (in general) a gift of land required a delivery of seisin, a gift to take effect upon the donor's death and not before could hardly be accepted, for the gift lacked the essential requirement of livery of seisin. Thus the *post obit* gift as such was doomed by ordinary principle. But the line between a death-bed gift (perhaps accompanied by livery), a gift *inter vivos* to take effect on death (the *post obit* gift), and a will which 'makes an heir' is not easy to draw, and it does not seem that the royal court in the twelfth century indulged in any subtle analysis; rather it condemned anything in the nature of a testamentary disposition, whatever form it took. In the thirteenth century the attitude changed. It was thought for a while that if a man gave lands to a man, his heirs, and his legatees, such a form of gift might give the alienee a power to leave it by will. Bracton vacillated upon this question, but in the end seems to be against allowing a power of devise to be attached to land by the *forma doni*. This view prevailed.[38]

Exceptions were, however, recognized under local custom, most frequently in the case of lands held in boroughs by burgage tenure. In connection with such customs the medieval courts built up a considerable body of law upon the nature of devises.[39] It is notable that to Littleton the chief peculiarity of such customary powers of devise was that, '. . . by force of such devise he to whom such a devise is made after the death of the devisor may enter into the tenements to him devised to have and to hold to him after the form and effect of the devise without any livery of seisin thereof to be made to him'.[40] The general prohibition of devises of land applied only to devises of the freehold; chattels real such as terms of years could be devised like other chattel interests. In effect landowners were able to enjoy a power of devise by means of the use of lands, as we shall see, so that the common-law attitude was not as important as it might seem. Quite why it was adopted is a difficult question; perhaps a desire to prevent disherison of heirs, coupled with a desire to prevent the loss of feudal incidents, influenced the royal judges.

[38] See Pollock and Maitland, II, pp. 26–7. Cf. Britton III, c. 20, 7, which implies that there could be no powers of devise except under local custom.
[39] See Kiralfy, *Source Book*, p. 100, *Faryngton* v. *Darrell* (1430).
[40] Littleton, sec. 167.

Covenants affecting Land

The rules which enable the benefit of covenants made upon the sale of a fee simple to run at common law derive ultimately from the medieval law of warranty. Before *Quia Emptores* (1290) the grantor of a fee, who would also be the grantee's lord, owed an obligation which arose from the relationship of lord and man, sealed by the ceremony of homage, to warrant or guarantee the grantee's title.[41] Apart from the duty to warrant which arose from the receipt of homage it was quite usual for a charter of feoffment to include express clauses of warranty, and after *Quia Emptores*, when feoffor and lord ceased to be the same person, express clauses of warranty became usual. The benefit of these clauses of warranty was annexed to the estate in the land, and could be relied upon in a number of ways. If the tenant was impleaded he could call upon the warrantor to defend the action (voucher to warranty), and if the warrantor lost then he was bound to recompense the tenant by conveying to him lands of equal value. If the tenant was impleaded by the warrantor he could plead the warranty as a bar to the action. The obligation to warrant was not a personal obligation; it descended upon the heirs of the original warrantor. When express clauses of warranty became common the tenant acquired an additional right to sue for damages for breach of the warranty, for the warranty was now a covenant (if made in a sealed instrument) and the covenantee could enforce it by writ of covenant. By a simple extension it became settled that not only the benefit of covenants of warranty but also the benefit of any covenant affecting land was annexed to the estate in land for the covenantee. The basis of the modern law was laid in *The Prior's Case*, or *Pakenham's Case*.[42] One Pakenham sued a prior for breach of a covenant that the prior and his convent should celebrate divine service in the plaintiff's chapel once a week. The covenant had been made with the plaintiff's great-grandfather, and the plaintiff claimed as assignee. The court upheld his claim, holding that he was entitled to succeed because the

---

[41] For a discussion of this rule and its effects see S. E. Thorne, 'English Feudalism and Estates in Land', [1959] *Camb. L. J.* 193, esp. at p. 196 *et seq.* See also S. J. Bailey, *op. cit.*, VIII *Camb. L. J.* 274, IX, 82.

[42] Y.B. 42 Edw. III Hil., pl. 14, f. 3.

benefit of the covenant was annexed to the manor of which he was tenant. The burden of covenants would of course pass to the heirs of the covenantor, but the law stopped short of allowing the burden to be annexed to land so as to bind not heirs of the covenantor but assigns of the land.

Mortgages

Pledges of land as security for a debt, whose function it is to give the creditor more extensive recourse against the debtor's lands than he would have as a mere judgment creditor, are very ancient; they are found in Anglo-Saxon times and in Domesday Book. It was, however, a very long time before the common law evolved a satisfactory form of mortgage, and in Glanvill's time the situation was no doubt complicated by the refusal of the Royal courts to interest themselves as a general rule in private agreements. Glanvill tells us that nothing in the nature of a charge was recognized; the mortgagor must convey the seisin in the lands to the mortgagee, who would then hold the lands *ut de vadio*—by way of pledge.[43] This was a peculiar way of holding lands; as lawyers say, the transaction was *sui generis*, in marked contrast to the later law in which mortgagees were given one of the ordinary estates, such as a fee simple or a term of years. The Glanvillian gagee was given a gage, and nothing else. If the arrangement was that the profits of the land should go to diminish the debt, then the gage was a *vivum vadium*, a living pledge, and an honourable transaction; if not, it was a *mortuum vadium*, a dead pledge and a usurious and sinful thing. Yet for all this the royal courts would recognize a *mortuum vadium*, for it was not an illegal transaction.

Glanvill tells us of a variety of forms of gage. The debtor may be given a set time to pay; this is a gage for a fixed term (nothing to do with the later mortgage under which a lease for years is made). At the end of this fixed period the parties may have agreed that the creditor shall not hold in gage but in fee, and such an agreement is effective. In the absence of agreement the creditor can come to the court at the end of the term and obtain an order that unless the debtor pay within a reasonable time, the land shall be held in fee; such an order resembles the decree of foreclosure of later law. If the gage is not accompanied

[43] Glanvill, X, 6–12.

by an agreed fixed term for payment, the creditor may apply for such an order at any time, but without such an order he cannot change his position from one who holds *in gage* to one who holds *in fee*.

It might have happened that the Glanvillian gage should develop in the common law; there would have been an estate in gage with its own peculiar incidents like the other estates in land. The reason why this did not happen is fairly clear; the interest of one who held in gage was not protected by novel disseisin. Thus Glanvill says that a gagee who is ejected even by the gagor is remediless. He has not the required seisin of a free tenement. It may be that in the early years of the assize the connection of the gage with usury did not help it to receive sympathetic treatment; the speedy remedy was introduced to protect free landholdings and not to secure the fruits of usury. More simply, a creditor money lender was not a feudal tenant, owing service and entitled to protection. By Bracton's time the practice has developed of creating real security by manipulating other interests in land. It was very usual for the debtor to convey a lease for years to the creditor; the conveyance would include a provision that if the debt had not been paid by the end of the term the fee itself should vest in the creditor. The conception of a lease which would swell into a fee simple in the future does not seem to have troubled the lawyers of the thirteenth and fourteenth centuries, and there are a number of authorities which support the view that such a form of mortgage was good. But as the doctrine of estates developed, such swelling leases came to be viewed with disfavour, so that other forms of mortgage became more common. Leases at a nominal rent were used, in which the creditor was given no right to the fee; he recouped himself solely by the right which the lease gave him to take the profits of the land during the term.

By Littleton's time, however, yet another form had become current. Land would be conveyed to the creditor in fee simple subject to the condition that if the debt be paid by a certain day the debtor could re-enter. This is the parent of the classical common-law mortgage, but it must be noted that it is not identical with it, for the mortgagor has a power of re-entry, and not a right to a re-conveyance. Littleton gives a new explanation of the term mortgage:

And it seemeth that the cause why it is called mortgage is, for that it is doubtful whether the feoffer will pay at the day limited such sum or not: and if he doth not pay, then the land which is put in pledge upon condition for the payment of the money, is taken from him for ever, and so dead to him upon condition. And if he doth pay the money, then the pledge is dead as to the tenant.[44]

The terms of such conditional feoffments were strictly construed by the courts, and in time this led to the extensive modification of the mortgage by the Chancery.

Besides the common-law forms of mortgage the medieval mortgagor very frequently made use of statutory devices. In the early common law a creditor could only distrain upon the lands of his debtor; the land itself was inviolate. A judgment creditor was however permitted by a statute of 1285 to choose to have execution levied against the lands of the debtor; he became tenant by elegit of half of the lands until the debt was paid, and had a statutory right to protect himself by novel disseisin.[45] The Statute of Merchants[46] gave even more extensive rights to merchants who had obtained an acknowledgment of a debt formally; non-payment led to the creditor's obtaining the whole of the debtor's lands as a security. Similar provisions were enacted in 1353[47] in the case of debts acknowledged in the Courts of the Staple. Creditors who made use of these provisions acquired a chattel interest in the land, which would descend to their executors and not to their heirs, which was an obvious advantage. In effect they obtained something in the nature of a charge over the land of their debtors from the time the debt was acknowledged, in the case of Statutes Merchant and Staple; the debtor remained until default in possession of the land, to the advantage of both parties. The use of these statutory forms of real security was very common, and tended to compensate for the deficiencies in the common law of mortgage.

---

[44] Littleton, sec. 332.

[45] Westminster II, c. 18, discussed in Plucknett, *Concise History*, p. 390, *Legislation of Edward I*, Ch. VI.

[46] 13 Edw. I (1285) and II Edw. I (1283); for the text see Fifoot, *History and Sources*, p. 239. See also Simpson, *History of the Common Law of Contract*, 87–8, 587–95.

[47] 27 Edw. III., st. 2.

VII

The Action of Ejectment and the Recognition of the Copyholder

By the close of the medieval period the real actions had become very unsatisfactory, and a way of escape from their complexities was found in the action of *eiectio firmae*,[1] a variety of the writ of trespass, that is to say by tort action for compensatory damages. We have seen how the termor was denied novel disseisin, and for long lacked any adequate protection against eviction by a stranger. But if he was unable to bring the assize and obtain specific recovery of his term, he was at least able to recover damages in an action of trespass, and for those who had bought terms of years to hold them as short-term investments damages would not be a wholly inadequate remedy.[2] Towards the end of the fifteenth century the opinion began to be expressed that the term itself might be recovered.[3] For theoretical reasons which have already been explained[4] this view could be justified only by erroneous arguments, but it was nevertheless held in *Gernes* v. *Smyth* (1499) on a writ of error from the King's Bench that specific recovery could be had, perhaps because of a fear that if the common-law courts failed to provide a satisfactory remedy for the husbandry tenant, the Chancellor would. The new view was maintained in the Commons Pleas in 1525 and again in 1530; it was never again questioned.[5] The termor now

[1] It is usual to confine the use of the English title, *ejectment*, to the developed action involving the Doe and Roe fiction, and to use the Latin title, *eiectio firmae*, for the action in its earlier state of development.

[2] This was first decided in 1320 (Y.B. 15 Edw. II, f. 458). See also Ames, *Lectures in Legal History*, at p. 226, where Y.B. 47 Edw. III Trin., f. 5, pl. 11, is cited. Mere tenants at will did not acquire the use of the action until 1440: see Y.B. 18 Hen. VI, f. 1, pl. 1. But copyholders, a special class of such tenants at will, were allowed to use trespass earlier than this: this is discussed later.

[3] By Paston J. in 1448 (Statham, *Abridgement, Non-Tenure*, pl. 7) by Brian C.J. and Fairfax J. in 1468 (Y.B. 7 Edw. IV Pasch., f. 6, pl. 16) and Hussey J. in 1481 (Y.B. 21 Edw. IV Mich., f. 10, pl. 2).   [4] See above, p. 93.

[5] We have no report of these cases; the source of information is Fitzherbert, *Natura Brevium*, p. 220. See now Baker, Selden Society, Vol. 94, at p. 181.

found himself more favourably placed than the freeholder. The procedure in *eiectio firmae* was less dilatory, trial was by jury, and the action allowed the question of title to arise in a simple form. The lessee who was ejected would recover his term if he could show that he had a better title than the ejector, and his title depended upon the title of the lessor who had granted the lease to him.

The Use of Ejectment by Freeholders

It was this which suggested the use of the newer action by freeholders. By allowing specific recovery in the action, the judges had of course conferred upon it one of the leading features of a real action. Suppose that Smith believes himself to be entitled to Blackacre, although Jones is actually in occupation. If Smith grants a lease of Blackacre to John Styles, and Styles gets into possession of Blackacre and is ejected by Jones, Styles will be able to bring *eiectio firmae* against Jones, and the issue decided in the action will be whether the plaintiff's lessor, Smith, or the defendant, Jones, is best entitled to Blackacre. This sort of situation could arise quite easily in the normal course of events, but towards the end of the sixteenth century, claimants of land had begun to grant leases to friends or professional attorneys solely in order to have their titles tried by *eiectio firmae*, rather than by the older real actions. The lease to John Styles would not be a serious lease, but would only be granted in order that John Styles could appear as plaintiff; if he won the action he would release his interest to his landlord Smith. Thus in *Gerrarde* v. *Worseley* (1580) we read of one Sir Robert, who 'made a lease for the term of seven years, to the intent to try the title in an *eiectio firmae*'.[6] The practice seems to have become fairly common in the 1560s and 1570s.

In order that this device might succeed, a number of conditions had to be satisfied. The nominal plaintiff, in order to use the writ, had to be a leaseholder.[7] Now *ex hypothesi* the real claimant to the land would be out of possession, for otherwise he would have no need to sue in the first place, and he was

---

[6] Dyer, 374a. This appears to be the earliest reference to the practice.

[7] The basic rule is that to use trespass at all the plaintiff must have had possession at the time of the trespass; this combines with the rule that to use trespass *de eiectione firmae* the plaintiff must have been a tenant for years.

therefore in a difficult position in attempting to grant a lease. So long as he had a right of entry (i.e. his entry had not been tolled or discontinued)[8] he could validly grant a lease, but before the lease took effect, and the grantee acquired a term[9] (and thus the required status as plaintiff) it was necessary for him to have acquired possession. Before this he only obtained the curious interest known as an *interesse termini*, and this was not enough for it did not rank as an estate, though it was an assignable legal interest. Finally it was essential that the nominal plaintiff be ejected from the land.

To bring all this about must have been a somewhat hazardous undertaking. In *Cooper's Case*[10] the technique is explained.

In an *eiectione firmae*, the case was that the husband and wife (the real claimants) had right to enter into certain lands in the right of the wife, and a deed of lease is written in the name of the husband and wife to one A (a friend, the nominal plaintiff) for to try the title, and also a letter of Attorney to B to enter into the land, and to deliver the said Deed of lease to the said A in the name of the husband and wife, . . . and entry and delivery is made accordingly; the said A enters, and upon ejectment brings an *eiectione firmae*. And the whole matter aforesaid was found by special verdict,[11] and the plaintiff had judgment to recover.

This extraordinary performance continued to be gone through for some time, and in spite of the inconvenience involved in the use of *eiectio firmae*, Coke was able to say in 1601 that 'at this day all titles of lands are for the greatest part tried in Actions of Ejectments'.[12]

In the early years of the seventeenth century we can see the beginnings of the process by which the need for an actual entry and ouster came to be removed. In *Merrell* v. *Smith* (1613)[13] it was held that the date of the ouster was immaterial; in *Wilson* v. *Woddel* (1609)[14] the courts relaxed the requirement that the

---

[8] See above, p. 41.

[9] Cf. Littleton, sec. 58. 'And when the lessee entreth by force of the lease, *then* is he tenant for tearme of yeares' (my italics).

[10] (1584) 2 Leon. 200.

[11] No doubt a special verdict was found so that the court could sanction a set form of proceeding in these cases.

[12] *Alden's Case*, 5 Co. Rep., 105b.

[13] Cro. Jac., 311.

[14] 1 Brown. and Golds., 143.

ejector must be the sitting occupant of the land and allowed an ejection by his servant to be pleaded. All this shows a readiness on the part of the judges to encourage the use of ejectment by treating the technical requirements of the action as unimportant; at the same time they showed that they were prepared to allow a looseness of pleading which would have been fatal in the old real actions.[15]

Messrs Doe and Roe

The perfection of the action is said to owe a great deal to the ingenuity of Chief Justice Rolle, who presided over the Upper Bench in the time of the Commonwealth, and who was apparently responsible for the introduction of the 'casual ejector' into the scheme of things.[16] The procedure he sanctioned was this.[17] The genuine plaintiff commenced an action in the name of a friend against another friend; we will call these two persons Doe and Roe, though it was some time before the names of wholly fictitious individuals came to be used. Doe alleged a lease by the genuine claimant, an entry under the lease upon the land in dispute, and an ejection by Roe (the casual ejector). Roe then informed the actual occupant of the land, who was the real defendant, that an action against him had been commenced, and that, as he had no interest in the affair he did not propose to defend the action, but rather to allow judgment to go against him by default. He advised the real defendant to defend the action, and this advice was sound, for if Doe did obtain judgment for Blackacre by default the judgment would be executed against the land, and the real defendant, whom we may call Jones, would find himself turned off his land. In the Upper Bench Jones would only be allowed to defend the action on condition that he did not deny the lease, entry, and ouster, and also on condition that he undertook to save the casual

---

[15] See Holdsworth, VII, pp. 4–8.

[16] See Blackstone, III, p. 202. The leading contemporary authority is a note in Style's *Reports*, p. 368, dated 1652. This notes the difference in practice between the Upper Bench (corresponding to the King's Bench) and the more conservative Common Bench (Common Pleas). In consulting Style's note the student must amend the text by reading *Defendant* for *Plaintiff* the second time the word *Plaintiff* occurs, or, better still, read 'the person applying to defend the action'.

[17] The final form of the fiction is set out with marvellous clarity by Blackstone, III, Ch. XI.

ejector Roe harmless of any costs. This latter condition was necessary because Roe would at this time be a real person, who would otherwise risk liability for costs if the genuine plaintiff won the action. If the real defendant Jones did defend the action on these terms, as he was in effect forced to do, the action went on under the description *Doe, on the demise of Smith, (genuine plaintiff)* v. *Jones,* and was confined to deciding whether Smith or Jones had the best title to the land. The whole ingenious rigmarole did away with the need for any actual lease or entry or ouster, and was obviously more convenient.

At first the Common Bench, traditionally conservative as it was, refused to accept the new technique, so that in our example Jones would be able to deny the lease, entry, and ouster. Thus one who wished to use ejectment in that court had to go through the whole absurd ritual, and not simply allege it. Inevitably the Common Bench had to capitulate or lose profitable litigation, and this soon happened. For some time, however, both courts insisted that the plaintiff's lessee and the casual ejector be real persons. By the end of the seventeenth century the fictitious Roe and Doe appear, and even Fairclaim and Shamtitle make a temporary appearance in the Reports.[18]

In a form of action so riddled with fiction, abuses were bound to occur. The courts very wisely took a stern line in such cases, and in one instance the legislature stepped in.[19] Perhaps the most serious of these abuses arose from an ostrich-like reluctance, which afflicted the courts for a while, to admit that the action of ejectment had in reality become a real action. Judgment in a personal action only operated as a bar to the parties from suing again on the same cause of action. Vexatious litigants took advantage of the fact that ejectment was theoretically a personal action of trespass, brought to remedy a single act of ejection, and a plaintiff who had failed to recover land in an action begun by Doe against Roe for Blackacre would at once initiate a new action in the name of Goodtitle against Roe; the fictitious causes of action were different and the judgment

[18] *Fairclaim* v. *Shamtitle* (1762) 3 Burr. 1290, *Goodtitle* v. *Tombs* (1770) 3 Wils.

[19] 11 Geo. II, c. 19 (1738), on which see Holdsworth, VII, pp. 14–15. The statute dealt with cases where a genuine lessee was sued in ejectment but failed to inform his landlord, or failed to defend the action; it both penalized such tenants and allowed the landlord to defend either alone or as co-defendant, to prevent his being defrauded out of his interest.

in the first action did not operate as a bar in the second. One litigant had no fewer than five bites at the cherry in this way.[20] This abuse was in part remedied by the issue of perpetual injunctions by the Court of Chancery restraining vexatious plaintiffs, and in part by the common-law courts adopting a more sensible attitude and refusing to allow subsequent actions in which the same title, or substantially the same title, was asserted.

The Death of the Old Actions

There were, however, situations in which recourse had still to be had to the older actions. In order to succeed in ejectment the plaintiff must show a right of entry; if this had been lost, then ejectment could not be brought with success. A Statute of Limitations of 1623 laid down that such a right of entry must be enforced, except in exceptional circumstances, not more than twenty years after it accrued,[21] but more generous periods of limitation applied to some of the older actions. Ejectment did not lie for incorporeal rights, unless appurtenant or appendant to land, for the action of ejectment was based on the fictitious possession of the plaintiff's lessee, and the plaintiff's right of entry. The judicial imagination boggled at attributing these notions to incorporeal rights. Finally there were a number of situations in which for complex reasons the older actions had still to be used. Examples of such survivals were the writs of dower, and of dower *unde nihil habet*. In general, however, the real actions died a rapid death, and occasional attempts to revive them met with little success.[22]

In 1833 the real actions were abolished,[23] with three exceptions: the two writs of dower and the writ of *quare impedit* (used

---

[20] *Earl of Bath* v. *Sherwin* (1709), 2 Bro. P.C. 373.

[21] 21 James I, c. 16 (1623). The real actions were still partially governed by a statute of 1540 (32 Hen. VII, c.2.). Thus the right to sue by writ of right, which did not depend upon the demandant's having a right of entry, was not affected by the twenty-year period of limitation in the statute of 1623, which only barred actions based upon rights of entry, and did not destroy the title of the person barred.

[22] Hargrave, in his notes to Coke on Littleton, remarks (Co. Litt. 239a [note 155]): 'Booth, who wrote about the end of the last century, mentions real actions as *then* worn out of use. It is rather singular that this should be the case, as many cases must frequently have occurred, in which a writ of ejectment was not a sufficient remedy.' The reference is to Booth, *Real Actions*, a work of great merit, written ostensibly to encourage the revival of the real actions. It remains the leading work on the subject.

[23] Real Property Limitation Act (1833), 3, 4 Will. IV, c. 27.

to try title to advowsons) were retained. The doctrines governing rights of entry and their loss were at the same time reformed, so that the need to use the real actions in cases when such rights had been tolled or discontinued no longer existed. The Doe and Roe fictions disappeared in the Common Law Procedure Act of 1852,[24] and the forms of action themselves in 1876.

Limitation of Actions and Ejectment

In every system of law some provision has to be made to restrict the enforcement of stale claims, and in no branch of the law is the limitation of actions more important than in the land law. With the rise of ejectment a new statutory regulation was needed, and an Act of 1623 restricted the exercise of a right of entry to a period of twenty years from the time when it accrued.[25] This obliquely restricted the action of ejectment, in which the plaintiff, as we have seen, had to have such a right. If the claimant to land did not have a right of entry, but only a right of action, he was forced back upon the real actions, and his right of action by real action was in general governed by a system of limitation set up by a statute of 1540,[26] under which the periods of limitation were considerably longer—thus in formedon in remainder the period was fifty years.[27] Neither of these statutes barred the *title*, only the right of entry or the right of action.

Around these statutes arose an extraordinarily complex body of law. Let us suppose that in 1650 Smith conceives that he had a right to Blackacre, and that Jones is currently in actual possession of the land. In order to apply the rules as to limitation it is necessary to decide when the period of limitation began to run, and this will depend upon the moment when Smith's right of action or right of entry accrued to him. Broadly speaking, time ran from the moment when Jones acquired a possession which was adverse to Smith; it will be adverse if it is incompatible with Smith's right to the land.[28] Then it is necessary to

[24] 15 and 16 Vict., c. 76.   [25] 21 Jac. I, c. 16.

[26] 32 Hen. VIII, c. 2. Some real actions were not dealt with—for example the writ of right of advowson and darrein presentment.

[27] In writs of right the period was sixty years; that for novel disseisin was thirty.

[28] Under the pre-1833 law the expression 'adverse possession' had a complex meaning; broadly it was so defined that an adverse possessor was bound to acquire seisin. Since 1833 'adverse' has acquired a simpler connotation.

determine whether this possession was acquired in such a way as to leave Smith with a right of entry, or a mere right of action. If it was acquired by a discontinuance[29] or a deforcement,[30] then Smith will have a right of action only and he must use a real action; if by a disseisin[31] or an abatement[32] or an intrusion,[33] then, unless it has been tolled,[34] Smith will have a right of entry, and can use ejectment, if he is still within the twenty-year period. Around these terms of art hung a massive body of subtle doctrine.

But even when Smith's right of action and entry are both barred he does not lose his title; if he somehow or other gets into possession of Blackacre his old title revives. Thus if Jones were to grant the land to Smith, Smith will be entitled to Blackacre not by a new title; he will be entitled by virtue of his original title. This survival of the old title has a serious consequence, for notwithstanding the Statutes of Limitation conveyancing is rendered uncertain by the existence of dormant titles to land; such dormant titles are inevitably mischievous, and frustrate the very purpose for which systems of limitation exist at all.

Theories of Title

Primarily systems of limitation do not create titles, in the way in which prescription does; they restrict the enforcement of titles. Thus in our example Jones also has a title to land from the time when he acquired (or his predecessor in title acquired) adverse possession. Until Smith's right of entry or action is

[29] An act which turns a right of entry to a right of action: an example is an alienation in fee by a tenant in tail, which puts the heir in tail to his formedon in descender. See Co. Litt. 325a.

[30] Defined in its narrow sense by Blackstone as 'such a detainer of the freehold, from him that hath the right of property, but never had any possession of the right' as does not amount to an abatement, intrusion, or discontinuance! For example, a squatter prevents a lord from entering lands which should come to him by escheat *propter defectum sanguinis*.

[31] 'A wrongful putting out of him that is seised of the freehold.'

[32] A wrongful entry of lands, left vacant upon the death of a tenant who died seised, before the entry of the heir or devisee who is entitled to enter.

[33] A wrongful entry on lands left vacant by the determination of a particular estate of freehold, before the entry of the remainderman or reversioner who is entitled to enter.

[34] Literally 'taken away'; if a disseisor died seised and his heir entered, the entry of the disseisee was taken away by the 'descent cast' on the disseisor's heir. Generally on the terms used in this paragraph see Blackstone, III, Ch. 10.

barred, Jones will have a title defeasible by the entry or action of Smith, but it is a title for all that. Any possession by Jones is prima facie[35] evidence of seisin in fee simple, and a possession acquired by discontinuance, deforcement, abatement, intrusion, or disseisin is bound to confer seisin on Jones, for these are ways of acquiring seisin. Seisin is the root of Jones's title, just as it must be the root of Smith's. But Jones, unlike Smith, actually has seisin, and thus has an estate in Blackacre, which he can alienate and deal with. Smith has a mere claim to be seised for an estate; no estate is vested in him, and under the old law he could not alienate his claim, be it represented by a right of entry or a right of action.[36] The law favoured the person seised, as it did in the medieval law, and there is much to be said in favour of a system which prevents dealings in Blackacre by a person who has not gone to the trouble of enforcing his claim to Blackacre.

The old system of limitation was radically altered by the Real Property Limitation Act of 1833. The Act, by abolishing the majority of the real actions,[37] left the action of ejectment in all but sole possession of the field. This made it necessary to do away with the situations in which a claimant to land was unable to use ejectment—thus the doctrine of discontinuance, and the tolling of entries by descent cast were abolished. But the old rule that a plaintiff in ejectment must have a right of entry was not altered; all that the statute did was to abolish the rules which might lead to the loss of a right of entry, and its conversion into a right of action only, for mere technical reasons. The legislature then provided that the claimant's right of action or entry (i.e. his right to bring ejectment or to enter, if he could)[38] must be exercised within twenty years.[39] This

---

[35] Thus a person in possession could be life tenant, and in such a case the presumption would be rebutted; one who enters wrongfully cannot, however, qualify his wrong, and claim a lesser estate than fee simple.

[36] Since 1833 both the right of entry and action can be alienated.

[37] The two writs of dower, and the writ of right of advowson survived until 1852.

[38] Forcible entry is still a criminal offence, but the law was wholly reorganized by the Criminal Law Act, 1977. If, however, one who has a right to enter does so forcibly he does not suffer any civil disadvantage in the modern law, so long as he uses no more force than is reasonably necessary. See *Hemmings* v. *Stoke Poges Golf Club* [1920] 1 K.B. 720. Cf. Y.B. 9 Hen. VI. f. 19 pl. 12, Fitzherbert, *Natura Brevium*, 248 H.

[39] The period is now in general twelve years, and has been since the Real Property Limitation Act, 1874. The matter is now governed by the Limitation Act, 1980. See Megarry and Wade, *Real Property*, pp. 1030 *et seq.*

period, however, was not to run from the moment when he acquired a right of entry, but from the moment when the defendant or his predecessor in title acquired possession. Thus in computing the period of limitation the acquisition of simple possession by the defendant, or his predecessor in title, is the only matter to be considered; whether he obtained seisin or not and when he obtained seisin became wholly irrelevant. Naturally this alteration in the law greatly reduced the importance of the old learning on seisin and its surrounding conceptions. The statute also provided that after time had run against the claimant his title, and not merely his right of action or entry, was wholly extinguished; it was no longer allowed to rest dormant.

If we look at the effect of the Limitation Act of 1833 upon the position of the occupant of the land some very difficult questions arise. Let us suppose a simple case. Smith is seised of Blackacre in fee simple, and he goes away on a holiday; when he returns he finds Jones in possession of the land. In twenty years' time Smith will have lost his title to Blackacre; we know this to be so without our having to ask whether Jones's acquisition of possession amounted to a disseisin or not. At the expiration of the period Jones will be safe from anything Smith can do to disturb him. Probably he will be absolutely safe, but we cannot be certain of this; there may be somebody else with a title to Blackacre who has not yet been barred; perhaps Smith's title was defective, for it may be that he was granted a fee simple by a fraudulent lessee holding under a ninety-nine year lease, and time will not run against the lessee until the lease ends—say in fifty years' time. Time only runs against a reversioner when the lease expires. It will not be correct to say that the squatter Jones has an absolute title; he has a title indefeasible by Smith, and that is all that can certainly be said. But what is the basis of Jones's title? For a time after 1833 it was rumoured that he acquired Smith's title by a 'Parliamentary conveyance', that is as a successor in title to Smith, but this view, though sensible enough, came to be abandoned.[40] The courts came round to the view that Jones's title was a new title, beginning in Jones, and in modern times have gone further in holding that a squatter does not obtain an interest commensurate with Smith's,

[40] See *Tichborne* v. *Weir* (1892), 67 L.T. 735, and Lightfoot, *Possession of Land*, pp. 272 *et seq.*

either.[41] Since there was nothing in the statute of 1833 or in any later statute which expressly abrogated the old common-law rule that mere possession is not a root of freehold title the traditionalist view was, and still is, that the root of Jones's title is not his possession, but his seisin; his possession counts as evidence of seisin, under the rule that possession is prima facie evidence of seisin in fee simple. In our example there is nothing to rebut the presumption; Jones is not a tenant for years, or at will, or for life, and so Jones is seised in fee simple.[42]

But this view was not consistently maintained in the nineteenth century, nor is it consistently held today, for some would reject the view that the post-1833 law should be analysed in this way.[43] It seems odd that the question whether Smith's title is statute-barred should involve simply a question of possession, whilst the root of Jones's title should be sought in seisin; surely, it is argued, it would be preferable to use the concept of possession in both contexts. There is much to be said for this view; what is difficult is to justify it on technical grounds. The strongest point in its favour is that it alone explains some conundrums which cannot be explained if the traditional view is held.

One example will have to suffice. Under the modern system of limitation if there is a tenant at sufferance on the land, time starts to run against his landlord from the moment when the tenancy at sufferance begins. At the end of the limitation period the landlord's title is barred. The tenant certainly has a title, but it cannot be based upon his seisin, for he never had seisin. Such a tenant is not a disseisor; throughout the period of limitation the seisin has been in the landlord, and unless one

---

[41] *Tichborne* v. *Weir* did not deal with the distinct question—does a squatter acquire an interest equivalent in *quantum* to the person whose title he bars? In *Fairweather* v. *St. Marylebone Property Co. Ltd.* (1963) A.C. 510 it was wrongly thought that to say that he does is to accept the Parliamentary conveyance 'heresy'.

[42] See A. D. Hargreaves, 'Terminology and Title in Ejectment', 56 *L.Q.R.* 376, and cf. Holdsworth's reply at p. 479. Cf. also S. A. Wiren, 'The Plea of Ius Tertii in Ejectment', 41 *L.Q.R.* 139, *Allen* v. *Roughley* (1955), 94 *C.L.R.* 98.

[43] Of the modern textbooks Megarry and Wade, and Cheshire (so it seems), take the view that possession and not seisin forms the only root of title in English land law. The only attempt to argue this view is that of Charles Sweet in 'Seisin', 12 *L.Q.R.* 239. R. M. Lightfoot, in *Possession of Land*, pp. 123 *et seq.*, 271 *et seq.*, adopts a compromise position. The few cases of modern date employ so bewildering and loose a terminology as to be all but valueless upon any point of principle. See B. Rudden, 'The Terminology of Title', 80 *L.Q.R.* 63.

has recourse to the discredited fiction of a Parliamentary conveyance there is no way of explaining how the tenant acquired seisin, or when. It seems simpler to base the new title on possession, and if this is done in one instance, why not in all instances?

The Position of Manorial Tenants

In one special field the rise of the action of ejectment had a particular importance: in the sixteenth century it was extended to protect the landholding of the copyhold tenants of manors, the heirs of the tenants in villeinage who in the twelfth century had been denied the freeholder's right to protection in the royal courts.

As we have seen, the royal justices, when, in Glanvill's time, they were working out the embryonic land law, took a momentous decision. They decided that the royal courts would concern themselves only with persons who held their lands by free tenure. Feudalism, as we have seen, imposed upon each lord the duty to administer justice to his tenants, and to hold a court in which they might litigate; as supreme lord the King, like any other lord, owed this duty to his own tenants in chief, whilst as King he had a duty to exercise a general supervision over all justice. We have seen how the Crown encroached upon seignorial jurisdiction, and how it took all freeholders under royal protection. It would have been possible for the Crown to have extended its jurisdiction still further, or at least to have attempted to do so; in the thirteenth century there was indeed some suggestion that his course might be adopted. The chance was lost, however, and until the very end of the Middle Ages the unfree tenants were excluded from the benefits of the common law; if they wished to secure justice and protection in their landholding they must seek it in the court of their lord, for the King's court studiously ignored their claims.

If we are to understand who these unfree tenants were, and what were the marks of their curious status, we must look at the history of that manorial system of economy which prevailed over a large part of England in the Middle Ages, and which, in some isolated instances, has lasted even up to the present day.[44]

[44] For further information on the medieval history of the unfree tenants and on unfree tenure see *English Historical Documents*, II, pp. 813 *et seq.*, esp. Nos. 172, 176, 179, 180, 205. See also P. Vinogradoff, *The Growth of the Manor* (1920), F. W.

At the time of the Conquest large parts of the country were not cultivated, and those that were, were not farmed by individual farmers acting independently of each other, each relying on his own resources, but by a communal system of agriculture which depended for its success upon the co-operation of all the members of a small village community, forming an economic unit which was largely self-supporting. From place to place such communities would differ in size, organization, and structure, but over large parts of the country, and particularly in the south of England, these differences were not so great as to prevent us speaking of a system of manorial economy, so long as we realize that the degree of local variation was very considerable.

The lands occupied by such a community would be partly cultivated and partly waste land. The arable land was farmed in accordance with a fixed customary system, in which one crop would be grown one year and another the next, and at regular intervals the land would be allowed to lie fallow, a practice which enabled it to be ploughed at a time appropriate for weed control. In this arable land the inhabitants of the manor had individual holdings, often consisting of scattered strips, each unfenced from those of his neighbour. The great open fields which were the result of this practice were cultivated and cropped uniformly in accordance with local custom. Over the waste land the villagers had customary rights to graze their cattle, dig turf, gather wood and the like, and they had similar rights over the open fields which were from time to time out of cultivation. The cattle pastured by day on the waste land, and at night moved on to the arable, thereby manuring the ground. Hence the rule that beasts in respect of which a right of common was claimed must be 'levant' and 'couchant' on the arable land to which the right was attached; they must go to bed there.

Before 1066 a high proportion of these communities had fallen under the domination of powerful individuals, but the precise relationship between such lords and the inhabitants of the manors varied enormously. Some would be slaves bound to the

Maitland, *Domesday Book and Beyond* (1921), P. Vinogradoff, *Villainage in England* (1892), Pollock and Maitland, I, pp. 356-83, 413-32, Poole, *Obligations of Society*, Ch. II, Holdsworth, III, pp. 198-216, H. S. Bennett, *Life on the English Manor*, Orwin and Orwin, *The Open Fields*. The account given in the text is necessarily simplified.

soil, but a large proportion of the humbler cultivators were men who were personally free, but who were bound by custom (which in individual cases may have originated in some form of contract) to perform services of an agricultural nature or supply produce to the lord. The agricultural services would usually take the form of a duty to cultivate the lands which the lord farmed as his own—the demesne lands, as they came to be called. The extent to which the relationship between the lord and the peasants of such a community can be described as tenurial in Anglo-Saxon times is disputed, but it is fairly obvious that the distinction between saying that Hugo 'owns' land in Kidlington, and is the man of Alfred, for whom he must work for three weeks a year, and saying that he *holds* his land in return for those services, is not a very great one, and after the Conquest the Norman administrators found little difficulty in expressing the situation in tenurial terms. Quite soon after 1066 the humble peasant class of cultivators had been fitted neatly into the universal tenurial system.

A distinguishing feature of a manor, as these village communities are called, is the fact that the landholding inhabitants of the manor are the tenants of a single lord, and sometimes such a manor was not a simple geographical unity, but rather a jurisdictional or economic entity, whose unity depended largely on the legal fact of subservience to a single powerful man. After the Conquest the personal status of many of the peasant landholders tended to be depressed, and many of those whose ancestors in Anglo-Saxon times had been free men came to be reduced to some form of personal subjection to their lord. Such men, the villeins of medieval law, came to occupy a curious position in consequence of the way in which the early lawyers worked out the legal implications of their status. Broadly speaking they became only relatively unfree. *Vis-à-vis* their lord they were unfree, though to some extent protected against ill usage, but *vis-à-vis* the rest of the world they were accorded the rights of free men. But not all the inhabitants of manors were depressed into this condition, and in most manors there was to be found a class of tenants who were in all respects free men. Some such men might hold their lands by services obviously appropriate to free men alone—by knight-service for example. In many cases, however, they might be bound to perform

agricultural work which did not differ noticeably from that required of villeins. When the royal courts adopted the view that
they ought not to encroach upon the seignorial jurisdiction of
lords to such an extent as to become involved in protecting the
landholding of villeins they were faced with a choice. They could
have made personal status the crux of the matter, and adopted
the rule that they would always protect a free man in his landholding, irrespective of the nature of the services by which he
held his land. Alternatively they could let the matter turn not
on the tenant's status, but on the nature of the services he
owed. The judges settled for the second alternative.

Villein Tenure

This meant that villein tenure and villein status became
divorced. The legal systematizers analysed the wide variety of
services which persons of villein status were found to owe by
custom, and eventually reached the conclusion that the characteristic feature of such services was their uncertainty. If it happened that a tenant was found whose services displayed this
quality he was said to hold by villein tenure. Having made this
analysis they were from time to time confronted with free persons whose tenure could only be described as villein tenure—
persons whom their analysis did not really fit, personal status
and form of landholding having diverged. Such persons' landholding was not protected in the royal courts, for it was the
nature of a tenant's tenure, and not his personal status, which
entitled him to protection by the real actions. Throughout the
course of the Middle Ages the number of villeins declined, and
the class became extinct by the beginning of the seventeenth
century: the law tended to encourage liberty, and there were
many ways in which a villein could become free.[45] The result
was that villein tenure and villein status drifted farther and
farther apart, for more and more free persons were holding
land by unfree tenure. In the end this forced the courts to alter
their attitude to such tenants, but this was not to happen until

---

[45] The last reported case is *Pigg* v. *Caley* (1618), Nov. 27. The disappearance of
villein status is still rather a mystery; there were still a considerable number in
Elizabeth's reign. See Holdsworth, III, pp. 501 *et seq.* I. S. Leadam, 'The Last Days
of Bondage in England', 9 *L.Q.R.* (1893) 348, A. Savine, 'Bondmen under the
Tudors', 17 *T.R.H.S.* 2nd Ser. (1902) 235.

the very end of the fifteenth century. The institution of villeinage was never in fact formally abolished, a fact of some significance in the history of the common law's attitude to colonial
slavery in the eighteenth century.

We have said that the courts in the end settled on the uncertain nature of the services owed as the mark of villein tenure,
but 'uncertainty' was given a special meaning. Thus a tenant
who owed his lord four dozen eggs at Christmas and four days
ploughing at Michaelmas was classified as a tenant by free
socage, whereas one who owed forty days unspecified labour in
the spring held by villeinage, though in a sense both requirements are certain enough. The distinction is something like
that between a contract of service and a contract for services in
the modern law. In one sense the services due by the villein in
our example are not uncertain at all, for although he must be
prepared to do as he is told on forty days a year the rest of his
time is his own. Though there would be oppressive lords, and
villeins whose complaints have not come down to us, yet in
general the services due from a villein tenant were as rigidly
fixed and probably as generally observed as those due from free
tenants. They were defined by local custom, which was thought
to be binding on lord and tenant alike. The common-law courts
took no cognizance of these local customs, but they were enforced in the lord's court of the manor, appropriately called a
customary court. With the spread of the practice of keeping
court rolls, and of making surveys of manors, the customs in
some manors came to be written down, and this assisted in
giving them fixity. But the common-lawyers, once they refused
to allow tenants in villeinage to use the real actions, were forced
into the position of saying that the seisin and freehold of lands
held in villeinage was in the lord, who alone could litigate about
them in the royal courts. The villein tenants were merely his
tenants at will, and he could therefore eject them at will, whatever might in fact be the recognized rights of the tenant. In
practice the villein tenant could be as well off as the tenant who
held by free tenure. His services were fixed and recorded, and
so were the various incidents of his tenure. Furthermore, manorial courts often modelled their procedure upon that of the
royal courts, so that actions imitating novel disseisin and the
other real actions were allowed in them. Some manors even

went so far as to copy statutory law, the most notable instance of this being the recognition of a custom allowing entails in some manors, in imitation of the statute *De Donis*.

In the course of the fourteenth century the practice of commuting rents and services in kind for money payments became widespread, and the process continued in the fifteenth and sixteenth centuries. Various factors have been selected by historians as being the causes of this phenomenon. In some manors commutation was probably introduced because it led to more efficient estate management; manorial lords found it better to rely upon hired labourers, over whom they had a power of selection, than upon villein tenants whom they could not choose, and who might be inefficient workmen, unsuitable to employ upon the lord's demesne. The Black Death[46] destroyed a large proportion of the villein tenants of manors, and the ensuing competition for labour amongst manorial lords brought into being a class of labourers prepared to hire out their services to the highest bidder they could find. Thus the regulation of the contract of service begins in 1349 with the Ordinance of Labourers. By the middle of the fifteenth century the mass of villein tenants no longer laboured for their lords, but paid him a fixed rent for their holdings in lieu of personal service. As the value of money fell, these quitrents became less and less burdensome and, just as with the free tenures, the incidents of unfree tenure and the lord's rights over manorial land, which both retained their value, gained an increased importance.

Copyhold Tenure

The commutation of services naturally enhanced the social status of tenants in villeinage, and, at the same time as it becomes common, we find the name villein tenure giving way to the more modern name of copyhold tenure.[47] This title derives from the increased recognition of the rights of tenants in villeinage in the customary court. The process of alienation

---

[46] 1348–9; it must be remembered that plague was endemic in England until the late seventeenth century; the last outbreak in England took place in East Anglia in 1910–18. It is thought that the disease is now extinct there, but only a bold person would tangle with a rat flea near the villages of Shotley, Trimley, or Freston. See L. F. Hirst, *The Conquest of Plague.*

[47] The term is common in the fifteenth century.

of villein lands adopted in these courts was that of surrender and regrant. The alienor surrendered the lands to the lord, who admitted the alienee to the land; the process was recorded in the court rolls. It became the practice to make a copy of the entries on the rolls, to save the inconvenience of looking them up if there was a dispute over the land, and so the villein tenant was said to hold 'by copy of the court roll', the copy being his title deed. The court roll itself became a sort of register of titles to copyhold land, for since all transactions were recorded upon the roll, it provided conclusive evidence of a copyholder's rights.

Littleton is very confusing about copyhold tenure. He devotes different sections of his book to tenants by copy of court roll and to tenants in villeinage, and the distinction between the two tenures is not at all clear.[48] It would be easy enough if the distinctive feature of villein tenure lay in the fact that the tenant was a villein and not a free man, but though Littleton regards this as normal it is not essential.[49] Rather he seems to have regarded copyholders as a class of peculiarly privileged free men holding land by unfree tenure, and not as a class which included all such men.[50] After his time the status of villeinage declined fairly rapidly, and this may have had something to do with the growth of the doctrine that all those who held by unfree tenure were copyholders. It may also have been the case that the distinctive feature of the copyholder—his use of a copy of the court roll as evidence of title—became more widespread soon after Littleton's time.[51]

There were good manors and there were bad, and in spite of the developments which took place in good manors a copyholder on a bad manor was very much at the mercy of a lord who cared to defy the custom, and either insist upon his common-law

[48] Secs. 172 *et seq.* deal with tenure in villeinage, secs. 73 *et seq.* with Tenant by Copie.

[49] 'Tenure in villeinage is most properly when a villeine holdeth of his lord . . .', Littleton, sec. 172.

[50] 'Tenant by copy of court roll is, as if a man be siesed of a manor within which manor there is a custom, which hath beene used time out of minde of man, that certain tenants . . . have used to have lands and tenements, to hold to them and their heirs in fee simple or fee taile or for terme of life at the will of the lord, according to the custom of the same manor.' Littleton, sec. 73.

[51] See Gray, *Copyhold, Equity and the Common Law*, pp. 5–10.

right to eject a mere tenant at will, or at least use the threat of exercising it to bring a recalcitrant copyholder to heel. In the fifteenth century the position began to improve, for both the common-law courts and the Chancellor started to interfere on his behalf; for some time this dual protection continued. The common law development originates in the late fifteenth century, when Danby C.J. in 1467 expressed the view that a lord had no right to eject a copyholder who performed his services,[52] in 1481 Brian C.J. went one stage farther and said that a lord who did so could be sued in an action of trespass.[53] Some hints of this liberal view appear in the original text of Littleton's *Tenures*, printed about 1481.[54] The text of Littleton published in 1530 incorporates the *dicta* of Danby and Brian, and by passing into the sacred text of Littleton the new view is almost assured success.[55] But the point was not apparently settled until 1566.[56] At first such an action would be for damages only, and lie only against a lord who evicted his copyhold tenant in breach of the custom of the manor. If evicted by some third party a copyholder was in a curious and unsatisfactory position, and indeed had been for a long time earlier. There was no question of his bringing any of the real actions in the royal court. The freehold and seisin of the copyholder's estate resided in his lord, and the legal theory on this point was far too deeply rooted to be disturbed. The copyholder had therefore to fall back upon the protection afforded in the lord's court or, if he wished to use the royal courts, he had to be satisfied with some form of remedy based upon his possession of land. If he were evicted

52 Y.B. 7 Edw. IV Mich., f. 19, pl. 16.

53 Y.B. 21 Edw. IV Mich., f. 80, pl. 27.

54 Littleton, sec. 77, up to '. . . But the lord cannot break the custom which is reasonable in these cases.'

55 Littleton, sec. 77. For an example of the citation of these dicta see *Anon* (1564) Moo. K. B. 60. There is a hint of protection in a case from the time of Cavendish C.J., who was C.J.K.B. from 1372 until 1381, when he was murdered in the Peasants' revolt; see Y.B. 13 Ric. II (Ames Foundation), p. 122. But the position in 1390 was stated by Thirning J. thus: 'In many manors there is a custom that those who are niefs and villeins shall inherit, and that their heirs shall have their lands after their death, and that they may have an action within the manor (such as mort d'ancestor or any other action) to claim the fee simple; and so also those who hold at will. But for all that the freehold is still in the lord, and a writ of false judgment is not maintainable in such a case, and has never been seen.' For Plucknett's comments on this case see his introduction to Y. B. 13 Ric. II (Ames Foundation), at p. xxxii.

56 Gray, 64, citing from a MS. report.

his lord might use the real actions on his behalf; otherwise trespass for damages could be employed by him personally, and this did not enable him to enjoy anything like the degree of security of the freeholder.[57] His position was strikingly similar to that of the leaseholder in the fifteenth century.

At the same time the Chancellor had also become involved in the protection of villein tenants, presumably on the basis that it was against good conscience for a lord to ignore their rights, and thus risk hell-fire. Petitions to him to redress the wrongs of villeins are found throughout the fifteenth century,[58] and it may be that it was the fear of losing business to Chancery which had an effect in provoking the common-law courts to act. C. M. Gray, in his important study of the history of this jurisdiction, has shown that the equitable protection of the copyholder was established in Henry VII's reign.[59] The situation in Henry VIII's time is summed up in a note in Cary's Reports.

Touching copyholders, Mr. Fitzherbert in his Natura Brevium . . . noteth well, that foreasmuch as he cannot have any writ of false judgment, nor other remedy at common law against his lord, therefore he shall have aid in Chancery; and therefore if the lord will put out his copyholder that payeth his customs and services, or will not admit him to whose use a surrender is made, or will not hold his court for the benefit of his copyholder, or will exact fines arbitrary when they be customary and certain, the copyholder shall have a subpoena to restrain or compel him as the case shall require.[60]

The equitable jurisdiction over copyhold land passed out of use in the later law where it was redundant, but some aspects of it, such as the granting of relief against forfeiture, survived to the very end.

In the late sixteenth century the court of King's Bench decided to allow copyholders to use *eiectio firmae*, and obtain specific recovery of their lands. Characteristically the Court of Common Pleas hesitated for a while before they came around to the same

---

[57] This was decided in 1400, Y.B. 2 Hen. IV, f. 12, pl. 49, when the point was treated as arguable. The lack of the freehold was used as an argument against giving a copyholder the action.

[58] See Gray, *op. cit.*, *passim* and Baker, Selden Society, Vol. 94, pp. 187–92, Selden Society, Vol. 10, p. xxxix. Cf. I. S. Leadam, 'The Security of Copyholders in the 15th and 16th Centuries', VIII, *E.H.R.* 684.

[59] Gray, *op. cit.*, p. 34.

[60] Cary 3.

opinion; in this branch of the law as in others they fought a losing battle. The chronology of this conflict is not easy to establish. The King's Bench allowed the action as early as 1573[61] and again in 1588 in *Rumnay and Eve's Case*,[62] and *Melwich* v. *Luter*.[63] The court was prepared to permit the action whether or not the custom of the manor in question permitted the copyholder to lease land without the lord's licence (a power to lease being essential to the use of ejectment), and so it was not necessary in any litigation to plead such a licence; this at least was Chief Justice Popham's opinion. In the Exchequer the action was allowed by 1596.[64] The Common Pleas at first did not permit the action at all; after recanting on this point they fought a rear-guard action, permitting the action if the custom of the manor permitted copyholders to lease lands, and this custom was pleaded, or if an express licence to lease was pleaded.[65] Their eventual capitulation may have been the result of the futility of resisting the judges of the other two courts; we have no dramatic capitulation recorded in the reports, and there was no real chance that the forces of conservatism should stifle development, as had been possible for a time in the case of the famous conflict over *assumpsit*.

Coming so late into the royal courts the copyholder brought with him a body of customary law which it was quite impossible for the common-lawyers to sweep away. They thus adopted the principle that the rules governing the landholding of a copy-holder were to be found in the custom of the manor concerned. These rules varied from place to place, and so copyholders were never subjected to a uniform system of land law; there

---

[61] Cited from MS by Gray, 65 and 202 note 22.

[62] Leon. 100.

[63] 4 Co. Rep. 26a. This case is the only one on the subject included in Coke's reports; it therefore comes to be treated as the leading case on the point. Gray, 242, prints a MS report.

[64] *Goodwin* v. *Longhurst* (1596), Cro. Eliz. 535.

[65] *Ever* v. *Aston* (1599), Moo. K. B. 271, *Stephens* v. Elliott (1596), Cro. Eliz. 484, *Petty* v. *Evans* (1610), 2 Brown 1. Eventually a compromise was reached. The courts held that by a general custom of the realm a copyholder might lease his lands for a year without the licence of his lord. This was enough to enable all copyholders to use ejectment. See Co. Litt. 59a, note (4). This compromise is quaintly stated by Richardson C.J. in 1629: 'And although by common law a copyholder may not make a lease for one year, yet since this is a general custom of all Manors in England, he can' (see *Turner* v. *Hodges*, Litt. 233). The general custom is treated not as common law, but as analogous to local particular custom, which abrogates common law.

never grew up anything which could be called a common law of copyhold. Inevitably, however, the tendency was towards uniformity; the reason why this was not achieved even as late as this century is that the copyholder did not achieve as full a legal protection as the freeholder until late in the sixteenth century, and when this protection was achieved the common-law courts deliberately adopted the role of protectors of local manorial custom, and not destroyers of it, for their intervention in the affairs of copyholders was justified upon the ground that they were doing for the copyholder what the copyholder's lord was primarily bound to do—respect the ancient custom of the manor.

Tenants in Ancient Desmesne

Half-way between tenants in villeinage and tenants by free tenure came a peculiar class of peasants known as tenants in ancient demesne. Such tenants, because of their peculiar history, did not acquire the right to use ejectment.[66] These were men who held land in manors which were Crown manors in 1066; the only proof admitted of the status of a manor was Domesday Book, and once it was shown that a manor formed part of the ancient demesne the peculiar customs which affected tenants in such manors continued to apply even if the King was no longer lord of the manor. Like tenants in villeinage, those who held in ancient demesne could not use the ordinary real actions, but unlike them such tenants could use a peculiar form of the writ of right (called the little writ of right close) and another writ, the writ of *Monstraverunt*. The former writ enables the tenant to claim lands in the manor; the latter protects him against any unlawful exaction of services. Thus the tenants in ancient demesne are especially privileged, and their privilege is not lost when the manor passes out of the King's hands, but continues to attach to their landholding. But privilege apart they were in much the same economic and social position as other villein tenants. It has been suggested that they represent a survival from an early period before the King's court had classified all tenures as free and unfree, men whose position was not depressed into that of mere tenants at will by the crude

---

[66] *Alden's Case* (1601), 5 Co. Rep. 105a.

simplifications of the lawyers, but who were protected from that fate by their close connection with the King. Tenure in ancient desmesne still exists, and special rights enjoyed by such tenants have been upheld in recent times.[67]

These tenants in ancient demesne simply did not fit into the categories of the medieval land law, and there was considerable difficulty in saying whether they were freeholders or not. In the fifteenth century it came to be said that if such a tenant by custom conveyed by feoffment he was a freeholder, presumably because the efficacy of a feoffment could be explained only if the seisin was in the tenant. Otherwise such tenants were held not to be freeholders when the matter was finally settled in the eighteenth century in connection with the restriction of the right to vote to freeholders,[68] this accorded with the view adopted by Blackstone.[69]

The Theory of Copyhold Tenure

If the freehold of copyhold land was not in the tenant it was in the lord, and such was the conclusion adopted by the common-lawyers of the Middle Ages as a theoretical explanation of the legal situation which arose on a manor. As freeholder the lord alone had the seisin. Yet clearly the unfree manorial tenants were in occupation, and the only way of describing the position in common-law terms was to say that the copyhold tenants were tenants at will of the lord. In Littleton this doctrine is accepted, as it had to be, but Littleton is only too well aware of the incongruity of it. A tenancy at will might well arise through the agreement of two persons. Thus Littleton defines such a tenancy in this way:

. . . tenant at will is, where lands or tenements are let by one man to another to hold to him at the will of the lessor, by force of which lease the lessee is in possession. In this case the lessee is called tenant at will because he has no certain or sure estate, for the lessor may put him out at what time it pleases him.[70]

When he discusses the position of a copyholder Littleton has to explain that this is hardly a full description of his position. He

[67] See *Iveagh* v. *Martin* [1961] 1 Q.B. 232.
[68] See 31 Geo. II, c. 14, and *Conolly* v. *Vernon* (1804), 5 East 51.
[69] Blackstone, *Law Tracts*, cited by Holdsworth, III, p. 265.
[70] Littleton, sec. 68.

calls him a tenant at will of the lord, but adds that he is more than this, for he holds at the will of the lord 'according to the custom of the manor', and can have 'an inheritance according to the custom of the manor'; in one passage he even says that a copyholder may have an estate.[71] The legal theory which made copyholders mere tenants at will was inadequate, for there was all the difference in the world between an ordinary tenant at will and a copyholder, who might by custom hold for life, in fee simple or in fee tail like a freeholder. Furthermore, the relationship between a copyhold tenant at will and his lord was the consequence of the existence of an unfree tenure between them, whilst between an ordinary tenant at will and his landlord it would be difficult to say that any tenure at all existed.[72] When the copyhold tenant came to enjoy the same degree of protection as the freeholder the legal theory which Littleton found difficult became simply impossible to maintain.

The rise of the action of ejectment had a profound effect upon the subsequent development of the common law. Freeholders, leaseholders, and copyholders acquired a single and adequate action for the protection of their interests in land. Inevitably this encouraged the assimilation of the law governing these three classes of landowners, and prepared the way for the simplification of the land law which was attempted in the 1925 legislation, and which will in time be carried still farther. The use of the action by copyholders brought into the royal courts a species of property which had been in exile for centuries, and enabled the courts to build up if not a common law of copyhold tenure, at least a common body of principle for the treatment of divergent customary copyhold law.

In doing so they were faced with a number of difficulties. Rooted firmly in the reports was the theory that a copyholder held at the will of the lord of the manor. When the courts came round to protecting the copyholder some drastic revision of the concept of the copyholder's tenancy at will had to be undertaken, for he was now a tenant at will who could not be ejected

---

[71] Littleton, secs. 73, 77.

[72] Fealty was incidental to tenure of any kind, Littleton (sec. 132) notes that '. . . he, which is tenant at will, according to the course of the common law, shall not do fealty: because he hath not any sure estate. But otherwise it is of tenant at will according to the custom of the manor. . . .'

at will. A form of words had to be found to express this anomaly. In Littleton were hints of the notion that a copyholder was a peculiar sort of tenant at will; thus Littleton, in the section of his book on 'Tenant by Copie', gives this definition of such a tenant,

. . . tenant by copy of court roll is as if a man be seised of a manor within which manor there is a custom which hath been used time out of mind of man, that certain tenants within the same manor have used to have lands and tenements to hold to them and their heirs in fee simple or fee tail or for term of life etc. at the will of the lord according to the custom of the manor.[73]

This pointed the way to the developed doctrine; the will of the lord was not a free will, but a will subjected to the custom. It came to be said that the lord was a mere instrument of the ancient customary observances of the manor. The legal position could be expressed only in a paradoxical way. Thus it is said that *in strict law* the copyholder remained a tenant at will, but *by the custom* could have an inheritance just as a freeholder could. Thus in the course of time the courts worked out a compromise between the old view, under which the lord was treated as 'owner' of the lands of his unfree tenants, and the new view, under which the unfree tenant was to be regarded as 'owner'. The lord was still the freeholder, but he became a very unusual freeholder, and the tenant remained a tenant at will, but became a very unusual tenant at will.

The lord continued to be regarded as the person seised of the copyholder's lands; he will normally be seised for an estate in fee simple. By the custom he has lost most of the benefits of seisin of a freehold estate, but he never loses them all. He is the freeholder for the purposes of electoral law; he has the vote. He retains, too, some of the rights of enjoyment of a freeholder, for the copyholder never goes beyond acquiring a customary right to occupy the land, and the land remains for some purposes the lord's land. Thus the lord has the right to mines and minerals and to timber, though he must not disturb the occupation of a copyholder by entering without leave to enjoy these rights. The copyholder, even if he holds an estate in fee simple by the custom, must not commit waste, upon pain of forfeiting his land;

73 Littleton, sec. 77.

the land is not his in the full sense in which a freeholder's land is his. Thus a copyholder in general had no customary right to lease his land for more than a year; if he wished to grant a longer term he must obtain the licence of his lord. If he exceeds his customary rights, for example by granting a longer lease, he loses his privileged position and becomes liable to forfeiture. And not only did copyholders not acquire the same freedom over their lands as freeholders; in addition they continued to be burdened by tenurial exactions long after these had ceased to trouble those who held by free tenure. In many manors the lord was entitled to a heriot on the death of his tenant; he could seize his tenant's best beast. Troublesome money rents were often payable, and the copyholder could be liable for a variety of customary dues and fines payable, for example, on alienation. Local ill feeling could be caused when a lord revived some exaction which had lapsed; stories were long told in the country of sudden demands for heriots. The survival of the trappings of tenure became increasingly resented in modern times, when they conflicted with more egalitarian notions. And a hierarchical and paternalistic system survived in many village communities well into living memory, though it was more commonly associated with the lease for years and the tied agricultural worker's cottages than with the more ancient tenurial arrangements of the medieval world.

The estates and interests which could subsist in copyhold land were modelled closely on the ordinary freehold estates; this, as we have seen, was recognized by Littleton to be the situation then existing in some manors, and the courts went some way towards generalizing such customs. In theory it was difficult to justify the recognition of estates tail in copyhold land. If recognition was justified by showing a customary power to entail, it conflicted with the theory that manorial customs should have existed since the beginning of legal memory in 1189, which was well before the statute *De Donis*, and it was very difficult to argue that *De Donis* was intended to apply to the unfree tenures. For a long time the recognition of entails was a matter for learned dispute. A customary power to entail was not recognized in all manors, but only in those which had anciently used such a custom. In manors which had not done so, the effect of a grant to a man and the heirs of his body created an estate which was modelled upon the fee simple conditional before *De Donis*, which could be alienated freely once issue were born. Copyholders who held in tail were allowed to secure a power of free alienation by various methods. Sometimes a customary common recovery was employed, in imitation of the common recoveries of the common-law courts, whilst in others the entailed land was surrendered to the lord and re-granted in fee simple. The Fines and Recoveries Act in 1833[74] introduced a uniform and simple method of barring entails in copyhold land, which made these expedients unnecessary.

Conveyances of Copyhold Land

The method by which copyhold lands were conveyed was peculiar. The copyholder surrendered his lands into the lands of his lord, who then admitted the grantee; the transaction was recorded on the court rolls by the steward of the manor. Originally the admittance of new copyhold tenants was performed in the court of the manor, which all the copyholders were bound to attend as suitors. The practice of actually holding courts passed out of use in many manors, and the need to hold them formally was abolished in 1841.[75] The surrender took the form of a symbolic delivery of the land to the use of the alienee, whose right to admittance was not recognized at common law.[76] Copyhold lands were devisable by the testator's making a surrender to the lord to the use of his will, but the need for a surrender was abolished in 1815 by statute.[77] The employment of surrenders into the lord's hand *to the use* of the alienee is a curious feature of the history of copyhold, which was already in operation in Littleton's time. The use thus created was probably enforceable in Chancery from the fifteenth century onwards, so as to secure the alienee's right to admittance. In 1615 it was held in *Forde* v. *Hoskins*[78] that no action lay at common law to compel admittance, at the suit of the grantee, though relief could be obtained in Chancery.[79] The grantor could, however, bring an

---

[74] 3 and 4 Will. IV, c. 74.
[75] Copyhold Act, 4 and 5 Vict., c. 35.
[76] *Forde* v. *Hoskins* (1615), Cro. Jac. 368, where an action was refused to the alienee.
[77] 55 Geo. III, c. 192.
[78] 1 Roll. Rep. 126. The common-law action lay only at the suit of the grantor.
[79] *Rothwell's Case* (1567), Dyer 264a.

action on the case against the lord for failing to admit the person to whose use the lands had been surrendered, though it is improbable that such actions were ever much employed. The equitable jurisdiction eventually became obsolete in the eighteenth century when the common-law courts began to allow writs of mandamus to be brought against a manorial lord to compel him to admit the intended alienee.[80]

The law of copyhold was always an intricate and specialized body of law, and the intricacy was in part due to the prevalence of special customs in manors. In Coke's time[81] the courts built up a set of principles upon the admission of such local customs affecting copyhold, and these principles had some effect in reducing the luxuriance of local custom. Thus the rule that an unreasonable custom was void, which is to be found in Littleton, was used to restrain harsh exactions by lords from their copyhold tenants, and the rule that custom must be of immemorial antiquity could have the effect of docking a local custom whose proof was rendered thereby impossible, and prevented the growth of new customs at variance with the common law. But the degree of uniformity which was reached was very limited. Even on the most elementary points there could be local variation: the fee simple, for example, was not universally accepted by manorial custom. The result was inconvenience, and the Real Property Commissioners in 1832, when they came out in favour in principle of the abolition of copyhold tenure (though they could find no ideologically acceptable way of bringing this about) laid particular stress upon this inconvenience: 'Each manor has for itself a system of laws to be sought in oral traditions, or in the court rolls or proceedings of the customary court, kept often by ignorant or negligent stewards.'[82] The inevitable result was litigation and insecurity. It was frequently difficult to tell if land was copyhold or not, so that either a

---

[80] E.g. *Roe d. Noden* v. *Griffiths* (1763), 4 Burr. 1952 at 1961. Uses of copyhold lands were not affected by the Statute of Uses.

[81] Coke wrote a chatty little book on copyhold—*The Compleat Copyholder*; it was published in 1630. The style is quite unlike Coke's other writings; the book ends, 'And so I conclude with Copyholders, wishing that there may be a perfect Union betwixt them and their Lords, that they may have a feeling for each other's wrongs and injuries, that their so little Commonwealth, having all its members knit together in compleat order, may flourish to the end.'

[82] *Report of the Real Property Commissioners*, p. 14.

disastrous mistake was made or the land had to be conveyed by two conveyances, one appropriate to freehold and the other to copyhold. The rules as to timber and minerals could prevent the proper development of the land, whilst the fines and exactions to which the copyhold tenant was liable led to friction and abuse, and discouraged copyholders from improving their land. The solution adopted in the nineteenth century by the legislature was that of passing a series of statutes encouraging and facilitating the voluntary extinguishment of copyhold tenure, and by slow degress the current of opinion eventually in 1925 came round to the decisive step of compulsory abolition,[83] though some of the lord's rights were nevertheless preserved for the future.

[83] For reference purposes the best book on copyhold law is Scriven, *On Copyholds*, 7th ed., 1896; see also Holdsworth, VII, pp. 296–312, and Williams, *Real Property*, pp. 438–83.

VIII

Uses and the Statute

THE conception of a use of lands differs little from that of a bailment of a chattel, and both transactions will be actuated by much the same sort of motives. I may hand over a book to a friend because I feel that it is safer in his custody, or because I am going abroad and cannot take it with me, or indeed for a multitude of honest and understandable reasons. I may also do so for dishonourable or fraudulent reasons—to keep a valuable book out of the hand of my creditors. Furthermore, I may hand over a book to a friend with some instructions requiring him to do something more positive with it—to read it to my small son at bedtime. In the course of time the law has evolved a number of remedies which protect me against sharp practice in such situations when I bail a chattel, and these remedies are common law remedies, though they have to some extent been supplemented by the intervention of equity. Unfortunately the medieval lawyers were incapable of devising suitable remedies when the same sort of transaction was carried out not with chattels but with land, nor did they find it easy to prevent such transactions being used for fraudulent purposes. In the Middle Ages it was the Chancellor who supplied the first defect and the legislature the second.

We meet with examples of uses of land back in Domesday Book;[1] by the time we reach the thirteenth century the practice of putting lands in use has become fairly common. The essence of such a transaction is that lands are conveyed to a person or persons (called the feoffee or feoffees to uses) with a provision that they be held for the benefit (*ad opus*) of a beneficiary. The beneficiary is described in law french as 'cestui a que use le feoffment fuit fait', and from this obtains his curious title 'cestui que use'. The plural of this term is often rendered charmingly

---

[1] For examples see Pollock and Maitland, II, p. 234, and, for the early history, II, pp. 228-9; also Maitland, *Collected Papers*, II, pp. 403-16, Plucknett, *Concise History*, pp. 575-8, Ames, *Lectures in Legal History*, Lect. XX.

as 'cestui que usent', an expression calculated to give a grammarian bad dreams. The beneficial enjoyment of the land is therefore separated from the legal title, for the feoffee is a mere passive recipient of title, often with no active duties to perform, who is not intended to benefit from the transaction in any way. His basic duty is the passive one of allowing the *cestui que use* to take the profits of the land; from this comes the other title sometimes given to the beneficiary—'the pernor of profits'. Sometimes the feoffee might have active duties imposed upon him—for example he might be instructed to reconvey the lands to another person; such a direction would create an active use. But passive uses were more commonly met with, and in the development of the law of uses they played a much more important part.

The Medieval Use

A variety of explanations have been given for the prevalence of feoffments to uses in the Middle Ages. The Crusades, it has been suggested, encouraged the practice by taking landowners out of the country and making it imperative that they left somebody at home in control of their lands. The friars of the Order of St. Francis found it convenient that property should be held by others to their use. Thereby they could, as St. Francis had enjoined, achieve both individual and corporate poverty. Like horses, which used but did not own their stables, the friars used, but did not own, the buildings they occupied.[2] Their resulting complete poverty was thought to imitate the poverty of Christ. Dishonesty also played some part.[3] One who was proposing to indulge in treasonable enterprises could seek to avoid the chance of his lands being forfeit to the Crown for treason by conveying them away to a blameless confederate, to be held to his use. By the fifteenth century it becomes clear that most uses were created for one of four main reasons: they could be

[2] See for an account of the Franciscans and the use J. R. H. Moorman, *A History of the Franciscan Order from its Origins to the year 1517*. The site of their house in Canterbury was thus held by aldermen to their use.

[3] Modern techniques of lawful tax evasion often resemble the techniques employed with the use, and succeed by separating title from enjoyment. For a contemporary account of the reasons for the prevalence of uses see St. Germain, *Doctor and Student*, II, c. XXII. And on the early history see J. L. Barton, 'The Medieval Use' 81 *L.Q.R.* 562.

employed to assist in simple fraud; they could be used to avoid feudal dues; they could be used to gain a power of devise over land; and they could be used to facilitate the creation of settlements of land. But before these reasons can be explained we must first see how the Chancellor came to protect the use and develop a body of equitable principles around the institution.

The use simply could not be fitted into the common-law scheme of things,[4] for the doctrine of estates and the doctrine of seisin left no place for the separation of beneficial enjoyment from legal title. The simplest form of use would arise when A enfeoffed B of Blackacre to the use of C. By the feoffment the legal estate vested in B, upon whom the seisin had been conferred by the livery of seisin. Until seisin had passed to C he could not possibly obtain any estate in the land, and if of course B did make a conveyance and pass the seisin to C, then B would step out of the picture completely, which was hardly A's intention. If B let C into possession without any formal conveyance then the only legal category into which C could be fitted was that of tenant at will of B, and this meant that C could be thrown out by B whenever B wished. The root of the common law's difficulty lay in the fact that the landowner's beneficial interest was protected by protecting seisin; the person who had seisin could recover that seisin specifically in the real actions if he were disseised, or disturbed in some other way. The *cestui que use* did not have seisin, and thus he could not use the actions which gave specific recovery, nor were there forms of action capable of protecting a beneficial interest divorced from seisin. It has been suggested that the common law could have protected the *cestui que use* by allowing him other actions—trespass and assumpsit for example—and it must be admitted that the same development which enabled trespass to be used to protect the termor might conceivably have been copied in relation to the *cestui que use*. But if the *cestui que use* was never let into possession by a dishonest feoffee, he could never have used trespass, which only protected one who had possession, and the employment

---

[4] There was some chance that in Bracton's time the common law might develop a remedy: see Holdsworth, II, p. 246, and B.N.B., pl. 1851 (1226), where an heir was not allowed to recover by mort d'ancestor land which his father had bought to the use of a third party. There is scant evidence that any notable progress was made towards the direct protection of beneficiaries.

of assumpsit in this connection would have required a very considerable degree of modification of the rules governing that action; for example, specific recovery would have had to have been introduced in it. We may well understand therefore, the helplessness of the common-lawyers in the matter, for they were bound to work within the scheme of actions provided by the Register of Writs.[5]

The intervention of the legislature was confined to the introduction of measures directed towards the prevention of fraudulent feoffments to uses. There is evidence of the enforcement of uses in the ecclesiastical courts, but, so far as the later history is concerned, the important forum was the Chancery, for it was to the Chancellor that petitions for the protection of uses were directed.[6] Since it was settled in the fifteenth century (and recognized earlier) that the common-law courts would not uphold uses as such, the person who made a feoffment to uses was clearly reposing a trust or confidence in the feoffee, which it was unconscionable, though not illegal, for him to break. Thus it was the very impotence of the common law which provided the basis upon which the Chancellor could intervene in the name of good conscience and, later, equity, and require the feoffee to hold the land for the benefit of the *cestui que use* and allow him to take the profits. He could enforce his decrees by threat of imprisonment, and his mode of procedure by interrogation under oath was a potent method for discovering the nature and scope of the trust reposed in the feoffee, and whether or not his behaviour was conscionable. We find the Chancellor intervening to protect a *cestui que use* in 1446, but the frequency of petitions before this date indicates that his intervention

---

[5] Some conveyances to uses could be treated as grants to the feoffees of estates upon condition. But this was of limited value; the remedy for breach of condition was entry by the feoffor, and only if the feoffor and the *cestui que use* were the same person was this remedy at all satisfactory. Just before the Statute of Uses certain common-lawyers were prepared to argue, and indeed decide, that uses were recognized by the common law, but this view was no more than a conceit. See Y.B. 14 Hen. VIII Mich., pl. 5, f. 4, and 27 Hen. VIII Pasch, pl. 22, f. 7. The common law courts had held in 1379 that uses as such could not be recognized at common law: see Holdsworth, IV, p. 416. The *cestui que use* in possession could not, however, be wholly ignored—since he was not a trespasser he was ranked as a tenant at will.

[6] R. H. Helmholtz, 'The Early Enforcement of Uses', 79 *Columbia L. R.* 1503. In 1402 (R.P., iii, 511) the Commons petitioned for a remedy against dishonest feoffees, but without success.

began earlier.[7] The early development and character of the Chancellor's jurisdiction remains largely obscure; the Chancellors were men trained in civil and canon law, and may well have acted upon legal principles, or upon the theories applied to the confessional. In the later half of the fifteenth century the Chancellors began to develop some consistent principles which governed their readiness to intervene, and once this begins to be the case it is clear that the *cestui que use* has come to obtain a species of protected interest which will be defended consistently and predictably—that is, a species of property.

Uses and Consideration

Besides being ready to protect those uses which arose through express creation, the Chancellor and the common-lawyers[8] evolved a doctrine of implied uses, which arose through operation of law, and the principles governing these implied uses came in time to be extremely important. It was a common practice in the fifteenth century for a landowner to convey his land to one or, more usually, a number of feoffees, and to remain in occupation of the lands for the time being, subsequently declaring the uses upon which the lands were to be held. Out of this practice grew the equitable presumption upon a conveyance of this sort, where the feoffees gave no value to the feoffor, that the feoffees should hold to the use of the feoffor, unless the feoffee or feoffees could show a contrary intention. The implied use which came back to the grantor in this way was called a resulting use. This doctrine is adumbrated in Littleton's book. Soon after his time it comes to be explained by reference to the rather obscure equitable doctrine of consideration, which was evolved in the late fifteenth and early sixteenth centuries. The absence of 'consideration', so it was said, caused the use to result back. One must be careful not to think of 'consideration' as if it was synonymous with 'recompense'; rather the word connoted some *sound reason* for the conveyance,

---

[7] For examples see Baildon, Selden Society, Vol. 10, p. xxxvi. The case in 1446 is *Myrfyn* v. *Fallan*, Cal. Proceedings in Chancery, Vol. II, p. xxi (Record Comm. 1827–32).

[8] A statute of 1484, as we shall see, brought litigation concerning uses into the common-law courts; hence the year books contain discussion of the doctrines concerning them. See A. W. B. Simpson, *A History of the Common Law of Contract*, Pt. II Ch. V, and J. L. Barton, 'The Mediaeval Use' 81 *L.Q.R.* 562.

and the payment of money by the feoffee was only one possible reason. Thus if land was given gratuitously to a prior or abbot, the obvious charitable purpose rebutted the presumption of a resulting use, for it furnished a consideration for the gift, and if the feoffor's intention was that a use should result back he must say so expressly. In 1505[9] it was argued, with what success we are not told, that the natural love of an elder son for a younger, and his obligation in natural law to look after him, might form a sufficient consideration, and in Henry VIII's reign it was settled that a marriage fell within the scope of the conception of good consideration. At the same time as it was being settled what considerations would rebut the presumption of a resulting use when there had been a feoffment or other conveyance, a momentous step forward was taken by the admission that a use might arise without there being any conveyance at all. This was first admitted in the case of a bargain and sale of lands. By 1535, if not earlier,[10] it was settled that if A bargained and sold lands to B, then, once the purchase price was paid, A would hold to the use of B, although there had been no conveyance executed. The underlying notion here is that it would be unconscionable of A to hold to his own use after he had been paid the money. This rule is a development out of the earlier rule that the payment of money rebutted a presumption of a resulting use arising on a feoffment, and the analogy between the two doctrines is drawn by saying that in both instances 'the consideration changes the use'. There is also an obvious analogy between the bargain and sale of lands passing the use and the bargain and sale of chattels, which, so some lawyers thought, passed 'the property'.[11] Once it was admitted that a bargain and sale passed the use it began to be suggested that any mere agreement would pass a use; that is to say that if A and B agreed that A should hold to B's use then a use would pass. This was felt to be carrying things too far, so the heresy was squashed by saying that a covenant (i.e. an agreement) must be supported by good consideration to have this effect, and the payment in the bargain and sale supplied this need.[12]

9 Littleton secs. 462–4, and Y.B. 20 Hen. VII Mich., f. 10, pl. 20.
10 Y.B. 27 Hen. VIII Pasch., f. 5, pl. 15, f. 7, pl. 22.
11 See Fifoot, *History and Sources*, Ch. 10.
12 Y.B. 21 Hen. VII Hil., f. 18, pl. 30.

What, then, would be good consideration? In the period just before the Statute of Uses the employment of uses in connection with family settlements again raised the question whether or not marriage and natural love and affection formed sufficiently acceptable reasons or considerations. In 1523 Hales J. held that a marriage to be celebrated at the same time as the use was agreed to pass or to be celebrated later would be a good consideration, but at the same time he introduced the doctrine that a past consideration (for example a marriage that had already taken place, or money previously paid) would be no good.[13] The underlying notion here is that although the agreement to pass the use might be the result of the past marriage (or whatever it was) the marriage could not have been the result of the agreement to pass the use. One could not therefore say that the past consideration had been furnished *because of*, or *in consideration of* the agreement to pass the use, and it was therefore ineffective. Upon this reasoning natural love was perhaps past consideration, and therefore insufficient. Later in the sixteenth century, however, Hales's doctrine, though it passed into the law of contract which developed around the action of assumpsit, was partly discarded in connection with uses, so that in *Sharrington* v. *Strotton* (1566)[14] it was settled that a person might covenant in consideration of natural love and affection to stand seised to the use of a close relative, and such a covenant was effective to pass the use. Thus the equitable doctrine of consideration embraced three forms of consideration—payment of money, marriage, and natural love and affection, and it is probable that a mere promise of money or marriage was admitted from 1523 onwards.

Uses and the Doctrine of Notice

The Chancellor also built up the doctrine of notice; this is the name given to the corpus of rules evolved to determine which holders of the land will be bound in equity to hold it for the benefit of the *cestui que use*. Clearly the feoffee himself was bound, and it was not necessary that the uses should be declared in any formal manner or in writing; whatever the informality the feoffee's conscience was still affected. Furthermore, the

[13] Brooke, *Abridgement, Feffements al uses*, pl. 54.
[14] Plowden 298.

uses need not be declared at the time of the feoffment, but could be specified after an interval.[15] But the Chancellor did not confine his interference to the original feoffee or feoffees. In 1482 we learn that it was a common practice in the Chancery to enforce uses against the heir of a feoffee, though the Chancellor seemed to be doubtful as to the propriety of doing so, and Chief Justice Hussey recalls that thirty years earlier this was not the practice.[16] In 1466 a note in the year book[17] states that a purchaser for value of the land from the feoffee will be bound by the use if he has express notice of it, and the wording of the note implies that one who took by conveyance from the feoffee without giving value would be bound anyway; the point of the note is to draw attention to the fact that *even a purchaser for value* might be bound. The justification for saying that a purchaser for value with notice was bound was that he was a party to the fraud of the feoffee who had sold the land. The reason why a purchaser for value without notice was not bound, and why a person who did not give value was, irrespective of notice, depend both upon the equitable doctrine of consideration. The general rule that one who gave consideration held to his own use was not displaced in the case of the purchaser for value without notice by any fraud, and so the use in favour of the *cestui que use* was extinguished in favour of the purchaser for value without notice, who thus acquired the seisin by common-law conveyance and the use in equity. The old books put this by saying that the use was changed (transferred from one person to another) because of the consideration. On the other hand, when the feoffee conveyed the land to another, and the conveyance was gratuitous or lacked consideration, the transaction at first sight might appear to fall under the general rule that upon a conveyance for which there was no consideration a use resulted to the grantor (here the feoffee to uses). But to apply

---

[15] The extreme example of this form of delayed declaration is the declaration of uses by will. Feoffments to the use of the feoffor's last will are commonly found from the early fifteenth century onwards. For an example from *c.* 1393 see Baildon, Selden Society, Vol. 10, Case No. 45.

[16] Y.B. 22 Edw. IV, Pasch., f. 4, pl. 18.

[17] Y.B. 5 Edw. IV Mich., f. 7, pl. 16: 'If J has enfeoffed A to his [own] use, and A has enfeoffed R, notwithstanding that he [A] sold him the land, if A gave notice to R of the intention of the prior feoffment, he [R] is bound by writ of Subpoena to perform the intent.'

this rule would have been absurd, for the feoffee, when he made the conveyance, was seised not to his own use but to the use of the *cestui que use*; the general rule was therefore modified so that the grantee held to the use of the original *cestui que use*. The lawyers put this by saying that the old or original use was not changed by a conveyance by the feoffee for which there was no consideration; on such a conveyance the seisin passed at law, but not the use. The first clear statement of the relationship between notice and consideration was by Pollard J. in 1522, and the doctrine he stated came to be revised to form in later law the doctrine of purchaser for value without notice, the basis for the distinction between legal and equitable ownership.[18]

The use had originated as a personal confidence or trust placed by one person in the other, and even when a use became a species of property it continued to bear marks of this origin. Thus it never came to bind the land itself; rather, it was conceived to bind the conscience of persons into whose hands the land came. This conception is illustrated by the rule that quite irrespective of notice a use was only binding upon persons who came to the land *through* those in whom the confidence had been originally reposed. Thus if a feoffee to uses sold the land to another who took with notice that person would be bound, but if the feoffee was disseised by some rogue, who might well know of the use, such a disseisor was not bound by the use. He came to the land *in the post*, he came to it after the feoffee, but he did not come to it *in the per*, he did not take through the feoffee, and only one who came *in the per* was bound. Another illustration of the same conception is to be found in the rule that no use could arise unless at the time of its creation there was some person in whom the creator of the use had reposed his confidence; there could be no use which attached simply to the land, and not to some person. Thus there was nothing to resemble the modern system under which a trust can arise without a trustee.

Uses and Wills

We know little of the ways in which the Chancellor allowed *cestui que usent* to deal with their equitable interest before the

---

[18] See Simpson, *History of Contract*, pp. 359-60, discussing Y.B. 14 Hen. VIII, M. f. 4, pl. 5.

Statute of Uses. The normal mode of alienation was for the *cestui que use* to instruct the feoffees to pass the lands by common-law conveyance to the alienee. It was their duty to do this. It seems clear that he allowed equitable estates to be moulded in imitation of common-law estates, so that there could be a *cestui que use* in tail or in fee simple, and so on, and it is probable that he did not look askance at the creation of equitable future interests which did not conform to any common-law models; for example it is probable that a use might be made to shift from one beneficiary to another upon the occurrence of some future event. On topics such as this we have no very clear information.[19] In one particular, however, there was a definite and extremely important settled rule, and that was that uses could be disposed of by will; common-law estates, of course, could not. Thus by conveying his lands to feoffees to his own use a landowner at once acquired what amounted to a power of devise over his beneficial interest, and it is generally admitted that this power of devise was the most potent attraction of putting lands in use. The theory of the matter was that a will, that is a declaration of the feoffors' wishes, operated as a delayed declaration of trust. A 'will', it must be understood, does not originally mean a piece of paper, but, literally, a will. A 'last will' is exactly that: a final expression of wishes by a dying person.[20]

Uses and Feudalism

The employment of the use to avoid the feudal dues was also widespread. Normally there would be a number of feoffees to uses, and they would hold as joint tenants. As an insurance against fraud, eminent lawyers were often used as feoffees and, no doubt, were paid for their services. By choosing such respectable persons and not putting his trust in a single feoffee

[19] It is hazardous to read back into the period before 1536 doctrines concerning uses which may never have been formulated in the Chancery; we know very little about the doctrines of equity before the seventeenth century. Most of the 'equitable' doctrines about uses before 1536 are known to us from common-law cases, and may well be the invention of common-lawyers. Equitable practice is quite another matter. An invaluable source of information is St. Germain's *Doctor and Student*.

[20] About the origin of this rule or its theoretical justification little at all is known; it seems to be accepted from as early as *c.* 1400. See Simpson, *History of Contract*, pp. 334–44, Baker, Selden Society, Vol. 94, pp. 192–203.

the feoffor could have considerable confidence that his wishes would be observed without the need for litigation. Now at law the feoffees were the persons who had the legal estate, and it was from them that the lord must look for his feudal services and incidents. By the fifteenth century the services were usually not worth exacting, but the incidents were. The plurality of feoffees had the effect, however, of denying to the lord wardship, marriage, relief, primer seisin, and escheat. This was because of the *ius adcrescendi*—the rule that when one joint tenant died his interest accrued to the surviving joint tenants, and did not pass to his heir, so that the legal estate never passed by descent at all; thus no minor ever inherited the legal estate so as to be in ward, and no heir ever had to pay relief and so on. Of course, the original joint feoffees would die out in the course of time, but whenever the number became dangerously low the *cestui que use* could instruct the remaining joint feoffees to enfeoff a few more and keep the number up. It was simple enough to ensure that they never all died out without heirs, so that there was never a risk of escheat *propter defectum sanguinis*. Escheat *propter delictum tenentis* could be avoided by using as feoffees persons who were unlikely to commit crime, such as judges. Thus the *cestui que use*, who beneficially enjoyed the land, could die, inherit, commit felony, and leave his interest by will even if he had no heirs; he never had to pay the incidents of tenure. When it is said that uses were used for fraudulent purpose it was the avoidance of the feudal incidents that is usually being referred to, though other frauds could be perpetrated by much the same technique of keeping the person beneficially entitled behind a screen of feoffees of undeniable respectability; frauds on creditors can obviously be carried out in this way.[21]

A number of statutes were passed to deal seriatim with these evasions.[22] Some prevented debtors conveying their lands to feoffees to their own use to avoid creditors, but were difficult to enforce because a cunning debtor could make it difficult to find out what lands were held to his use, since no formality was required in the declaration of uses.[23] Others dealt with the

---

[21] See generally Bean, *The Decline of English Feudalism*, pp. 1215–540, esp. Ch. V. See Plucknett, *Concise History*, p. 579, Baker, Selden Society, Vol. 94, pp. 192–203.

[22] E.g. 51 Edw. III, c. 6 (1377), 2 Rich. II, st. 2, c. 3 (1379), 3 Hen. VII, c. 5 (1488), 19 Hen. VII, c. 15 (1504).   [23] E.g. 15 Rich. II, c. 5 (1392).

evasion of the Statute of Mortmain,[24] and with feoffments designed to impede litigation. Evasion of feudal incidents was also tackled; thus a statute of 1489 made the *cestui que use* liable in some circumstances for wardship and also for relief.[25] One statute (that of 1 Rich. III, c. 1) allowed a *cestui que use* to make conveyances of the legal estate. It was probably simply aimed at the protection of purchasers, but it had the effect of giving common-law courts official cognisance of uses. In the case of the feudal incidents the loss caused by feoffments to uses fell more and more on the Crown, and from the 1520s onwards a confused position developed. Some argued that uses should be recognized at common law. Others thought they should be extirpated as fraudulent devices. Thus in 1535 an attempt was made to argue before the Exchequer Chamber and the Chancellor the general proposition that manipulation of uses calculated to defraud the Crown of feudal revenue was covinous and void, or as we should say, contrary to public policy.[26] Under pressure, the judges agreed, taking the view that wills of uses were in principle impossible. But the position of uses could hardly be left to rest on one coerced decision, and shortly afterwards an attempt was made to tackle the problem of uses by radical legislation.

The Statute of Uses

Such legislation was forced through Parliament in 1536 in the form of two statutes: the Statute of Uses[27] and the Statute of Enrolments.[28] The second of these two statutes is best considered as a sub-provision of the first. The basic principle embodied in this legislation was brilliantly simple in conception—it was to vest the legal estate in the *cestui que use* and take it away from the feoffees.[29] This approach was not entirely without precedent.

---

[24] E.g. 1 Rich. II, c. 9 (1377), 4 Hen. IV, c. 7 (1403), 11 Hen. IV, c. 3 (1410).

[25] 4 Hen. VII, c. 17.

[26] *Lord Dacre's Case*, Y.B. 27 Hen. VIII Pasch., f. 7, pl. 22. Selden Society, Vol. 93, pp. 228–30, discussed Simpson, *History of Contract*, pp. 334–6, Baker, Selden Society, Vol. 94, pp. 196–202, E. W. Ives, 'The Genesis of the Statute of Uses', 82 *E.H.R.* 673.

[27] 27 Hen. VIII, c. 10. The text is available in Digby, *Real Property*, p. 347, together with valuable notes.

[28] 27 Hen. VIII, c. 16.

[29] An account of the political history of the statute, and of other proposed legislation is given by Holdsworth, IV, pp. 450–61 and more recently by Ives, cited note 26

Earlier statutes had adopted the expedient of treating the *cestui que use* (for some purposes) *as if he had* the legal estate. The most far-reaching of these statutes was that of 1484,[30] which enacted that the *cestui que use* could make legal conveyances of the land held to his use, and thus, like the Settled Land Act of 1882, gave to the person beneficially entitled a power of disposition over something which in strict law he did not have. But this statute, quite apart from the obscurity of its wording, made the grave error of leaving the feoffees with their power of disposition too, with the result that both feoffees and *cestui que use* could both convey the same land.[31] The resulting muddle can well be imagined, and the statute was not successful. It did, however, proceed upon the principle of treating the beneficial owner *as if* he were legal tenant, and lawyers justifiably treated it as the source of the expedient employed by the statute of Uses, which went one step further by actually making the *cestui que use* legal tenant.

The vesting of the legal estate in the *cestui que use* was described as 'executing' the use; the seisin was taken from the feoffees and passed to the *cestui que use* by the statute. The courts saw the statute as a Parliamentary conveyance, and conceived of Parliament as having done no more than a feoffee to uses could have done lawfully beforehand.[32] For if A held Blackacre to the use of B before the statute, it could not be said that he had acted in breach of trust if he conveyed the legal estate to B by an

above; the text of draft bills is added in Appendix IV. There is a valuable study of the statute by P. Bordwell, 'The Conversion of the Use into a Legal Interest', in 21 *Iowa L.R.* at p. 1.

[30] 1 Rich. III, c: 1; for the connection between the two statutes see D. E. C. Yale, 'The Revival of Equitable Estates in the Seventeenth Century', [1957] *Camb. L.J.* 72. A statute of 1484 (1 Rich. III, c. 5) had transferred the seisin vested in King Richard as feoffee to uses before his accession to the beneficiaries; Richard could, of course, have done the job himself, and the statute merely saved him the trouble. A statute of 1485 (1 Hen. VII, c. 1) allowed formedon to be brought against the *cestui que use*, thus making him the representative of the land; he was allowed all the protection which a tenant at law had in this action.

[31] The statute allowed *cestui que use* to alienate either to the use of the alienee, or to his own use, or to the use of a third party. Such alienations bound the *cestui que use* and his heirs, or any person holding *only* to the use of the alienor. The word *only* bred considerable difficulty. The policy behind this curious piece of legislation has never been satisfactorily explained; the text is available in Digby, *Real Property*, p. 345, note 2.

[32] See *Wimbish* v. *Taillebois* (1551) Plowden 59, discussed Gough, *Fundamental Law*, p. 25.

ordinary private conveyance, and the Statute of Uses could be portrayed by lawyers as if it had avoided any dangerous Parliamentary meddling with private property; they said it did no more than a feoffee could lawfully have done privately before it was passed.[33] But, of course, this way of looking at the statute is deceptive, for it was drafted with the intention of clearing the feoffees to uses out of the picture in all cases, and thus abolishing generally the separation of the legal estate from the equitable estate. By doing this the frauds on private persons (in which Henry VIII was probably not very interested) and the evasion of feudal incidents (in which he certainly was) would be prevented, for those frauds and evasions all depended upon this separation of legal title from beneficial enjoyment. At the same time the power of devise would be destroyed, for a legal estate, which was what the *cestui que use* now held, could not be devised. This too would prevent evasion, for a landowner who died in possession of his lands could no longer devise his interest by will; his lands would therefore pass to his heir who would take by descent, and one who took by descent would be liable to pay the feudal dues, such as relief. Thus an incidental effect of the statute was to reintroduce primogeniture *in fact* into Tudor society.

The statute opens with a long preamble given over to a diatribe against the supposed evils attendant upon the creation of uses. It is quite clear, however, that this is mere propaganda, and that the realities of the matter are that Henry VIII was by 1529 becoming short of money, and resolved to meet his need by turning to the feudal revenues which were his as supreme lord, but whose collection was frustrated by the prevalence of uses. He proposed a number of expedients in 1529 in a draft bill but met with strong opposition from landowners and lawyers, and it was only after some years manœuvring, characterized by a combination of threats and compromise, that he was able to secure the support of the common-lawyers and secure the passage of the Statute of Uses in 1536, which benefited them as lawyers by bringing back into the common-law courts all that litigation concerning uses which had previously been conducted in Chancery, and so clipping the wings of the Chancellor,

---

[33] Even so far as to treat the feoffees to uses as the donors of the seisin.

whose encroachments were not at this time popular in West-minster Hall. The alarming decision in *Lord Dacre's Case* (1535) that wills of uses were impossible may have secured common-law support for the legislation.[34]

The statute then goes on to provide a remedy for the evils attendant upon uses, and the substance of this remedy appears as the first section of the Act, which lays down that,

> . . . where any person or persons stand or be seised, or at any time hereafter shall happen to be seised of and in any . . . lands . . . to the use, confidence or trust of any other person or persons . . . that in every such case all and every such person and persons . . . shall from henceforth stand and be seised . . . of and in the same . . . lands . . . to all intents constructions and purposes in the law, of and in such like estates as they had or shall have in use, trust or confidence of or in the same.

Having thus transferred the seisin and legal estate to the *cestui que use* the statute then makes it quite clear that the feoffees are to be deprived of all their interest by providing that,

> . . . the estate, title, right, and possession that was in such person or persons (who were seised to another's use) be from henceforth clearly deemed and adjudged to be in him or them that have or hereafter shall have such use, confidence or trust, after such quality, manner, form, and condition as they had before, in or to the use, confidence or trust that was in them.

This first section contains the meat of the statute, and upon its interpretation depended the success of the legislation. Upon the skill of the draftsman in executing his brilliantly simple design opinions have differed, but the modern view seems to be that of Bacon, who regarded it as 'the most perfectly and exactly conceived and penned of any law in the book'.[35] Yet in the self-same *Reading* in which Bacon expressed this view he admitted that nobody was really certain how it ought to be interpreted, and in the century following its enactment the reports are full of cases attempting to deal with the difficulties it raised.[36] We

---

[34] See Holdsworth, IV, pp. 450-61, and note 26 above.

[35] Bacon, Reading (1600). In Spedding's edition at p. 416.

[36] 'I have chosen to read upon the Statute of Uses . . . a law whereupon the inheritances of this realm are tossed at this day, as upon a sea, in such sort that it is hard to say which bark will sink, and which will get to the haven: that is to say what

may distinguish two sources of these difficulties. In the first place the statute contains gross errors both of commission and omission, and in the second place new devices for its evasion were developed which the draftsman could not possibly have envisaged. Furthermore, the abolition of the power of devise produced such violent political opposition that within a few years it was restored by the Wills Act (1540),[37] which in its turn was evaded too.

Secret Conveyancing

That a bargain and sale of lands passed a use to the purchaser was well established in 1536, and the draftsman realized that this meant that after the statute the purchaser would obtain a legal estate upon the conclusion of the bargain, since the use in his favour would be executed by the statute. There would therefore be no need in future to convey lands by feoffment with livery of seisin, with its attendant notoriety, for a secret bargain and sale would suffice. Now secret conveyancing helped the perpetration of frauds, and was a hindrance to a King anxious to recover feudal dues, for it made it difficult to tell who was legal tenant of land. To prevent this the Statute of Enrolments was passed; it provided that bargains and sales of freehold land should be void unless enrolled in public registries set up for the purpose. The immediate effect of the Statutes of Uses and Enrolments was therefore to restore notoriety to conveyancing, and in practice the bargain and sale enrolled—a registered conveyance—replaced the feoffment; by the use of a nominal consideration it could be used for conveyances which were gifts in all but name.

With this piece of prescience the draftsman contented himself. Now even before 1536 it had clearly been suggested that if A convenanted to stand seised to the use of B in consideration of marriage, or in consideration of natural love and affection, such a covenant might raise a use in favour of B[38] and if this were to

---

assurances will stand good, and what will not.' Bacon's *Reading* was published in 1642; the text is bad and incomplete, and the reasoning difficult to follow. The best edition is by Spedding.

[37] 32 Hen. VIII, c. 1.

[38] Y.B. 20 Hen. VII, f. 10, pl. 20, 21 Hen. VII, f.18, pl. 30.

be accepted it was clear that the effect of the statute would be to vest the legal estate in B without more formality. The statute of Enrolments made no provision for the registration of such covenants, no doubt because the draftsman doubted their validity. But by 1566[39] the validity of both types of covenant had been admitted, and secret conveyancing was once more established in the law. To covenant to stand seised became the normal method of making a family settlement, and the restoration of notoriety to conveyancing was frustrated. It is difficult not to blame the draftsman of the statute for his failure here, for such covenants were not unknown when he framed the Statute of Enrolments.

Even worse was to come. It was impossible to employ such a covenant to convey land to a stranger, for in the cold estimation of the law one could have no natural love and affection for persons outside the family. Conveyancers therefore exercised their ingenuity in the search for some form of bargain and sale which would fall outside the scope of the Statute of Enrolments, and therefore be valid without public registration. Now the statute only mentions bargains and sales of *freeholds*, so that if A bargained and sold a term of years to B, A would at once be seised to the use of B for that term. The Statute of Uses executed the use, and B obtained a legal term of years without any need for entry on the land; such a bargain and sale, since a term was not a freehold estate, did not need to be enrolled, and was thus an effective secret conveyance. Now suppose that A was tenant in fee simple and, having thus secretly passed a term to B, he wishes to convey to him his reversion in fee simple—all he now needs to do is to execute a deed of release to B, and B will become tenant in fee simple without more ado. For since a release is effective without any livery of seisin a simple deed of release is all that is required. To Serjeant Moore is attributed the realization that such a bargain and sale of a lease, followed by a release, offered a mode of secret conveyance which escaped the Statute of Enrolments and which could be used as a

---

[39] *Sharrington* v. *Strotton* (1566), Plowden 298. It was held in *Callard* v. *Callard* (1597), 2 And. 64 (and see Popham 47) that the covenant must be under seal. See also the resolution of the judges in Edward VI's reign, noted in Popham 48, and *Lord Burgh's Case* (1542), Dyer 55a, *Bainton* v. *The Queen* (1553) Dyer 96a, *Marmaduke Constable's Case* (1553), Dyer 101b.

mere conveyancing device by bargaining and selling a nominal term of six months or a year, and following this a day or so later with a release of the fee simple.

Such a transaction had another advantage over a straight-forward bargain and sale, for it could be used to create settlements, whereas the bargain and sale of freeholds could not. For reasons which we shall explain the courts held that they would not execute a use on a use. In its crudest form such a use upon a use would arise if A enfeoffed B to the use of C to the use of D, and if this was done then D's use was void, and C obtained the legal estate by force of the statute. When A bargained and sold the fee simple in Blackacre to B, A held to the use of B, and this use was executed by the statute; if A purported to sell to B to the use of C, C's use was a use on a use, and therefore void. But in the bargain and sale with lease and release it was possible to declare uses *on the release*, which was conveyance effective at common law, and not dependent upon the statute. Hence, such uses were not uses on a use, but uses declared on a legal conveyance of the fee simple in reversion, just like uses declared on a feoffment in fee simple. Thus A could bargain and sell a term of one year to B, and B would acquire at once a legal term; next day he could release the fee simple reversion to B to the use of his son for life, remainder to his son's son in fee simple. These uses would be valid, and were uses of freehold; they would therefore be executed by the Statute of Uses, so that the son obtained a legal life estate and the son's son a legal remainder in fee simple. The whole transaction could be completed in the privacy of a lawyer's office, and nobody need ever know. The perfected form of this conveyance was sanctioned by the courts in *Lutwich* v. *Mitton* (1621),[40] and thereafter it became the most usual form of conveyance, making the Statute of Enrolments a dead letter. One can hardly blame the draftsman for not fore-seeing the employment of this device, though it must be admitted that its success depended upon doctrines of law which were perfectly well known in 1536; if only he had not used the fatal term 'freehold' in his statute it could never have happened.

---

[40] Cro. Jac. 604.

The Restoration of the Power to Devise Land

The attempt to abolish the power of devise failed for political reasons. The outcry against its abolition reached its peak in the rebellion known as The Pilgrimage of Grace, in 1536, in which some of the landowning gentry were involved. It is not difficult to see why. A rigid doctrine of primogeniture was entirely anachronistic in the sixteenth century, and landowners were not prepared to sacrifice their younger children to it. There had been two ways of avoiding its consequences. A father could give lands to his other children in his lifetime, or he could employ a conveyance to uses which would enable him to devise his beneficial interest and postpone his generosity until it no longer cost him anything. Any student of human nature will realize that the latter method was preferred. Further, a power of devise offers all sorts of attractive possibilities in the way of power to the devisor; until the very last moment the family may be kept in order, and devises hedged about with conditions of residence, celibacy, and so on enable a devisor to die happy that even from the grave his wisdom may endure to govern and restrain the youthful folly of his children. It must have been irritating enough to the landowners to be frustrated in their tax evasion by the Statute of Uses, but to deprive them of the power of devise must have seemed the last straw. In 1540 Henry VIII recanted, and the Statute of Wills[41] allowed landowners to devise two-thirds of their lands held in knight-service, and all their lands held in socage. The statute, however, ensured that the King would not lose by this concession, for those taking by devise under the statute were to be liable for the feudal dues just as if they had taken by descent as heirs. But even this provision was eventually evaded by a device whereby a landowner could convey lands to a friend to his own use, the use in his favour being executed in the form of a legal fee simple determinable on his death. On the same conveyance the landowner reserved a power of appointment of further uses exercisable by will.[42] On his death he had nothing left to devise by will, for his

---

[41] 32 Hen. VIII, c. 1.

[42] It will be noted that an incidental effect of the statute was to introduce legal powers of appointment. Before the statute a feoffor to uses could reserve a power to declare the uses subsequently, and the effect of the statute was to vest the legal estate in

fee simple determined *eo instanti* with his death, but he could appoint further uses in that will, which would be executed by the Statute of Uses and thus could, in effect, devise his land. Since, however, the exercise of this power was not technically a devise it did not rely on the Statute of Wills, and so the provisions of that statute which preserved the feudal dues did not apply, so that the Crown lost its dues. This, perhaps the most artificial of the evasions of the Statutory settlement, was finally upheld in the same case of *Lutwich* v. *Mitton* in 1621[43] which upheld the bargain and sale with lease and release; but the subtleties upon which it depended were quite unknown to the draftsman of the Statute of Wills in 1540, or indeed to any lawyer of the time.[44]

The Separation of Legal and Equitable Ownership

We must now turn to an evaluation of the success of the attempt to end the separation of legal and equitable ownership. Now it is fairly clear that there was in the legislation no attempt to abolish uses in the sense of *preventing* or rendering *void* future conveyances to persons *to the use* of other persons. The provisions for the enrolment of bargains and sales are unintelligible unless the draftsman envisaged that implied uses would still be held to arise, and if implied uses, why not express uses? What was envisaged was simply that whenever uses arose in future they would be executed; that the separation of legal and equitable ownership would be impossible. As one judge later put it, the use was to be *transubstantiated* into a legal estate. But the wording of the Act cannot be said to have made even this much clear, and a reader in the Inner Temple soon after the statute argued the contrary.[45]

the person in whose favour a use was declared. Legal powers of appointment became impossible when the statute was repealed in 1925.

[43] Cro. Jac. 604.

[44] See Megarry, 'The Statute of Uses and the Power to Devise', 7 *Camb. L. J.* 354. It must not be supposed that the statute failed to abolish the power to devise, or that the Statute of Wills was redundant. What is described is a device which is not technically a devise at all, though it serves the same function.

[45] Or so it seems from the account given by Bacon (*Uses*, 423). 'And this was the exposition, as tradition goeth, that a reader of Grays Inn which read soon after the statute was in trouble for, and worthily; who, I suppose, was Boyse, whose reading I

A very strong case could be made for the less startling view that it was anticipated that only the implied use which arose on a bargain and sale would survive the statute. We may well suspect that the draftsman thought that many forms of conveyance to uses would simply die out. Thus before the Act if A conveyed his fee simple to B without consideration B would be seised to A's use; such a transaction was no mere fatuity, for A could now devise his use or alienate it informally, things he could not do with a legal estate. After the Act such a conveyance would be pointless, for the use in A's favour would be executed, and so A would end up as tenant in fee simple, just as he was before he started. It must have looked as though express conveyances to uses would die a natural death; now that it was no longer possible to separate the legal and the equitable estate, why bother to try? That this was the anticipated result is indicated by the fact that the legislature only made provision for the survival after the Act of one type of use—that arising by implication on a bargain and sale. It was obvious that in future a bargain and sale would, under the provisions of the statute, operate as a conveyance and would be preferred to the more cumbersome feoffment; its future status was therefore dealt with in the Statute of Enrolments. But why trouble to provide for a future feoffment to A in fee simple to the use of B in fee simple, which would in future be a pointless way of conveying the legal fee simple to B?

If this was the way the draftsman looked at the matter, then the skill with which he went about his task may be given a coherent evaluation, for we may say that he made two grave mistakes. For the first we may blame him, and it was that he failed to word the first section so as to execute *all* uses; thus his assumption that the separation of legal and equitable ownership would in future be impossible was wrong. In consequence there was still point in creating those uses which would not be executed by the Statute. The second was that he failed to anticipate correctly the way in which the courts would deal with limitations of those uses which were executed by the statute. We may take these two points in turn.

could never see.' John Boise's opinion was still held by some diehards at the time of Bacon's Reading: his reading has never been found in any MS collection. Bacon mistook the Inn. See Baker, Selden Society, Vol. 94, p. 203.

Uses outside the Statute

In 1580 the judges and chief baron were asked by the Chancellor whether uses declared on a term of years were executed by the statute, as where lands were conveyed to A for a term of a thousand years to the use of B and his heirs. Their opinion was that such uses were not covered by the statute.[46] The doctrinal explanation of this, as it came to be settled, was that a termor was not seised, and the statute clearly only spoke of situations where one person was *seised* to the use of another, and omitted to mention situations where one person was *possessed* to the use of another. In the early seventeenth century the Court of Chancery came to protect such uses, under the name of trusts; the position is stated in this way: 'Although *cestui que use* of a term of years be not within the Statute of Uses, rather therefore he shall have remedy in Chancery'.[47] In fairness to the draftsman, however, it must be said that it is by no means clear that the termor's lack of seisin was the reason for the decision in 1580, or indeed that every lawyer at that date would have said that a termor lacked seisin (as opposed to seisin of the freehold).[48] Furthermore it was arguable in 1536 that some uses of leasehold were void in any case under the provisions of a statute of 1488.[49] As late as 1593 there was some doubt (quite apart from statute) whether a use of a chattel interest was possible at all.[50]

---

[46] Dyer 369a.

[47] Cary 11, no date.

[48] The conveyance known as bargain and sale with lease and release, discussed above, p. 189, may depend upon the theory that a lessee for years is seised. But Littleton's text is against this view; see sec. 459 and cf. secs. 447 and 460. See below, p. 247.

[49] 3 Hen. VII, c. 4. The statute in terms makes uses of chattels in favour of the settlor void, but it was restrictively interpreted in a case in 1556. See Brooke, *Abridgement, Feffements al Uses*, pl. 60 [amend the text, reading H.7 in place of R.3].

[50] *Sir Francis Inglefield's Case*, 1 And. 293, pl. 302. See also Holdsworth, IV, pp. 463, 465, note 2, 472, and the literature there cited. Much confusion has been caused by the incorrect view that all references to the employment of long terms of years to evade feudal dues necessarily refer to conveyances *limiting uses* on long terms. In fact long terms could be employed for evasion without limitations to uses at all; consider the results on the royal revenues if a tenant in chief alienates to a friend in fee simple and takes back a term of 1,000 years at a peppercorn rent, bearing in mind that terms are devisable. The real reason why uses of terms were not executed by the statute was probably this: if A granted lands to B for a term of 1,000 years to the use of C and his

Quite soon after 1536 another form of use which was not executed was discovered. If a feoffee to uses had active duties to perform, as if lands were conveyed to B to collect the rents and profits and pay them to C, then the use was not executed.[51] The explanation was that the feoffee could not in such a case have conveyed the lands to C without a breach of trust, and the statute only did universally what the feoffee could himself have done privately without breaking trust. These uses did not generally form a large or important class, and represent only a minor fault in the statute. They included, however, uses for charitable purposes, such as the relief of poverty, where there existed no specific beneficiary. These were important.

A third type of use which was not executed was the use limited upon a use; such a use would arise if lands were conveyed to A to the use of B to the use of C. If such a use was limited, the common-law courts treated the second use as 'repugnant' to the first, and by this they meant that it was simply a contradiction of the first use, and could not stand with it. The invalidity of the second use was settled in *Jane Tyrrel's Case*[52] (1557), in conformity with the prevailing view before the statute.[53] Until 1634[54] there is no indication that the second use would be enforced by the Chancellor, so that nobody would deliberately declare a use upon a use in the hopes of getting round the statute by producing a separation of the equitable and legal estate. Where the use on a use arose, it arose by accident. We may say then that it was perhaps a reproach to the draftsman that he

heirs, and the use *was* to be executed, both A and C would hold the fee simple simultaneously, and this theoretically horrible result could not be accepted in 1580. The problem requires elaboration which cannot be attempted here.

[51] Brooke, *Abridgement, Feffements al Uses*, pl. 52 (1545). 'A man makes a feoffment in fee to his own use for term of life, and then, after his death, J. N. is to take the profits. This creates a use in J. N. [i.e. one that will be executed]. It is otherwise if he says that after his death his feoffees are to take the profits and deliver them to J. N. This creates no use in J. N., for he is not to have them except through the hands of the feoffees.' The decision is influenced by the common form definition of a use as 'a liberty to take the profits'. The words used in the statute, read in good faith, cannot be said to support this decision.

[52] Dyer 155a; for discussion see Holdsworth, IV, pp. 469–73.

[53] Brooke, *Abridgement, Feffements al Uses*, pl. 40 (1533). The doctrine was taken to apply to any use upon a use, and not only to express uses in contradiction to uses implied by law—as in *Tyrrel's Case*. There are, however, slight inconsistencies in the application of the doctrine.

[54] *Sambach* v. *Dalston*, Tothill 188, discussed below.

never dealt with uses declared on a term, but that his other two failings were not at once very important, and it is indeed unfair to treat his silence on the use upon a use as a failing at all.[55]

Shifting and Springing Uses

We now turn to his failure to predict the way in which the courts would deal with limitations of uses declared after 1536. Since a limitation to uses now vested a legal estate in the *cestui que use*, it might reasonably have been anticipated that legal estates so created would be governed by exactly the same rules as governed the limitation of legal estates by ordinary common-law conveyances. These rules governing the limitation of legal estates have already been mentioned. One example is the rule that at common law, once a fee simple tenant has alienated his fee simple, he has exhausted his power of alienation; thus a feoffment 'to A and his heirs, but if A marries B, to C and his heirs' confers a fee simple on A but is void as regards C, for having given a fee simple to A the feoffor has nothing left to give. Now before the Statute of Uses there seem to have been no such clear rules governing what could or could not have been done with uses, so that a feoffment of X 'to the use of A and his heirs, but if A marries B to the use of C and his heirs' might well have been accepted as it stood by the Chancellor, and the use (called a shifting use for obvious reasons) enforced exactly as limited. What were the common-law courts after 1536 expected to do with such a limitation? The statute gives no guidance whatsoever, and the only possible explanation for this extraordinary omission must be that the draftsman thought it obvious that, since the *cestui que use* now obtained the legal estate, the rules of the common law would apply; thus the use in favour of A would be executed, but the shifting use in favour of C would be void. But this is not at all what happened, for soon after the statute we find the courts upholding shifting uses, which broke common-law rules. We also find what came to be called springing uses upheld and executed too. Such a springing use arose in this way. At common law it was not permissible to enfeoff B and his heirs *when he becomes 21*, for such a feoffment would cause an abeyance of seisin—a period when

---

[55] Uses of copyhold interests were outside the statute, as the copyholder lacked seisin. This exclusion was no doubt deliberate.

nobody was seised of the lands in question. But probably in equity one could enfeoff X to the use of B at 21, and in the meantime, whilst B was a minor, a use would result to the grantor. After the statute such springing uses were allowed to be good, and the effect of the limitation mentioned would be that the grantor would hold the legal fee simple until B attained the age of 21, and it would then spring up in B or, if you like, shift over to B. Furthermore, devises taking effect under the Statute of Wills were allowed the same freedom from common-law rules, and this freedom was attributed to the words of that statute which allowed devises at the free will and pleasure of the devisor. This extraordinary relaxation of the rules previously governing the limitation of estates naturally led to the continued employment of conveyances which employed the magic words 'to the use of', which had so important an effect in giving a landowner a licence to break the strict common-law rules.[56]

Why, then, did the courts adopt this attitude? There seems to be a plausible explanation, though it cannot be directly based on any reported case. In cases arising soon after the Statute of Uses the courts would be dealing largely with conveyances to uses drawn up before the statute, drawn by conveyancers who relied on the then practice of the Chancellor. As we have seen the courts deliberately minimized the extent to which the statute interfered with private property by suggesting that the vesting of the legal estate in the *cestui que use* would not have been a breach of trust by the feoffee before 1535. To be consistent in this reasoning they had to hold that the legal estate after the statute vested automatically in the same person who, in the view of equity, would have had the use before. Once they took this view in the case of pre-1536 conveyances they could find nothing in the Statute of Uses to indicate that they ought to apply any different rule to post-1536 conveyances to uses. Thus anybody who would have been equitable owner before 1536 must obtain the legal estate after 1536, common-law rules as to the limitation of estates notwithstanding.

---

[56] The earliest example of a shifting use appears to be the case in Brooke, *Abridgement, Feffements al Uses*, pl. 59 (1556). The first instance of a shifting fee is *Hinde* v. *Lyon* (1577), 3 Leon. 64, and the first springing use is in *Mutton's Case* (1568), Dyer 274b, Moo. K. B. 517. See E. G. Henderson, 'Legal Rights to hand in the Early Chancery' 26 Am. J.L.H. 97.

The new-found flexibility in the manipulation of legal estates was not lost on the conveyancers and the landowners who employed them, and the late sixteenth and early seventeenth centuries may justly be called the age of the fantastic conveyance, for if the old common-law rules could be bypassed by using the formula 'to X to the use of . . .', what rules *were* to limit a man's powers of disposition over his land? Could he make it inalienable for ever, or could he make the fee simple in it jump from person to person a hundred years after his death? The chaotic state of the land law on points such as these was all the more lamentable during a period of social upheaval marked by an increase in the prosperity and social status of the lesser landowners, which, in its turn, brought an accompanying desire to 'found families' and ensure that the family estate should not be alienated out of the family in the future. The courts were brought face to face with the fact that the wide powers of disposition which their interpretation of the Statutes of Uses and Wills had conferred upon landowners were being employed for their own destruction.[57] This is the basic problem of perpetuities, and it was not for well over a century after 1536 that a consistent solution of this problem began to emerge.

The Subsequent Fate of the Statute of Uses

The Statute of Uses was primarily a statute designed to prevent the evasions of the feudal revenues, and an integral part of this design was the setting up in 1540 of the Court of Wards and Liveries, to supervise and control the collection of these dues.[58] Economic studies have shown how efficiently the new system worked, and how heavily the archaic burdens of feudalism pressed upon the landowning class as a form of taxation outside regular parliamentary control.[59] In 1612 an attempt was made to abolish these dues and compensate the Crown with other taxes, but this proposal, known as the Great

---

[57] As we shall see (Ch. IX) in the late sixteenth century the idea that limitations to uses should be restrained by the rules governing legal limitations before the statute was revived, notably by Coke, and this idea was temporarily accepted in *Chudleigh's Case* (1595), 1 Co. Rep. 113b.

[58] 32 Hen. VIII, c. 46.

[59] See H. E. Bell, *Court of Wards, passim*; J. Hurstfield, 'The Revival of Feudalism in Tudor England', 37 *History* (*N.S.*) (1952), p. 131, 'The Profits of Fiscal Feudalism 1541–1602', 8 *Econ. Hist. R.* p. 53.

Contract, foundered. In the struggles between Crown and Parliament which led up to the Civil War the existence of the Crown's feudal revenues assisted the King in dispensing with Parliamentary taxes, and hence with the need to summon Parliament at all. When eventually Charles was forced to summon the Long Parliament one of its first acts was a resolution for abolition of the feudal dues, and in 1645 both houses passed resolutions to this effect. These were confirmed by an Act in 1656, which in its turn was confirmed at the Restoration by a new Act, the Tenures Abolition Act of 1660,[60] the Crown was simultaneously compensated for the loss of the feudal revenues. The effect of the Act of 1660, which is extraordinarily ill drawn, was to abolish knight-service and grand serjeanty, and convert these tenures into free and common socage—that is into socage tenure where no services were due and no special customs applied. The statute expressly abolishes all the burdensome incidents of military tenure which mattered in practice, except forfeiture and escheat. The honorary incidents of grand serjeanty were preserved, frankalmoin was not affected at all, and existing socage tenures were largely unaffected.[61] The Act did not in any way affect copyhold tenure. An incidental and important effect of this statute was that land held before in knight-service, of which only two-thirds had previously been devisable, could now all be devised by will. Hence all freehold land came to be devisable by will, apart only from entailed property, it being impossible to bar an entail by will.

The Origin of Trusts

In effect, therefore, from 1645 onwards the only free tenure of any importance which remained was socage, and the preservation of the feudal revenues had ceased to be of any importance. The economic purpose of the Statute of Uses had disappeared. This was bound to have an effect upon its treatment by the courts. Very probably it accelerated the rise of the passive trust, which is the most notable of all the evasions of that ill-used statute. By about 1700 it had become possible to create trusts

---

[60] 12 Car. II c. 24; for the text see Digby, *Real Property*, p. 396, and Ch. IX for an account of the legislative history of the statute.

[61] The effect of the statute on petit serjeanty is uncertain, though practically unimportant.

which apparently differed only in name from uses, but which were not executed by the statute. Such trusts were enforced in Chancery just as uses had been before 1536, so that the separation of legal and equitable ownership was again possible. Such trusts were created by a conveyance 'to A, unto and to the use of A, in trust for B', and by adopting this simple variant on the formula 'to A to the use of B' a conveyancer was allowed to create equitable estates just as he had been before the statute.

The history of the steps by which trusts came to be recognized forms an intriguing but still somewhat obscure chapter of legal history.[62] As we have seen, not all uses were executed by the statute. Uses declared on a term of years were not, and were well known in the sixteenth century, but some Chancellors were not prepared to enforce them; they regarded them as fraudulent evasions of the Statute of Uses, since such uses were created to deprive the Crown of revenue. With the disappearance of the feudal revenues it was natural that such uses came to be enforceable in Chancery, and they came to be known as 'trusts' to distinguish them from uses which could be executed by the Statute of Uses. No doubt the existence of such trusts, created by a conveyance of a term of years 'to A to the use of B', or 'in trust for B' had something to do with the revival of trusts of freehold, but no very direct connection has ever been shown. It must, however, have occurred to lawyers that there was no very sensible distinction between allowing A to convey a term of 1000 years to B, to be held on a passive trust for C, and allowing A to do the same with a fee simple, whatever the technical distinctions between the two situations may be; the one institution may well have pointed the way to the other. Certainly it is only such trusts created on terms of years which can be said to have anything like a continuous history from the time of the Statute of Uses: after 1660 they became a common feature of conveyancing.

Trusts of freehold have a lesser-known history. We have seen how the common-law judges refused to execute active uses, where the feoffees were given duties to perform which went beyond the mere passive duty of allowing the *cestui que use* to

[62] See J. L. Barton, 'The Statute of Uses and the Trust of Freeholds', 82 *L.Q.R.* 215, 'The Use upon a Use in Equity 1558–1625' (1977), 93 *L.Q.R.* 33, Milsom, *Historical Foundations*, pp. 233–9.

take the profits. One form of active trust would arise when land
was conveyed to A and his heirs with a direction to convey it to
B and his heirs.[63] Though but rarely met with, such active
trusts to convey seem to have been readily enforceable in
Chancery, particularly if the direction was actuated with a
charitable motive.[64] In such cases the consequence of enforcement was that precisely the same result was achieved as if there
had been a normal conveyance 'to the use of B', for in either
case B obtained the legal estate. There would therefore be no
purpose in a conveyancer deliberately attempting to evade the
statute by imposing a trust to convey. Another form of active
trust arose when land was conveyed to trustees to collect the
rents and profits, and use them for the payment of debts. Such
trusts were charitable, in that the payment of debts was
beneficial to the debtor's soul, and in the late sixteenth century
trusts of this sort were enforceable in Chancery.[65] Thus by the
early seventeenth century the Chancery would be familiar at
least with these two forms of trusts as well as with charitable
purpose trusts, which lacked a beneficiary with capacity to take.

One other sort of use or trust was not executed by the statute
—the use upon a use. Until the eighteenth century no conveyancer ever deliberately conveyed land to A to the use of B to the
use of C, except perhaps when the second use was secret. But
this might be the accidental effect of what he did. Since the
statute a bargain and sale passed a legal estate, and had the
effect of a feoffment. Ignorant conveyancers sometimes forgot
the reason why this was so, and treated it as an equivalent of a
feoffment. Thus in *Jane Tyrrel's Case* in 1557[66] Jane Tyrrel
bargained and sold lands to her son in fee simple to her own use
for life, with remainders over. When analysed, the situation
now was that Jane was seised to the use of her son to the use of
herself, and so she, or her conveyancer, had limited a use on a

---

[63] Such a gift could be construed as a common-law feoffment upon condition, so
that if the condition was not fulfilled the feoffor or his heir might enter. But B had
no remedy, for a right of re-entry could not at common law be reserved in favour
of a stranger. For an early attempt at enforcement see *Young* v. *Leigh* (1577-8), Cary,
67.

[64] *Sir Moyle Finch's Case* (1600), Coke, 4th Institute 85-6, *Forde* v. *Hoskins* (1615), 2
Bulstrode, 337.

[65] Holdsworth, IV, 438.

[66] Dyer, 115a, I And., 313.

use.[67] The common-law courts would not execute the second use, but said it was a mere contradiction of the first,[68] and the Chancellor would not protect it in equity; no doubt he realized that if he did so, such second uses would before long be deliberately created. But this attitude on the part of Chancery was hard and unsympathetic, for everybody knew that the use on a use had only arisen through a mistake, and in *Sambach* v. *Dalston* (1634),[69] where a similar slip was made, we find the first instance of equity intervening. But this intervention did not take the form of a holding that whilst the first *cestui que use* had the legal title yet he must hold the legal estate in trust for the second *cestui que use*. The Chancellor simply ordered that the legal estate be conveyed to the second *cestui que use*. This amounts to saying that since the Statute of Uses fails to execute the second use, yet, since it was unconscionable not to execute it, equity would insist upon its execution by private conveyance. The decision in *Sambach* v. *Dalston* did not therefore open any doors to deliberate evasion of the statute's design to end the separation of legal and equitable ownership. Even earlier than this, back in Elizabeth's time, there is some evidence for the enforcement of passive secret trusts, when good

[67] But *quaere* whether this analysis was the only possible one. If A bargained and sold lands to B an implied use in favour of B arose by operation of law, and was executed by the statute. Some conveyancers may have thought, quite reasonably, that the implied use might be rebutted by an express statement that the lands were to be held to the use of some other person—for example to the use of A for life, remainder to the use of B and his heirs. But this view was rejected by the courts.

[68] More mysterious explanations are given by some; common-lawyers have always been tempted to let metaphors rule their thinking; Thus Saunders C.J. in *Tyrrel's Case* (see Dyer 155a) says that 'a use cannot be engendered of a use'. Cf. too the doctrine that a use could only be limited on a fee simple, and not for example on a fee tail or life estate, because the existence of a tenure between the grantor and grantee in such cases implied a use in favour of the grantee, and any limitation of further uses was merely contradictory. See Y.B. 27 Hen. VIII Pasch., pl. 22, at f. 10 where Mountague C.J. notes a recent decision (i.e. *c.* 1530) that a use could not be limited on an entail. This doctrine may have caused the draftsman of the Statute of Uses to believe that a use could not be limited on a term of years, *sed quaere*.

[69] Reported briefly in Tothill at p. 188. The correct title to the case is *Sambach* v. *Daston*, but it is convenient to retain the traditional title. A fuller report has been identified in Nelson 30 under the name *Morris, Lambeth et Margery ux.* v. *Darston*; see J. E. Strathdene, 'Sambach v. Dalston; an Unnoticed Report', 74 *L.Q.R.* 550. See also D. E. C. Yale, 'The Revival of Equitable Estates in the Seventeenth Century', [1957] *Camb. L.J.* 72. The account given in the text is deliberately simplified; the case did not involve a bargain and sale.

conscience appeared to require this.[70] But the evidence for general enforcement is weak.[71]

After the Statute of Tenures the next step was taken. In *Ash* v. *Gallen* in 1668[72] there was another blunder. The parties to a conveyance had intended to convey by feoffment to uses, but the conveyance had been mismanaged and there had been a bargain and sale to uses; thus inadvertently but incompetently they had limited a use upon a use. It was suggested that the second use could be enforced as a trust, and in the context this seems to envisage the first *cestui que use* holding in trust for the second, rather than actually conveying the land. The case was compromised without a decision. About this time, however, it is clear from a number of sources of information that the second use would be so enforced in Chancery, probably by an order to convey. Equity dispensed with the need for the conveyance, which at first had been insisted upon, around 1700.[73] In the late seventeenth century equity was developing too a doctrine of implied trusts, where good conscience led to the conclusion that the wrong person had come into the legal title to lands. One situation of this sort arose where A had bargained and sold lands to B, but C had provided the purchase money. At law A held to the use of B, and the Statute of Uses passed the legal estate to B. Equity, however, held that B held in trust for C by implication.[74] The trust in favour of C, even if it had been recognized at law, would be a use upon a use, but in equity it was enforceable as a trust. Again the Chancellor could have ordered a conveyance to C, but instead he preferred to protect the *cestui que trust*, who obtained his interest under the doctrines of equity, by purely equitable means. By the close of the century it was recognized that a use upon a use deliberately created would be enforced as a trust, as '. . . where lands are limited to

---

[70] See note 69 above.

[71] See Barton in 93 *L.Q.R.* 33, instancing a case in 1560.

[72] 1 Ch. Cases 114.

[73] See *The King* v. *Holland* (1671), Aleyn 15, Style 40; Hist. MSS. Commission, 7th Report, App. Pt. i, 3, No. 16 (1670)—'the trust is now the same that uses were before'; *Sympson* v. *Turner* (1700), 1 Eq. Cas. Ab. 383, *Daw* v. *Newborough* (1715), Comyns 242. The rule is stated by Lord Nottingham in *Grubb* v. *Gwillim* (1676) thus: 'If an use be limited upon an use, though the second use be not good in law nor executed by statute, it amounts to a declaration of trust and may be executed in Chancery', Selden Society, Vol. 73, p. 347.

[74] E.g. *Anon* (1683), 2 Vent. 31.

the use of A in trust to permit B to receive the rents and profits'.[75] But uses upon uses deliberately created in this way were rarely met with in practice; the only passive trusts to be deliberately created at all commonly were trusts limited on a term of years, not trusts of freeholds.

With the growing recognition of trusts some terminological confusion was cleared up. In 1536 the terms 'trust' and 'use' were interchangeable.[76] It became the practice in the seventeenth century to employ the term 'use' solely for uses executed by the statute. The term 'trust' became appropriated for interests protected in equity only. Thus it became proper to speak of a conveyance of a term of years 'to A in trust for B', and of a conveyance 'to A to the use of B in trust for C'. This terminological usage must not be allowed to obscure the fact that the trust concept and the use concept were basically the same, nor that the trust is nothing else but the old use, slightly modified, in a new guise.[77]

In the eighteenth century trusts of freehold became more common, and a new formula was devised for their limitation. Instead of a conveyance 'to A to the use of B upon trust to allow C to take the rents and profits', A was removed from the picture by conveying 'to B unto and to the use of B in trust for C'.[78] From what has been said about the identity of the trust and the use it may be wondered why such a limitation did not give C a use which would be executed by the statute, so that he would obtain the legal and not the equitable estate. In substance, though not in form, this limitation looks just the same as one 'to B to the use of C'. But this was not the way the courts construed such a limitation. At common law the better view

[75] *Sympson* v. *Turner* (1700), 1 Eg. Cas. Ab. 383.

[76] Thus the Statute of Uses speaks of persons being seised 'to the use, confidence, or trust of any other person'. For an early suggestion that trusts and uses were separable, see *Sir Francis Inglefield's Case* (1593), 1 And. 293, pl. 302.

[77] For Lord Nottingham's argument that the trust and the use differed intrinsically, see Yale, *op. cit.* The argument, though ingenious, can hardly be supported; like all great lawyers, Lord Nottingham was sometimes compelled to rewrite a little history.

[78] Hence Lord Hardwicke's statement that 'by this means a Statute made upon great consideration, introduced in a solemn and pompous manner, by this strict construction, has had no other effect than to add at most three words to a conveyance'. (*Hopkins* v. *Hopkins* (1738), 1 Atk. 581 at p. 591). The remark, though famous, is mere bombast. For a slightly different account of the matter see Hargreaves, *Introduction*, p. 99.

was that if A conveyed land to B and his heirs unto and to the use of B and his heirs, B took a fee simple by the common law, and not under the provisions of the Statute of Uses. The use in his favour was not executed, and the only point of saying 'unto and to the use of B and his heirs' was perhaps to make it clear that B was not to hold to the use of the grantor A, by way of resulting use. In such a grant 'the use and the estate go together', and this was decided in *Meredith* v. *Joans* (1631).[79] Bacon, in his *Reading* on the statute had been of the same opinion.[80] Later in the seventeenth century the effect of a grant 'to B, unto and to the use of B, in trust for C' came to be considered by the common-law courts. To Chief Justice Hale it seemed unimportant to decide in such a case whether B took a common law (e.g. by force of the words 'to B') or under the Statute of Uses (e.g. because he was *cestui que use* by force of the words 'unto and to the use of B', the statute executing the use). What he was quite certain of was that the trust in favour of C was a use upon a use, and could not be executed at common law. He put the matter thus, 'whether feoffees take by the common law or by the Statute yet where the Use is once disposed of to them and their heirs (whether the Statute executes it or not) there cannot be a use upon a use nor a trust upon such a use to be executed by the Statute'.[81] Hale's idea was simply that however the matter was looked at the use or trust in favour of C was a second use, and could not be executed by the statute; it was a use upon a use within the rule in *Tyrrel's Case* even if the first use was not one which the statute executed. Later opinion vacillated over the first use. Holt C.J. thought it was not executed by the statute, but agreed with Hale that the second use was a use upon a use.[82] Lord Talbot, giving the first reported Chancery decision on the subject in 1723, seems to have thought it was executed, but again agreed that the second use was a use upon

---

79 Cro. Car. 244.

80 Bacon, *Uses*, 439, 440: the point was not of purely theoretical interest, as Bacon says, 'Now let me advise you of this, that it is not a matter of subtlety or conceit to take the law right, when a man cometh in by the law in course of possession, or when he cometh in by the Statute in course of use', and he gives reasons at p. 441. Cf. p. 425, and see 2 And. 136 and Moo. K. B. 45.

81 *Tipping* v. *Cosins* (1695), Comb. 313, citing *Pybus* v. *Mitford*.

82 *Tipping* v. *Cosins* (1695), Comb. 313.

a use, and therefore only enforceable as a trust in Chancery.[83] The final received doctrine was that enunciated by Holt C.J., but the vacillations over the first use did not affect the view taken of the second, which, as Hale had stated, was not recognized by the common-law courts and therefore was only enforceable as a trust in Chancery. Thus it became usual to create trust estates by the form 'to trustees and their heirs, unto and to the use of the trustees and their heirs, in trust for C'. As late as 1827, however, an attempt to attack the validity of this form of limitation was made, but by then its general use made it impossible for the courts to do anything but uphold it.[84]

The general recognition of trusts was followed by the intricate process of working out the details of the system of equitable ownership. In essence the new trust was the old use in a new guise, but the Chancery did not follow precisely their ancient model. In part this was perhaps the consequence of the dearth of information on the incidents of estates in use before the Statute of Uses; in part it happened because the rule that equity follows the law led to different results now that the common law had become so different from the old common law which had served as a model for the late medieval Chancellors. From the late sixteenth century too the Chancery developed trusts for a wife's 'sole and separate use', giving married women of property a new independence.[85] Thus there came to be important differences between the old equitable ownership of the use and the new equitable ownership of the trust. Trusts were not so restricted in their enforceability; they would bind not only those who came to the property *in the per* but also those who came *in the post*. The trust bound the land into whosoever's hands it came, excepting only the purchaser for value without notice, so that even a squatter could be bound. Trusts could arise although no personal confidence had ever been reposed by one person in another, an impossibility with the use. In general, the Chancellors modelled the incidents of equitable ownership upon the common law; thus, for example, the equitable interest could be split up into analogous estates, requiring the same words of limitation for their creation. An

[83] *A.-G.* v. *Scott*, Cases Temp. Talbot 138.
[84] *Doe* v. *Passingham*, 6 B. and C. 316.
[85] *Sanky* v. *Golding* (1579) Cary 87.

equitable fee tail could be barred by an equitable recovery, and could be fashioned according to the common-law variations. But at the same time the Chancellors refused to copy the more unjust and indefensible doctrines of the common law; for example, no conveyance of an equitable interest could have a tortious operation. Here there was nothing to recommend the common-law rule, which offended against the same principle *nemo dat quod non habet*; it was in fact an archaic survival of the pre-eminence attached to seisin in the medieval law. The Chancellors refused to perpetuate this archaism in the new field of trust estates.[86] But the basic distinction between legal and equitable ownership, resting upon the doctrine of purchaser for value without notice, in its essentials dates from Henry VIII's time, as we have seen.

[86] Generally see Holdsworth, V, p. 304, VI, pp. 640-4.

IX

Future Interests, Perpetuities, and the Family Settlement

THE term 'perpetuity' has been applied at various times in the history of the law to refer to various arrangements made by conveyancers to enable landowners to restrict the power of free alienation of land, by imposing upon that land forms of settlement which made it impossible for their successors in title (usually their children) to deal with it as freely as they themselves had been able to do. Such attempts can be viewed as an abuse of the power of free alienation, for a settlor who makes such an attempt is using the freedom which the law gives him to deprive others of the same freedom; in consequence at most periods of English legal history the courts have set limits upon the degree to which landowners should be permitted to impose such restrictions. Indeed some writers have claimed that the common law has had a bias, whatever that means, in favour of freedom of alienation.

But there are ups and downs in the history of legal thought upon the matter which are extremely difficult to explain in sociological terms—for example, in terms of a struggle between an entrenched hereditary landed class and a mercantile class eager to see land on the market so that they might become 'squires by purchase'. In a fairly fluid society in which there always seems to have been land for sale such an analysis into 'haves' and 'have-nots' fails to convince, for people move too rapidly from one category into another. Thus a young lawyer could work his way up the profession from relatively humble origins and amass an enormous fortune; this he would wish to put into land, and indeed many an English landed family goes back to a successful Inns of Court man. Such a man's attitude to the alienability of land is likely, however, to be inconsistent. Naturally enough he wants there to be land on the market to purchase, but at the same time he wants to entrench his family by making sure that the land he has purchased will remain within the family in the future, and not be sold. At no point in his active career will he find himself wholly for or against free alienability of land. The lawyers and judges who moulded the more modern rules upon perpetuities in the period between 1450 and 1700 were themselves great purchasers and settlors of land; it could thus be that the rules worked out in the courts represent an attempt to balance the conflicting desires of their authors, and produce a body of law which indulged to some extent both the desire for an active land market and the desire to retain land in the family. We may therefore see the law as expressing a compromise between conflicting pressures, and one worked out in a society in which the dynastic ambitions of the propertied were viewed sympathetically. Many settlements of property were created on the occasion of a marriage between dynastic families, and here what was needed was compromise between the interests of the families concerned. Given the legal subservience of women, the bride's family required of property law some security both for their daughter and for her children and grandchildren. This could only be achieved if the husband's property rights over the family land were in some degree restricted, so that the landed endowment of the family would pass down to the next generation. Indeed the whole history of settlements can only be made intelligible if we remember that although the family as such was not treated as a legal entity by the common law, which dealt only in individual property rights, landed society did nevertheless view property as ultimately belonging to the family in some moral sense, and the legal system reflected this.

Unbarrable Entails

The problem is first met in connection with the entailed estate, for the statute *De Donis*, as interpreted by the courts, enabled a landowner to settle land in such a way that it would be for ever inalienable, so long only as the issue of the tenant in tail continued. By limiting remainders after the first limitation in tail, so that even if the issue of the first tenant in tail died out the land would pass inexorably to a remainderman in tail, and thus continue to be inalienable, a settlor could impose his will upon the land for generations after his death. To what extent the perpetual entail ever in fact became a problem we do not at present know. But the evils of allowing one man to impose his will permanently over the devolution of the family endowment seem to have been soon recognized.[1] In the absence of legislative intervention,[2] the courts evolved means of barring entails, and eventually the common recovery afforded a convenient way of doing this which superseded the complications and uncertainties involved in the use of collateral warranties and other devices. As we have seen, the common recovery was established in the 1470s. But this was not the end of the matter, for conveyancers at once began to search for some device which would prevent the barring of entails, and inserted into settlements clauses designed to prevent the use of recoveries or warranties to break settlements. An early example comes from a case in 1495. 'Land was given in tail, remainder in fee, on condition that if the donee or his heirs alienated to the damage of the issue, the donor and his heirs might re-enter. And the opinion of the court was that the condition was good.'[3]

The reason given was that the condition was in accordance with the general law, for statute forbade the tenant in tail to alienate; a similar condition in general restraint of alienation attached to a fee simple was thought to be bad, for the converse reason.[4] Such clauses of perpetuity were developed in the sixteenth century with the hope of securing two results. One was to prevent any act by a tenant in tail which was substantially, though not in name, an alienation, notably the suffering of a common recovery; the other was to allow the remainderman to enter if such an alienation was attempted, rather than to allow the donor to have the land back. This could not be done by the

---

[1] A recurrent feature of the complaints against the entail is that it deprives a father of parental control over his children; thus Bacon (*Use of the Law*, p. 490) says, '. . . the land being so sure tied upon the heir of his father could not put it from him, it made the son to be disobedient, negligent, and wasteful, often marrying without the father's consent, and to grow insolent in vice knowing there could be no check of disinherison over him'.

[2] Legislation reduced the other inconveniences of entails; for example, they became forfeitable for treason in 1534 by 26 Hen. VIII, c. 13, and certain leases were made binding on the heir in tail in 1541 by 32 Hen. VIII, c. 28; all legislative interference is post-medieval. For a discussion of the entail in relation to conscience see St. Germain, *Doctor and Student*, I, Chs. XXVI to XXXII. See also J. H. Baker, Selden Society, Vol. 94, pp. 208–9.

[3] Y.B. 10 Hen. VII Mich., pl. 28, f. 11; cf. 13 Hen. VII Pasch., pl. 9, f. 22.

[4] See also Littleton, *Tenures*, sec. 360.

reservation of a power of re-entry, for such a power could only be reserved in favour of the donor and his heirs; the medieval lawyers saw that such a power reserved in favour of a stranger would in effect amount to the limitation in his favour of a contingent remainder which would operate by cutting short the preceding estate.[5] In their final form clauses of perpetuity used to be included in settlements in which estates tail were limited to the settlor's eldest son, with remainders to his younger sons, and the clause would provide that if the eldest son did, or began to do, any act whatsoever which would, if completed, have the effect of barring his entail, then his estate would at once cease as if he were dead without issue, thus enabling the younger son to enter as remainderman; similar clauses would restrain the other sons.[6] The validity of such clauses, with their variants, was tested in a series of cases at the end of the sixteenth century, and they were held invalid.[7] The reasoning which tended to this view is much too complicated to reproduce here, but behind it all lies the acceptance of the basic principle that an entailed estate was to be regarded as an estate which carried with it an inherent liability of being barred, and that any device which tended to prevent its being barred was *ipso facto* bad. This has remained a root principle of the doctrine of estates thereafter.[8]

[5] See Littleton, sec. 720–3, for a discussion of the attempt of Rickhill (a Justice of the Common Pleas 1389–1407) to create a perpetuity; this took the form of a gift to the settlor's sons successively in tail, with a proviso that if the eldest son should alienate in fee simple his estate should determine and the next son enter. Other devices used contractual forms; the tenant in tail might enter into a covenant not to bar, or oblige himself by penal bond.

[6] But it is to be noted, that since these notable remedies provided by the statute [i.e. the Tudor Statutes of Fines, 4 Hen. VII, c. 24 and 28 Hen. VIII, c. 36] there is started up a device called a perpetuity; which is an entail with an addition of a proviso conditional, tied to the estate, not to put away the land from the next heir; and if he do, to forfeit his own estate.' Bacon, *Use of the Law*, p. 491. There were other devices too; see *Hunt* v. *Gateley* (1581), 1 Co. Rep. 61b, *Wiseman's Case* (1585), 2 Co. Rep. 10a.

[7] *Corbet's Case* (1599), 1 Co. Rep. 83b, *Mildmay's Case* (1606), 6 Co. Rep. 40a, *Mary Portington's Case* (1614), 10 Co. Rep. 35b. *Corbet's Case* was fictitious, though the judges who determined it were ignorant of this; Coke suppressed this fact, though he must have known it. *Portington's Case* reversed *Scholastica's Case* (1572), Plowden 408, and *Rudhall* v. *Milwards* (1586), Moo. K. B. 212; the decision was a naked piece of judicial legislation.

[8] See generally P. Bordwell, 'Alienability and Perpetuities, III', 24 *Iowa L.R.* 1, at pp. 59 *et seq.*

A settlor who confined his activities to a manipulation of the common-law estates—basically the fee simple, the fee tail, and the life estate—and who confined himself to vesting these estates in persons from the moment when the settlement took effect, and did not experiment with postponed vesting (which would involve the use of contingent remainders), could tie land up for a considerable period of time, but within very definite limits. Thus the father of a family could contrive to make himself life tenant, and his elder son life tenant in remainder, with a remainder in tail to a living grandson, but once he died his son and grandson, if of age, could join in suffering a common recovery and the settlement could be broken. If the son was unwilling to break the settlement the grandson would be able to do so once he became tenant in tail in possession, and could bar the entail on his own; this would of course mean that the settlement remained unbroken for a period which might be as long as half a century. In real life there would be powerful family pressures involved in addition to legal controls, and, one suspects, they may have been in practice more significant.

Contingent Remainders

As we have seen, the medieval lawyers were very chary of admitting the validity of contingent remainders, and in the end were only prepared to accept a limitation to the heirs of a living person provided that the living person died before the precedent estate determined. Such remainders might have helped our settlor had it not been for the rule in *Shelley's Case*. Thus he might settle land on his son for life, remainder to the heirs male of his son, in the hope of preventing his son joining with a grandson to break the settlement, but the effect of the rule was that under such a limitation the son became a tenant in tail in possession at once, and could at once disentail. It is indeed a good exercise for a student of the history of real property to try to contrive a perpetuity under the rules of the medieval law[9]; he will find that he cannot do so. In the sixteenth century the courts began to allow contingent remainders which depended upon other contingencies than the death of a living person; the

---

[9] In a sense a medieval entail was a 'perpetuity', and to this extent the statement in the text needs qualification; however, there were as we have seen devices for breaking entails.

case which settled this was *Colthirst* v. *Bejushin* in 1550.[10] Soon after, they enunciated a number of rules which severely limited the usefulness of contingent remainders to settlors wishing to tie up lands for long periods.[11] Technically the decision holds that a provision which makes an interest (which purports to be a remainder) commence upon a contingent event is to be construed not as a *condition* cutting short the precedent estate and allowing an entry for condition broken, but as a *limitation*, specifying the time when the interest should vest by way of remainder. If construed as a *condition* giving a right of entry, such a provision would have run into the rule that only the donor or his heirs could enter for breach of condition. But to call such a proviso a *limitation* was strange, for in an obvious sense it does not delimit *what* is granted, but indicates *when* what is granted vests. The decision was probably influenced by the doctrines applied to springing uses.

These rules were as follows:

(*a*) The limitation of a remainder must be preceded by a limitation of a vested estate of freehold. This is another way of saying that the settlor cannot execute a conveyance which leaves nobody seised of the land at all. Thus he could settle land on A for life, remainder to B (aged 10, say, at the time of the settlement) in tail at 21, for the seisin passed to A, but he could not alienate to B at 21 *simpliciter*, for then there would be nobody seised at all until B came of age. This rule follows from the general principle that no conveyance is valid if it must create an abeyance of seisin.

(*b*) A contingent remainder must not operate so as to cut short a precedent estate. Thus a gift to A for life, but if A ceases to reside in the manor house at Dale to B for life, is bad. This follows from two principles. The first is the ancient rule that a man may not derogate from his grant. Having granted an estate for life to A the settlor cannot take it back by making it possible for A's life estate to last a shorter period than his life, by being cut short. The second is the rule that it is impossible

---

[10] Plowden 21. Perhaps this view was taken earlier, in 1535. See Y.B. 27 Hen. VIII Mich., pl. 2, f. 24, and the information added to the year book report by Mountague C.J. in Plowden at p. 34.

[11] Notably in *Archer's Case* (1597), 1 Co. Rep. 63b, and *Chudleigh's Case* (1595), 1 Co. Rep. 120a.

for a grantor to reserve a right of entry in favour of a stranger, and this is substantially what he has tried to do.

(*c*) Once he has parted with the fee simple a grantor has nothing left to grant, for he has exhausted the whole *quantum* of his interest. Thus if A grants a fee simple to his son, he cannot go on to limit a remainder in fee to another son if the son ceases to reside in the manor house at Dale.

These rules governed the limitation of contingent remainders, and if they were infringed the limitation was void *ab initio*. Deductions from them had a more serious effect, by making it possible for contingent remainders to be destroyed *ex post facto*.

Of the rules governing the destructibility of remainders we may notice the two most important. They were:

(*a*) The remainder must vest before the precedent estate determined, so that there was no abeyance of seisin. Thus in a grant to A for life, remainder in tail to B at 21, if it happened that B failed to attain his majority by the time A died the remainder failed.

(*b*) A contingent remainder was said to depend upon the precedent estate of freehold, which was essential to its validity. If this estate was destroyed, then the contingent remainder would be destroyed too. Such destruction could occur accidentally in a number of ways which are explained in any modern textbook, but what is important is that destruction could be deliberately engineered.

The combination of these rules limited the usefulness of contingent remainders very severely. Thus a father might settle Blackacre on his son John for life, remainder in tail to his grandson James at 30. Until the remainder in tail vested in James the settlement was to some extent protected, for since James had no entail he could do nothing to bar it. But the risks were patent. If John died before James became 30, then the settlement would fail utterly. Furthermore, when the father dies, his son John, if he is the eldest son, will inherit the reversion in fee simple; this will merge with the life tenancy and the contingent remainder will be destroyed with the disappearance of the precedent life estate on which it depends. The possibilities mentioned are only illustrative of some of the ways in which by accident or design the simple settlement chosen could fail. Contingent remainders therefore provided a very speculative device for tying up land, and so long as the courts were prepared to resist any relaxation of the rules which governed their creation and destructibility there was no great danger that they could be employed to create unbreakable settlements.

The Perpetual Freehold

The most extreme example of an attempt to keep within the contingent remainder rules and nevertheless maintain land in a permanently inalienable state is represented by the form of limitation known as the perpetual freehold, which was attempted by a number of conveyancers in the late sixteenth century. This took the form of a limitation 'to A for life, remainder to his son for life, remainder to that son's son for life' and so on *ad infinitum*. Such limitations do not in their inception obviously break the rules governing the limitation of contingent remainders, but if upheld would establish what would be in effect an unbarrable entail.[12] In *Lovelace* v. *Lovelace* (1585)[13] it was held that all the remainders must vest before the determination of the first life interest, or fail, for this was the estate upon which they depended, and this effectively dealt with the problem. In the course of time a variety of other explanations were found for the invalidity of limitations of perpetual freeholds. One is the general principle that anything which amounted to the limitation of an unbarrable entail was bad, but this rule was not recognized until the decision in *Mary Portington's Case* in 1614. Another is the shortlived rule against 'double possibilities', which is that a contingent remainder must not depend on more than one contingency.[14] But these formulations all come into the law after the crucial decision in *Lovelace* v. *Lovelace*, which was based upon a rigorous application of the rule that all contingent remainders must vest in good time—that is, before the determination (or *eo instanti* with the determination) of the particular vested estate upon which they depend.

---

[12] See *Perrot's Case* (1594), Moo. K. B. 368, and cf. *Manning and Andrew's Case* (1576), 1 Leon. 256.

[13] Cited in *Perrot's Case* at p. 371 from Justice Windham's M.S. reports; the same point was decided in *Haddon's Case* (1586 for 1576), unreported.

[14] The *Rector of Chedington's Case* (1598), 1 Co. Rep. 148b; the connection between this supposed rule and the rule restated in *Whitby* v. *Mitchell* is wholly fanciful.

The Rule in Whitby v. *Mitchell*

From the decision in *Lovelace* v. *Lovelace* can be traced in a confused way the rule in *Whitby* v. *Mitchell*[15]—that after a limitation for life to an unborn person any further limitation to his issue is bad *ab initio*. Soon after 1585 the courts, in a different context, accepted the general principle that any limitation which tended to set up an unbarrable entail was void; this position was reached, as we have seen, by 1614. The earlier cases which had struck at limitations of perpetual freeholds could now be viewed as particular applications of this general principle, rather than as applications of the technical rule that contingent remainder must vest in good time. If they were so regarded, then limitations of perpetual freeholds were not simply futile upon the practical ground that the string of life estates could not in fact vest in due time, but rather void *ab initio*, because of their tendency to produce a perpetuity. In the seventeenth, eighteenth, and nineteenth centuries conveyancers were aware of the fact that perpetual freeholds were useless to attempt, but the theory of their fragility became confused. Cases are few and far between.[16] Courts confronted with limitations of perpetual freeholds struck down such limitations consistently enough, and seem to have taken the view that such limitations were void *ab initio*, but their reasons for doing so are inconsistent; sometimes there is talk of a wide general principle against perpetuities, and sometimes there is talk of a rule against double or remote possibilities. What is wholly forgotten is the original basis for the futility of attempts to create perpetual freeholds—the ordinary 'wait and see' principle that a contingent remainder must vest in good time, which made such limitations precarious but not invalid.[17] To some extent

---

[15] (1890) 44 Ch.D. 85. The basis of the decision, according to Cotton and Lindley L.JJ. was the 'rule against double possibilities', though Lindley L.J. confesses himself unable to understand the theoretical justification for this 'rule'. Lopes L.J. suggested that the rule upon which the decision was based had a 'feudal' origin, but goes no farther. The case has provoked an extensive literature; see in particular Holdsworth, VII, p. 209, C. Sweet, 'The Rule in Whitby v. Mitchell', 25 *L.Q.R.* 385, P. Bordwell, 'Alienability and Perpetuities', IV, 25 *Iowa L.R.* 1, Morris and Leach, *Perpetuities*, Ch. 10.

[16] See *Humbertson* v. *Humbertson* (1716), 1 P. Wms. 332, *Duke of Marlborough* v. *Godolphin* (1759), 1 Eden 404, *Mainwaring* v. *Baxter* (1800), 5 Ves. 458.

[17] Such limitations were futile, but not invalid *ab initio*. Consider a limitation to A for life, remainder to his heir male for life, and so on *ad infinitum*. Such a limitation is

this forgetfulness may have been encouraged by the blurring of the distinction between contingent and vested remainders in the decision in *Dormer* v. *Packhurst* in 1740, and to some extent it may have been encouraged by the development of the modern rule against perpetuities, which rejected a 'wait and see' approach.

In *Whitby* v. *Mitchell* the court was confronted with an apparently guileless and innocuous limitation;[18] nobody could have suggested that the settlor had intended to create a perpetuity or a perpetual freehold as the sixteenth-century lawyers understood the concept. The court was faced with what it conceived to be a borderline case, and had to enunciate a clear rule; it could not talk generally about unbarrable entails, or perpetual freeholds, for it had to decide precisely how far a settlor could go, or, to put it another way, the court had to say what precisely counted as an unbarrable entail or perpetual freehold. The ruling we know as the rule in *Whitby* v. *Mitchell* is the result. Frankly bemused by the history of the matter the court gave a ruling quite divorced from the normal contingent remainders rule of timely vesting; the connection was quite forgotten. This had important consequences. The court conceived itself to be enunciating an independent, arbitrary, technical rule of law: a dogma with a life of its own but no purpose. Thus the statutory modifications of the common-law rules governing legal contingent remainders are never mentioned; had they been thought to be relevant the decision would have been different, for by 1890 a contingent remainder did not have to vest in good time; this was the broad effect of the Contingent Remainders Act (1877). Furthermore, the rule in *Whitby* v. *Mitchell* allowed no 'wait and see'; a limitation which infringed the rule was void *ab initio*. Once firmly established, so anomalous a rule had to be abolished by statute at the first opportunity.[19]

---

absurdly risky, for only the lineal heirs born in the lifetime of A can take, for only their estates will vest in time. In practice A's son and grandson may qualify, but there is no practical chance that A's lineal heirs *ad infinitum* will do so.

[18] In effect, to H and W for life successively, remainder to their unborn child for life, remainder in fee simple to the children of the unborn child. The last limitation, made in exercise of a special power of appointment, was such that the children were bound to be ascertained within the lifetime of H and W: thus it did not infringe the rule against perpetuities. The facts, which are complex, are more fully stated in the report in 42 Ch.D. at 494; see Morris and Leach, *The Rule against Perpetuities*, p. 256.

[19] Law of Property Act (1925), s. 161.

Chudleigh's Case *and Executory Interests*

Such then were the rules of the common law, and they effectively prevented settlors from creating settlements which would
fetter the free alienation of land for excessively lengthy periods.
But, as we have seen, the courts in construing the Statute of
Uses did not require estates limited by way of use to conform to
these rules. The position of uses in tail before the statute was
passed was highly controversial and unsettled; some thought
such uses unbarrable, others impossible. So far as successive
interests were concerned the normal common-law rules seem
not to have been applied at all. Thus a settlor by employing the
machinery of the statute could make even a fee simple pass
from one person to another, and there seemed to be no limit to
the remote future date at which this might happen. Unless
some check was put upon the powers thus conferred on settlors
it would be possible to subject the free alienation of land to
restrictions lasting indefinitely, so that there never was a
beneficiary who was able to do as he liked with the land.
Towards the end of Elizabeth I's reign the courts reacted to a
fear of the possibilities of such extravagant settlements. In
Chudleigh's Case (1595)[20] they reversed the legal development of
the previous half-century by holding that the intention of the
legislature in passing the Statute of Uses had been to make
limitations by way of use subject to precisely the same rules as
governed the limitations of estates at common law.[21] By this
decision the whole problem of perpetuities would be solved, for
the common-law rules would prevent perpetuities being
created by limitations to uses. Unhappily it could be argued

---

[20] 1 Co. Rep. 113b. Bacon's argument is printed in Spedding, *Lord Bacon's Works,*
Vol. VII (1859), at p. 613. *Chudleigh's Case* is also reported as *Dillon* v. *Freine* in
Popham at p. 71 and I And. 314.

[21] Bacon (*Uses*, p. 395) does not indicate his own view, but in his argument in
Stanhope's Case (Spedding, Vol. VII, p. 562) he says, 'for although it be said in Freine
and Dillon's Case, and in Fitzwilliam's Case, that it is safe to construe the statute of 27
H. VIII as that uses may be made subject to the rules of the common law, which the
professors of the common law do know, and not leave them to be extravagant and
irregular: yet if the late authorities be well marked, and the reason for them, you shall
find this difference, that uses, in point of operation, are reduced to a kind of conformity
with the rules of the common law; but that in point of exposition of words, they retain
something of their ancient nature, and are expounded more liberally according to the
intent'. For *Fitzwilliam's Case* see 6 Co. Rep. 32a., esp. at 33b.

that this ruling was *obiter*, for *Chudleigh's Case*, though it concerned a settlement by way of use, dealt with limitations which did not infringe in their inception the rules governing the limitation of contingent remainders. In the course of the seventeenth century[22] the ruling in *Chudleigh's Case* was whittled down until it became the rule in *Purefoy* v. *Rogers*[23]—that if a limitation by way of use did not on the face of it break the common-law rules as to the limitation of contingent remainders, then it would be subjected to the common-law rules, which allowed the destruction of such remainders. Thus a limitation 'to A to the use of B for life, remainder to the use of C at 21' did not on the face of it break these rules, and so it was precarious—for example it would fail if C did not attain his majority before the death of B. On the other hand, a limitation 'to A to the use of B for life, remainder to the use of C in tail one year after the death of B', violated the rule which required contingent remainders to be limited so that they were capable of vesting at the determination of the precedent estate, so that such a limitation escaped the rule in *Purefoy* v. *Rogers*. The quaint result therefore of the whittling down of the ruling in *Chudleigh's Case* was that limitations by way of use which broke the contingent remainder rules, and which were therefore dangerously likely to produce over-lengthy settlements, were not governed by any restrictions at all as to the manner in which they might be limited. Such limitations were called limitations of legal executory interests,[24] and formed the most important class of future interests for which some sort of rule against perpetuities had to be developed.

The Destructibility of Executory Limitations and Devises

Now one way of dealing with these executory interests was to say that although they need not be limited in accordance with the rules of the common law, yet they were nevertheless destructible (though not in the same way as were contingent remainders) by the combined action of the feoffees to uses and those who had vested interests. The theory which allowed

[22] See *Woodliff* v. *Drury* (1596), Cro. Eliz. 439, *Pells* v. *Brown* (1620), Cro. Jac. 590. The point was still arguable in 1694; see *Davies* v. *Speed*, 12 Mod. 39.

[23] (1671) 2 Wms. Saunders 380, a case concerning limitations by will.

[24] 'Executory' as opposed to 'executed' by the statute; if all went well an executory interest would in time become executed. In the sixteenth century it is usual to contrast executed uses with 'contingent' uses or 'uses in futuro'.

executory interests to be destroyed before they vested was never very clearly agreed, but depended, broadly speaking, on this reasoning. Suppose a feoffment to X to the use of A for life, remainder to the use of B one year after A's death. Under the Statute of Uses it was clear that A obtained his seisin from the feoffee, X, by force of the statute. But where was B to obtain his? Not from A, for A was never seised to B's use. The only source left was X, but the statute said that X was to be left with nothing. At this point the conundrum seems unanswerable, but one view which obtained a certain degree of support, and which gave rise to perhaps the deepest of all the mysteries of the common law, was that some mysterious vestige of right remained in X, from which B would obtain his seisin a year after A's death. Thus if this mysterious '*scintilla iuris*', this spark of title, was destroyed, then B's use would be destroyed too, and be incapable of ever vesting.[25] From this it was argued, and indeed accepted in *Brent's Case*,[26] that if A made a feoffment (which he alone, being seised, could do) and persuaded X to join in it, X's participation destroyed his 'right'; thus there was no source from which B could ever obtain seisin, and so the contingent use in his favour was destroyed. *Chudleigh's Case* gave some support to this metaphysical reasoning, and until the decision in *Pells* v. *Brown* in 1620,[27] and indeed later, there was a current of opinion to the effect that executory future interests were destructible by a feoffment involving the co-operation of the person seised (normally a life tenant) and the feoffee or feoffees; vested interests, entails apart, could be destroyed, of course, only with the co-operation of the person in whom the interest was vested.

At the same period as the courts were vacillating about the law relating to executory limitations taking effect under the Statutes of Uses and Wills which concerned freeholds, they

[25] The best modern account is that of P. C. Bordwell, 'The Conversion of the Use into a Legal Interest', 21 *Iowa L.R.* 1.

[26] (1575) Dyer, 339b; see also *Chudleigh's Case*, 1 Co. Rep. 113b, for an entertaining dispute about the *scintilla*. Some supposed that the spark of title in the feoffees gave them a right of entry, sufficient to support contingent uses in the same manner in which a legal contingent remainder could be supported by a right of entry; there were variants on the doctrine. In 1860 Lord St. Leonards persuaded Parliament to abolish the doctrine by 23 and 24 Vict., c. 38, s. 7; the statute poses a problem of a sort in analytical jurisprudence.

[27] Cro. Jac. 590.

were also doing much the same in relation to leaseholds. Leaseholds were chattel interests, and at common law one could not carve estates out of terms of years; thus a grant of a term of 100 years to A for life, remainder to B in tail, simply counted as an absolute gift to A.[28] The Statute of Wills, however, allowed a person to devise 'at his free will and pleasure', and attempts were made by testators to devise long terms with similar limitations, in the hope that the courts would allow them to do by will what they could not do at common law by conveyance *inter vivos*. Such executory limitations of long terms were sometimes rejected and sometimes upheld in the sixteenth century,[29] but in *Manning's* and *Lampet's Cases* in 1609 and 1612[30] it was held that a term of years could be devised to one person for life, with a gift over to another after the death of the devisee for life. This looks like the recognition of a power to carve estates out of a chattel interest—a reversal of the well-established common-law rule that estates could not subsist in chattels—but the courts avoided openly going so far. The gift over did not take effect by way of remainder—it was not treated as a slice of cake. Instead it was said to take effect as a 'quasi-remainder'; on the death of the devisee for life the *whole term*, which had previously been in the hands of the devisee for life, jumped over to the 'quasi-remainderman'. The cake was passed about, not sliced up. The courts went beyond holding that such executory devises of terms were valid—which was startling enough—for they also held that they were indestructible. That is to say, that there was nothing which the devisee for life could do to destroy the executory devise; he was unable to obtain an unfettered power of alienation over the term.

This disability was the more striking in view of the fact that the devisee for life in theory had the whole term, whilst the quasi-remainderman had no vested interest in it, but only a mere possibility of obtaining the residue of term in the future. To put it another way, the quasi-remainder was contingent, and it was curious indeed that the courts thus came round to

---

[28] *Anon* (1537), Dyer, f. 7a.

[29] See *Anon* (1568), Dyer, 277b, *Weleden* v. *Elkington* (1578), Plowden 519, where such limitations were upheld, and compare *Anon* (1553), Dyer, 74b, and the opinion of Coke in *Mallet* v. *Sackford* (1607), Cro. Jac. 198. See generally Holdsworth, VII, p. 129.

[30] 8 Co. Rep. 94b, 10 Co. Rep. 46b.

permit indestructible contingent interests in leaseholds when they had in the past gone to such trouble to make contingent interests in freeholds destructible under the elaborate contingent remainder rules.

The peculiarity of this clearly struck the judges of the time; now that at least some forms of executory devises of leasehold were both good and indestructible, there seemed little point in having a different law for freeholds.

The whole question came to a head in *Pells* v. *Brown* in 1620.[31] The case concerned a devise of a freehold interest in property to A and his heirs, but if A should die in the lifetime of B, then to B and his heirs. A attempted to destroy the limitation in favour of B by conveying to X by common recovery. The judges reached two important conclusions. The first was that such a limitation was not bad *ad initio*, although it broke the common-law rules as to the limitation of estates by limiting a fee simple after a fee simple. This decisively rejected the opinion expressed in *Chudleigh's Case* that the limitation of uses must conform to the common-law rules. Secondly, they held that the executory limitation in favour of B was indestructible without B's consent, and although this ruling was concerned with the effect of a common recovery only, it was taken to embody a general principle. Thus executory limitations of freeholds were held to be both good, and indestructible by the first taker.

The decisions in *Manning's* and *Lampet's Cases*, and in *Pells* v. *Brown*, marked the failure of the courts to control settlors by subjecting their settlements to the old common-law rules. In the case of leaseholds, indestructible future legal interests had been let into the law in the form of executory devises taking effect under the Statute of Wills, and the old rule forbidding estates in leaseholds had been sidestepped, though not directly abrogated. In the case of freeholds, executory limitations operating under the Statute of Uses, and executory devises operating under the Statute of Wills, could now escape the rules governing the limitation of contingent remainders, and were both valid and indestructible—valid although they broke those rules, and indestructible because they broke them. Furthermore, the Chancery in the seventeenth century came to deal with future trusts—usually trusts of leasehold, which were not executed by the Statute of Uses, and these future trusts were not obviously confined by any rules. It was clear to contemporaries that settlors would have to be confined by some rules if they were not to employ executory limitations and devises to tie up land for undue periods, but some new approach to the problem of perpetuities was needed if an effective body of rules was to be built up.

The Background to the Modern Rule

What this approach should be was not for some time apparent. The majority of the decisions before *The Duke of Norfolk's Case* in 1681[32], which was to settle the form of the modern rule against perpetuities, concern executory devises of leaseholds.[33] In dealing with them the common-law judges seem to have woken up with some horror to the dangers involved in their decisions in *Manning's Case* and *Lampet's Case*. They had allowed the creation of what was in effect, though not in theory, a life estate in a lease; they resolved to go not one inch beyond those decisions, and in particular to permit nothing in the nature of an entail of a lease. The fear of allowing one was reasonable enough, for such an entail would be unbarrable by common recovery, a leaseholder being unable to create a 'tenant to the praecipe' against whom a collusive real action could be brought. *Manning's Case* had involved an executory devise after a life interest; in *Childe* v. *Bailie* (1618–23)[34] the judges were confronted with a similar executory devise after a purported entail of the term. The executory devise was held to be bad. The basis of the decision was simple enough; it was the common-law rule that estates could not be carved out of leaseholds, which were chattel interests. The purported gift to the entail was thus ineffective, and operated as an outright, absolute gift of the term; any limitation over after it was simply void, for there was nothing left to give. Thus the common-law rule on executory devises of leasehold became clear enough—such a devise was

---

[32] 3 Ch. Cas 1, 2 Swanston 454. The best account of the history of the rule up to Lord Nottingham's time is that of D. E. C. Yale, Selden Society, Vol. 73, pp. lxxiii *et seq.* See also Bonfield, *Marriage Settlements 1601–1740*, esp. Ch. 2.

[33] Exceptions are *Pells* v. *Brown* (1620) Cro. Jac. 590; also *Snow* v. *Cutler* (1664), 1 Lev. 135, 1 Keble 752, 800, 851, 2 Keble 11, 145.

[34] Palmer 48, 333, W. Jones 15, Cro. Jac. 459.

good if it followed a life interest, and bad if it followed any greater interest. In the case of executory limitations and devises of freeholds there was a dearth of clear authority beyond *Pells* v. *Brown*.[35] Clearly the leasehold rule did not apply, for in *Pells* v. *Brown* the executory limitation had followed a gift of a fee simple and had been upheld; nobody, in fact, really knew what the limits were.

In argument in *Childe* v. *Bailie* a quite different approach to the matter had been suggested, though unsuccessfully, by Bridgman and Davenport, the counsel for the losing side. They had pointed out that in the will upon which the litigation arose the gift over after the entail had been so worded that it was bound to take effect, if at all, in the lifetime of the first taker; the substance of the limitation in the will was a gift to A in tail with a gift over to B if A died without leaving issue alive at his death. Thus, it was argued, the gift over was no more 'remote' than a gift over after a life interest, which had been held good in *Manning's Case*, and was no more objectionable than such a gift—the term only remained fettered by a clog on its alienability for one lifetime. It could thus be argued that there was no more danger of a perpetuity in such a case than there was in a straightforward common-law grant for life, which also tied up land for a lifetime, and was regarded as innocuous. This argument was not accepted, but it did suggest a concentration upon remoteness of vesting which was later to be taken up by Lord Nottingham. In the years following *Childe* v. *Bailie* the common-law courts steadfastly maintained their position with only the slightest modification in detail, and we may sum up the common law on the subject in these propositions:

(*a*) Following *Pells* v. *Brown*,[36] an executory limitation of freehold taking the form of a gift over after a fee simple was good *perhaps* if it was bound to take effect, if at all, within the lifetime of the first tenant in fee simple. How far beyond this a settlor could go was uncertain, for there was a dearth of case law authority.

(*b*) An executory devise of a leasehold interest was good if it took the form of a gift over after a gift for life, and would take

---

[35] Cro. Jac. 590.   [36] Cro. Jac. 590.

effect, if at all, during the continuance of the life interest or immediately on its determination.[37]

(c) An executory devise of a leasehold interest could not be limited after any interest greater than a life estate or interest.[38]

(d) Any number of life interests in leaseholds could be devised one after the other, so long as they were all given to persons *in esse*.[39]

(e) Any set of limitations which in substance amounted to the entail of a term was bad.[40]

The Duke of Norfolk's Case

The position in Chancery over future trusts was not, however, settled, and there was no inflexible rule that equity should follow the law; and when *The Duke of Norfolk's Case*[41] came before Lord Nottingham in 1681, the law, and the position in equity, were in a considerable state of confusion, lacking any clear unifying principle which could be used to explain these rules and give some guidance for the future; in consequence he was able to utilize this confusion to justify a new approach to the problem of perpetuities. This Lord Nottingham was able to provide by enunciating a new rule, which would apply to executory limitations both of freeholds and leaseholds. The case itself concerned a limitation of leasehold property by way of devise to trustees, on trust for the settlor's second son in tail, but if the settlor's eldest son should die without issue male *in the lifetime of the second son*, or if the settlor's earldom should descend to the second son (which again must happen in that son's lifetime), then the leaseholds were to be held on trust for the settlor's third son. Lord Nottingham held these gifts over good, because the interest limited in favour of the third son must vest, if at all, in the lifetime of the second son. To do this he had to disapprove rule (c), which was established by *Childe* v. *Bailie*. He was prepared to do this, for it enabled him to enunciate a

---

[37] *Manning's Case* (1609), 8 Co. Rep. 94b, *Lampet's Case* (1612), 10 Co. Rep. 46b.

[38] *Childe* v. *Bailie* (1618–23).

[39] *Goringe* v. *Bickerstaff* (1662), 2 Freeman 163, 1 Ch. Cas. 4, Pollexfen 31, Cf. the dictum of Twisden J., 'if all the candles be lighted at once it is good'. *Love* v. *Wyndham* (1670), 1 Mod. 50, at p. 54. Jones's argument in this case anticipates Lord Nottingham's concentration upon remoteness of vesting.

[40] *Apprice* v. *Flower* (1661), Pollexfen 27.

[41] 3 Chan. Cas. 1, 2 Swanston 454.

single principle which would govern limitations both of freehold and leasehold—that an interest which is bound to vest, if at all, within the lifetime of a person in being when the settlement takes effect is validly limited. This ruling of Lord Nottingham's concentrated attention on the remoteness of time at which the future interest must vest, and on this alone; it is just possible that the earlier rules which have been listed did so in the case of freeholds (rule (*a*)), though this was nowhere clearly stated. But in the case of leasehold they concentrated rather on the nature of the interest preceding the contingent limitation (rules (*b*) and (*c*)), thus making a unified doctrine impossible.

Lord Nottingham believed that so long as settlors were prevented from vesting estates in persons at too remote a time in the future, the problem of perpetuities would be solved. His objection to perpetuities was grounded in natural law. Human laws should be appropriate to the nature of man, and man, unlike God, possesses only a limited ability to foresee what will happen in the future. Hence a landowner should not be allowed to settle the devolution of family lands too far into a future which he could not foresee. Hence perpetuities 'fight against God, by effecting a stability which human providence can never attain to'.[42] There is no reason to suppose that Nottingham was concerned about inalienability of land as inimical to a free market economy. He left it to later judges to decide the utmost limits of time within which vesting might be postponed, and they settled eventually on the period of a life or lives in being and a period in gross of twenty-one years, borrowing this period by analogy with the time within which the fee simple might be made inalienable at common law by using legal contingent remainders.[43] As the rule developed its function was differently conceived; it came to be valued as favouring a free market in land.[44]

---

[42] 2 Swanston 460. The same idea is expressed by Dodderidge J. in *Pells* v. *Brown* (1620), 2 Rolle Rep. at 221.

[43] For an account of the later developments of the rule see Morris and Leach, *Perpetuities*, pp. 9–11. *Stephens* v. *Stephens* (1736) Cases temp. Talbot 228 added a minority to the period; *Cadell* v. *Palmer* (1833) 1 Cl. and F. 372 a period of twenty-one in gross; and *Thelluson* v. *Woodford* (1805) 11 Vesey Jun. 112 ruled that the lives need have no connection with those beneficially interested.

[44] For discussion of the rationale of the rule see Morris and Leach, *Perpetuities*, pp. 13–17; G. L. Haskins, 'Extending the Grasp of the Deal Hand: Reflections on the

When new law is made in a system based upon precedent, the old cases have to be refashioned to provide authority for the innovation, and Lord Nottingham's arguments in *The Duke of Norfolk's Case* contain some extremely ingenious examples of the process. He did his best to distinguish *Childe* v. *Bailie*, which was, after all, a solemn decision of the Exchequer Chamber, but he hardly claimed to have succeeded. He justified his decision positively largely by two cases—*Pells* v. *Brown* (1620) and *Wood* v. *Saunders* (1669).[45] The former case was certainly reconciliable with his rule on remoteness of vesting, but there is not a glimmer of evidence that the judges who decided it were in the least influenced by any such conception; in the reports of the case nothing is made to turn upon the fact that the shifting fee simple was bound to vest, if at all, within a life in being. The argument from *Wood* v. *Saunders* is equally specious. In that case there was a limitation of a term by will (in effect) to A for life, then to B for life, then to C absolutely, but if C died before A and B, to D in tail. C did so die, and the question was whether D took the term. It was held that he did, and at first sight this seems to run counter to *Childe* v. *Bailie*, for the devise to D appears to follow a devise of the term for more than a life; Lord Nottingham was thus able to argue that the gift to D was good because it was bound to vest, if at all, within a life in being. But the ground upon which the decision actually proceeded was not this at all; it was that the rule in *Childe* v. *Bailie* did not apply. *Childe* v. *Bailie* had held bad a gift over after a vested absolute devise of a term (a devise purporting to be a devise in tail counting as an absolute devise). In *Wood* v. *Saunders* the devise to C was held to be contingent—it depended upon C surviving A and B—and the contingency never occurred. The devise to D, which the court upheld, did not follow a vested absolute devise to C, for the term had never vested in C; thus the gift over to D could not be objected to upon the ground that the term had already been given absolutely to somebody else—the basis of the objection to the gift over in *Childe* v. *Bailie*. The truth is that Lord Nottingham's rule against remoteness of vesting was an innovation, and only the barest shreds of authority for the doctrine

Origins of the Rule against Perpetuities', 125 *Univ. of Pennsylvania L.R.* 19, Simpson, 'Entails and Perpetuities', 24 *Juridicial Review* (*N.S.*) 1 (comparing Scots law).

[45] Cro. Jac. 590, 1 Ch. Cas. 131.

could be dragged out of the earlier cases which he reviewed, though many could be explained retrospectively as illustrating it. It is a striking mark of Lord Nottingham's genius that he was able to impose his new theory on the law.

Remoteness and Alienability

Lord Nottingham was not, as we have seen, concerned about inalienability of land as such—his worry was with vesting of interests at periods remote from the settler's knowledge of the family circumstances. His rule did, indirectly, tend to favour alienability, and came to be valued for this. It is not always obvious why a control over remoteness of vesting is capable of preserving the alienability of land. Suppose Jones to be tenant in fee simple of Blackacre. In settling Blackacre he may limit as many estates, or interests for life, in tail or in fee as he cares, but all must vest if at all within the perpetuity period. During this period he can contrive to make the land inalienable for longer than any one person's life, by keeping it in the possession of life tenants, and he may contrive to vest a life estate in a person who is a baby or even an unborn infant at the end of that period. But then the sands begin to run out. At the end of the perpetuity period there must be a vested remainderman in fee tail and a vested remainderman in fee simple, or there must be a vested remainderman in fee simple alone; alternatively there may be a reversioner. Sooner or later the last life tenant dies, and inevitably a remainderman or reversioner in fee tail or fee simple will be entitled in possession. Either will have a full and unfettered power of disposition over the whole fee simple in Blackacre, and the full freedom of alienation with which the settlor started will exist again. Theoretically at any rate, control over remoteness of vesting will have the result which Lord Nottingham anticipated. His decision, which was given in defiance of the views of the common-law judges,[46] was reversed by his successor[47] and eventually restored by the House of Lords in 1685. Thereafter English lawyers both in the common-law courts and in Chancery followed the lead he had indicated, and the basic rule against

[46] See 3 Ch. Cas. at pp. 14–26.
[47] 1 Vernon 163.

perpetuities became a rule against remoteness of vesting. With the measure of success it enjoyed we shall deal in discussing the classical settlement of land which was evolved in the eighteenth century.

Trustees to Preserve Contingent Remainders

We have seen how it was that the courts, when they grudgingly admitted contingent remainders into the law in the sixteenth century, developed rules which made them destructible, and how under the rule in *Purefoy* v. *Rogers* a large category of limitations by way of use and by way of devise were caught by these rules. The result of this was that settlors who employed legal contingent remainders were playing with fire, for such remainders were wholly precarious. With the recognition of the wide powers of disposition available to a settlor who employed executory limitations the position became somewhat absurd. Thus Jones could validly devise a term of a thousand years to his son for life, with remainder in tail to his eldest grandson living at his son's death, and the grandson's interest was indestructible. But if he devised a freehold in the same way the son could destroy the contingent remainder to the grandson. Thus when the conveyancers set out to devise some way of preventing the destruction of contingent remainders their efforts met with the sympathy of the courts. According to a legal tradition developed in the eighteenth century, Sir Orlando Bridgman is said to have invented the device known as 'trustees to preserve contingent remainders' which achieved the desired end. Bonfield has however shown that the evidence for this is weak.[48] Instead of limiting land, say, to A for life, remainder to A's eldest son living at his death in tail, and thereby risking the destruction of the contingent remainder if the precedent estate was prematurely determined, the conveyancers added after the limitation to A a limitation of a remainder to trustees for the life of A, making this remainder expectant upon the determination of A's life interest before his death, with some provision that the trustees should accumulate the rents and profits and hold them in trust for the next remainderman to take. Thus if A's life estate was

---

[48] Bonfield, *Marriage Settlements 1601–1740*. Ch. 4, contains an exhaustive discussion of the matter.

to determine prematurely—for example by forfeiture—there was still the estate *pur autre vie* of the trustees upon which the contingent remainder in tail could be said to depend, so that it escaped destruction. This device is found in use as early as 1641, and is fairly common in settlements drafted in the 1650s. But there was one possible flaw in the design. It was essential that the courts should hold that the remainder limited to the trustees was vested, for of course if it were itself contingent both it and the remainder in tail would be equally destroyed by the determination of the precedent life estate, and the whole device would fail. The courts obligingly did eventually so hold, and the House of Lords upheld this view of the law in *Dormer* v. *Packhurst* in 1740.[49] Immense ingenuity has been devoted to showing that this decision either was or was not justifiable.[50] The reality of the matter is that the holding was motivated by expediency and nothing else, for by 1740 the device had become common form in settlements, and a contrary decision would have had a disastrous effect upon hundreds of settlements. Various modifications of this method of preserving contingent remainders were devised to suit the requirements of settlors, with the practical result that contingent remainders became once more a usual and reliable feature of conveyancing. Their use was not controlled, and did not need to be controlled, by the rule against perpetuities, for the old rules governing the limitation of such remainders adequately dealt with the risk of perpetuities. In practice they could be limited after a life estate

[49] 6 Bro. P. C. 351, upholding *Duncomb* v. *Duncomb* (1697), 3 Lev. 437. The trust was enforced in Chancery earlier than this. See Bonfield, pp. 71-2, 76-81.

[50] See Challis, *Real Property*, pp. 142-7. The true position would appear to be this. The question whether an estate be vested or contingent can be asked of a particular moment in time only in relation to a particular person, and all that is being asked is if a certain person has an estate or not. At the moment when a settlement takes effect the trustees do not have an estate, and thus all they 'have' is a bare possibility of obtaining an estate in the future. If it is asked whether they will have an estate in the future if the prior estate determines prematurely, the answer is that they will. The problem for decision then becomes: does this fact suffice to protect the succeeding and admittedly contingent remainders? The solution of this problem must turn upon whether these admittedly contingent remainders depend upon the estate of the prior life tenant or upon the limitation in favour of the trustees, and upon principle they can obviously depend only upon the prior life tenancy, which alone was vested when the settlement took effect. Thus the decision in *Dormer* v. *Packhurst* was 'wrong'. Of course, it is possible to devise a definition of a vested remainder which fits the decision in that case, but such a definition is perverse and is, of course, bound to fit the very case which it is designed to fit.

given to a living person, in which case the remainder either
vested within a life in being or failed, or after an entail, in
which case the remainder, before or after it vested, could be
barred by a common recovery. Thus such remainders could
not produce problems of remoteness.[51]

The Old Rule Against Perpetuities

Before leaving this account of the treatment of perpetuities
by the courts we must say something about the contrast which
is often drawn between the so-called *old* rule against perpetuities
and the *new* rule developed from *The Duke of Norfolk's Case*, for
this contrast can be dangerously misleading. There never was a
single old rule, or a single body of doctrine, which was comparable to the new rule against remoteness of vesting; instead there
were a number of interrelated rules and principles, some of
them of uncertain scope, which together checked the excesses
of settlors. Thus there was the principle which laid down that
the entail was a barrable estate, the rules governing the contingent remainder, the uncertain antecedents of the rule in
Whitby v. *Mitchell*, the rule in *Purefoy* v. *Rogers*, the general
principle that the fee simple was alienable, and so forth—all
this medley of doctrine added up to 'the old rule' against perpetuities. Underlying it was the general reluctance to permit
any arrangement which amounted in substance to an unbarrable entail. For the ordinary conception of a perpetuity was
that of an unbarrable entail—the most obvious example of a
permanent or nearly permanent inalienable interest in land.
But any disposition of land which put the power of alienation of
a fee simple tenant into abeyance for an over-lengthy period
was included in the concept, and viewed with dislike too. The
newer rule against perpetuities simply added to the existing
body of doctrine upon the subject, and was designed to catch
forms of future interest which escaped the other rules. Although
it tackled the subject in a different way, by concentrating upon

---

[51] For the history of legislative intervention in this field see Megarry and Wade,
Real Property, pp. 1183–86. Broadly speaking the Real Property Limitation Act of 1833
and the Real Property Act of 1845 protected contingent remainders against deliberate
attempts to destroy them, and the Contingent Remainders Act of 1877 protected them
against the risk of failure to vest in good time. It was held by *In Re Frost* (1889) 43
Ch. D. 246 that the rule against perpetuities applied to legal contingent remainders;
the decision produced much controversy.

remoteness of vesting alone, it was closely related to the older rules, and in the eighteenth century this was well realized—so much so that lawyers saw in all the rules directed against perpetuities a single policy and a single principle—that the power to dispose of the fee simple in possession of a parcel of land ought not to be put in abeyance for a longer period than was normal in the traditional strict settlement, which is a period of a life in being plus twenty-one years. But by then it was beyond the wit of any lawyer to unify the various threads and produce one rule which would produce this result. In part the root of the trouble lay in the fact that the law compromised with the desire of landowners to tie up their estates; the law *against* perpetuities in reality *permitted* them, within limits. In part the trouble lay in the inability of lawyers to treat the problem of perpetuities openly for what it was: a problem about the alienability of land and estates in land. Instead, the problem is tackled obliquely, as a problem about remoteness of vesting, or a problem about the derivation of estates, or attempts are made to solve it by reviving an archaic medieval rule about the construction of words of limitation, as happened in *Shelley's Case*. The lawyers were driven to these shifts by the burden of concept and theory which they inherited, and in particular by the unhappy interpretation put upon the Statutes of Uses and Wills, which irrevocably destroyed the fundamentally simple structure of the medieval land law.

Mysteries of Property Law

Thus by the end of the seventeenth century the law of future interests is becoming something of a tangle. The settlor could employ no less than three different types of future interest—legal contingent remainders, executory limitations, and trusts—to effect his purposes, but in doing so he must read warily through a jungle of various doctrines, some of uncertain ambit, which imposed different and sometimes apparently pointless restrictions upon his powers. The modern rule against perpetuities was not yet fully formulated; older rules against perpetuities still had an uncertain existence, the definition of a contingent remainder was not settled, the rule in *Shelley's Case* might frustrate perfectly reasonable dispositions for no obvious reason, and if we were to go into the minutiae of the law we might reasonably be led to agree with Cromwell's verdict that the law of real property was an ungodly jumble. Glancing for a moment at other parts of the law, confusion deepens. To bar an entail a tenant must go through a fantastic rigmarole, which even judges thought it better not to investigate too closely,[52] litigation had to be conducted through the medium of absurd fictions, and at every turn a slight failure to attend to some technicality or other could ruin a conveyance. Thus a limitation 'to A in fee simple' had the extraordinary effect of giving A a life estate, to give but one illustration. To laymen the system was wholly unintelligible and the remedy which would occur to us—legislative reform—was impossible in the climate of thought of the eighteenth century. To the lawyers, who alone had sufficient grasp of the law to have done something about it, the law of property, and particularly the law of future interests, became a great mystery, an elaborate network of rules so interrelated that any radical legislative interference might destroy the assumed coherence of the whole, and throw men's security in their property into confusion. What enabled them to adopt this position was the extraordinary mastery of the law exhibited by the leading conveyancers of the late seventeenth and eighteenth centuries, whose model conveyances were imitated by the lesser members of the profession, and whose practice was treated with reverence by the courts. Their conveyances so manipulated the rusty machinery of the land law as to produce the social consequences desired by the more important and influential landowners. And, no doubt, the deeper the mysteries involved, the more money lawyers could extract from their clients for their arcane services. The way in which they achieved this is best shown by an examination of the classical eighteenth-century settlement.

The Family Settlement

In the medieval period the family settlement was a relatively simple affair. A new family might be provided for by a gift 'in frank marriage', which would relieve it of the burden of feudal exactions for three generations, or by land given subject to

---

[52] See *Martin d. Tregonwell* v. *Strachan* (1744), 1 Wils. 73, where Willes C.J. remarked of Pigott's book on Common Recoveries, 'Mr. Pigott has confounded himself and everybody else who reads his book.'

some form or other of entail, which would ensure that the lands remained in the family and passed down from generation to generation. Perhaps it was the growth of devices for barring entails which led to settlors employing the more complex form of settlement under which a life estate only was given to the first beneficiary, with an entail in remainder to his eldest son, and successive remainders to his younger sons; settlements of this type are met as early as the fourteenth century, but appear not to have been commonly employed. In so far as is known, the typical medieval settlement involved a series of entails to named descendants. There were a number of variant forms; for example, after a life interest a remainder in tail might be limited not to the eldest son by name (he might well not be born when the settlement was made) but to 'the right heirs' of the life tenant—such a form gave rise to the rule in *Shelley's Case*. In general it may be said that the medieval settlement relied upon straightforward use of the life estate and the entail, and, since contingent interests were only grudgingly recognized, the beneficiaries took vested interests. In the fifteenth century there are signs of an increasing elaboration; settlors became more preoccupied with attempts to keep land in the family. The courts recognize and indeed encourage devices which make the entailed estate alienable, so that settlors can no longer treat it as an estate which *is* a settlement in itself. We know of two judges who made elaborate attempts to make unbreakable settlements—Thirning and Rickhill[53]—and there are a number of indications in the year books that they were not alone in these attempts. Furthermore, the use of lands, now that it is regularly protected in Chancery, came to be commonly employed by settlors; not only is it possible to deal more freely with an equitable estate than with a legal estate, but uses may be devised, so that settlements by will become generally possible. The Statute of Uses in 1536 made it possible to deal as freely with the legal estate as it was possible to deal with the use beforehand; and the Statute of Wills conferred a wide freedom upon testators. In addition the Statute of Uses made it possible for settlors to employ legal powers of appointment. Before the statute, the Chancellor

[53] See Co. Litt. 377b. For other examples of medieval settlements see A. D. Hargreaves, *Shelley's Ghost*, 54 *L.Q.R.* 70.

allowed a landowner to convey lands to a feoffee to such uses as he, or some other person, might declare; after the statue such a declaration or appointment conferred a legal estate upon the person in whose favour the appointor might exercise his power. Other developments in the sixteenth century contributed to the increased power of settlors; particularly important was the recognition of legal contingent remainders. All this led to increased elaboration in the form of settlements of land.[54]

The sixteenth century saw the rise of a new aristocracy and a new landed gentry, which seems to have been obsessed with a desire to entrench its position in society. The landowners, many of whom were lawyers themselves, aided by their conveyancers, attempted expedient after expedient to give permanence to their families; the confused state of the land law and the passion for litigation gave rise to case after case in which this or that form of settlement came under review, to be upheld or struck down for reasons which appeared incomprehensible at times to lawyers, let alone to their clients. Towards the end of the seventeenth century, however, the activities of a number of eminent conveyancers—notable amongst them was Sir Orlando Bridgman, who, it is said, 'betook himself to conveyancing in the time of the Civil Wars'—produced some order by designing model conveyances which satisfied the desires of the landowners and kept within reasonably well settled doctrines of the law;[55] there arose a conveyancing tradition, and in the courts a respect for that tradition, which has continued to this day.[56] The most notable achievement of the conveyancers was the classical strict settlement.

Basically the strict settlement, under which landed property could be kept within a family for generation after generation, depended upon one simple principle: a tenant in tail must never be allowed to come into the possession of the family land, which must always be kept in the possession of a life tenant. Once a tenant in tail of full age came into possession he could break the entail by common recovery, and secure a power of

<hr>

[54] For sixteenth-century settlements see *Calthrop's Case*, Moo. K. B. 101 (1535,) 1 Co. Rep. 67b–68b (1587), 120a–120b (1566), 162b–163a (1568), *Holcroft's Case*, Moo. K. B. 486 (1555). Other examples are given by J. H. Baker in Selden Society, Vol. 94, pp. 204–8, and an analysis of the forms is given by Bonfield, *op. cit.*, pp. 8–9.

[55] His model conveyances were published completely in 1690, after his death.

[56] On the early history of this tradition see Bonfield, *op cit.*, pp. 64–6.

unfettered disposition over the fee simple. Out of possession he could disentail by fine on his own volition, but a fine only created a base fee, and a base fee was not a valuable interest; it could be sold, but not for very much. Thus a tenant in tail out of possession was not so dangerous a person as a tenant in tail in possession, that is in the eyes of a settlor who wished to tie up his land. A life tenant in possession, on the other hand, could only lawfully alienate for an estate for his own life; if he wrongfully alienated in fee simple the land could be recovered by the next remainderman from the alienee so long at least as there was a vested remainder. Thus a settlor who could contrive to keep a succession of life tenants on the family lands *ad infinitum*, son succeeding father, would achieve the ideal settlement.

The technique by which this was done was ingenious. Suppose the settlor, Lord Doe, has a son John Doe; Lord Doe is tenant in fee simple of Blackacre, and wishes to settle this property on his son John. He will convey it to John for life, with remainder in tail to John's as yet unborn eldest son, with similar remainders to John's younger children, and a final remainder in fee simple to his own right heirs. The remainders in tail are of course contingent, not vested. Until John marries and has a son the land is safely tied up, for the settlement will always include a limitation to trustees to preserve the contingent remainders in favour of the unborn sons of John, and this device makes it impossible for John to destroy them by destroying his life estate. If he attempts to do so, then the *estate pur autre vie* given to the trustees is sufficient to preserve them—it is a vested estate upon which they can depend. Trustees who took steps to destroy contingent remainders would commit a breach of trust. It is the limitation to trustees which makes the settlement *strict*, that is to say unbreakable by the life tenant. Settlements employing a life estate followed by a contingent remainder to the life tenant's unborn son are found in the middle of the sixteenth century, and earlier, but it is not until the 1650s that the ingenious mechanism which saves the remainder from the risk of destruction becomes generally used.

If a son is born he will obtain a vested entail in remainder. As a young man he will require an income; this the settlement does not give him. He can, of course, bar the entail by fine, and sell or mortgage his resulting base fee to obtain money, but his father will suggest a better course. To suffer a common recovery and break the settlement requires the co-operation of the tenant in possession (the father) and the tenant in tail (the son). Hence with the father's co-operation the son can bar the entail by common recovery and resettle the land, including in the resettlement a provision giving him an income. The father will, however, only co-operate if the resettlement ties up the land for another generation. The form the resettlement will take will be that a life estate is given to John Doe, a life estate in remainder to the son, and an entail in remainder to the son's as yet unborn son at 21; the limitations will include a provision giving the son an income charged on the lands. This process of resettlement can be repeated each generation. Although the common law in theory knew no perpetual unbarrable entail, the process of settlement and resettlement which was invented by the conveyancers produced much the same effects, by keeping large family estates in the hands of a succession of limited owners for generation after generation.

The form of the strict settlement presented here in a simplified form[57] was perfected in its main essentials by the mid-seventeenth century, and was in common use by the end of its century. It has altered little up to the present day, though the effects of taxation have made it unpopular. Around the basis of the life estate followed by the entail, coupled with the resettlement each generation, it was possible to build up a series of provisions which provided for the requirements of the dynastic landholding family, whilst ensuring as far as possible that the family lands pass down intact from generation to generation to the eldest son. The life tenant's wife was usually provided for after her husband's death by the grant of what was known as a jointure. This was a rent-charge or an annuity secured on the land. In her husband's lifetime she might be given a smaller annuity by way of pin money. The younger children, who were not to have the lands, were recompensed by the payment of capital sums, called portions. To secure them their portions a long term of years was limited to trustees who were to raise these sums by accumulating the profits of the lands; in practice the eldest child would, if he was able, pay the

[57] Blackstone, in Appendix II to Vol. II, gives a standard form precedent for a strict settlement.

portions out of his own pocket; once they were paid the term ended and he could come into his inheritance and enjoy the family estate, so that he has every incentive to raise them as rapidly as possible. In some settlements greater flexibility was achieved through the use of powers of appointment; for example, the life tenant could be left to appoint the first remainder in tail to whichever of his children he wished, so that he could choose a successor who was in his eyes a worthy head of the family; such a power, especially if exercisable by will, had the additional advantage of enabling father to keep his children in order.

Although family land might be put under settlement at any time by a landowner who possessed a power of disposition over it, the strict settlement was essentially a mechanism for the regulation of property rights on the occasion of a marriage. In aristocratic circles marriage involved a complex treaty between different families, viewing each other then, as they do today, with a combination of nervousness, hostility, and fear of loss of status. In the negotiations, the bride's family offered their daughter and a financial contribution for the endowment of the new family; the groom's family, in turn, their son and their part of the endowment. Granted the legal subservience of women, it was essential, if the bride and her children were to be protected from the risk that the groom might prove unreliable, and her family's status protected, that the groom's power of disposition over the family landed endowment be restricted. The mechanisim for achieving this result was the strict settlement, whose function it was to ensure that the lady and her future offspring were kept in the manner in which they were accustomed, or entitled. For the groom's point of view the settlement was the price that had to be paid to make a good marriage. The pressure to settle property is thus explicable. But marriages take place every generation, and if the next round of matchmaking was to be handled satisfactorily, there must be new treaties and new prices to pay. In the dynastic world therefore, there needs to be a chance to readjust matters each generation, and the system of settlement and resettlement achieved just that. In substance the strict settlement functioned as an entail of unlimited duration, subject to revision by family conference at appropriate intervals.[58]

58 See Simpson, 'Entails and Perpetuities', 24 *Juridical Review* (*N.S.*.) 1.

The strict settlement, by perpetuating and consolidating the wealth and power of the wealthy families, and by preserving their estates intact through the years, had an immense effect upon the social and political life of the country until very recent times. Precisely what effect is somewhat controversial.[59] The settlement was the legal regime of the landed interest, powerful in both national and local political life; there is inevitably a problem in saying whether the legal institution was cause or effect of the political and social phenomenon. Death duties have in this century brought about the destruction of the social structure which the strict settlement enshrined, though the institution still lingers on.

Whatever may be said in favour of the system it is clear that there were grave disadvantages in subjecting a large portion of the land of the country to the management of a series of life tenants. At common law a life tenant had severely limited powers. He was liable for waste; thus he was unable to cut timber, or open new mines, or plough up ancient meadow land; at the same time he was under no liability to prevent permissive waste, so that he could let the land fall into poor condition, with impunity. He could only alienate the land for his own life, so that he was quite unable to tap the full capital value of one part of the settled land even if he intended to apply the capital to develop the remainder. His own capital was frequently absorbed in paying extravagant portions, so that he had little left to devote to good management; the fact that his interest determined on his death did not encourage life tenants to invest their private moneys in settled land. To a great extent these disadvantages could be overcome by the insertion in settlements of clauses which conferred wider powers upon the life tenant. In Bridgeman's model conveyance[60] the life tenant is made unimpeachable for waste, and during the eighteenth

---

[59] Bonfield, *op. cit.*, provides a full bibliography. In particular see H. J. Habakkuk, English Landownership 1680–1740'. 10 *E. H. R.* (1940), E. Spring, 'The Settlement of land in Nineteenth Century England', 8 *Am J.L.H.* (1964) 210, G. Mingay, *English Landed Society in the Eighteenth Century* (1963), F. M. L. Thompson, *English Landed Society in the Nineteenth Century* (1963), L. and J. Stone, *An Open Elite? England 1540–1880* and ensuing controversy in 17 *Albion* (1985) 149–66 C. E. and D. Spring), 167–80 (L. Stone) *et seq.*, and E. Spring, 'Law and the Theory of the Affective Family' 16 *Albion* p. 1.

[60] Bridgeman's *Conveyances*, 2nd ed., p. 196, reproduced as Appendix III to Holdsworth, VIII; see also Holdsworth, VII. at p. 377, for an earlier form.

century the best-drawn settlements regularly enlarged the life
tenant's powers. A precedent in Hayes's *Introduction to Conveyancing*,[61] published in 1840, gives the life tenant a wide power of
leasing, selling, and exchanging the settled land. But all too
often such powers were not included, and in the nineteenth
century there arose a widespread dissatisfaction with the effects
of such ill-drawn settlements upon the welfare of settled land.
The economic development of the country was being hindered
by the prevalence of land which it was impossible to utilize fully,
so that both the beneficiaries under strict settlements and the
country at large suffered.

Settlements and Perpetuities

The strict settlement in its classical form keeps well within the
rule against perpetuities, or the rules governing legal contingent
remainders, from which the perpetuity period was taken by
analogy. Normally the conveyancer employed the conveyancing
device of lease and release; the provisions of the settlement were
declared on the release, and took effect under the Statute of Uses,
so that the beneficiaries took legal estates. Under the rule in
Purefoy v. *Rogers* the normal limitations were treated as if they
were limitations of legal contingent remainders, for they did not
overtly break any of the common-law rules governing such remainders. The effect was that nobody could dispose of the fee
simple in possession until the life tenant's eldest son attained his
majority, and at the worst this would not happen for a lifetime
and a period of twenty-one years after the death of the life tenant;
usually it would take a generation, which is about twenty-five
years. No single person, acting alone, could dispose of the fee
simple in possession at the earliest until both the life tenant died
and the remainderman in tail attained his majority—at the worst
a period of a life in being and twenty-one years. If the settlement
gave the beneficiaries trust estates, or involved limitations not
governed by the rule in *Purefoy* v. *Rogers*, then the ordinary rule
against perpetuities applied to it. It will be seen that a settlor with
the best possible intentions may sterilize an estate for a very long
period, say sixty or seventy years, even without intending to do
so; a determined eccentric could tie up land for close on a cen-

---

[61] Hayes, *Introduction to Conveyancing*, Vol. II, No. 14, at pp. 68 *et seq.*

tury. Until the position was altered by statute in 1800 by Thelluson's Act, a settler could also direct an accumulation of income for the perpetuity period, so that nobody in the interim was entitled to the product of the property.[62] Even when the time was reached when the life tenant and the remainderman in tail were able to break the settlement, and had the option of resettling or of disposing of the fee simple, the land would usually be burdened by subsisting third party rights—widows' annuities for example—and the social pressure to do as the family had always done and resettle was extremely strong. Modern textbooks as well as historical works tend to portray the law of real property as a body of law which has zealously protected the power of free alienation of land, and the rule against perpetuities (and associated doctrines) as an effective curb against attempts to destroy this power in landowners. In reality the rule against perpetuities permits them, and it is important to realize that the strict settlement ingeniously removed the power of free alienation from a large number of the landowners of the country; it required statutory intervention to restore it to them.[63]

[62] See *Thellusson* v. *Woodford* (1799), 4 Vesey 227, arising out of the will of the eccentric Peter Thellusson. A mass of uninvestigated papers dealing with the subsequent litigation survives in the Treasury Solicitor's papers in the Public Record Office.

[63] On the whole subject-matter of this chapter see the series of articles, 'Alienability and Perpetuities' by P. Bordwell in the *Iowa L.R.*, 22 at p. 437, 23 at p. 1, 24 at pp. 1, 635, 25 at pp. 1, 707.

X

The Later Development of Commercial Interests in Land

The Mortgage

THE post-medieval law of mortgages falls into two parts—the changes in the form of the mortgage, and the transformation in its nature which was brought about through the intervention of the Chancellor. The former is relatively unimportant. From the very early period until the 1925 legislation introduced the *charge by way of legal mortgage*[1] the law of property has never known a mortgage as such; mortgages have always pretended to a greater or less degree to be something which they are not, for they have been created by the manipulation of ordinary common-law estates. Conveyancers have employed a large number of different techniques in order to make land into a security for a debt, but after Littleton's day two main forms of mortgage were commonly employed. By the first the mortgagor conveyed his lands outright in fee simple to the mortgagee, with a covenant for reconveyance if the debt was repaid on time. This is the classical common-law mortgage, and it was in general use until 1926. It seems to have come into prominence in the sixteenth century, when the Chancellor became ready to enforce the covenant specifically.[2] At common law the remedy for breach of covenant was an action for damages only, and it was no doubt the availability of specific performance in equity which allowed this form of mortgage to supersede the older form of mortgage which it resembles, in which the mortgagor grants a fee simple with a condition for re-entry on payment, instead of a covenant for reconveyance. The second main form of mortgage involved the grant of a lease to the mortgagee. Of

---

[1] Law of Property Act 1925, s. 87.

[2] Or perhaps earlier; see Turner, *Equity of Redemption*, p. 21, and the Introduction by Hazeltine at pp. xl *et seq.* There is a case in 1456, Selden Society, Vol. 10, p. 137, *Bodenham* v. *Halle.* Cf. Ames, *Lectures in Legal History*, Lect. XXII.

such mortgages by demise there were variants.[3] The mortgagor might grant a long lease of, say, five hundred years, to the mortgagee, with a provision that until he defaulted he could retain possession. If he paid on time the conveyance specified that the lease should be void. Alternatively, the grant of a long lease was followed by a regrant by the mortgagee of a sub-lease back to the mortgagor at a fixed rent, with a provision for the forfeiture of the sub-lease if the rent fell into arrears. Mortgages by lease were popular in the seventeenth century and until after Blackstone's time;[4] probably they were more frequently employed than was the classical mortgage. They had the advantage that they could be used for both freehold and leasehold property; they also conferred a chattel interest upon the mortgagee, which on his death passed to his executors, who were the persons entitled to the debt. This was more convenient than the classical form, because a fee simple conveyed by way of mortgage descended upon the mortgagee's heir, unless steps were taken to prevent this, thus separating the security from the debt. Mortgages by demise caused difficulty, however, because the fee simple reversion was left in the mortgagor even if he defaulted, and about the end of the eighteenth century they largely fell out of use.[5] Besides these two common-law forms of mortgage the use of statutes merchant and statutes staple and of tenancy by elegit survived for a while, but passed out of use in the seventeenth century.

Equitable Modification of Mortgages

The intervention of equity radically transformed the nature of mortgages. The common-law courts construed mortgage transactions strictly and unsympathetically. If the mortgage provided that the mortgagor was to lose his land through

---

[3] An ingenious form is found in *Bamfield* v. *Bamford* (1675), Selden Society, Vol. 73, p. 183.

[4] Cf. Blackstone, II, Ch. 10, III. See Simpson, *History of Contract,* pp. 126–35, 87–8 on statutes merchant and staple.

[5] See the notes to Co. Litt. 204b, 'These [mortgages by demise] are attended with this particular advantage, that on the death of the mortgagee, the term and the right in equity to receive the mortgage debt vest in the same person: whereas in cases of mortgages in fee, the estate, on the death of the mortgagee, goes to the heir, or devisee, and the money is payable to his executor or administrator . . . On the other hand, in cases of mortgages for years, there is this defect, that, if the estate is foreclosed, the mortgagee will only be entitled for his term.'

defaulting in payment upon a fixed day then that was that; it mattered nothing that he defaulted by a single day, or that the property was worth infinitely more than the debt. In the mid-fifteenth century the Chancellor began to intervene to protect mortgagors in peculiarly scandalous cases, and inevitably his readiness to intervene grew with time. At first the mortgagor was given redress when the mortgagee had been in possession, and had been satisfied by the rents and profits,[6] though not by payment, or when the mortgagor had paid on time but the mortgagee refused to reconvey.[7] In Elizabeth I's reign the Chancery begins to relieve mortgagors who had defaulted, and lost their land for ever at common law; they were allowed to redeem the land upon payment.[8] Such cases at first probably involve some particularly hard circumstances; the mortgagor has paid the major part of the debt on time, or has been robbed, or has paid late by accident.[9] By the time of *Emmanuel College* v. *Evans* (1625)[10] the requirement of special hardship has been dropped, and the Chancery has come to give relief against forfeiture of the land as a matter of course. The recognition of an equitable right of redemption in the mortgagor inevitably produces the correlative right of foreclosure in the mortgagee; this is first mentioned in 1629, in *How* v. *Vigures*.[11] The protection accorded to mortgagors was viewed as one aspect of a general policy of providing relief against penalties and forfeitures, and protecting persons from the unconscionable enforcement of legal rights.

---

[6] The earliest known case is *Bodenham* v. *Halle* (1456), Selden Society, Vol. 10, at p. 137. The whole matter is discussed by Turner, *Equity of Redemption*, pp. 21 *et seq.* Cf. the accountability of the mortgagee in possession, noted in *Holman* v. *Vaux* (*c.* 1616), Tothill 133.

[7] Y.B. 9 Edw. IV Trin., f. 25, pl. 34; here the plaintiff sued to recover a debt, and the defendant pleaded that he had enfeoffed the plaintiff of lands in fee simple on condition that the plaintiff should take the profits until the debt was paid, and then reconvey the land. He alleged that he was ready to pay the debt when the plaintiff was willing to reconvey. In the course of argument it was noted that the duty to reconvey was enforceable by subpoena.

[8] *Langford* v. *Barnard* (1594), Tothill 134, and cf. *Hammer* v. *Lochard* (1612), Tothill 132, 'a mortgagor relieved after the day of redemption, notwithstanding it was in infant's hands, and a purchase'.

[9] See Cary, 1.

[10] 1 Ch. Rep. 18.

[11] 1 Ch. Rep. 32.

The interference of equity was at first strongly resented, and an attempt was made to limit the right to redeem to a period of one year after forfeiture of the land at common law,[12] this failed, and after the Restoration the Chancery was allowed to develop its new creature without statutory interference.[13] By the end of the seventeenth century the conception of the debtor's power to redeem was developed into the conception of the equity of redemption,[14] a peculiar form of property which could be dealt with by the debtor like other forms of equitable property. Thus in *Roscarrick* v. *Barton* (1673)[15] it was held that it could be entailed in equity.

In the eighteenth century the final touches were put upon the conception; the equity of redemption is spoken of as an estate in the land, and the mortgagor is regarded as the owner in equity of the land. In his celebrated judgment in *Casborne* v. *Scarfe* (1738)[16] Lord Hardwicke described it in these terms:

An equity of redemption is considered as an estate in land; it will descend, may be granted, devised, entailed, and that equitable estate may be barred by a common recovery. This proves that it is not considered as a mere right, but as such an estate whereof, in the consideration of this court, there may be a seisin, for without such a seisin, a devise could not be good.

As soon as equity began to recognize a right of redemption, steps were taken to ensure that redemption was not hindered by provisions in the mortgage or by the activity of the mortgagee; any clog upon the mortgagor's right to redeem was simply void. The sense of clog here is of a piece of wood attached to an animal or even person to restrain movement. The principle was vigorously insisted upon by Lord Nottingham,[17] and it is only in

[12] In 1653 a Bill was introduced; it became an ordinance in 1654, but did not survive the Restoration.

[13] Lord Nottingham's contribution to this body of doctrine is discussed by D. E. C. Yale in Selden Society, Vol. 79, pp. 1–62.

[14] The expression is first found in 1654 in *The Duchess of Hamilton* v. *The Countess of Dirlton*, 1 Ch. R. 165.

[15] 1 Ch. Cas. 217.

[16] 2 J. and W. 194, cited Turner, *op. cit.*, at p. 66.

[17] See, for example, *Howard* v. *Harris*, I Vern. 1. The doctrine of clogs on the equity is found in 1639 in *Bacon* v. *Bacon*, Tothill 133. 'The court will relieve a mortgage to the tenth generation . . . and in some cases where the mortgagee will suddenly bestow unnecessary costs upon the mortgaged lands, of purpose to clogg the lands, to prevent the mortgager's redemption. . . .'

very modern times that any sort of inroad has been made upon it. The general theory accepted in Chancery from the seventeenth century onwards was that a mortgage, whatever its outward form, was no more than a security for a debt, and that the mortgagee's rights to the land must be so limited in Chancery as to ensure that he obtained a security and no more. Upon this theory the major part of the equitable interference with the mortgage can be justified; it was constantly used as the guide when new problems arose. The result was that the Chancery freely interfered with mortgage transactions with a complete indifference to the terms agreed by the parties; in no branch of the law was the sanctity of agreement less regarded.

The growth of the conception that a mortgage was but a security was accompanied by the practice of allowing the mortgagor to remain in possession of the land until he defaulted. This appears to have become usual from the end of the sixteenth century,[18] very frequently mortgage deeds expressly provided that it should be so. The medieval mortgage had been both in form and in fact a pledge; the land was actually handed over to the creditor. In form the mortgage continued a pledge, or at least adopted a form appropriate to a pledge; thus in the classical form of mortgage the fee simple was conveyed to the mortgagee. In substance, however, the nature of the transaction changed; it became a hypothecary transaction, in which the entry into possession of the mortgagee was an unusual step. Equity encouraged this development by developing the doctrine that a mortgagee in possession was strictly accountable for the profits of the land. The tendency in effect was for the mortgagee to rely more upon his rights over the land, which equity treated as the land another, than upon his legal estate in the land. This was encouraged too by the widespread custom of giving the mortgagee a power of sale over the land, which became the most valuable of his rights.[19] In equity the hypothecary charge was developed, but the common law was unable to develop the

[18] See *Stone* v. *Grubham* (1615), 2 Bulstrode 225, and generally Turner, *op. cit.*, Ch. V.

[19] At common law the mortgagee could sell his interest, be it a fee simple or a term, for it was *his*. But in equity he could not sell free from the equity of redemption, and to obviate this difficulty express powers of sale were inserted in mortgage deeds. The use of such powers dates from the early eighteenth century; see *Tucker* v. *Wilson* (1714), I P. Wms., at p. 262.

notion; not until the 1925 legislation was the realistic charge by way of legal mortgage introduced as an alternative to the mendacious legal mortgage.[20]

Landlord and Tenant

When, at the end of the Middle Ages, the lessee or termor acquired a right to obtain specific recovery of his lease, and became as well protected as a freeholder, the medieval doctrine that his interest was a mere chattel interest began to wear a strange look. In the early sixteenth century the security of tenure of the lessee was considerably improved. It had been the law that the lessor's feudal lord could evict the lessee during the wardship of his heir. After considerable vacillation this was changed by judicial decision.[21] The protection of lessees was taken a step farther in 1530,[22] when a statute put a stop to a device which had been tolerated before whereby a lessee could be ousted by the use of a collusive recovery by his landlord. Statute[23] also gave lessees who had been granted leases by limited owners some measure of protection against ouster by their landlords' successors in title.

In the sixteenth century the whole nature of the lessee's interest was reviewed in a number of cases, and a very confused body of law resulted.[24] The better view in the early sixteenth century was that the lessee was seised—a view that is historically correct.[25] Thus in a case in 1537[26] a lessor made a feoffment of some land whilst the lessee was on the land, and the question at issue was whether the feoffee acquired a freehold. Baldwin and Fitzherbert JJ. thought not, 'for the lessor has nothing to do with the possession during the term; and the livery and seisin are nothing but a gift of the possession, which the lessor cannot make without wronging the termor'. They concluded that the

---

[20] On the concept of usury, which applied to mortgages, see Simpson, *History of Contract*, pp. 113–17, 510–18.

[21] See Baker, Selden Society, Vol. 94, p. 182.

[22] 21 Hen. VIII, c. 15; see Co. Litt. 46a. This statute closed the gaps left by the statute of Gloucester.

[23] 32 Hen. VIII, c. 28, which, *inter alia*, allowed a tenant in tail to make a lease for twenty-one years which would bind the heir in tail.

[24] See Challis, 'Leaseholds, Are they Tenements?', 6 *L.Q.R.* 69.

[25] See above, pp. 71, 194, and cf. Littleton, sec. 567; but Littleton may be thinking of a lease accompanied by livery of seisin in this section.

[26] *Anon*, Dyer, 33a.

lessor should have granted the freehold reversion by deed, and this decision assumes that the seisin is in the lessee.[27] By Coke's time, however, this had all changed; 'seisin is a word of art, and in pleading is only applied to a freehold at least, as *possessed* for distinction sake is to a chattell real or personal'.[28] Yet some traces of the older conception that the lessee was *seised*, though not *seised of a freehold* survived in the law; thus a release by deed of the freehold reversion to a tenant for years is quite effective without livery of seisin; the rule is inconsistent unless the tenant for years already has seisin. In short the lessee is said not to be seised, but is treated for some purposes as if he is.

Chattels Real and the Doctrine of Estates

The most important consequence of the medieval rule that a term was 'but a chattel' was that on the termor's death his interest passed to his executor, and not to his heir,[29] he had no freehold and he had no estate of inheritance. The old common-law rule was that estates could not be carved out of chattel interests, so that a lessee, however long his lease, could not grant his interest to another in tail, for example, nor could he limit remainders in it.[30] With the fuller protection granted to lessees this old rule began to look anomalous, but it was maintained in the sixteenth century in respect of grants *inter vivos*.[31] The modern explanation for the rule that a leasehold could not be entailed is that a leasehold is not a *tenement* (a subject of tenure) and thus falls outside *De Donis*,[32] which speaks only of tenements, but whether this is historically correct is a difficult question: in the fifteenth and sixteenth centuries there was

[27] Cf. *Metteford's Case* (1578), Dyer, 362b, a decision only reconciliable with the view that a lessee has seisin.

[28] Co. Litt. 200b.

[29] The descent to the heir was the leading characteristic of 'real' property, but naturally a life estate cannot so descend: this may be one of the reasons why life estates and terms are treated as closely analogous.

[30] Y.B. 37 Hen. VI Trin., pl. 11 (an attempt to limit remainders in a mass book). There was a current of authority, beginning with this case, for the view that the *enjoyment* or use of chattels, though not the property, could be limited at common law by way of quasi-remainder; see a note in Owen's Reports at p. 33 (1565). This theory was rejected in *Manning's Case* (1609), 8 Co. Rep. 94b.

[31] See *Anon* (1552), Dyer 74a, *North* v. *Butts* (1557), Dyer 139b, *Woodcock* v. *Woodcock* (1600), Cro. Eliz. 795.

[32] See Challis in 6 *L.Q.R.* at p. 69.

doubt.[33] The truth is that leaseholds were treated as partaking of the nature of real property to the extent of being the subject of tenure, but not to the extent of being the subject of estates; they are half one thing and half the other.

The hybrid quality of leaseholds comes out again in connection with the Statute of Wills. This allowed devises 'at the free will and pleasure' of the testator, and the courts were disposed to take a generous view of this power. What was to happen if a testator devised a lease to one person with a remainder over to another? The common-law rule was that the gift of a chattel for an hour was a gift for ever,[34] but it was hard to maintain this dogma now that the interest of a lessee (particularly if he held under a long lease) looked so like an estate in land. For a long time there was doubt on the matter; thus in 1551 a case is reported thus:

Note that according to Mountague and Molyneux JJ. if a man seised of a term devises this to his wife for her life, the remainder to his son and his heirs male that this is a good remainder, notwithstanding that it is only a chattel. Hales J. to the contrary, for it is contrary to the nature of a chattel to be entailed.[35]

In the end a compromise solution was reached in *Manning's* and *Lampet's Cases*.[36] A testator was allowed to leave a leasehold by will to one person for life with a gift over to another; loosely speaking he was permitted to create remainders in leaseholds. But he was not allowed to carve estates of inheritance out of leaseholds; he could not make a leasehold descend to an heir, for to this extent a lease was treated as a chattel, which passed to the executor or administrator of a deceased lessee. Thus an

---

[33] Littleton, sec. 132, says there is a tenure, and his view was approved by Coke, Co. Litt. 93b. Contra Y.B. 5 Hen. V Hil., f. 12, pl. 30; 10 Hen. VI Mich., f. 13, pl. 44; 9 Edw. IV Pasch., pl. 1, f. 1. On Littleton's side are 9 Hen. VI. Mich., f. 43, pl. 22; 21 Edw. IV Pasch., pl. 24, f. 29; 5 Hen. VII Hil., pl. 2, f. 10. Cf. 40 Edw. III Trin., pl. 17, f. 34.

[34] Brooke, *Abridgement, Done et Remainder*, pl. 57. This rule is connected, of course, with the absence of any remedy for the remainderman, though detinue could have been adapted easily enough.

[35] From Rawlinson MS. C.112 (Bodleian Library), Hilary 4 Edw. VI. These reports are variously attributed to Harper J. and Dalison J., and were probably written by neither. Baker in his *Introduction to English Legal History* at p. 256 cites other MS. authority from this period.

[36] (1609) 8 Co. Rep. 94b, (1612) 10 Co. Rep. 46b; earlier cases are conflicting. See Lord Nottingham's history of the matter in 2 Swanston at p. 464.

entail of a leasehold was not possible.[37] This meant that the doctrine of estates was not applied to leaseholds; one could not be said to have a fee simple in a leasehold, so that if a leasehold was devised to A for life, remainder to B and his heirs B took by quasi-remainder only. B did not have any interest until A died, and then he took the lease, which was viewed as passing over to him. This was quite unlike the theory applied when a tenant in fee simple granted to A for life, remainder to B and his heirs, for there B obtained a fee simple in remainder at once. He had a present interest in the land, though one which did not entitle him to seisin until A died.

Thus it was that the leasehold interest in lands came to be treated in part as an interest in land, as real property, and in part as a chattel interest; it became a chattel real. It could not really be fitted into the scheme of things at all. Blackstone defines the lease oddly; he calls it,

a contract for the possession of lands and tenements, for some determinate period: . . . these estates were originally granted to mere farmers or husbandmen, who every year rendered some equivalent in money, provisions or other rent; but, in order to encourage them to manure the ground, they had a permanent interest granted to them, not determinable at the will of the lord. And yet their possession was esteemed of so little consequence, that they were rather considered as the bailiffs, or servants of the lord . . . than as having any property of this own.[38]

Since 1926 a lease has become an estate, and it may be that in the end English Law will evolve a law of property,[39] and not a law of real property and a law of personal property. If one had to point to a modern legal problem which is closely analogous to the problem posed by leasehold to the old lawyers, the modern position of the contractual licence springs to mind, for it lies, as leasehold once did, on the boundaries of contract and property.

---

[37] Finally settled in *The Duke of Norfolk's Case* (1681), 3 Ch. Cas. 30. Cf. *Childe* v. *Bailie* (1618–23), Palmer 48, 333, Cro. Jac. 459.

[38] Blackstone, Bk. II, Ch. 9. I. M. S. Arnold, 'Fourteenth Century Promises' 1976 *Camb. L.J.* at 323–30, deals with the earlier history of this approach.

[39] See F. H. Lawson and Bernard Rudden, *The Law of Property*, for a bold attempt to treat the law of property as a whole.

With the decay of the feudal tenurial system and the full recognition of the lease for years as an adequately protected interest in land, the lease for years became the legal institution under which a very great proportion of the land of the country was held. The landed gentry retained freehold interests, commonly under settlement, and exploited the land at one remove, and left a class of tenant farmers in actual occupation of the soil. They in their turn employed labourers, landless men, hired periodically, who might live in or have their own tied cottages. At its best this system could be an acceptable one. The landlord and tenant divided between them the burden of providing capital for agriculture, and a progressive landlord could do a great deal to encourage, and indeed insist upon, good husbandry. The system at its worst can be seen in the melancholy history of Ireland, where some of the English landlords rarely visited their estates, and were only concerned to extract from their tenants rents which would enable them to live in affluence in England. In the course of time the legislature has found it necessary to intervene to protect tenants against the abuses which rapacious landlords could readily perpetrate under the common law. In particular the legislature has intervened to give tenants a security of tenure beyond the term fixed by their lease, and to enable limited owners, particularly life tenants, to grant leases of longer duration than would have been possible at common law. With the exception of a statute of 1540, of restricted scope,[40] these interventions begin in the nineteenth century with the series of statutes dealing with settled land. At an earlier period the difficulties inherent in the lease could be dealt with only by private action. Thus settlements could include a grant of leasing powers to the life tenant, so that he could grant leases to endure beyond his life; covenants for renewal could be inserted into leases to give security to the tenant farmer. In one respect conveyancing practice in the sixteenth century curiously anticipated the modern position of the tenant farmer, for it was customary to grant leases for life rather than for years,[41] a custom which long survived on conservatively managed estates.

[40] 32 Hen. VIII, c. 28.

[41] But a lease for life, since it operated to pass the freehold, could not be limited to take effect in the future, whereas a lease for years could. A lease for life created a tenure between the tenant for life and the reversioner in fee, and upon this tenure rent service could be reserved.

Forms of Lease

In the sixteenth century the practice of granting farming leases for periods of twenty-one years became increasingly common. There are vague hints that extremely long leases were void at common law,[42] but by the seventeenth century it is clear that there were no restrictions upon the possible length of terms. Very long terms, however, are usually employed only as conveyancing devices. The longest customary period for a lease which is not merely a device is the building lease, customarily fixed by the nineteenth century at ninety-nine years. Local conveyancing custom has settled the usual terms for other purposes, and it varies today in different parts of the country and in different estates, as it has always differed.

Before the Statute of Frauds[43] a lease could be validly created by parole, whatever its length. In practice parole leases were probably not common. Conveyancers could use a number of possible formalities; for leases for fixed terms a bargain and sale in writing, or a simple indenture, were both commonly employed. The advantage of using a bargain and sale of a lease, which took effect under the Statute of Uses, was that it obviated the need for entry[44] by the lessee to complete the conveyance. Any other form of conveyance conferred upon the tenant a curious interest known as an *interesse termini*[45] until he entered, and this could produce inconvenience; for example, a sub-lease could not be created on an *interesse termini*. This troublesome doctrine survived until 1926.[46]

In Littleton's time it was clearly settled that a fixed duration was essential to a lease. A person who was let into possession of land by the freeholder but who was not granted any certain term

---

[42] Co. Litt. 45b, 46a, and cf. *Cotton's Case* (1613), Godbolt 192. Long leases were treated with suspicion in the sixteenth century because they could be used to defraud the Crown of feudal dues.

[43] (1677) 29 Charles II, c. 3.

[44] Littleton, sec. 58, 'And when the lessee entreth by force of the lease, *then* is he tenant for tearme of years'. The need for entry by the lessee is to be distinguished from the need for livery of seisin by the grantor when a freehold was conveyed; see Littleton, sec. 59. Livery of seisin to the lessee in addition to entry was necessary if freehold remainders were limited after the lease. Littleton is very difficult on the lessee's seisin. See secs. 456, 459, 460, 59, 60, 567.

[45] Co. Litt. 46b, Littleton 459 and Co. Litt. 270a.

[46] Law of Property Act (1925), s. 149 (1), (2).

was ranked as a tenant at will, and a tenancy at will could be determined at any time, though two special categories of such tenants, copyholders and *cestui qui usent*, came to be protected. Other tenants at will[47] were given some degree of protection by the law relating to emblements; if ejected after they had sown a crop, they had a liberty to enter the reap what they had sown. Otherwise they had a wholly precarious interest, and this made tenancies at will extremely unsatisfactory. Now in the developed law the periodic tenancy is recognized as a form of lease; the typical example is the yearly tenancy, which will continue until it is determined by six months' notice on either side, and such tenancies are extremely common. Such periodic or 'running' leases obviously pose a problem in legal analysis which is glossed over in modern textbooks, for in a sense they do not conform to the rule which requires a lease to be for a fixed term—they are in effect leases for an uncertain duration, determinable by notice. They are not leases for a fixed term with an option to renew; such an analysis is quite unrealistic. In short they are anomalous, and when they first came before the courts at the end of the fifteenth and the beginning of the sixteenth centuries they provoked a great deal of controversy. In 1506 a lease for one year, and then from year to year as the parties pleased, at a fixed rent, was held to be a lease at will only.[48] A case in 1522[49] on the same type of lease provoked a long discussion in the Common Pleas, and the judges were divided. Upon grounds of convenience, for such arrangements were common, Brudenell C.J. and Pollard J. were prepared to hold that by such an arrangement a lease for one year was created at once, followed by successive one-year terms for each year in which the arrangement was continued; if the tenant, with the consent of the landlord, continued in possession for one day of a new year, then a fixed term for the whole of that year was created. Fitzherbert and Brooke JJ. were not so sympathetic. Such an arrangement, in their view, created a lease

---

[47] Littleton, sec. 68, 'Tenant at will is where lands or tenements are let by one man to another to have and to hold to him at the will of the lessor, by force of which lease the lessee is in possession. In this case the lessee is called lessee at will, because he has no certain or sure estate, for the lessor may put him out at what time it pleaseth him.'

[48] Y.B. 21 Hen. VII Mich., f. 38, pl. 47. Cf. 13 Hen. VIII Trin., f. 15, pl. I.

[49] Y.B. 14 Hen. VIII Mich., f. 10, pl. 6, a lease 'for term of one year, to commence at the feast of St. Michael, to last to the end of the said year, and so for the next year, from year to year as long as the parties pleased'.

for one year and no more; thereafter the tenant who remained in possession became a tenant at will only. If the arrangement was expressed as a lease for *years* 'at the will of the parties', or 'for as long as the parties pleased', then they would treat it as a lease for a fixed term of two years (to give effect to the plural 'years') followed by a tenancy at will. For two centuries thereafter the dispute as to the nature of periodic tenancies continued its arid course. In 1601 Gawdy and Fenner JJ. adopted the view of Brudenell C.J. and Pollard J.[50] Popham C.J. introduced another quaint construction, for he held that a lease 'from year to year as the parties pleased' created a term of two years (from year to year = two years) followed by a tenancy at will. Popham's view was adopted in 1606,[51] where the court was confronted with a lease 'for a period of one year and so from year to year for as long as both parties should please'; three years are mentioned, and these are added up to confer a term of three years followed by a tenancy at will. This sort of absurd construction would lead one to say that a lease from 'year to year to year to year' would create a term of four years; neither common sense nor logic recommends it. Eventually the view of Brudenell and Pollard triumphed when the great Holt C.J. adopted it in 1702,[52] and in the course of the eighteenth century the dispute died out.

This paved the way for a new and important development. In the absence of an express arrangement for a periodic tenancy the courts were ready to imply one instead of a mere tenancy at will, so long as this could be justified, as it could be if rent had been paid and accepted by the year. Thus Blackstone says:

The law is however careful, that no sudden determination of the will by one party shall tend to the manifest and unforeseen prejudice of the other . . . courts of law have of late years leaned as much as possible against construing demises, where no certain term is mentioned, to be tenancies at will; but have rather held them to be tenancies from year to year so long as the parties so please, especially where an annual rent is reserved; in which case they will not suffer either party to determine the tenancy even at the end of the year, without

---

[50] *Agard* v. *King*, Cro. Eliz. 775.
[51] *The Bishop of Bath's Case*, 6 Co. Rep. 35b.
[52] *Leighton* v. *Theed* (1702), 1 Ld. Raymond 707.

reasonable notice to the other, which is generally understood to be six months.[53]

The terms upon which leases were granted naturally varied enormously. In the seventeenth century it became customary for the lessor to covenant that he had the right to demise, that the lessee should have quiet enjoyment, that the lessor should make further assurance if any difficulty over the title arose, and that the property was free from incumbrances. The lessee's basic obligation was the absolute duty to pay rent. In the sixteenth century there was a considerable development in the law which governed the extent to which covenants in a lease would run with the land and with the reversion. By extension of the rules relating to the running of covenants made on the sale of a fee simple it was settled by Coke's time that not only the benefit but also the burden of covenants ran with the lease. What medieval authority there was hardly concerned the running of the burden of covenants, but in *Spencer's Case* (1583)[54] the same rule was applied to both on the ground that he who takes the benefit should also take the burden. There were, however, limitations. The covenant must touch and concern the land, and not be merely collateral. The covenant must relate to something in being; the metaphysical bent of the sixteenth-century lawyers required that the covenant must annex itself to something concrete. Finally, the covenant must be expressed to be made with the assigns of the lessee.

The running of covenants with the reversion came to be recognized through a curious accident of history. When Henry VIII despoiled the monasteries he found that a large part of their lands had been leased; in order to dispose profitably of the reversions he decided to make statutory provisions enabling the grantees of the reversions to enforce the covenants in the leases, and to make the assignees of the reversions reciprocally liable to the burdens of the covenants. Thus was passed the statute of 1540.[55] The Act was not well drawn, and its precise scope was difficult to determine; upon it the courts performed a very intelligent process of interpretation and extension to produce the

[53] Blackstone, Bk. II, Ch. 9, sec. II.
[54] 5 Co. Rep. 16a.
[55] 32 Hen. VIII, c. 34.

modern situation. The major defect which eventually required statutory intervention was the rule that when the reversion was severed as regards the land the benefit of a condition in the lease was was not severable, and this inconvenient rule lasted until the nineteenth century.[56]

Restrictive Covenants

The starting point for the modern development of restrictive covenants is, of course, the case of *Tulk* v. *Moxhay* in 1848;[57] from that decision there has been developed a body of law which proved to be, if not an unmixed blessing, yet of very great importance in regulating the urban development of the country before the introduction of modern planning legislation, for it became possible to impose upon land by private treaty a wide variety of restrictions upon user and development. Today the older system of private regulation continues alongside the modern system of public regulation, and both have their distinctive merits, and their distinctive disadvantages.[58]

Tulk v. *Moxhay* was not, however, an entirely new departure, and if we are to understand the history of the equitable doctrine we must go back a little and examine not only the doctrines of equity but also the doctrines of law on the running of covenants. We have seen that in medieval law the benefit of covenants could run with land of the covenantee, even in the absence of privity of estate. Whether the burden of covenants could run was uncertain, and this uncertainty long continued; there was a tenuous line of authority to the effect that it could.[59] In *Keppel* v. *Bailey* (1834)[60] the enforceability of the burden of a covenant came before Lord Brougham in a suit in equity; the action arose between parties who were not the original covenantor and covenantee. Lord Brougham took the view that equity should follow the law and only enforce the covenant if it

[56] Law of Property (Amendment) Act (1859), s. 3. Conveyancing Act (1881), s. 12.
[57] 2 Ph. 774.
[58] Planned towns, such as Winchelsea, date back to the Middle Ages; planning law in its modern term is a product of this country, starting with the Housing, Town Planning etc. Act of 1909. In the previous two centuries 'planning' was conducted principally through private bill legislatior
[59] See the judgment of Lord Brougham in *Keppel* v. *Bailey*, 2 My. and K. 517 at pp. 540 *et seq.*
[60] 2 My. and K., p. 517.

was enforceable in a common-law court. After a masterly review of the authorities he came to the conclusion that the burden of such covenants did not run at law, a conclusion which has been vindicated in modern cases. He therefore held that the burden did not run in equity either. Lord Brougham did not, however, base his decision solely upon technical grounds, but went on to consider the matter on principle. He argued that to allow the burden of covenants to run with land would have very unsatisfactory consequences. 'It must not be supposed that incidents of a novel kind can be devised and attached to land at the fancy and caprice of the owner.' If this were to be permitted a person would be able to impress upon land whatever peculiar restrictions and impositions he wished, and they would burden the land in perpetuity into whosoever hands the land should afterwards come; in effect an owner could impose a tenure upon land by such covenants. The evils of allowing landowners so unrestricted a power was, in Lord Brougham's view, obvious enough, and his argument is an extremely convincing one. It must be noted that he was dealing with a composite covenant, partly negative and partly positive,[61] and the evils which he envisaged are more obvious in the case of positive covenants. But even in the case of negative covenants there is a great deal to be said in favour of Lord Brougham's opinion. The effect of restrictive covenants is to sterilize the use of a parcel of land permanently; in principle it is not at all clear that a private landowner ought to be allowed to do this without public control of his activities. Whatever their merits, restrictive covenants can have a very detrimental effect on the free development of land, which is not in all cases in the public interest.

In spite of the decision in *Keppel* v. *Bailey*, the question both in law and in equity remained unsettled, and it is clear that there existed a body of conveyancing opinion which was opposed to the decision. In 1838, after Lord Brougham had ceased to be Chancellor, and Lord Cottenham held the office, the Vice-Chancellor, Sir Lancelot Shadwell, acted on the view that the burden of a covenant could run in equity in *Whatman* v. *Gibson*.[62] In 1846 he gave a similar decision in *Mann* v.

---

[61] The covenant in question imposed, amongst other things, an obligation to pay money. [62] 9 Sim. 377, 196.

Stephens,[63] and this was upheld by Lord Cottenham; the only reason why this decision is not treated as a leading case is that the reasons of Lord Cottenham are not fully reported. Two years later the same point was decided in the same way by Shadwell V.C. and upheld by Lord Cottenham in *Tulk* v. *Moxhay*.[64]

Lord Cottenham approached the matter in an entirely different way from Lord Brougham. He did not dispute Lord Brougham's view that the burden of covenants did not run with land at law. The reason why in his view, an injunction could be obtained in a court of equity was quite unrelated to any doctrine about the running of covenants with land; equity here was not following the law, but relying upon the peculiar equitable doctrine of notice. He took the view that it would be inequitable to allow a purchaser of the land who bought it with express notice of the covenant to act in defiance of it. The reason why he thought it was inequitable was that if the purchaser of the land from the original covenantor was able to escape from liability under the covenant this would allow the covenantor to make an unfair profit; having bought Blackacre for £1,000, its value when burdened by the covenant, he could resell for £1,200, its unburdened value. Lord Cottenham also relied upon the principle *nemo dat quod non habet*. If a landowner could, by selling his land, convert it from burdened land to unburdened land, he would transfer something he had never himself owned. '. . . if an equity is attached to the property by the owner no one purchasing with notice of that equity can stand in a different situation from the party from whom he purchased.' The Chancellor did not in his judgment consider, as Lord Brougham had done, the social expediency of allowing burdens to be shackled upon property 'at the fancy or caprice of the owner', nor is there any indication whatever that he regarded the fact that the covenant was restrictive made any difference; all his reasoning would apply both to positive and negative covenants.

Nor indeed was his reasoning particularly convincing. If a sale of the land to a person who took free from the covenant was an objectionable transaction because of the unfair profit, this

---

[63] 15 Sim. 377.
[64] 2 Ph. 774; see also 1 Ha. and Tw. 105.

would be a reason for penalizing the vendor, not the vendee, for the unfair profit was destined for his pocket. Again, the argument from the principle *nemo dat quod non habet* begs the whole question, for it assumes that the equity *is* attached to the property, though this is the very question for decision. The argument in the judgment in *Tulk* v. *Moxhay* can equally well be applied to any contract affecting any property, and the wider issues which were involved in the case were simply not appreciated. It is not surprising that the decisions which followed upon the case produced a very unsatisfactory body of law. Thus the doctrine was applied to both negative and positive covenants,[65] the person enforcing the covenant did not have to retain land for whose benefit the covenant was entered into in the first place,[66] and the doctrine was even belatedly applied outside the sphere of real property.[67] It is unhistorical to regard these decisions as *extensions* of the rule in *Tulk* v. *Moxhay*. Only the second is in any way inconsistent with Lord Cottenham's reasoning, for it cannot be reconciled with the Chancellor's attempt to justify his decision by pointing out that unless the burden of covenants was attached to land in equity it would be impossible for the original covenantee to maintain the value of the land retained. But this justification has achieved far more prominence in the later law than it had in Lord Cottenham's judgment, where it occupies a very minor position.

In the course of time a reaction set in against so extreme a doctrine. Thus the courts limited the rule to negative covenants, they insisted that the new equitable right be modelled on the analogy of legal easements, so that there must be a dominant as well as a servient tenement.[68] The extension of the doctrine to chattels has been repudiated.[69] In the typical manner of lawyers a new history was invented to give plausibility to these restrictions. Jessel M.R. said that the doctrine was 'either an extension in equity of the doctrine of *Spencer's Case* to another

---

[65] *Morland* v. *Cook* (1868), L.R. 6. Eq. 252, *Cooke* v. *Chilcott* (1876), 3 Ch. D. 694.

[66] *Luker* v. *Dennis* (1877), 7 Ch.D. 227, *Catt* v. *Tourle* (1869), 4 Ch. App. 654.

[67] *De Mattos* v. *Gibson* (1858), 4 De G. and J. 276, *Lord Strathcona S.S. Co.* v. *Dominion Coal Co.*, [1926] A.C. 108.

[68] *Haywood* v. *Brunswick Permanent Benefit Building Society* (1881), 8 Q.B.D. 403; See *L.C.C.* v. *Allen*, [1914] 3 K.B. 642.

[69] *Port Line Ltd.* v. *Ben Line Steamers Ltd.* [1958] 2 Q.B. 146.

line of cases, or else an extension in equity of the doctrine of negative easements'.[70] It is true that the modern body of law on the subject can be viewed as Jessel M.R. suggests, but there is no historical truth in the belief that the decision in *Tulk* v. *Moxhay* itself owes anything whatever to these two analogies.

At the same time as this pruning of the equitable doctrine was being undertaken it was finally settled that the burden of covenants could not run at law,[71] that is in the absence of privity of estate. Conversely, the rule that the benefit could run was elaborated; although this was a common-law rule, the elaboration of the rule was mainly the work of the Chancery judges, for two reasons. The first was the fact that the normal remedy sought for breach of covenant was an injunction, which brought most cases into Chancery even where a legal remedy was available. The second was the consequence of the decision in *Tulk* v. *Moxhay*, which enormously increased the demand for injunctions, by increasing the range of potentially enforceable covenants. In general, the Chancery judges followed closely the legal rules on the subject, such as they were; the major innovation here was the peculiar rules applied to building schemes, which may be traced back to *Whatman* v. *Gibson* in 1838.[72] It is indeed in the building scheme that the restrictive covenant has proved to be most beneficial and at the same time, paradoxically, most objectionable. A restrictive covenant can be brought to an end by the agreement of the dominant and servient owner, but where a building scheme exists the number of persons who must consent is so large that in practice the area is subjected to a local law which may be incapable of alteration, unless the original scheme provides for some power of variation vested in trustees, which is sometimes the case. To some slight extent modern statutory powers have dealt with the problem of the obsolete covenant, but the power of compulsory discharge is very limited. This is all the more unsatisfactory in view of the failure of the Chancery judges, when they invented the whole doctrine, to impose any limitations upon the eccentricity of owners of land in imposing covenants upon land.

---

[70] *London and S.W. Rly.* v. *Gomm* (1882), 20 Ch. D. 562, at 583.
[71] *Haywood* v. *Brunswick Permanent Building Society* (1881), 8 Q.B.D. 403.
[72] 9 *Sim* 196: see also *Western* v. *MacDermot* (1866), L.R. 1 Eq. 499.

Easements and Profits.

The nineteenth century saw the settlement of the modern law of easements and profits, particularly of the former. Profits are essentially incidental to a system of agriculture which is no longer in use in most of the country, though in hill-farming country the right to pasture sheep on moorland commons remains essential to the type of farming practised. But in general, profits do not now have the importance which they had in the Middle Ages, when the basic rules governing them were settled. The decline in the importance of rights of common, the most usual form of profit, goes hand in hand with the spread of the enclosure movement and with the more frequent use of the lord's right to approve commons. Until the nineteenth century, enclosures were brought about by private act; more modern agricultural practice favoured the cultivation of land in separate fields, which was obviously more efficient. A series of public acts from 1801[73] onwards facilitated enclosures. In 1845[74] the need for private legislation was done away with altogether, and a Board of Inclosure Commissioners was set up to regulate schemes presented to them. Soon it was realized that the result of this legislation was that the country was being deprived of open spaces, which were of immense value for public recreation. Through the activities of the Commons Preservation Society, founded in 1865, the process was checked, and the Commons Act of 1876[75] severely limits the rights to enclose; schemes must be approved by the Board of Agriculture, and the private right to approve has been restricted though not abolished. But although the Act of 1876 practically halted the enclosure movement, the destruction of the ancient manorial structure of villages had by then been almost completed. The economic and social consequences of this process were very considerable, and remain controversial.[76] The only parts of the country where common

[73] 41 Geo. III, c. 109.

[74] 8 and 9 Vict., c. 118. See A. H. Manchester, *Modern Legal History*, pp. 315–19, *Sources*, pp. 342–5, Holdsworth, XIII, pp. 352–4.

[75] 39 and 40 Vict., c. 56.

[76] The starting point is J. L. and B. Hammond, *The Village Labourer 1760–1832*, on which see G. E. Mingay's introduction to the 1966 edition of E. C. K. Gonner, *Common Land and Enclosure* (1st ed. 1912); J. D. Chambers and G. E. Mingay, *The Agricultural Revolution 1750–1880*.

rights are still the backbone of the agricultural system are those mountainous areas where hill sheep-farming is practised. Elsewhere common rights are rarely of great importance, nor is it normal today to grant new profits to be enjoyed in severalty. Contracts now do the job which grants of property did in earlier times, so that, generally, surviving profits wear an archaic look. The Prescription Act (1832)[77] chose fairly long periods of prescription for profits, and the Act does not extend to profits in gross; the policy it adopted has tended against the perpetuation of profits in modern times.

The law relating to easements was greatly developed in the nineteenth century. The progressive urbanization of the country has had a great deal to do with this; so too has the process of enclosure, which made it necessary to define more closely the reciprocal rights and duties of the owners of separate holdings of lands. In the days of the common fields there was for example no need for many of the rights of way which exist today, for the local population could wander where they wished through the unfenced countryside without causing annoyance or injury, and the modern desire for privacy was hardly known. Thus Charles J. Gale, who in 1839 published the first treatise on the law of easements, wrote in his preface that

. . . the difficulties which arise from the abstruseness and refinements incident to the subject have been increased by the comparatively small number of decided cases affording matter for defining and systematizing this branch of the law. 'Upon some points indeed there is no authority at all in English Law'.

The rules which there were had grown up around the action on the case for nuisance and the older assize; until his book was written no attempt had been made to knit together a body of principle since Bracton attempted the task in the thirteenth century. Largely as a result of Gale's book the courts built up a body of law which owes a great deal to Roman and Continental Law, whose influence has been felt both through the borrowings from that system in Bracton, which Gale used, and from the direct recourse which Gale had to the Digest.[78]

---

[77] 2 and 3 Will. IV, c. 71.
[78] For an illustration see my discussion of the rule in *Wheeldon* v. *Burrows*, in 83 *L.Q.R.* 240, a piece embarrassingly marred by an error as to gender.

Thus the nature of an easement, and the salient differences between easements and other rights of a similar character, were settled in a series of cases. Since 1868 the law has been that an easement cannot exist in gross; there must be a dominant and a servient tenement, as in Roman Law.[79] The courts recognized that although easements must be analogous to the established types, yet so long as a right claimed was capable of benefiting the dominant land *as land*, new varieties of easement could be recognized to fit the changed conditions of society.[80] The position is perhaps best explained by saying that new *species*, but not new *genera*, may be added to the incidents of property. A curious example from a case in 1864 is a right to have the bowsprits (or, more correctly, jib booms) of ships projecting over adjoining land.[81] With one exception, the duty to fence easements could not be created which involved the servient owner in the expenditure of money; the essentially negative character of easements was well recognized, and suggested the restriction of the equitable rules which sprang from *Tulk* v. *Moxhay* to *restrictive* covenants only.

The distinction between easements and those natural rights which are attached by common law to all ownership of land, goes a long way back into the law, but the implications of the distinction were not fully appreciated until the nineteenth century. A series of cases drew the distinction between natural rights which might be confused with easements, and easements proper. An instance is the natural right which a landowner has to the support of his land in its natural state, and the easement of support which can be acquired in respect of buildings; for the former there is no need to show a grant or to prescribe, whilst for the latter there is.[82] The terminology which speaks of natural rights is now,

---

[79] *Rangeley* v. *Midland Rly. Co.*, L.R. 3 Ch., App. 306. Cf. *Hill* v. *Tupper* (1863), 2 H. and C. 121. See also Challis, *Real Property*, p. 54, note IV by Sweet, who suggests that a way in gross can be granted expressly, and cf. *Senhouse* v. *Christian* (1787), 1 T.R. 560, with *Thorpe* v. *Brumfitt* (1873), L.R. 8 Ch., App. 650.

[80] See the valuable discussion in Megarry and Wade, *Real Property*, pp. 838–9. Students should beware of the citation of Lord Brougham's dictum in *Keppel* v. *Bailey* (1833), 2 My. and K. 517, at p. 535, in this context; Lord Brougham's view that 'It must not be supposed that incidents of a novel kind can be devised and attached to property, at the fancy and caprice of any owner' was totally rejected in *Tulk* v. *Moxhay*, which allows landowners to do precisely what Lord Brougham condemned.

[81] *Suffield* v. *Brown* (1864), 4 De G. J. and S. 185.

[82] See *Dalton* v. *Angus* (1881), 6 App. Cas. 740, for a classic illustration of the difficulties of the distinction.

however, suspect; it is simpler and more intelligible to talk of the situations in which a landowner can sue in tort without proving the existence of a servitude,[83] than to speak of natural rights and attempt to list these. The confusion between the two arose, as we have seen, because the action for nuisance can sometimes be used to protect servitudes and sometimes to protect 'natural rights'; when the law of servitudes was thought to be no more than a commentary on a form of action it was easy to fall into the error of forgetting its dual function. A similar confusion is to be found in modern textbooks, where it is said that nuisances can be legalized by prescription. Were this true the definition of a nuisance would be the same as the definition of an easement, for it is easements, a form of property, which can be acquired in this way. What has happened here is that the law of torts (which deals with actions for wrongs) has been confused with the law of property (which deals with the subjects of property rights, amongst other things). Of course, some easements do permit the dominant owner to commit what would otherwise be a private nuisance. But not all easements do, for a right of way allows the dominant owner to trespass, not to commit nuisance. Again, some acts which prima facie amount to a nuisance (or to a trespass) can by acquiescence give rise to a prescriptive title to an easement, but there are also some acts, such as the repeated emission of foul smells, which can never found a prescriptive claim, for there is no easement of malodour.

Licenses Affecting Land

The distinction between easements and licences, as had been recognized in the fifteenth century,[84] lay in the fact that an easement was a right of property, whereas a licence was a revocable permission to commit some act which would otherwise be unlawful. The difference was lucidly set out by Vaughan C.J. in *Thomas* v. *Sorrel* in 1674. 'A dispensation or licence properly passeth no interest, nor alters or transfers property in any thing, but only maketh an action lawful, which without it had been unlawful.'[85] There was no chance of confusing a licence

---

[83] A good example of a decision which illustrates the distinction is *Tenant* v. *Goldwyn* (1705), 2 Ld. Raymond 1090, 6 Mod. 311.

[84] Y.B. 20 Edw. IV Trin., pl. 2, f. 4.

[85] Vaughan 330, at p. 351; cf. *Webb* v. *Paternoster* (1620), Palmer 71.

with a lease, for any arrangement which conferred a right of possession of land even if the possession was terminable at will, would create some form of tenancy; a bare permission to occupy would give rise to a tenancy at will. The present day 'licence with exclusive possession', which has caused so much confusion, would have caused merriment if it had been suggested fifty years ago. What did cause some difficulty in the nineteenth century was the revocability of licences which were coupled with the grant of an interest. In *Wood* v. *Leadbitter* (1845)[86] it was settled that such a licence could not be revoked prematurely; unfortunately, in that case it was not made sufficiently clear that the interest must not be an interest in the colloquial sense, but an interest in property, and this led to the decision in *Hurst* v. *Picture Theatres* in 1915.[87] At the same time the application of equitable doctrines of estoppel, largely the invention of Sir John Romilly, led to decisions which made inroads upon the common-law doctrine of the revocability of licences.[88] Once it was admitted that some licences could be irrevocable, there arose a risk that licences might become elevated into property rights, of which irrevocability is one feature. Modern cases have to a large degree resolved the confusion which the irrevocability of licences might have caused, by adopting the sensible view that licences granted by contract cannot be revoked in breach of contract; this does not elevate licences into property rights, for the irrevocability applies only as between the parties to the contract. But there are modern cases which have tended to elevate some licences into property rights, capable of binding persons other than licensor and licensee.[89] The relative vagueness and fluidity of the concepts involved enables courts to fashion fair results in situations in which those involved have neglected formalities, often through acting without proper legal advice. The future form of the law affecting licences has become uncertain, and this uncertainty can be traced back to the decision in *Wood* v. *Leadbitter*, and the evolution of the doctrine of equitable estoppel in the mid-nineteenth century.

[86] 13 M. and W. 838.
[87] [1915] 1 K.B. 1.
[88] See for example *Dilwyn* v. *Llewelyn* (1862), 4 De G. F. and J. 517.
[89] E.g. *Errington* v. *Errington,* [1952] 1 K.B. 290, a decision which is very confused in its reasoning. On the whole subject see Megarry and Wade, *Real Property,* pp. 806–8.

Prescription

The acquisition of easements was to some extent simplified by the Prescription Act; the defects of this statute can be followed out in any modern textbook, but for all its defects the Act certainly did improve the position. It was passed, so tradition has it, because of Lord Tenterden's dislike of the fiction of the lost modern grant. This fiction dates from the middle of the eighteenth century;[90] the earliest reported case is *Lewis* v. *Price* (1761), and it may be that Wilmot J. was the father of the device.[91] The reasoning behind the doctrine was ingenious and plausible. Under the Statute of Limitation then in force[92] twenty years' occupation of land normally operated as a bar to an action of ejectment. The Statute of Limitation could not possibly be interpreted to cover actions connected with easements, but the eighteenth-century judges thought that it was rather ridiculous that although twenty years' enjoyment usually sufficed to render an occupier of a house secure, enjoyment since 1189 had to be shown before the same person could acquire an easement of light in respect of the same house.[93] In thinking that this situation was anomalous the judges were surely right, and it is curious that the similar anomaly which exists in the modern law passes with so little comment. To remedy this situation judges began to direct juries that if twenty years' user, or more, could be shown, they would be entitled to treat this as evidence of the grant of an easement.[94] This way of putting the matter

---

[90] It has been suggested that the fiction can be traced back to *Bedle* v. *Wingfield* (1607), 12 Co. Rep. 4, a decision that a grant of an incorporeal thing—an advowson— would be presumed from long user, but the case turns on its own special facts. The advowson in question was shown to exist in 1303, and there was no evidence that it did not exist in 1189, nor was the immemorial antiquity of the advowson in dispute. The question at issue was this: had the advowson passed to the plaintiff's predecessor in title in 1303 by a Crown grant? The words of the surviving charter were not apt to pass the advowson, but in view of the enjoyment since 1303 by the plaintiff's predecessors in title it was held that another grant by deed at that date must be presumed. Nobody doubted that the advowson existed; the question was, who had title to it?

[91] 2 Wms. Saunders 175. The introduction of the fiction is connected with the relaxation of the rule that he who relies on a deed in litigation must produce it; see *Read* v. *Brookman* (1789), 3 T.R. 151.

[92] (1623) 21 Jac. I, c. 16.

[93] See *Lewis* v. *Price* (1761), 2 Wms. Saunders 175, *Campbell* v. *Wilson* (1803), 3 East 298.

[94] See, for example, *The King* v. *Jollife* (1823), 2 B. and C. 59.

was the only one theoretically open to them, for any title to an easement had to depend upon a grant at some time, but there were judges who were prepared to go even further, and to hold that twenty years' user actually operated as a bar to any action by the servient owner,[95] a doctrine which was repudiated in *Campbell* v. *Wilson* (1803).[96] Up to the passing of the Prescription Act the theory of the matter was quite settled: twenty years' user gave rise to a presumption of a grant, and in the absence of special circumstances a judge was correct to direct juries fairly strongly to find a grant proved. The presumption could, it was said, be rebutted, but it was not quite clear how; nor is it clear today.[97]

For some reason or other the lost modern grant fiction is said to have upset the judges of the early nineteenth century; why they should have been more conscience-striken about this than they were about the equally ludicrous prescription since 1189 has never been clear, if indeed there is any truth in the story.[98] In consequence of criticism in the First Report of the Real Property Commissioners, and the enthusiasm of Lord Tenderden, the Prescription Act[99] was passed; the Act did not however exactly follow the recommendations of the commissioners. The object of this statute was to do away with the need for the fiction, but to preserve the effect of it, and to render obsolete prescription at common law.[100] Thus the statutory rules for the acquisition of easements by the twenty-year period[101] represent an attempt to codify the rules governing the lost modern grant doctrine. Before the Act twenty years' user

[95] *Holcroft* v. *Heel* (1799), 1 Bos. and Pull. 400.

[96] 3 East 298, and cf. *Darwin* v. *Upton* (1786), 2 Wms. Saunders 175.

[97] See *Angus* v. *Dalton* (1877), 3 Q.B.D. 85, and the same case in the House of Lords, 6 App. Cas. 740.

[98] See Thesiger L.J. in *Angus* v. *Dalton* (1878), 4 Q.B.D. 162, at p. 171, and cf. *Bright* v. *Walker* (1834), 1 C.M. and R. 211.

[99] (1832) 2 and 3 Will. IV, c. 71.

[100] The account given in the text seems to the writer to be the only intelligible reconstruction of Lord Tenterden's intentions, and is based in part on the terms of the Act and partly on Lord Tenterden's speech in the Lords (15 March 1831), *Hansard*, 3rd Ser., Vol. III, c. 442. It is clear that the idea that Lord Tenterden was largely motivated by a desire to preserve jurors from moral contamination has been exaggerated; he simply wanted to tidy up an unsatisfactory branch of the law. An alternative text of his speech is given by Campbell, *Lives of the Chief Justices*, Vol. II, p. 325; both texts present difficulties.

[101] Secs. 1 and 2.

nec vi nec clam nec precario gave rise to a rebuttable presumption
of a grant; presumably the presumption could be rebutted in a
variety of ways, as a claim under the ordinary rules for
common-law prescription could be rebutted, but the one
defence to a claim by lost grant which was clearly not open to a
defendant was to show that the user commenced after 1189.
The Prescription Act attempted to maintain this existing position. Again, the easement of light was treated anomalously[102]
because the cases before the act so treated it,[103] and the statute
attempted to reproduce the existing law. It is true that the lost
modern grant fiction was not abolished in terms, but the clear
intention of the statute was to abolish it; why should anyone
employ a revolting fiction to produce the same effects as the
statute? The Act did go beyond mere codification by its provisions for the acquisition of easements by the forty-year
period, which was intended to supplant prescription at common
law, and by its provisions as to the acquisition of profits, but it
was not clear that the lost modern grant fiction was applicable
to profits at all.

Why, then, did the lost grant fiction survive the Act? To
understand this we must see what advantages the fiction retained which made it worthwhile for claimants to continue to
plead a lost grant. The first reason was that the Act was so badly
drafted that it was not at all clear what easements could be
claimed under it.[104] The second was the requirement under the
act of showing twenty years' enjoyment immediately before an
action was brought, which is the fatal flaw in the scheme of the
statute. The explanation of the draftsman's choice of the period
before an action was brought is simple enough: he confused the
working of a system of limitation of actions with a system of
acquisitive prescription, and instead of producing a Prescription Act he produced a cross between a Prescription Act and a
Statute of Limitations. It is not entirely reprehensible that he
did so. The lost grant fiction was developed by analogy with the
Statute of Limitation of 1623 and, as we have seen, there was

---

102 Sec. 3.
103 See *Cross* v. *Lewis* (1824), 2 B. and C. 686, where it is pointed out that the only way
in which a landowner can prevent the acquisition of a right to light is to obstruct his
neighbour's windows, since the enjoyment of light is not an actionable wrong.
104 See Holdsworth, VII, p. 352.

some authority in the cases for two explanations of the effect of twenty years' enjoyment of a servitude. The one which was best supported was the fiction of the lost grant—twenty years' user gave rise to a prescriptive title. The other was that twenty years' user operated as a bar to the servient owner's right of action.[105] The draftsman confused the two, and although the Prescription Act should have adopted the first in all its particulars, he fell into the error of being influenced by the second theory and treated the twenty-year period as if it was a period of limitations of an action.

Thus it was that the lost modern grant fiction had to be preserved, for otherwise great injustice would have been done in cases where a claimant could show twenty years' user, but could not show twenty years' user immediately before he brought his action.[106] The survival of the oldest method of prescription, which depends upon user since 1189, is the result in part of the same deficiencies in the Prescription Act which preserved the lost modern grant, and in part the result of the rule that the lost modern grant is only to be employed as a last resort.[107] Thus although the same facts which will base a claim on immemorial user will always suffice to establish a claim by lost modern grant a claimant must always try immemorial user first.

The nineteenth-century judges no doubt did their best to interpret the Prescription Act so as to avoid injustice, but it is hardly surprising that they produced a disorderly and uncertain body of laws, and that many simple and obvious points remain unsettled to this day. The Act is a classic example of an incompetent attempt to reform the law.

[105] See *Holcroft* v. *Heel* (1799), 1 Bos. and Pull. 400.
[106] Per Lord Blackburn, *Angus* v. *Dalton* (1881), 6 App. Cas., at p. 814.
[107] See *Bryant* v. *Lefever* (1879), 4 C.P.D. 172.

XI

The Nineteenth-century Movement for Reform

It is difficult in a short account of the history of the leading doctrines of the land law to give any convincing impression of the extreme complexity achieved by the beginning of the nineteenth century. To some extent this complexity was not special to land law, but also existed in other branches of the system, for example in the law of procedure and pleading. But the law of landed property, formed centuries earlier in feudal conditions, harboured many ghosts of the past, and this was one reason why the disease was there particularly gross. Another reason was that the refined elaboration of legal principles and distinctions is carried furthest in those branches of the law where the richest pickings are to be had, and landed wealth was still the principal form of wealth.

The Earlier Reforms

Consciousness of the defects of the post-medieval law, and the possibility of improving it by legislation or judicial decision, long predate the nineteenth century. Thus the seventeenth century saw what has been called a popular movement for law reform,[1] and under the Commonwealth a variety of proposals were advanced for simplifying the law. In particular it was proposed that fines and recoveries be abolished and the barring of entails simplified, fines for alienation of copyhold lands restricted, the half-blood allowed to inherit, and a system of registration of conveyances and descents of lands established locally. Such proposals did not all originate with radicals who were hostile to lawyers as such; professionals such as William Sheppard and Matthew Hale, the latter presiding over a law reform committee in 1652, were involved. But the only sub-

[1] See D. Veall, *The Popular Movement for Law Reform 1640–1660*, esp. ch. X, Holdsworth, VI, pp. 412–23.

stantial changes in the law which occurred in the seventeenth century were embodied in the Statute of Tenures in 1660, and the Statute of Frauds in 1677. The former re-enacted Commonwealth legislation of 1656; military tenures had in fact gone by Parliamentary order in 1646. The latter did not originate under the Commonwealth; its function was that of insisting upon formality in more important legal transactions.[2] It required writing for transactions conveying freehold interests in land, or terms of years, with the exception of leases for less than three years at a rent equal to two-thirds or more of real value. The statute also regulated the making and revocation of wills of real estate requiring signed writing and attestation; there were exceptions, for example wills by mariners at sea. Declarations and creations of trusts of lands were also to be 'manifested and proved' by signed writing; so too were assignments. Somewhat modified, these provisions remain in force,[3] though the Real Property Act of 1845[4] required a deed for conveyances where the Act of 1677 required only writing. The Statute of Frauds also required written evidence of contracts to convey interests in land, such contracts being formerly actionable even if by parole only. This provision was in effect modified by the evolution of the mysterious equitable doctrine of part-performance, which emerged shortly after 1677.[5]

The eighteenth century was, so far as land law is concerned, a period of legislative quiescence, but even then there were some stirrings. Thus Lord Mansfield attempted, although without success, to modify the practical effect of the archaic rule in *Shelley's Case* by treating it as a rule of construction only, which could be bypassed by evidence of contrary intention.[6] This attempt at law reform by judicial decision foundered amidst much esoteric controversy, and the celebrated and pointless rule survived until 1926. Blackstone, himself no great radical, found fault with the absurdities of fines and recoveries, though without immediate effect. And repeated attempts were

[2] For discussion see Holdsworth, VI, pp. 379–97, Simpson, *History of Contract*, pp. 599–620.   [3] Megarry and Wade, *Real Property*, pp. 478, 636–38.

[4] Replacing the Transfer of Property Act of 1844.

[5] For discussion see Simpson, *History of Contract*, pp. 613–16, P. Hamburger in 27 Am. J.L.H. 254–285.

[6] See *Perrin* v. *Blake* (1770), 4 Burr. 2579, *Foxwell* v. *Van Grutten*, [1897] A.C. 658; also Holdsworth, III, p. 109.

made to secure legislation establishing either a general system of registration of conveyances, or local registries.[7] In 1739, indeed, a bill to establish a general registry actually passed the Commons. Out of all of this came however only local registries for Yorkshire and Middlesex, established in the early eighteenth century—the Yorkshire system starting with the West Riding in 1703 and that for Middlesex in 1708.[8] The East Riding and Kingston-upon-Hull obtained the same system in 1707, and the North Riding in 1735. Ireland acquired a similar system in 1707.[9] But after this movement in the early eighteenth century, legislative modification of the land law during the rest of this period was of a minor nature, such as legislation in 1741[10] curing certain formal defects in the levying of common recoveries.[11]

The resistance to reform arose from a number of factors. There was amongst laymen a reluctance to suggest interference with so incomprehensible a mystery of the law of property, which they could not hope to understand. Until the *Commentaries* of Blackstone appeared in the 1760s there was no way of acquiring the elements of the law of property, unless one was prepared to become a practitioner. Even amongst the practitioners only a few possessed an extensive grasp of the law, which was essential to any intelligent proposals for reform. Those who did understand the system encouraged the view that it was dangerous or even beyond the wit of man to meddle with so elaborate a structure, upon which the sacred property rights of the people were based.[12] The property-owning classes saw that the system could be made to work, at a price, and realized that the system of primogeniture enshrined in the strict settlement was the very basis of their whole way of life. Even if they were sympathetic to schemes to reduce the expense and delay involved,

[7] The best account is that of Charles Fortescue-Brickdale in the article 'Land Registration' in the 13th edition of the *Encyclopaedia Brittanica*. See also Holdsworth, VI, p. 532, note 9, XI, pp. 586–8.

[8] 2 and 3 Anne c. 4, 7 Anne c. 20.

[9] The Registration of Deeds (Inland) Act.

[10] 14 Geo. II. c. 20.

[11] Holdsworth, XI, pp. 586–94, summarizes this legislation.

[12] When it was proposed to abolish Fines and Recoveries, whilst preserving their effect, Sir Edward Sugden, later Lord St. Leonards and one of the outstanding property lawyers of the period, thought that it would prove beyond human ingenuity to draft a bill to achieve this result. Mr. P. B. Brodie achieved the impossible. See Campbell's *Lives of the Chancellors*, VII, p. 565.

they were not anxious to interfere with the fundamentals of the law.

In the expense and delay the common run of lawyers had, of course, a vested interest: simple cheap conveyancing and certainty of titles do not increase the emoluments of attorneys. Originally conveyancing was not reserved for lawyers, nor indeed for anyone else; the matter was not legally regulated. In 1712, however, the members of the Company of Scriveners acquired a monopoly in the City of London, and the attorneys and solicitors resented this. The Society of Gentleman Practisers in the Courts of Law and Equity (formed in 1739) succeeded in ending the monopoly in 1760, and in 1804 persuaded Pitt to support legislation monopolizing conveyancing for gain for lawyers—including barristers—as a concession at a time when stamp duty for practising certificates was being increased. Thereafter, lawyers, and eventually solicitors, had a special interest in maintaining an elaborate system of private conveyancing.[13]

Yet for all this there was a growing desire for reform of the whole system of English Law which bore fruit in the second quarter of the nineteenth century and thereafter. The factors which encouraged the general movement for reform are intricate and a matter for general history, posing the problem of whether to seek an explanation primarily in the world of ideas, or rather in the logic of economic forces and realities. In the case of the land laws we can note only those which were of particular importance. After 1832 the political influence of the country landowning classes diminished, albeit very slowly, and there was in consequence a better chance for reforming measures designed to bring the land law into line with the needs of a commercialized, industrial nation. The reform of the law governing settled land is an apparent illustration of this shift in political power, though the reform initially worked in favour of the landowning classes. The belief in the value of a free market economy inevitably had implications for the land law, suggesting, for example, the need for reforms which would cheapen and facilitate the transfer of landed property. It was

[13] See B. Abel-Smith and R. Stevens, *Lawyers and the Courts*, pp. 19–24, and generally. The decline in conveyancing by barristers dates from the late nineteenth century; *op. cit.*, 213–14, 222, 440–1.

also very important that a number of able and influential lawyers allied themselves to the movement for reform, these men had the immense advantage of attacking the abuses of the system from within, and of having the technical competence to suggest and draw up concrete proposals for reform, instead of merely inveighing against this or that absurdity. Particularly important was the involvement of Henry Brougham, whose celebrated six-hour speech on the state of the law, delivered as Lord Chancellor in 1828, led to the establishment of the Real Property Commissioners, and of James Humphreys, whose *Observations on the Actual State of the English Laws of Real Property, with the outlines of a Code* had been published in 1826, and received the approval of Jeremy Bentham, the arch advocate of rationalization of the law and of codification.[14]

The Real Property Commissioners

The Real Property Commissioners were appointed in 1829 in response to Brougham's speech, their chairman being John Campbell, later Lord Chief Justice of the King's Bench and Lord Chancellor. Proceeding by taking both written and oral evidence they produced four massive but extremely lucidly presented reports in 1829, 1830, 1832, and 1833.[15] Nothing comparable had been produced before, or, for that matter, since. The first report dealt with inheritance, dower, curtesy, fines, recoveries, prescription, and limitation. The second was concerned with the proposal to establish a general registry of deeds and instruments affecting land. The third dealt with tenures, contingent remainders, future interests and perpetuities, and with covenants and the limitation of church rights. The fourth dealt with wills and probate.

All the reports reflect a general philosophy of law reform in the field of the land law which is set out explicitly in the first

---

[14] See generally A. H. Manchester, *Modern Legal History*, esp. Ch. I. Other important figures were Charles Butler (1750–1832), a Catholic conveyancer, John Campbell (1779–1861), later Lord Chief Justice and Lord Chancellor, Richard Bethell (1800–73), Hugh McCalmont Cairns (1819–82), and Joshua Williams (1813–81). See entries in Simpson, *A Biographical Dictionary of the Common Law*.

[15] These reports are most generally available in the microfiche edition, the references being *British Sessional Papers* 1829 (263) X 1, 1830 (575) XI, 1, 1831–2 (484) XXIII 321, 1833 (226) XXII 1. The figure in bracket refers to the sessional number, and is not needed to locate the report.

report. Essentially the commissioners argued that a distinction needed to be made between the mechanisms for the transfer and creation of rights in landed property, which were gravely defective, and the substance of what could be created and transferred, which was in all essentials more or less perfect. Hence they reported:

We have the satisfaction to report that the Law of Real Property seems to us to require very few essential alterations; and that those which we shall feel it our duty to suggest are chiefly modal. When the object of transactions respecting land is accomplished, and the estates and interests in it which are actually created and secured, the Law of England, except in a few comparatively unimportant particulars, appears to come almost as near perfection as can be expected in any human institution.

In accordance with this philosophy they rejected such radical proposals as the abolition of primogeniture in favour of partibility, the abolition of the doctrine of tenure, or of copyhold tenure, or the introduction of a codified system of property law, much less any redistributive modification of the law. Rather, said the commissioners:

We dread the shock that would be occasioned by any precipitate attempt at emendation, and we recollect that it is as impossible suddenly to change the laws as the language of any country . . . We shall study to interfere as little as possible with established rules, and in all new enactments to preserve the spirit and analogies of existing institutions.

Hence the recommendations of the commissioners were designed either to abolish anachronisms, pointless rules and distinctions, and absurdities of one kind and another—essentially a pruning job—or, more positively, to establish a system of private conveyancing of a simpler kind, its simplicity resting upon a scheme of registration of deeds and instruments.

The Abolition of Anachronisms

It would be impossible here to list all the specific recommendations of the commissioners. They included the abolition of the rule that inheritances could never ascend, and that the half-blood could not inherit, the abolition of dower *ad ostium ecclesiae* and *ex assensu patris*, the abolition of fines and recoveries and of all the real actions, the simplification of the law of limitation of actions around a twenty and a forty-year period, and the abolition of gavelkind, borough english, tenure in ancient demesne. Extensive modifications were recommended to simplify the rules governing dower and curtesy, acquisition of title by adverse possession, and acquisition of easements and profits by prescription. The varied systems for the making of wills—there were ten different ones—were to be assimilated. In the extraordinarily complex world of future interests and perpetuities it was recommended that contingent remainders should cease to be destructible by the premature ending of the precedent estate, and that in the law of perpetuities the 'lives in being' for the purpose of the rule should be restricted to those which 'might be in any manner connected with the objects of the settlement, or the dropping of which might furnish the motive of one of its limitations'. The report contains a long and interesting discussion of the problems raised by Peter Thelluson's will,[16] and by the new forgotten litigation in *Bengough* v. *Edridge* (1826–7).[17]

The legislation which followed the reports implemented some, but not all of, these suggestions; thus the abolition of gavelkind and borough english had to wait until the reforms of 1925, and tenure in ancient desmesne may still exist. The principal legislation based on the reports comprised six acts. The Inheritance Act of 1833 implemented most of the relevant recommendations.[18] The Fines and Recoveries Act[19] of the same year, drafted by one of the commissioners, P. B. Brodie, abolished these venerable institutions. The Act did away with the mumbo-jumbo of the common vouchee and the mass of ill-understood mysticism which surrounded these ancient methods of barring entails, and set up instead a simple system which

[16] Peter Thelluson's will, and the ensuing litigation is discussed by Morris and Leach, *Perpetuities*, 2nd ed., pp. 266–7, who list the reported cases. Papers connected with the litigation exist in the Public Record Office (Treasury Solicitor's Papers). See also Holdsworth, VII, p. 230.

[17] I Sim. 173, 57 E.R. 544. On Lady Denison's will see 4 Vesey 286, 11 Vesey 115.

[18] 3 and 4 Will. IV, c. 106. A later Act of 1859 (22 and 23 Vict., c. 35) implemented a recommendation not adopted in 1833, whereby if on intestacy no heirs of the last purchaser could be found, descent could be traced from the person last entitled.

[19] 3 and 4 Will. IV, c. 714. This Act is still in force. See Megarry and Wade, *Real Property*, p. 83.

faithfully preserved the substance of the old law, shorn of its absurdities. The Real Property Limitation Act, again of 1833,[20] abolished all the real actions, with three exceptions. They were the writs of right of dower, dower *unde nihil habet*, and *quare impedit*, used to settle disputes as to advowsons. The action of ejectment was no substitute for these actions, and the commissioners' recommendation that they should be replaced was not implemented until 1860, when the Common Law Procedure Act abolished the last of the real actions.[21] By 1833 the real actions were in general of course not used, except when ejectment was statute barred. Such actions, the commissioners explained: 'have generally originated in schemes of unprincipled practitioners of the law to defraud persons in a low condition of life of their substance, under pretence of recovering for them large estates, to which they have no title'.[22] More positively, this Act established, subject to certain exceptions,[23] a standard period of limitation of twenty years for the limitation of actions affecting real property, and very considerably simplified the intensely complex law of adverse possession, abolishing the arcane doctrines of descents cast, discontinuances, and continual claim.

The Dower Act of 1833[24] in general implemented the recommendations of the commissioners, which were based upon the belief that since a widow's right to dower had come to be barrable by the husband, albeit by various complex devices, the law might as well openly recognize this fact and render these expedients unnecessary. The right to dower was not formally abolished,[25] but it only applied to property to which the husband was beneficially entitled at death, and only if he had not abrogated it either by deed in his lifetime, or in his will. In short, the widow's right was now formally placed at her husband's mercy. Dower went finally only in the 1925 legislation.[26]

[20] 3 and 4 Will. IV, c. 27.

[21] 23 and 24 Vict., c. 145.   [22] Cf. the celebrated Tichborne Case.

[23] The exceptions dealt with cases where the claimant was under disability, or entitled in remainder or reversion. Special periods applied to claims to advowsons, claims by corporations sole, and claims to recover crown lands, the latter being regulated by the Crown Suits Act of 1769.   [24] 3 and 4 Will. IV, c. 105.

[25] Indeed it was extended to equitable estates.

[26] Subject to the bizarre exception of an adult who was a lunatic by 1925 and dies a lunatic since: such persons could still exist. The legislation was not retrospective, and doweresses may still be encountered.

The Wills Act of 1837[27] again broadly followed the recommendations of the fourth report, and considerably simplified the complex law of testamentary disposition. Before it was passed, to give one example of the difficulties which it removed, a will only affected land which the testator had at the time of the execution of the will; thus a landowner had continually to make new wills to avoid dying intestate. The Wills Act introduced the ambulatory will which takes effect upon the testator's property as at death. The Act also went some way towards assimilating the law of real and personal property, in anticipation of the 1925 legislation. The Act did not, however, implement proposals to abolish the jurisdiction of the ecclesiastical courts over probate and administration, and transfer this business to the Court of Chancery; the jurisdiction survived until the establishment of the Court of Probate in 1857. Finally the Real Property Act of 1845[28] carried into law some recommendations which had not been dealt with by the earlier acts. Thus the need for the older forms of conveyance was obviated by the enactment of the rule that corporeal hereditaments should in future lie in grant; a simple deed would now transfer the seisin in land to a purchaser. The position of a disseised tenant was improved; he was allowed to alienate his right of entry and his right of action to recover the land, whilst the tortious effect of a feoffment was abolished. Incidentally, much of the intricate law of seisin and disseisin fell into oblivion. The combined effect of the Real Property Limitation Act and the Act of 1845 was to abolish a mass of abstruse law concerning seisin and disseisin, and to reduce the theoretical advantages which the old law had conferred upon a person seised as against a disposed person with superior title, though by the time of the legislation these advantages had largely gone in practice.[29] The law of future interests was simplified by a provision that contingent remainders should no longer be liable to destruction by forfeiture, merger, or surrender, and contingent and future

[27] 7 Will. IV and I Vict., c. 26. Students of jurisprudence regularly follow H. L. A. Hart in instancing section 9 of this Act as an example of a power conferring rule, failing to notice that its repeal would enlarge and not abolish the power of testamentary disposition.

[28] 8 and 9 Vict., c. 106.

[29] See C. Sweet, 'Seisin', 12 L.Q.R. 239, and F. W. Maitland, 'The Beatitude of Seisin', 4 L.Q.R. 24, 286, Coll. Pap. I p. 407. And see above, pp. 40.

interests, and possibilities coupled with an interest, became alienable by deed.

The Prescription Act of 1832,[30] which began life as part of a bill which also dealt with titles, has already been discussed. It partially followed the thinking of the first report of the commissioners, who had proposed that a sixty-year period of enjoyment before the commencement of litigation should operate as conclusive evidence of a right to an easement or profit, and twenty years' enjoyment as prima facie evidence, rebuttable by proof of disability, the existence of a lease or of a life tenancy. It was also proposed that non-user for a twenty-year period should similarly operate as prima facie evidence of the extinguishment of the right. Lord Tenderden's Act only imperfectly followed these suggestions, though both he and the commissioners are vulnerable to the criticism that they confused prescription and limitation, if the criticism is fair.[31]

At one level there is undoubtedly an air of triviality about the legislation promoted by the reports, which reflects the commissioners' extreme caution. What is remarkable about common recoveries to twentieth-century eyes is not that they were abolished in 1833, but that they lasted so long; the same is true of the real actions. It is astonishing to find that John Roe and Richard Doe escaped the axe, and continued their antics until 1852, as if the lawyers could not bear to bid their old friends and benefactors goodbye.[32] When the liability of contingent remainders to destruction was altered in 1845 by the Real Property Act, the draftsman, presumably deliberately, stopped short of providing that they could not be destroyed by failure to vest before the natural determination of the precedent estate; thus he stopped short of quite assimilating them to executory interests and dug a pitfall for any conveyancer foolish enough to think that contingent remainders were immune from the risk of natural destruction. Into it a conveyancer obligingly fell, and a whole family of children were deprived of their property in the lamentable case of *Cunliffe* v. *Brancker*.[33] This provoked the

---

[30] 2 and 3 Will. IV, c. 71 on which see above pp. 267-9.

[31] See above p. 267, Holdsworth, VII, pp. 351-2; Megarry and Wade, *Real Property*, pp. 878-92.

[32] They were assassinated by the Common Law Procedure Act of 1852.

[33] (1876) 3 Ch. D. 393.

Contingent Remainders Act of 1877, but even that statute displays a perverse ingenuity in failing quite to assimilate contingent remainders to legal executory interests, although no conceivable purpose was served by retaining in the law two forms of future interest where one would have done.

Mainly we are dealing here with patchwork legislation, confined essentially to the mechanics of the law, in conformity with the basic approach adopted by the commissioners. Thus the enactment in 1845 by the Real Property Act that corporeal hereditaments should lie in grant looks as if it fundamentally altered a basic rule of the common law. In effect the old rule that corporeal hereditaments lie in livery had been obviated for centuries by the employment of conveyances operating under the Statute of Uses, such as the bargain and sale with lease and release; feoffments with livery of seisin had been practically unused since 1536. All that the Real Property Act did was to regularize the position, and slightly simplify it. Again, the Fines and Recoveries Act hardly altered the substance of the law at all, and its machinery still survives. This tradition of cautious piecemeal legislation, which meddles with the law as little as possible, has survived even in the 1925 legislation, which in places displays an extreme conservatism.

Registration of Deeds and Transactions

In their second report the commissioners, whilst confining themselves to the mechanics of the law, did commit themselves to the establishment of a General Register of Deeds and Instruments Affecting Land, a proposal which they characterized as one which: 'appeared to us to exceed in magnitude and importance all the other subjects within the scope of our Commission . . .'. The idea of recording in official, national, or local registers all transactions transferring or creating property interests has a long history.[34] The function of such a system is to provide easy and reliable access to information, to ensure 'the manifestation

[34] See the article by C. Fortescue-Brickdale on 'Land Registration' in the *Encyclopaedia Brittanica*, 13th ed. A history of the subject is appended to the first report at p. 523 (original pagination), and there is one by F. W. Sanders appended to the Report of the Registration and Conveyancing Commission (1847); see *British Sessional Papers* 1850 XXXII at p. 232 (original pagination).

of all the documents necessary to complete the title'. Thereby the system will reduce the costs of search, and obviate the risk of suppression, accidental non-production, or non-discovery, forgery and alteration, and loss of documents. To ensure that documents are registered there must be sanctions, and the basic approach to this need in the report is merely to give preference to rights created by registered transactions. Such a system does not amount to a system of title transfer by registration (often called registered title) such as we now have. In such a title-transfer system the function of the register is not to *record* transactions, but to operate as the only mechanism for the transfer of the rights in question. It is the entry on the register which is itself dispositive. Such a scheme was not proposed by the commissioners. Their proposals were carefully thought out, and involved an alphabetical system for the indexing of the register of wills, and a title system for indexing other transactions. But attempts by Campbell to secure legislation both in 1830, and again in 1831, failed.

Pressure was however maintained,[35] aided by the ideological commitment of economic liberals to the establishment of a free market in land, an ideology which naturally favoured simplified conveyancing. There were commissions and committees,[36] the most significant being the Royal Commission appointed under Palmerston in 1854, which reported in 1857. This first came out in favour of title transfer by registration (registered title), as contrasted with the registration of deeds and instruments only, an idea first suggested by one T. G. Fonnereau back in 1831. This was to be voluntary, but also compulsory in this sense: 'that, as to all land once put on the register, *the subsequent dealings and title should always continue on the register*'. This is the essential characteristic of such a system. Curiously enough this report reached Australia just at the time when the legislature in South Australia was considering enacting a system of registration devised by Robert Torrens, the 'Torrens

[35] Campbell tried again in 1845 and 1851. Lord Cranworth introduced a bill in 1853. There were numerous other attempts.

[36] There is a select committee report in *British Sessional Papers* 1852–3 (889) XXXVI 397 and commission reports in 1850 XXXII 79, in 1857 (2215 Sess. 2) XXI 245, and 1870 (c. 20) XXVIII 595.

System',[37] which passed into law that year, and was later adopted in many other jurisdictions.[38]

In 1862 a general system of registration of title based on the report of 1857 was introduced in Lord Westbury's Act, after an earlier attempt by Hugh Cairns in 1859 had failed, but the experiment was a failure.[39] The Act provided for the voluntary registration of indefeasible titles after strict examination; such titles, once accepted for registration, were to be guaranteed. It soon proved to be a dead letter, for the examination required before registration was too stringent. Landowners were not prepared to go to the trouble of submitting to it, especially as it was notorious that the titles to many estates were in some respect deficient; they preferred to rely upon the normal conveyancing methods. The standard required of a registered title was in fact set too high, particularly as registration was not compulsory. In 1875 Lord Cairns' Act went to the other extreme, by allowing the registration, voluntarily, of mere possessory titles.[40] Such titles could not, of course, be made to provide a guaranteed security to a purchaser. But in theory such a title, once registered, would improve as time went on, so that eventually reference to the register would be all that was required to prove a title. In practice the system was little used. A recently registered possessory title was valueless for conveyancing purposes, and landowners were not ready to use the machinery set up for the sake of possible benefits to the conveyancers of the twentieth century. The Act also provided for the registration of absolute and qualified titles, and all registration was voluntary. It was unpopular and little used; by 1879 only forty-eight titles of any kind had been registered. It became plain that only a compulsory scheme could ever replace private traditional conveyancing, which was based upon investigations into the history of the property.

[37] On Sir Robert Richard Torrens see an article in Simpson, *Biographical Dictionary*. His system is variously claimed to have been based on the Hanseatic system, or on the system of registration of title to ships.

[38] The Torrens System does not differ fundamentally from the modern English system, but relies much less on internal administrative action by the registrar, goes further in making a registered title indefeasible, and though simpler for the public to operate apparently generates much more litigation.

[39] 25 and 26 Vict., c. 53. See Holdsworth, XV, pp. 185–6.

[40] 38 and 39 Vict., c. 87. See Holdsworth, XV, pp. 186–8.

After these two unhappy experiments the next successful attempt was made in the Land Transfer Act of 1897. This adopted the expedient of compulsory registration, but registration was not enforced upon the whole country;[41] it was made compulsory at once only in the County of London and extended to the City in 1902. The system could be extended to any part of the country, however, upon a local request for extension. There were in fact no requests for extension before the 1925 legislation, which set up a new system, and since the beginning of compulsory registration in 1897, progress has been slow. The basic reason for this was the continuous opposition of the solicitors and their Law Societies.[42] The Act of 1897 does mark the beginnings of a successful system of registered title to land, and there is little doubt that in time compulsory registration will come to be extended to the whole country. The statute introduced the important innovation of a compensation fund for persons who suffered through any mistake on the register, though the right to compensation is very restricted. It provided for the registration of a variety of titles—an absolute title, a qualified title, and a mere possessory title—and its provisions applied to leasehold land as well as to freehold, subject to exceptions. The experience gained in the working of the registry formed the basis of experience upon which the present system of registration was established.[43]

The Land Question, Primogeniture, and the Strict Settlement

Law reform promoted by professional lawyers is unlikely to express a radical stance; indeed the concept of a radical lawyer is scarcely intelligible. In nineteenth-century thought outside the conveyancers' world a spirit of radicalism flourished, and the land laws were an obvious target. Wealth, and therefore power, traditionally resided with the landed classes; those outside the charmed circle attacked a system of land law which appeared to them to be the basis of the status of the landed

---

[41] Attempts to introduce compulsory registration failed on numerous occasions between 1873 and 1897.

[42] For discussion see Abel-Smith and Stevens, *Lawyers and the Courts*, pp. 196–206, A. Offer, 'The Origins of the Law of Property Acts 1910–25' (1977), 40 *M.L.R.* 505.

[43] The working of the act was reviewed in a Royal Commission Report of 1911 (*Cmd.* 5483).

interest.[44] Curiously enough, the continuous controversy centred upon the rule of primogeniture, nothwithstanding the fact
that since the abolition of military tenures in 1660, primogeniture was purely optional, applying only in the event of
intestacy. But the survival of primogeniture, even in this attenu-
ated form, was viewed as symbolic, and repeated attempts to
abolish it provoked a level of acrimony which is today almost
incredible. When eventually abolished by the 1925 legislation,
primogeniture passed into oblivion with no controversy at all;
its abolition was earlier presented as a certain road to national
ruin.

More rationally radical liberals favoured the existence of free
trade in land, and the aristocratic institutions of the entail and
strict settlement, coupled with the extraordinary power of the
dead hand, enshrined in the misnamed rule 'against' perpetuities, for the rule permits them, stood in opposition to their
policies. The views of the classical economists, widely
accepted, suggested that social improvement would follow from
the establishment of a free market in land, and the fearful supposed that revolution might be headed off by the breakup of the
great estates, held from generation to generation under strict
settlement. Attempts were indeed made to abolish entails and
strict settlements, though less frequently than symbolic attacks
were launched on primogeniture. All failed.

What happened instead was that a series of Acts progressively
increased the management powers of the tenant for life of lands
held under strict settlement—'tenant for life' here means the
family member currently entitled to possession of the settled
lands, whatever precise legal or equitable estate was vested in
him. The effect of this legislation was progressively to assimilate
the position of the life tenant, so far as management powers were
concerned, to those of a fee simple owner, whilst providing that
for the purposes of beneficial enjoyment the life tenant remained
a limited owner, entitled only to the income of the settled estate,
not the capital, and unable freely to alter the beneficial provisions of the settlement. The early steps were taken when drain-

[44] See F. M. L. Thompson, 'Land and Politics in England in the Nineteenth Century', *Transactions of the Royal Historical Society*, 5th Ser. 15 p. 23, E. Spring, 'The Settlement of Land in Nineteenth Century England', 8 *Am. J. L. H.* 209, 'Landowners,
Lawyers and Law Reform in Nineteenth Century England', 22 *Am. J. L. H.* 40.

age acts[45] gave limited owners the power to make capital improvements to their land with the leave of the Court of Chancery in connection with drainage schemes; additional powers were conferred in 1864 by the Improvement of Land Act.[46] In 1856 and 1877 powers of leasing, selling, exchanging, and partitioning settled land were conferred on life tenants, again with the leave of the court.[47] The Act of 1877 went a little further by allowing twenty-one year leases to be granted without leave, but the settlor could expressly deprive the tenant for life of this power. Then, in 1882, the legislature took a bold step forward: substantially full powers of management were put in the hands of the life tenant, and the life tenant was enabled to employ these powers, for the most part, at his own unfettered discretion. The statute radically altered the whole nature of limited ownership and the whole nature of a settlement; broadly speaking it made it impossible in future to ensure that specific landed estates were compulsorily kept within a family by the traditional methods, and converted the rights of beneficiaries under a settlement by operation of law from rights in land to rights in a shifting fund, whose content was to be determined for the most part by the life tenant, for the time being. The development of English Law here may have been influenced by Irish experience. There the existence of run-down and unmanageable settled estates had led in 1849[48] to legislation under which a special court could authorize the sale of incumbered estates, the purchaser acquiring a title free from third-party rights, legislation without which, such estates were quite unmarketable. The impetus for this was of course the conditions produced by the potato famine of the late 1840s, but what could be done in Ireland for one reason could be done in England in 1882 for a somewhat similar reason—the agricultural depression brought about by the import of cheap corn from the American prairies. Ironically the Settled Land Act was not passed to attack the landed interest, but to protect

---

[45] 3 and 4 Vict., c. 55, 8 and 9 Vict., c. 56.

[46] 27 and 28 Vict., 114.

[47] 21 and 22 Vict., c. 77, 40 and 41 Vict., c. 18. Both are called Settled Estates Acts, the latter being called Marten's Act after Sir Alfred Marten. There were also Limited Owners Residences Acts of 1870 (33 and 34 Vict., c. 56) and 1871 (34 and 35 Vict., c. 84), and an Act of 1877 (40 and 41 Vict., c. 31) dealing with Reservoirs and Water Supplies.

[48] 12 and 13 Vict., c. 77. See J. C. W. Wylie, *Irish Land Law*, para. 1.42.

it, and the powers compulsorily imposed by legislation on all settlements merely reflected what had long been the practice adopted voluntarily on the better managed estates.[49] The radical change lay in the coercive force of the Act of 1882.

The substance of the Settled Land Act of 1882, with slight amendment, was reproduced in the 1925 legislation, though the machinery of the strict settlement has been much modified.[50] But all legislation was largely irrelevant to the decline in the power of the landed interest, which came about as a consequence of changes in taxation and other economic factors in the early years of this century.[51]

Landlord and Tenant

No changes took place in the law of landlord and tenant in the nineteenth century to rival those which have, in modern times, largely abolished private landlordism in the case of residential property, radically transformed the position in the case of business and agricultural premises, and provided for beneficial enfranchisement in the case of some long leases. So far as residential property is concerned, modern rent control and security of tenure legislation dates back to 1915,[52] and was generated by problems related to the First World War. Nineteenth-century legislation in this field was concerned not with notions of social justice or redistributive socialism, but simply with public health, primarily in cities, which was thought to be threatened by overcrowded and insanitary housing. Such diseases as cholera were no respecters of persons. Statutory interference with private contract in the case of business lettings only starts in 1927 with the Landlord and Tenant Act of that year.[53]

[49] The technique of conferring additional powers on the life tenant, and of protecting the beneficiaries by establishing trustees to oversee the management of the property and hold capital money, can be traced back to the seventeenth century.

[50] For an account of the policy and provisions of the Settled Land Acts of 1882 and 1925 see Megarry and Wade, *Real Property*, pp. 311–84; *Bruce* v. *Marquis of Ailesbury* [1892] A. C. 356, discussed by E. Spring, 'Landowners, Lawyers and Law Reform in Nineteenth Century England', 22 *Am. J. L.H.* 40 at 54–5.

[51] See F. M. L. Thompson, *English Landed Society in the Nineteenth Century*, pp. 332 *et seq.*

[52] The Increase of Rent and Mortgage Interest (War Restrictions) Act 1915. See M. Partington, *Landlord and Tenant*, 2nd ed., pp. 152 *et seq.* See now D. Englander, *Landlord and Tenant in Urban Britain 1838–1918.*

[53] 17 and 18 Geo V., c. 36.

Only in the case of agricultural lettings was any serious inroad made into the sanctity of private contract, and this in two areas. The first concerned compensation for improvements. At common law a tenant had no right to be compensated for improvements made to the land if the tenancy came to an end, unless an express term of the lease conferred such a right; that is to say the matter was regulated by private contract. The process by which the position came to be changed followed a pattern which has come to be familiar:

In the earlier stage the law places upon some kind of contract an interpretation supposed to be specially favourable to one of the parties, but allows them to negative such construction by the express terms of the agreement between them. In the later stage the law forbids the parties to vary, by the terms of this contract, the construction placed upon it by the law.[54]

This process can be traced through the Agricultural Holdings Acts 1875 to 1895.[55] But this legislation did not touch security of tenure or the regulation of rent, both first dealt with by the Agricultural Holdings Act of 1947.[56] The second concerned the right to shoot game, which was normally reserved in agricultural leases to the landlord. A continuous source of grievance in the nineteenth century was the fact that this made it unlawful for farmers to shoot creatures which to their way of thinking were simply pests, or so at least their love of shooting was rationalized. In 1880 the position was altered by the Ground Game Act, which gave the occupier a right, quite unamenable to private contract, to shoot hares and rabbits, but not more elegant creatures, such as pheasants. This legislation, passed 'in the interests of good husbandry, and for the better security of capital and labour invested in the cultivation of the soil', provoked a level of controversy which today seems extraordinary, for it did clearly expropriate a right which was, no doubt for class reasons, highly valued.

In Ireland, where grievances related to the relationships of landlord and tenant were of profound political significance, there were changes in the law of a much more fundamental

---

[54] A. V. Dicey, *Law and Public Opinion in England During the Nineteenth Century*, p. 265.
[55] The critical act was that of 1883.
[56] 11 and 12 Geo. VI, c. 63. There had earlier been some wartime protection under the defence regulations.

character than any which took place in England and Wales. In particular the Land Law (Ireland) Act of 1881 introduced security of tenure and are imposed "fair" rents.[57] The reasons for this legislation belong to general Anglo-Irish history. It is curious however how Irish legislation, attempting to cope with a situation which was the consequence of a form of colonialism, anticipated the differently based attack on landlordism which has, in the twentieth century, so profoundly altered the nature of leases.

The Conservative Spirit of Land Law Reform

If one excepts the Married Woman's Property Act of 1882,[58] which belongs to the special history of family law, one cannot but be struck by the air of caution which characterizes the nineteenth-century reforming legislation. The legislation was indeed very tender to the rights of property, and there are only a few instances where anything which could be viewed as expropriation, or as direct attacks on freedom of contract, took place. This spirit of caution may be seen particularly in Parliament's approach to the problem of copyhold tenure. The survival of this form of tenure was in general simply a nuisance; the only substantial advantage possessed by a copyholder was the fact that the court rolls of the manor furnished him with a local register to title, which freeholders lacked. A series of Acts from 1841[59] onwards felt their way to its abolition, but never actually took the decisive step. At first copyhold could be enfranchized if both lord and tenant agreed; after 1852 either was able to compel enfranchisement. Thus the tenure gradually became less and less common, but only by slow degrees. Final abolition had to wait until the 1925 reforming legislation.

So far as the deep mysteries of the law were concerned it has been argued by Holdsworth that the new technique of limitation, and the final triumph of ejectment in the Real Property

---

[57] See for a brief account, J. C. W. Wylie, *Irish Land Law*, paras. 1.42 and 1.48–9, also discussing legislation of 1870 applying Ulster right to all tenancies by operation of law.

[58] For an excellent short account see Dicey, *Law and Opinion in Nineteenth Century Britain*, pp. 371–95.

[59] There were passed Copyhold Acts in 1841 (4 and 5 Vict., c. 21) 1843 (6 and 7 Vict., c. 23), and 1844 (7 and 8 Vict., c. 55) which allowed voluntary enfranchisement.

Limitation Act of 1833, altered the fundamental conception of title to freehold property. He maintained that the action of ejectment brought with it into the law a conception of 'absolute ownership' of land,[60] but the arguments with which he supported this view were shewn by Hargreaves to be untenable.[61] It was as if Holdsworth was searching desperately for some fundamental effect to attribute to the reforming legislation, though no such effect in reality took place. Sweet, with much greater plausibility, contended that the Act had been designed to make the concept of seisin irrelevant to title to land, and that it had produced this effect,[62] Challis thought of 'coming out with bell, book, and candle against the heretic', but unhappily never did so.[63] Hargreaves repaired this omission. Lightfoot attributed to the Real Property Limitation Act most curious results in his efforts to make sense of the nineteenth-century decisions.[64] It would be hopeless in a book of this size to attempt any critique of the views of these learned authors; the student must read their writings for himself. In doing so he must bear in mind the fact that the judges since 1833 have not been able to mould the theories of the law anew around the reforming statutes. The academic controversy indeed reflects the uncertain state of the law and, perhaps more deplorably, a loose and confusing terminology.

If the most striking feature of the nineteenth-century legislation on the law of real property is the way in which it was designed to leave the fundamentals of the law unchanged, this was not because more radical changes were not suggested. Thus in 1862 the conveyancer Wolstenholme suggested that reduction of legal estates to two, the very scheme eventually adopted in the 1925 reforms. The complete abolition of entails had its supporters, as it still has. Primogeniture was attacked by many, including Maitland in a paper in 1879. Pressure groups, such as the Land Law League, campaigned against perpetuities and favoured a degree of social control of land.[65]

---

[60] See Holdsworth, III, pp. 62 *et seq.*, 'Terminology and Title in Ejectment: A reply', 56 *L.Q.R.* 479.

[61] A. D. Hargreaves, 'Terminology and Title in Ejectment', 56 *L.Q.R.* 376.

[62] C. Sweet, 'Seisin', 12 *L.Q.R.* 239.

[63] See Challis, *Real Property*, Sweet's note to Appendix III.

[64] Lightfoot, *Possession of Land*, pp. 123 *et seq.*, 271 *et seq.*

[65] See Manchester, *Modern Legal History*, pp. 307–8.

The legislature was slow to respond to these proposals and in 1905 Dicey wrote: 'The paradox of the modern English Land Law may be thus summed up: the constitution of England has, whilst preserving monarchical forms, become a democracy, but the land law of England remains the land law appropriate to an aristocratic State.'[66] The reasons for this are various, but there is one great characteristic of the nineteenth-century reforming statutes which gives some clue to the explanation. The greater part of them were drafted and conceived by conveyancers, and dealt with the simplification of conveyancing; very naturally they employed the traditional techniques of the private conveyance. Thus the draftsmen were not concerned to alter the substantive doctrines of the law, but rather to manipulate them in such a way that conveyancing was simplified in conformity with the philosophy of the Real Property Commissioners. Even when substantial changes were made in the law, as by the Settled Land Act of 1882, orthodox conveyancing methods were employed; the tenant for life was given powers which he might have been given by private conveyance. In general the conveyancers, who alone were in a position to make concrete proposals for reform, were not much interested in remodelling the law of property upon any new scheme of interests; even if there had been a greater readiness on their part to co-operate in widespread reform the influence of the greater landed gentry was against it. It was not until the end of the First World War that professional opinion came round to the view that 'the main defects in the existing system of Conveyancing do not lie in the Conveyancing Acts or in the practice of Conveyancing, but in the general law of Real Property'.[67]

The shift in opinion made it possible to carry out an overhaul of the land law, which incorporated many reforms which had been suggested at an earlier date,[68] and built upon the dis-

---

[66] Dicey, 'The Paradox of the Land Law', 21 *L.Q.R.* 239.

[67] *Report of Sir Leslie Scott's Committee* (1919) Cmd. 424.

[68] For accounts of the genesis of the 1925 Reforms see Megarry and Wade, *Real Property*, pp. 1059 *et seq.*, Holdsworth, 'The Reform of the Land Law', 42 *L.Q.R.* 158, A. Underhill, 'Lord Birkenhead's Law of Property Bill', 36 *L.Q.R.* 107, H. W. Elphinstone, 'On the Transfer of Land', 2 *L.Q.R.* 12, T. Key, 'Registration of Title to Land', 2 *L.Q.R.* 324. On the history of the reform of the land laws see also A. Underhill, 'Changes in the English Law of Real Property during the Nineteenth Century', Vol. III, *Select Essays in Anglo-American Legal History*, p. 673, and by the same author, 'Property', 51 *L.Q.R.* 221.

connected reforms of the nineteenth century. Extraordinary political battles long impeded the reforming legislation, and Offer, in a brilliant study, has shown how the solicitors in the end gave way to a policy of reducing the costs of land transfer so long as these savings were not, in the short term at least, passed on to the public.[69] No student of the modern law can but be struck by the evolutionary character of many of the provisions of the modern legislation. The Settled Land Act of 1925 in many particulars simply improves upon the earlier Act of 1882; the device of keeping equities off the title is greatly extended but is in no way new. The abolition of copyhold completes a process which began as far back as 1841. Even section 56 of the Law of Property Act, which in the opinion of some is far-reaching and revolutionary, turns out on closer examination to have a long legislative history. The new form of mortgage is not new at all; it resurrects the form current until the late eighteenth or early nineteenth centuries. The old concepts of the law are not roughly handled; the definitions of Littleton and Coke still find their place in a modern textbook; lawyers can still gravely dispute the modern effects of *Quia Emptores*. For all the legislative interference which it has suffered, the law of property continues to display an extraordinary measure of historical continuity. It is as if nothing fundamental has changed. Yet the economic and social changes of the period of the Industrial Revolution could not possibly have taken place without some encroachments upon private property rights. The mechanism whereby this was achieved was not private property law, reformed or unreformed. It was the Parliamentary legislative power, harnessed by entrepreneurs through private bill legislation, which made development possible. But an account of that process lies outside the scope of a book of this character.[70]

[69] A. Offer, 'The Origins of the Law of Property Act, 1910–1915', 40 *M.L.R.* 505, *Property and Politics 1870–1914* (1983).

[70] See my 'Legal Liability for Bursting Reservoirs: The Historical Context of Rylands v. Fletcher', 13 *Journal of Legal Studies* 209, for an introductory account.

A List of Books Referred to in the footnotes

The edition is the one I have used; for a fuller bibliographical guide see A Legal Bibliography of the British Commonwealth of Nations, *Vols. I and II, by W. H. Maxwell and L. F. Maxwell, 2nd ed., 1955, London*

AMES, J. B., *Lectures on Legal History and Miscellaneous Legal Essays,* 1913, Camb., Mass.

BACON, F., 'Reading on the Statute of Uses', *The Works of Francis Bacon,* Vol. VII, edited by Spedding, 1859, London.

BAKER, J. H., *An Introduction to English Legal History,* 2nd ed., 1979, London.

BEAN., J. M. W., *The Decline of English Feudalism 1215-1540,* 1968, Manchester.

BELL, H. E., *History and Records of the Court of Wards and Liveries,* 1953, Cambridge.

BENNETT, H. S., *Life on the English Manor,* 1937, Cambridge.

BLACKSTONE, W., *Commentaries on the Laws of England,* 15th ed., 1809, London.

BLOUNT, T., *Fragmenta Antiquitatis; Antient Tenures of Land and Jocular Customs of some Mannors,* 1679, London.

BONFIELD, L. *Marriage Settlements 1601-1740, the Adoption of the Strict Settlement,* 1983, Cambridge.

BOOTH, G., *Nature and Practice of Real Actions in their Writs and Processes, both Original and Judicial; etc.,* 2nd ed., 1704, London.

BRACTON, H. de, *De Legibus et Consuetudinibus Angliae,* edited by Sir Travers Twiss in six volumes, 1878–83, London. Edited by G. E. Woodbine in six volumes, 1915–42, New Haven.

BRIDGMAN, O., *Conveyances; Precedents of Deeds and Instruments etc.,* 2 Vols., 2nd ed., 1689, London.

BRISSAUD, J., *History of French Private Law,* 1968, South Hackensock.

BRITTON, edited by F. M. Nichols in two volumes, 1865, Oxford.

BROOKE, R., *La Graunde Abridgement,* 2nd ed., 1576, London.

Calendar of Proceedings in Chancery in the Reign of Elizabeth, 3 Vols., Record Commission, 1827–32, London.

CAMPBELL, J., *Lives of the Chief Justices of England from the Norman Conquest till the death of Lord Tenderden,* 3 Vols., 1849–57, London.

CHALLIS, H. W., *Law of Real Property,* 3rd ed., by Charles Sweet, 1911, London.

CHAMBERS, J. D. and MINGAY, G. E., *The Agrarian Revolution, 1750–1880*, 1966, London.

CHESHIRE, G. C., *The Modern Law of Real Property*, 7th ed., 1954, London.

CHEW, H. M., *The Ecclesiastical Tenants in Chief and Knight Service*, 1932, London.

COKE, E., *The First Part of the Institutes of the Laws of England, or, A Commentary on Littleton*, 18th ed., 2 Vols., 1823, London. With notes by Hale and Nottingham, edited by Francis Hargrave and Charles Butler.

DICEY, A. V., *Law and Public Opinion in England during the Nineteenth Century*, 1926, London.

DIGBY, K. E., *An Introduction to the History of the Law of Real Property with Original Authorities*, 5th ed., 1897, Oxford.

English Historical Documents, Vol. II, 1042–1189, edited by D. C. Douglas and G. W. Greenaway, 1953, London.

ENGLANDER, D., *Landlord and Tenant in Urban Britain 1838–1918*, 1985, Oxford.

FARRAN, C. D. O', *The Principles of Scots and English Land Law*, 1958, Edinburgh.

FEARNE, C., *Essay on the Learning of Contingent Remainders and Executory Devises*, 1st ed., 1772, London.

FIFOOT, C. H. S., *History and Sources of the Common Law*, 1949, London.

FITZHERBERT, A., *The New Natura Brevium*, 9th ed., with a Commentary by Hale, 1793, Dublin.

FORTESCUE, J., *De Laudibus Legum Angliae*, edited by S. B. Chrimes, 1942, Cambridge.

GALE, C. J., *The Law of Easements*, 1st ed., 1839.

GANSHOF, F. L., *Feudalism*, 3rd English ed., 1964, London.

GLANVILL, R. de, *Tractatus de Legibus et Consuetudinibus Regni Angliae*, edited by G. D. G., Hall, 1965, London.

GONNER, E. C. K., *Common Lands and Inclosure*, 2nd ed. by G. E. Mingay, 1966, London.

GOUGH, J. W., *Fundamental Law in English Constitutional History*, 1955, Oxford.

GRAY, C. M., *Copyhold, Equity and the Common Law*, 1963, Camb., Mass.

HAMMOND, J. L. and B., *The Village Labourer 1760–1832* (with introduction by G. E. Mingay), 1978, London.

HARGREAVES, A. D., *An Introduction to the Principles of Land Law*, 3rd ed., 1952, London.

HAYES, W., *An Introduction to Conveyancing*, 5th ed., 1840, London.

HIRST, L. F., *The Conquest of Plague*, 1953, Oxford.

HOLDSWORTH, W. S., *A History of English Law*, 13 Vols. (to date), various editions 1922–1952. I have used principally Vol. II, 3rd

ed., 1923; Vol. III, 3rd ed., 1923; Vol. IV, 1st ed., 1924; Vol. VII, 1st ed., 1925, London.
Historical Introduction to the Land Law, 1927, Oxford.

HURSTFIELD, J., *The Queen's Wards: Wardship and Marriage under Elizabeth I*, 1958, London.

JOHN, E., *Land Tenure in Early England*, 1960, Leicester.

KIRALFY, A. K. R., *A Source Book of English Law*, 1957, London.

LAWSON, F. H. and RUDDEN, BERNARD., *Introduction to the Law of Property*, 2nd ed., 1982, Oxford.

LENNARD, R., *Rural England, 1086–1135*, 1959, Oxford.

LIGHTFOOT, J. M., *Treatise on the Possession of Land*, 1894, London.

LITTLETON, T., *Tenures*, edited by E. Wambaugh, 1903, Washington.

LONGRAIS, J. des, *La Conception Anglaise de la Saisine, du XIIᵉ au XIVᵉ Siècle*, 1924, Paris.

MADOX, T., *Formulare Anglicanum*, 1702, London.

MAITLAND, F. W., *Collected Papers*, 3 Vols., edited by H. A. L. Fisher, 1911, Cambridge.
Domesday Book and Beyond, 1897, Cambridge.
The Forms of Action at Common Law, edited by A. H. Chaytor and W. J. Whittaker, 1954, Cambridge.

MANCHESTER, A. H., *Modern Legal History 1750–1950*, 1980, London.
Sources of English Legal History 1750–1950, 1984, London.

MEGARRY, R. E., and WADE, H. W. R., *The Law of Real Property*, 5th ed., 1984, London.

MILSOM, S. F. C., *Historical Foundations of the Common Law*, 1981, London.
The Legal Framework of English Feudalism, 1976, Cambridge.

MINGAY, G. E., *English Landed Society in the Eighteenth Century*, 1963, London.

MOORMAN, J. R. H., *A History of the Franciscan Order From Its Origins to the Year 1517*, 1968, Oxford.

MORRIS, J. H. C., and LEACH, W. B., *The Rule against Perpetuities*, 1962, London.

ORWIN, C. S. and C. S. *The Open Fields*, 3rd ed., 1967, Oxford.

PALMER, R. C., *The Whilton Dispute 1264–1380*, 1984, Princeton.

PIGGOTT, N., *Common Recoveries, their Nature and Use, etc.*, 1739, London.

PLUCKNETT, T. F. T., *A Concise History of the Common Law*, 5th ed., 1956, London.
Early English Legal Literature, 1958, Cambridge.
Legislation of Edward I, 1949, Oxford.
Statutes and their Interpretation in the First Half of the Fourteenth Century, 1922, Cambridge.

POLLOCK, F., and MAITLAND, F. W., *The History of English Law before the time of Edward I*, 2nd ed., 2 Vols., 1952, Cambridge.

POOLE, A. L., *Obligations of Society in the XII and XIII Centuries*, 1946, Oxford.
From Domesday Book to Magna Carta, 1951, Oxford.

PRESTON, R., *Elementary Treatise, by way of essay on the quality of Estates*, 1791, Exeter.

ROBERTSON, A. J., *Anglo-Saxon Charters*, 1939, Cambridge.

ST. GERMAIN, *The Doctor and Student*, edited by W. Muchall, 1886, Cincinnati. (There are many other editions.)

SANDERS, I. J., *Feudal Military Service in England*, 1956, Oxford.

SCRIVEN, J., *A Treatise on the Law of Copyholds*, 7th ed., by A. Brown, 1896, London.

Selden Society, Publications of the, (still current), London, various volumes.
There is a *General Guide to the Society's Publications*, 1960, by A. K. R. Kiralfy and G. H. Jones, which summarizes the contents of each volume up to 1960.

Select Essays in Anglo-American Legal History, 3 Vols., 1907–9, Boston, Mass.

SIMPSON, A. W. B., *A History of the Common Law of Contract. The Rise of Assumpsit*, 1975, Oxford.
editor *A Biographical Dictionary of the Common Law*, 1984, London.

STATHAM, *Abridgement*. The only reliable edition is the first, printed in Rouen and published by Pynson, *c.* 1490; it is very rare. There is a modern translation by Klingelsmith, 2 Vols., 1915, Boston, Mass.

STENTON, F. M., *The First Century of English Feudalism*, 1932, Oxford.
Anglo-Saxon England, 1943, Oxford.

STUBBS, W., *Select Charters and other illustrations of English Constitutional History*, 9th ed., by H. W. C. Davis, 1913, Oxford.

SUTHERLAND, D. W., *The Assize of Novel Disseisin*, 1973, Oxford.

THAYER, J. B., *Preliminary Treatise on Evidence at the Common Law*, 1898, Boston, Mass.

THOMPSON, F. M. L., *English Landed Society in the Nineteenth Century*, 1963, London.

TURNER, R. W., *The Equity of Redemption*, 1931, Cambridge.

VEALL, D., *The Popular Movement for Law Reform 1640–1660*, 1970, Oxford.

VINOGRADOFF, P., *The Growth of the Manor*, 1911, London.
Villainage in England, 1892, Oxford.

WILLIAMS, J., *Principles of the Law of Real Property*, 19th ed., by T. C. Williams, 1901, London.

Table of Cases from Year Books and Abridgements

Table of Modern Cases

Table of Statutes

1874	37 & 38 Vict., c. 57 (Limitation)	152
1875	38 & 39 Vict., c. 87 (Registration)	282
1876	39 & 40 Vict., c. 56 (Enclosures)	261
1877	40 & 41 Vict., c. 18 (Settled Land)	285
	c. 33 (Contingent Remainders)	217, 231, 280
1881	44 & 45 Vict., c. 41 (Conveyancing Act)	256
1882	45 & 46 Vict., c. 38 (Settled Land Act)	285–6, 290
1897	60 & 61 Vict., c. 65 (Land Transfer)	63, 283
1925	15 & 16 Geo. V, c. 20 (Law of Property)	217, 252, 271, 83–4
	c. 23 (Administration of Estates)	24
1927	17 & 18 Geo. V (Landlord and Tenant)	286
1939	2 & 3 Geo. VI, c. 21 (Limitation)	24

Index